ANSWERS FOR TODAY

DAVE NESS

A Division of House to House Publications

About the Cover: Looking Toward Home

For six years, this was the view we had on the way home. We would climb the winding road to Cape Horn, come around a corner, and be presented with a blasting vista of ever-changing beauty. Such was life in the Columbia River Gorge. On the left side of the Columbia River is Washington; on the right side, Oregon. The promontory standing alone in the distance is Beacon Rock, second largest free standing monolith in the world, a landmark for the weary travelers of decades ago who were looking for a new life in Oregon. It must have been quite a sight for them to finally see Beacon Rock and know they were close to home. They had come the right way.

Those of us who follow Jesus need all the encouragement we can get along the way. We need answers, and we need them for our present situation, for today. Once in a while we can sure use a breathtaking glimpse of home. If we'll fix our eyes on Jesus, we will reach heaven. God will get us home. Along the way, the view will not always be glorious, we can't yet see what lies around the next bend, but Christ is our Beacon Rock. If we're facing toward Him, we can know we are heading in the right direction. He will furnish all the answers we need–the answers for today. He will lead us home. And home (heaven) will astound us. .

—Dave Ness

Answers for Today

P.O. Box 1747
Longview, WA 98632
www.PrayingforAmerica.org

ISBN 10: 0983156085
ISBN 13: 978-0-9831560-8-6

Partnership Publications
A Division of House to House Publications
www.H2HP.com

For my Dad
I didn't need just any father; I needed *you*.
I still do.

Foreword

For forty days, the largest Philistine anyone had ever seen growled out his trash-talking challenge to the Hebrews, taunting them to take him on in one-on-one combat or a suicide mission, depending on one's preference of term. Who knows? A near-sighted Israelite might have considered going for it the first few days, but after weeks of listening to this, all thoughts of rising up had evaporated and the Israelites were left only with a thorough knowledge of Goliath's favorite derogatory terms for them and their God. All thoughts of resistance had ceased.

Enter David. Shepherd boy, just a kid, idealistic and inexperienced in battle or politics. He's never even seen a giant before, much less killed one. But compared to the lion and bear David had already dispatched, Goliath must have looked decrepit. And compared to the God from whose presence David had just emerged, the giant must have seemed feeble and puny.

For what David needed to do, it was a case of "the less information, the better." He didn't need someone to hand him a Goliath trading card, complete with the giant's physical stats and records, including the recent surge in his HRO average (Hebrews run off). This was also not the time to head out to battle in "not-being-used-anyway" armor borrowed from his fearful king. David wisely chose to go back to what was familiar and solid—a well-worn sling, five smooth stones, his reliance upon God. The rest is history, in one of my favorite chapters in the Book (1 Samuel 17). Moral of the story? If you defy the living God, you'd better duck, especially if approached by a God-loving kid bearing a slingshot!

Another moral: Avoid TMI (Too Much Information). Especially when it comes to our Enemy, there's a lot we don't really need to know! If we spend most of our time concentrating on how bad things are around us, it's easy to become transfixed by our problems, when we need to be recharging our spirit around the God who can do anything! If we put our focus on God, not our problems, we'll do better. This includes in our personal lives, our families, our churches, our nation and beyond.

Sure, we have problems, and at every level. All the more reason to keep our eyes on God. A favorite professor of mine, Dr. Robert Sawyer, used to say, "If you have big problems, you have a little God. And if you have a big God, you have little problems."

Amen.

The last I checked, the God who helped David defeat Goliath is the exact same God who calls to us, inviting us to live for Him, with the promise of His ever-present support. My favorite verse in the Bible is 2 Chronicles 16:9, which says in part: "For the eyes of the LORD search to and fro throughout the whole earth, to show Himself strong in behalf of those whose heart is perfect toward Him."

Would the God who came alongside David come alongside us, too?

It starts with a daily relationship with Him, where we get to know God on a personal level. It continues when we refuse to concentrate on the size of the problem or the lies of the Enemy, and instead focus on the truth of God. The next step is being willing to go out on a limb for God, in the confidence that He will show His strength through us, as we depend on Him. It's a simple plan, and it beats whining about giants.

I've tried both. I've spent years whining about "How bad can things get?!" I've also spent years praying for an Awakening. I started this book nearly a decade ago, at about the same time I resigned my pastorate in order to pursue the spiritual transformation of America, thinking a community-based approach had to be more effective than trudging along in a local church ministry. At the end of six faith-filled years, most of what I had to show for the journey was that I had been available and obedient to God. He led me back into pastoral ministry once more, with many invaluable lessons learned along the way.

In 2004, I thought what we lacked in America was the "answer," the key to the puzzle of what we were supposed to do, where we fit, and how to get an Awakening in America. I was even going to call this book "The Puzzle," because I would, with God's help, put all the confusing information in order and be able to point to the finished product and say, "There it is. See where you fit? This is us, and this is what you do. And if we will all simply do what God is showing you to do through me, we'll have an Awakening, and we'll get our country back."

It didn't take long to notice how few people were looking to me to solve America's spiritual problems. More bothersome, it didn't seem God was counting on me for that, either! All He seemed to ask was availability and obedience. Then, as I pursued the answers to my questions which I knew must be in the Bible, I noticed how God almost always had His own plans, rarely delegating out strategy or planning to anyone else. God always had a plan. Seldom did He ask anyone to make a plan; usually, their job was simply to trust and obey. He always blessed their obedience.

So He wasn't counting on me to figure out how to turn America around?

Guess not.

The journey has been far from fruitless, though! I feel like a different person from the one who began Servant Connection in 2005, with the vision of "the spiritual transformation of America." I feel like I've been in school! God gave me the answers I needed, and so much more. I discovered anew the lifetime's wealth of wisdom contained in the Bible. I learned again the joys (and terrors) of living by faith when there's no backup plan. I found more answers than would fit in many books, and knew I was only scratching the surface. And I got my plan, the key to "the puzzle." God showed me what to do! He revealed to me the strategy which would spiritually transform my nation!

Here it is:

FOLLOW JESUS.

That's the plan.

Just as in Old Testament times, when the newly-freed Israelites in the Wilderness longed for a syllabus, a schedule, a map, any kind of plan which would show them where they were and what was coming next, and all they got was "Follow the cloud," so we Christians in the 21st century are getting "Follow me" as "The Plan" from Jesus. It was enough for our ancestors; it's enough for us.

If we go with the plan and follow Jesus, He will get us wherever we need to be, teach us what we need to know, inspire us to do the great things in His name He has already planned for us. If we follow Jesus, we will love people, because Jesus will teach us to love people. If we follow Jesus, we will be walking receptacles of the Holy Spirit. If we follow Jesus, we will be transformed, and people will notice. If we follow Jesus, we will be spiritually awake, which will awaken others. If we follow Jesus, we will have all the answers we need: we will have the answers for today.

God bless you as we follow Jesus, together. He will get us home.

Dave Ness
Seattle, Washington

CHOICES FOR A GREAT DAY

This devotional book begins with a section of "Choices for a Great Day." I have developed these over the years, and found them to be extremely helpful as a tool to set the dials of my mind in a good direction at the beginning of each day. Others have benefitted from them, as well, as I have shared them with various groups through the years. Any one of the choices can be focused upon, or any combination of them. I have found it helpful to say them out loud each morning. The point is, anything we do which helps to point our minds toward God will bring us benefit in the end. Here are some choices which will help a lot in having a great day!

DAY 1

Choices for a Great Day

I Choose to Come into the Light

This is the message we have heard from him and declare to you: God is light; in him there is no darkness at all. If we claim to have fellowship with him, yet walk in the darkness, we lie and do not live by the truth. But if we walk in the light, as he is in the light, we have fellowship with one another, and the blood of Jesus, his Son, purifies us from all sin.

If we claim to be without sin, we deceive ourselves and the truth is not in us. If we confess our sins, he is faithful and just and will forgive us our sins and purify us from all unrighteousness. If we claim we have not sinned, we make him out to be a liar, and his word has no place in our lives.

My dear children, I write this to you so that you will not sin. But if anybody does sin, we have one who speaks to the Father in our defense–Jesus Christ, the Righteous One. He is the atoning sacrifice for our sins, and not only for ours but also for the sins of the whole world. 1 John 1:5-2:2 (NIV)

"It's not my fault!"

This way of dealing with responsibilities and sins has been both common and ineffective ever since the Garden of Eden, when a formerly perfect man and wife ate the forbidden fruit and committed the first sin, quickly followed by the first excuses.

Adam's response when the Creator asked him about his sin? It's not my fault. This woman you gave me... (In a way, God, it's your fault since I was doing fine until you gave me this woman...)

Eve's response? It's not my fault! The snake made me do it!

Sin quickly caused the first humans to prefer hiding from God to walking with God. Sin always has that effect on us. People filled with guilt want to dive for cover, not come into the Light. But only in the Light do we find forgiveness.

The first step in getting forgiveness is admitting we need it. When we switch from "Not my fault!" to "I did it; please forgive me," peace follows. Relief comes when we quit blaming wives and snakes and God, and accept responsibility for our sin. Relief comes when we come into God's Light, instead of hiding in the darkness and pretending it's light.

God wants to have a relationship with His children, but it doesn't happen when we're hiding from Him. The first step in having friendship with God is to come into the Light. He takes it from there.

Choice #1: I choose to come into the Light.

DAY 2

Choices for a Great Day

I Choose to Love and Forgive Everyone

Pray then like this:

Our Father in heaven,
hallowed be your name.
Your kingdom come,
your will be done, on earth as it is in heaven.
Give us this day our daily bread,
and forgive us our debts,
as we also have forgiven our debtors.
And lead us not into temptation,
but deliver us from evil.

For if you forgive others their trespasses, your heavenly Father will also forgive you, but if you do not forgive others their trespasses, neither will your Father forgive your trespasses. Matthew 6:9-15

"I can't go on in life because of what they did to me!"

How do I free myself when I've been wronged, I'm "stuck" with anger, hurt and resentment, and no apology is in sight? In fact, it seems they refuse to even acknowledge their trespass, much less ask my forgiveness! Is there any release?

The release button is forgiveness; the one in control of the button is me. Should the perpetrator come asking my forgiveness, I can grant it, of course, but should they blithely skip through life, ignoring me, I don't have to wait for an apology before I can proceed with my life. I can choose to forgive, even if they don't ask. Forgiveness enables me to go on, regardless of their actions or inaction.

Forgiveness is like the release button on the seat belt after the accident. When I choose to forgive, it sets me free. I'm no longer trapped in the wreckage of "what happened." I am free to go on.

Forgiveness frees. Meanwhile, it has been said that, "Bitterness is like eating rat poison and hoping the other person dies." The choice to love and forgive everyone is a powerful choice which frees me to continue in life, no matter what happens, no matter what anyone does to me. Love and forgiveness are the keys to a free life. No wonder Jesus commanded His disciples to use them.

Choice #2: I choose to love and forgive everyone.

DAY 3

Choices for a Great Day

I Choose to Be Thankful

Rejoice always, pray without ceasing, give thanks in all circumstances; for this is the will of God in Christ Jesus for you. 1 Thessalonians 5:16-18

There is something so powerful about thanksgiving! Meanwhile, there is something so odious about ingratitude, envy and complaining.

The choices are before us in a never-ending array. A hundred times each day we choose to be grateful or resentful, to praise or find fault, to focus on thanksgiving or on complaining. The results of those choices are life-changing.

The individual under the grip of "I deserve better!" who has succumbed to a critical spirit will be shorn of countless blessings a mere change of attitude would have triggered. When less than ideal circumstances produce quick resentment and faultfinding becomes habitual, the ever-increasing collection of faults and poor circumstances form a perfect seedbed for bitterness, a homeless shelter for hard knocks. Unrecognized blessings tend to dry up. Complaints attract more complaints.

Meanwhile, the person who chooses to approach life with the dial of his inner mind set to "thankful" is an individual who can't be stopped. Circumstances can't do it; Satan himself can't do it. The power of gratitude overcomes the undertow of life's various griefs and disappointments. The buoyant hero bobs along, out of reach of the enemy. His very thankfulness is what keeps him afloat. Bitterness tries in vain to gain a foothold. Anger doesn't even bother. Friends surround the person who values their company and excuses their faults. God commands blessings which cannot be revoked. Life is good for the grateful, even when it's not!

Lord, help me set the dial of my mind on gratitude as a default. Then help me not to change it, though circumstances or frustrations try to wear me down. I want to be a grateful person, not just when I feel like it, but in the times when it is a sacrifice and an act of worship to "give thanks in all circumstances." It's your will for me. It's also one of the greatest defenses I have against the enemy of my soul.

I choose to be thankful, not as a trick to ward off bad karma or something, but because I am.

Choice #3: I choose to be thankful.

DAY 4

Choices for a Great Day

I Choose to Be Joyful in the Lord, Regardless of Circumstances

Rejoice in the Lord always. I will say it again: Rejoice! Let your gentleness be evident to all. The Lord is near. Do not be anxious about anything, but in everything, by prayer and petition, with thanksgiving, present your requests to God. And the peace of God, which transcends all understanding, will guard your hearts and your minds in Christ Jesus.
Philippians 4:4-7 (NIV)

Satan had convinced me. I could never be happy again. At the ripe age of 21, my life had already crashed and burned. Day after day, I wallowed in the smoldering ruins of a romantic relationship turned rejection, sifting through the ashes in a half-hearted search for hope. Finding none, I trudged through the remainder of a year of despair and torment I had called "The Year of Survival," and awaited a New Year which promised even bleaker prospects for the return of the circumstances on which all my joy had been based.

Things were not looking good. I was roadkill on the Highway of Love. The depression had been around so long, it had become my new identity. I had grown accustomed to milking my misery for all it was worth. One by one, all the ideal circumstances of a year ago had crumbled, with a domino effect on my psyche. I had always based any sort of happiness I felt on my circumstances. Now I could no longer find any reasons to be happy. I was now hoping to get hit by a truck.

I got hit by a car, instead. An 18-year-old ran a red light and t-boned me in my new car. Neither my car nor my hip ever really recovered. Life continued its torturous downward spiral. I bounced along the bottom, no longer even looking up.

God saved me. He reached out to me in my misery, asked me if I wanted to get well, and I told Him I did. He pulled me out of the pit of depression without changing my circumstances, and He taught me some life-changing lessons, one of them being that I could choose to be joyful in Him, regardless of my circumstances.

It was a new way of living, for me. Not one circumstance had changed for the better, yet I found myself filled with a new joy which could not be taken away! No longer did I need a reason to be happy; in this old world made new, I had a constant Source for an unending joy. I still do. It's my relationship with Jesus.

Choice #4: I choose to be joyful in the Lord, regardless of circumstances.

DAY 5

Choices for a Great Day

I Choose to Be Content

I am not saying this because I am in need, for I have learned to be content whatever the circumstances. I know what it is to be in need, and I know what it is to have plenty. I have learned the secret of being content in any and every situation, whether well fed or hungry, whether living in plenty or in want. I can do everything through him who gives me strength.
Philippians 4:11-13 (NIV)

If there is anything which limits the enemy's arsenal against us, I think it must be contentment. When someone like the Apostle Paul lands in jail (again), yet writes to the church in Philippi about being content, what's a devil to do?! Put him in jail?!

When we've arrived at contentment regardless of circumstances, we find ourselves in an impregnable fortress of peace. No longer longing for the circumstances where we can at last be satisfied, we choose contentment now–*in our present circumstances*–and avail ourselves of a peace which cannot be taken away. To live content is to live fear-free. The future is no longer tainted by fears of loss or disappointment. The present is satisfactory, without alteration. We are free to improve our circumstances, but we will be content regardless of the outcome. Contentment makes us free! Contentment is a powerful choice which invites peace and joy, while at the same time disarming our enemy from nearly every weapon he can use against us.

As long as I'm stuck in "I can't be happy until...!" Satan has an advantage over me. In order to keep me miserable, all he has to do is keep me away from the prized circumstances on which I have placed my hopes for happiness. It's simple. If my hope is in my circumstances, all Satan need do is take away those circumstances–*or let me live in fear of losing them*, and he steals my joy. The end-run around the devil's entire tool box of tricks is to choose contentment. If my joy is based on my relationship with Jesus, rather than my nifty toys and cool achievements, if I've chosen contentment in spite of miserable circumstances, what can he do to me, now? Answer: Not much.

The choices of gratitude, joy and contentment create a stronghold of peace around my entire life: mind, soul and body. It really doesn't matter what happens. An insulating cover of peace surrounds my life. The peace comes from God. I just choose to live in it.

Choice #5: I choose to be content.

Choices for a Great Day

I Choose the Fruit of the Spirit

But I say, walk by the Spirit, and you will not gratify the desires of the flesh. For the desires of the flesh are against the Spirit, and the desires of the Spirit are against the flesh, for these are opposed to each other, to keep you from doing the things you want to do. But if you are led by the Spirit, you are not under the law. Now the works of the flesh are evident: sexual immorality, impurity, sensuality, idolatry, sorcery, enmity, strife, jealousy, fits of anger, rivalries, dissensions, divisions, envy, drunkenness, orgies, and things like these. I warn you, as I warned you before, that those who do such things will not inherit the kingdom of God. But the fruit of the Spirit is love, joy, peace, patience, kindness, goodness, faithfulness, gentleness, self-control; against such things there is no law. And those who belong to Christ Jesus have crucified the flesh with its passions and desires. Galatians 5:16-24

Following Christ is so much more than repeating a "sinner's prayer." To follow Christ means the end of an old life. It means willingly putting to death *"the flesh with its passions and desires."* That one has been often skipped over in recent decades, in America. I've not heard that much about "death to self," nor have I often preached it, myself. It hasn't disappeared from the Bible, though. What was it Jesus said was required of His followers? And he said to all, *"If anyone would come after me, let him deny himself and take up his cross daily and follow me. For whoever would save his life will lose it, but whoever loses his life for my sake will save it."* (Luke 9:23-24) In case we wonder if He was serious, Jesus expressed these exact sentiments on multiple occasions, in multiple ways. He meant it.

Something will grow in my life; the only question is, "What?" The answer: whatever I want to grow. If I feed the flesh, I will reap a bumper crop of what the flesh produces: sin, in every variety. And sin always brings death. The fact that the death is not always immediate doesn't change its inevitability.

Then there's life in the Spirit. When I choose to say goodbye to the old life and its desires and I begin to crave the fruit of the Spirit, this is what I find growing in my life, in place of sin: Love. Joy. Peace. Patience. Kindness. Goodness. Faithfulness. Gentleness. Self-control. When I want God's Spirit to grow in my new life so much that I choose the fruit of His Spirit on a daily basis, an unbelievable transformation occurs. A life formerly ruled by sin increasingly looks like one ruled by God. This is the life I choose. I want God's Spirit to grow in my life.

Choice #6: I choose the fruit of the Spirit.

DAY 7

Choices for a Great Day

I Choose to Put Others First

If you have any encouragement from being united with Christ, if any comfort from his love, if any fellowship with the Spirit, if any tenderness and compassion, then make my joy complete by being like-minded, having the same love, being one in spirit and purpose. Do nothing out of selfish ambition or vain conceit, but in humility consider others better than yourselves. Each of you should look not only to your own interests, but also to the interests of others.

Your attitude should be the same as that of Christ Jesus:

Who, being in very nature God, did not consider equality with God something to be grasped, but made himself nothing, taking the very nature of a servant, being made in human likeness. And being found in appearance as a man, he humbled himself and became obedient to death–even death on a cross! Philippians 2:1-8 (NIV)

I can't have it both ways. What's a member of the "Me" generation to do?

Raised on a daily drip of self-esteem and rights, my tribe winces at the thought of not being the center of the Universe, even momentarily. The tyranny of "Me, first" has plagued each and every aspect of our lives: marriage, career, economics, relationships of every kind... Perhaps most difficult of all is the dilemma of having to choose between living for ourselves and relinquishing all our rights in order to follow Jesus as Lord. We struggle with that one. Why can't we have both? We've always been able to have both. Why not what we want, and heaven, too?

Jesus couldn't have both. Why should we? Jesus couldn't hold onto the rights of heaven and rescue humanity from their sin at the same time. He had to choose: keep the rights of being God, or give up *everything* to become our Savior?

He chose us.

He laid aside every right, made Himself *nothing*, and lived not a moment on earth for Himself, but only did the will of the Father. Jesus' entire earthly existence was devoted to *others*. He calls us to follow Him. It's a big stretch for former slaves to the "tyranny of me," but He will help us, if what we really want is to be like our Lord, and live for others instead of ourselves. We can have what we want, and heaven, too, if what we want is to be like Jesus. Others first.

Choice #7: I choose to put others first.

DAY 8

Choices for a Great Day:

I Choose to Think About What is Good

Finally, brothers, whatever is true, whatever is noble, whatever is right, whatever is pure, whatever is lovely, whatever is admirable–if anything is excellent or praiseworthy–think about such things. Philippians 4:8 (NIV)

Of all the disciplines the Lord taught me when He raised me out of my lifestyle of depression and taught me victory, this may have been the most helpful.

The pattern I had formed over the course of a bleak "Year of Survival" had become: "Think of my losses. Dwell on how good my circumstances used to be and how awful they were, currently. Wallow in self-pity and sadness, which invited even worse circumstances. Repeat the process."

The process was killing me. My prayers (mostly complaints) always included pleading with God for the return of the girl. I could not imagine ever being happy again until the romantic relationship upon which I had based my happiness was restored. Dwelling on her for only minutes resulted in days-long depression.

This is the habit God broke, in me. In the New Year I was calling "The Year of Victory," God had guided me to an entire page of "resolutions," designed to break me free from Satan's headlock of despondency and depression. The resolutions included everything from improving my exercise and eating habits to scripture memorization (the entire book of Philippians), to this very specific instruction regarding the principal source of my pain: I couldn't dwell on it or her. Whenever the girl or the relationship crossed my mind—which was pretty much constant—I could pray for her, then I had to go on. I couldn't think of her, but only pray for her, no matter how frequently I had to repeat the process. Pray, then go on. Replace thoughts of good times gone bad with *"whatever is true, whatever is noble, whatever is right, whatever is pure, whatever is lovely, whatever is admirable—if anything is excellent or praiseworthy—think about such things."*

It changed me. It was like four wheel drive. Just put it in praise and get out of there! Previously, all it took to trigger days of depression was the gentle reminder from the devil that things were not as they used to be. God taught me what to do with depressing thoughts: Pray, then go on. Don't dwell on darkness. Dwell on light. Discipline the mind to think about what is good.

Hope-filled decades have passed since then. The girl never came back. Neither did the grip of depression. I have practiced this discipline thousands of times, in many circumstances. It's still one of the best lessons God ever taught me.

Choice #8: I choose to think about what is good.

DAY 9

Choices for a Great Day

I Choose to Use This Mind and Body to Serve Jesus

I appeal to you therefore, brothers, by the mercies of God, to present your bodies as a living sacrifice, holy and acceptable to God, which is your spiritual worship. Do not be conformed to this world, but be transformed by the renewal of your mind, that by testing you may discern what is the will of God, what is good and acceptable and perfect. Romans 12:1-2

Jesus died for me so that I might live for Him. Although I may one day be called upon to die for my faith, which I am willing to do, I am definitely called to *live* my faith, which means using the mind and body currently on loan to me from God, and registered to Him, as mere instruments at His disposal. This is all quite scriptural, too: *We have the mind of Christ.* (1 Corinthians 2:16) *Do you not know that your bodies are members of Christ?* (1 Corinthians 6:15) And many more.

The general idea is that when we traded in our old, sinful life, the thing died—*we* died. The old, sinful man, enslaved to the passions of this world, no longer exists. In his place there is a new man, raised from the dead by Jesus Christ, who lives not for himself but for the One who saved him. He is a new creation, totally belonging to God. This includes both mind and body. The new man is filled with the Holy Spirit. We are vessels through which Jesus can work. He is the Master.

If I remember whose body this is, it helps greatly in keeping me out of trouble. Is what I'm contemplating a good use of a body which belongs to Jesus Christ? Is the entertainment I'm taking in a good thing to put into a mind on loan from God? Hmm. It makes a lot of choices pretty easy. The trick is in making it a choice, rather than defaulting to the old, sinful mindset which assures me that "it's my body and I can do what I want to." Nah. That was the old guy. He's gone. The new guy lives for Jesus. Thoughts are seized and taken captive. Either they submit to the Lord or they go! This mind and body belong to Jesus Christ. It's not an easy way to live, but it's a great way. And the rewards to come? Out of this world. Not only that, but it makes for great days and decisions, right now.

Choice #9: I choose to use this mind and body to serve Jesus.

DAY 10

Choices for a Great Day

I Choose to Be a Blessing to People

Therefore encourage one another and build one another up, just as you are doing. 1 Thessalonians 5:11

The people God uses to bless people are most often those doing it on purpose. They are some of my biggest heroes. My Bible favorites include Abraham, whose obedience God promised would bless the entire world (and it has), who also patiently blessed and rescued and re-rescued his nephew Lot for no other reason than that he cared about him. Abraham even went to the extent of bargaining with God, on Lot's behalf! The greatest blessing in Lot's life was his Uncle Abraham.

Another biblical favorite of mine: Boaz. Who? One of the main characters in the book of Ruth. Boaz had chosen blessing as a way of life. It came out of him everywhere! Ditto for Ruth, a foreigner who defined loyalty. In what I think is the sweetest book of the Bible, God brings two "blessers" together as husband and wife, Boaz and Ruth, and they wind up in the earthly genealogy of Jesus!

A third Blessing Hero of mine is Barnabas. His story begins in Acts 4, where he bails the Church out of financial straits by selling land and handing over the money. His real name was Joseph, but everyone called him Barnabas, which means "Son of Encouragement." Now there's a nickname I would like! Barnabas chose to be a blessing, a "Son of Encouragement." God helped him to wildly succeed.

It just occurred to me that "Barnabas"—"Son of Encouragement"—is cleverly close to the name of one of the greatest encouragers and blessers God ever brought into my life: Bernie Colby. Bernie is with His Lord in heaven, now, but while he was here, the guy blasted a trail of encouragement through thousands of lives, including mine. It was impossible to not like Bernie. He encouraged people on purpose; not just a few people—everybody. He always had a joke, a kind word, a listening ear. You loved to see him coming, hated to see him go. He would listen for your greatest aspiration, think up the ultimate affirmation to go with it—the thing you hoped beyond hope might be true—then repeat it to you sincerely and often until you began to believe it. To be around Bernie Colby was to be marked for life by blessing—kind of like being Abraham's nephew. Bernie blessed people on purpose. His mission in life was to encourage, and He did it better than anyone I know. I want to be a Son of Encouragement, like Bernie, Barney, Boaz and Abraham.

Choice #10: I choose to be a blessing to people

DAY 11

Choices for a Great Day

I Choose to Live on Earth as if I Were in Heaven

Pray then like this:
"Our Father in heaven, hallowed be your name,
Your kingdom come, Your will be done,
on earth as it is in heaven." Matthew 6:9-10

But our citizenship is in heaven,... Philippians 3:20

What would happen if I chose to live on earth as if I were already in heaven? What if God's will was done in my life while still living in this earthly body, just as it would be done if I were in His presence in heaven? Would this be a better way to live? What if I lived as a citizen of heaven who happened to be stationed on earth for the time being? Hmm. I see possibilities.

To live on earth as if I were in heaven would be to live as Jesus did while He was stationed here. What did Jesus do during His ministry on earth? Only the will of the Father. That was it. Even the words He spoke were straight from the Father. He lived a perfect life because He only did the will of the Father.

One perfect life on this earth was sufficient; that's not my responsibility, nor a possibility, but what is quite possible and reasonable is that I would learn to live as a citizen of heaven before I get there. How? By praying as Jesus taught His disciples to pray, for one thing: *Your will be done, on earth as it is in heaven.* Then I just need to live out my prayer. How would all of heaven respond to the will of the Father? I would suspect quite rapidly, and with a very good attitude!

How could I better live as a citizen of heaven? Lots of ways. By focusing more on the eternal, less on the temporal. By asking, "Will this matter in heaven?" By holding very loosely to the things of earth, since I'll soon be letting go, anyway, and heading for home. By concentrating on doing the will of the Father, promptly and with a good attitude. By not having a shadow agenda of my own, trying to feed a set of ambitions and desires at the same time I'm trying to live for Jesus.

It's all a pretty tall order. That's O.K. I don't have to do it perfectly; Someone already did that. But I'm sure it would please Him if I chose to live on earth as if I were already in heaven. It would bring a little more of heaven to earth.

Choice #11: I choose to live on earth as if I were in heaven.

DAY 12

Choices for a Great Day

I Choose to:
1. Listen. 2. Love.

And he said, "He who has ears to hear, let him hear." Mark 4:9

How many times did Jesus say that? I got that message, too, at the beginning of 2010. I had been asking the Lord for instructions regarding the coming year. He gave me a clear message, complete with numbering:

1. Listen. 2. Love.

Even I could remember that! Those two words gave me helpful guidance on many, many occasions throughout that year and beyond. They hang in my office today. When it comes to resolving sticky situations or pursuing deeper relationships, I've not found a better default plan than 1. Listen. 2. Love.

Listen to whom? Well, it starts with God, then goes on to include practically everyone else we encounter. If we listen first, we will better understand. If we understand, we can better show love in a way that feels like love. 1. Listen 2. Love brings a calming effect to nearly every situation. When people feel they're being heard, on top of knowing you really love them, they have to work at staying mad at you! We learn so much when we really listen. Then we know how to love.

God's two-word instruction guide for the whole year was a blessing in every way, but the most enjoyable part of all was when I renewed the discipline of listening to Him in a "Listening Journal" I kept on my computer. I've always enjoyed asking God questions, then writing down the answers. That's also the way I study the Bible—by writing down a question, then scouring the Word for the answer. My Listening Journal has been anything but a disappointment. When I opened my heart and mind to listen to God, He gave me answers!

I wrote "Good morning, Lord," then a short prayer. Then came listening time. "Do you have anything to say to me, Lord?" Often I wrote out a question for God. Listening, I was ready to write whatever God brought to my mind. Sometimes, what I wrote was clearly from me; other times, it was clearly from God. Often, it seemed to be a mixture of the two, as I worked through questions and problems like a student with a tutor. My Tutor seemed intent on letting me figure it out for myself, instead of just giving me the answer. He only spoke up to give me hints or guidance, as needed. Simple questions turned into pages of peace.

1. Listen. 2. Love. I'm still using the plan God gave me. It brings peace.

Choice #12: I choose to 1. Listen 2. Love.

DAY 13

Choices for a Great Day

I Choose to be Spirit-led

And they went through the region of Phrygia and Galatia, having been forbidden by the Holy Spirit to speak the word in Asia. And when they had come up to Mysia, they attempted to go into Bithynia, but the Spirit of Jesus did not allow them. So, passing by Mysia, they went down to Troas. And a vision appeared to Paul in the night: a man of Macedonia was standing there, urging him and saying, "Come over to Macedonia and help us." And when Paul had seen the vision, immediately we sought to go on into Macedonia, concluding that God had called us to preach the gospel to them. Acts 16:6-10

The story of the Early Church is one of being Spirit-led. This kind of thing was common for them! Their own plans, if they made any in the first place, seemed to customarily end up in the trash, replaced by some sort of divine intervention. It happened time and again. It turned out God was always right. They got into the habit of just following Him.

Would that could be said more of us! When I think of the way Christianity is practiced in my own country, these days, "Spirit-led" is not what comes to mind! Yet there is no thrill quite like knowing we are being guided by the Holy Spirit. Talk about a sense of adventure! Anyone who has ever been Spirit-led has some stories!

Does this mean we're not supposed to ever make plans? On the contrary, I think it means we make even more plans—the difference is that in every single step of the planning, we seek the Spirit's guidance and inspiration and correction. Too often, the planning I've seen (and done) is a matter of coming up with ideas on our own and asking God to bless them. It seldom works well that way, and when it does, the tendency to capitalize on our apparent genius by cranking out more self-made plans in an attempt to replicate groovy results usually backfires.

A better plan? Follow Jesus. Be Spirit-led. Trust God totally, including when He trashes our plans, replaces them with something which doesn't even make sense to us, or leads us in ways we don't want to go. He is a trustworthy God. He knows everything. If we allow Him to direct our paths, He will—flawlessly. And we will know the joy and excitement of being Spirit-led. I have some stories to tell!... I want more.

Choice #13: I choose to be Spirit-led.

DAY 14

Choices for a Great Day

I Choose to Work Six Days a Week, and Rest One

Remember the Sabbath day, to keep it holy. Six days you shall labor, and do all your work, but the seventh day is a Sabbath to the LORD your God. On it you shall not do any work, you, or your son, or your daughter, your male servant, or your female servant, or your livestock, or the sojourner who is within your gates. For in six days the LORD made heaven and earth, the sea, and all that is in them, and rested the seventh day. Therefore the LORD blessed the Sabbath day and made it holy. Exodus 20:8-11

Of all of the Ten Commandments, why is this one of the most difficult to keep?!

Because this one is so daily. Work six days a week, rest one. That pretty well covers all the days! Other commandments deal with less regular temptations, such as avoiding homicide. Temptations to either laziness or overwork—hey, that's every day!

It is apparent that God would like us to get on His rhythm and stay there. So, He designed the Sabbath. God's pattern of "Work six days, rest one" has countless physical benefits associated with it; He purposely attaches blessing to the keeping of the Sabbath; it's a sign of His ownership over us. Any of these alone would be reason enough to observe the Sabbath. Yet Sabbath remains elusive to us. When God says "Rest," excuses multiply as to why this is not a good idea, or the right time. And for many of us, when God says "Work," meaning physical work (or exercise!), excuses go into hyper-drive!

It's why this is one of my "Choices for a Great Day." Months ago, the Holy Spirit gently reminded me, "If you don't take care of your body, your body will fail you." I knew He was talking mostly about exercise, the very first thing to get tossed off my to-do list whenever choices must be made. Like most pastors, I struggle to wrestle a regular day of rest from my schedule, Sundays being an automatic work day, each week. Still, I've enjoyed much more success in that realm than in the area of exercise! It turns out I struggle with both sides of the Sabbath commandment—maintaining a regular day of rest and disciplining myself to put in at least a little time each day in exercise or physical work. (Pushing computer keys down doesn't count).

Sabbath is the gift of God's rhythm. I want to be an instrument for His use. That means I tune my life to Him. And we go on His timing, not mine.

Choice #14: I choose to work or exercise six days a week, and rest one.

DAY 15

Choices for a Great Day

I Choose Holiness (Instead of "Not That Bad")

But you were washed, you were sanctified, you were justified in the name of the Lord Jesus Christ and by the Spirit of our God.

"All things are lawful for me," but not all things are helpful. "All things are lawful for me," but I will not be enslaved by anything.

I Corinthians 6:11-12

"It's not that bad."

"It's not as bad as ______."

"It could be worse."

"This probably won't hurt my relationship with God all that much."

"Everyone else is doing it."

"It doesn't say anything in the Bible about not doing this."

"I need to be able to relate better to my people."

"God will forgive me."

"I'm not going all the way down this road–just a little."

"I'm strong, so this won't affect me."

"We shouldn't be legalistic. This is O.K. for me."

"I can handle this, and I'll still be fine."

"My __________ says this is O.K."

Holiness is pursued in the center of the Light, not the edges. Some things help me love God. Some things are sin, at least for me. Some things are "not that bad." I love God. I choose holiness (instead of selfishness, bad, or "not that bad.").

Choice #15: I choose holiness (instead of "not that bad").

DAY 16

Choices for a Great Day

I Choose to Keep No Record of Wrongs

The steadfast love of the LORD never ceases;
his mercies never come to an end;
they are new every morning;
great is your faithfulness.

Lamentations 3:22-23

The bad pile is a bad place to be.

The "bad pile" is the pile of grievances held against us when we get on the wrong side of someone. Once the determination is made in someone's mind that we are untrustworthy and despicable, everything we say or do, everything we don't say or do—it all gets added to the bad pile! Each action or inaction on our part is used by the other person as evidence that we are, indeed, a jerk, not to be trusted. Each time we see them, the mountain of ill will toward us has grown. No matter that we may well have formerly been in their good pile; our perceived sins are guaranteed to haunt our future relationship with that person to death or beyond, unless the pile is bulldozed by forgiveness and we get to start over.

With God, we get to start over every day! Talk about Someone who would have a few (legitimate) grievances against us! Yet, the Bible tells us His mercies toward us are new every morning. It's as if we had never sinned! Each day brings fresh forgiveness and acceptance from God, as if the many missteps of days past had not even happened. It's like first-time forgiveness. Every day is like that.

What if I treated others like God treats me, on this subject? He never throws back in my face my old sins, even the fresh ones from yesterday! His mercies are new every morning. It's like the Bible says in 1 Corinthians 13:5 (NIV): "Love... keeps no record of wrongs." God can never seem to find my rap sheet.

What if I copied God on this one? When it comes to keeping track of the offenses of others, what if I purposely lost the ledger? Instead of letting grudges and hurts stack up like old emails into a big pile, what if I deleted them at the end of every day? Would that be biblical? Would it be Christlike? Yeah. And it would free up a lot of space in my life for stuff like praise, grace, love... New mercy sounds like a lot more fun than no mercy. There's also less record keeping. I choose to be like God on this one. I choose to keep no record of wrongs.

Lord, help me approach everyone as if they had never done me wrong in my whole life. Help me go through my days with fresh, new mercy like yours.

Choice #16: I choose to keep no record of wrongs.

DAY 17

Choices for a Great Day

I Choose to be a Faithful Steward

His master said to him, 'Well done, good and faithful servant. You have been faithful over a little; I will set you over much. Enter into the joy of your master.' Matthew 25:23

I want to be that guy. I want to be the servant who can come up to my Master at the settling of accounts and present to Him a life lived for His purposes—not selfishly, not characterized by laziness, greed or envy—a life of faithful stewardship, lived for Jesus. That's what I want.

It won't happen by accident. If it happens, it will be by choice—mine. Nor is this a one-time thing I can just decide and get it over with. No, the choice to be a faithful steward is one I must make not only daily, but multiple times, each day.

Steward of what? Of everything entrusted to me: possessions, money, time, opportunities, relationships, talents, body, mind, words. To be a faithful steward means I treat all these things as belonging to someone else, and not my own.

A good bank teller handles thousands of dollars each day of other people's money, without peeling off so much as a dollar bill for herself. It's not her money. Her faithful stewardship of other people's money is what makes her a good teller.

The perfect example of faithful stewardship is Jesus' earthly ministry. He took everything entrusted to Him and used it *only* according to the Father's will. That included time and speech. Jesus *only* did what the Father showed Him to do. He *only* said what the Father showed Him to say. *And the word that you hear is not mine but the Father's who sent me.* (John 14:24) Everything Jesus did or said was directly from the Father. He didn't take days off as the Messiah. He didn't ad lib.

He was the perfect steward, who came to earth to do one thing: the will of the Father. Jesus, fully God, fully man, had all the power in the Universe at His disposal. He used *none* of it for Himself. He used it all for the glory of God and the salvation of man. He was a perfect Son, and a perfect Steward.

I can see where this is going, Father. You want me to follow Jesus. This means letting go of the things of this world, getting ready for the next. It means learning to be a faithful steward of everything you have placed in my hands, living not as a part-time hired hand, who puts in a few hours of service for you, then goes and does his own thing the rest of the time, but someone who is learning to be a faithful steward in everything. Thank you for teaching me. I'll try to learn. I want to live as a servant of the Most High God.

Choice #17: I choose to be a faithful steward.

DAY 18

A Love We Can't Shake

But Ruth said, "Do not urge me to leave you or to return from following you. For where you go I will go, and where you lodge I will lodge. Your people shall be my people, and your God my God. Where you die I will die, and there will I be buried. May the LORD do so to me and more also if anything but death parts me from you." Ruth 1:16-17

Of all the books in the Bible, I find the tiny book of Ruth the sweetest. It's the story of how God takes tragedy and bitterness and turns it all around, using human kindness and commitment. The story of how God restored Naomi's life is the story of how He restores ours.

The book begins with five devastating verses. First, there's famine. That alone would cause many to feel God-forsaken. Naomi's husband, Elimelech, determined it would be best for his family to be homeless refugees, rather than starving locals. They moved to the country of Moab. There was no welcome wagon. Then he died. Now a widow in a foreign country, at least Naomi has her two sons. They marry Moabite girls, Orpah and Ruth. For ten years, Naomi copes with her grief and takes comfort in what remains of her life: her sons. They both die.

Without husband, children or grandchildren, numb with grief, Naomi prepares to return to Israel. She remembers a life which seemed "full," even in a famine. Now it is an empty life. God has turned against her, she thinks. Even her name, Naomi, which means "pleasant," has become a cruel joke she can no longer bear to hear. "Call me Mara ('bitter')." It's all over. Bitterness has consumed her.

But God is about to turn this around. He starts with commitment. Naomi tries to send her daughters-in-law away, in fairness to them, but one won't go. Ruth not only stays—she commits herself unequivocally to Naomi for life! "I'll be buried where you are buried." It's one thing to commit yourself to a pleasant person. It's quite another to willingly commit yourself to an angry, broken person who offers nothing but bitterness. She did, though. Ruth's commitment to Naomi was the beginning of the turnaround.

Ruth's commitment to Naomi is like God's commitment to us. Jesus promises to never leave or forsake us. He laid down His life for us while we were still unrepentant sinners, He took upon Himself all our sin and grief and bitterness. He offers us a new life. Most of all, He offers us Himself—forever. There's nothing we can do to shake His love. He won't go away just because we are angry or bitter. We can blame Him and make everything His fault, and still He loves us. He absorbs our pain. He accepts and understands. It's a love we can't shake, even if we try.

The Bottom Line: God loves us with a love we can't shake.

DAY 19

Throwing Your Life Away

She said to them, "Do not call me Naomi (Naomi means 'pleasant')*; call me Mara* (Mara means 'bitter')*, for the Almighty has dealt very bitterly with me. I went away full, and the LORD has brought me back empty. Why call me Naomi, when the LORD has testified against me and the Almighty has brought calamity upon me?"* Ruth 1:20-21

Ruth? Are you sure about this? If you were going to commit to someone for life and promise them that nothing but death would separate you, couldn't you at least have picked someone in a better mood? Here you are, a penniless widow in a foreign country, and you've bound yourself for life to another penniless widow who is obnoxiously bitter. Not only that—she's your mother-in-law. You said goodbye to your homeland and your relatives for this? Yup.

Bless you. People weren't exactly standing in line to be Naomi's friend. Bitter people don't attract people; they drive them off. "Why choose to commit yourself to someone like that? Don't you know you'll be miserable? You're throwing your life away." No, you're *giving* your life away. There's a difference, a big one.

"Throwing your life away" is letting the hard knocks of human existence steal your joy and being content with being a victim. "Giving your life away" is what Jesus did for us when He offered Himself as a sacrifice for our sin. Ruth *chose* to commit herself for life to her bitter mother-in-law, and gave her what she needed more than anything in the world, right then: a friend. It changed them both. Kindness was desperately needed, but it had to begin with commitment.

When unbelievers run up against the Church, what do they sense? Warm acceptance? Or is the disapproval pretty strong? Not just disapproval of sin, but disdain for the sinner? Message received? "You don't like me or accept me; neither does your God." Bitterness grows.

Too often, the attitude extended toward unbelievers by the Church is similar to that expressed by the religious people in Jesus' parable of the Good Samaritan. "Don't get too close." "They probably deserved it." "Glad it's not me."It's the despised foreigner who comes to the rescue, the Samaritan who knows good and well that if it were him in the ditch, he shouldn't be expecting any Jews to lend a hand. He gets involved, inconveniences himself, makes a financial investment and a risk, and rides off, un-thanked, anonymous and immortalized.

We're followers of God. He loves the crabby, the stupid, the careless. When we lock on and commit ourselves to be kind to someone, *regardless*, something wonderful happens. We find ourselves channeling God's kindness.

The Bottom Line: When we give our lives away, we're channeling God's kindness.

DAY 20

Mr. and Mrs. Blessing

So Boaz took Ruth, and she became his wife.... and the LORD gave her conception, and she bore a son. Then the women said to Naomi, "Blessed be the LORD, who has not left you this day without a redeemer, and may his name be renowned in Israel! He shall be to you a restorer of life and a nourisher of your old age, for your daughter-in-law who loves you, who is more to you than seven sons, has given birth to him."

They named him Obed. He was the father of Jesse, the father of David. Ruth 4:13-15,17

If there's a story in the Bible which is "cute," this is it. By the end everyone is smiling. It's a "happily ever after" story, except it's true and God arranged it.

Years ago, we took our young daughter to Disneyland. Her biggest wish was to see Cinderella. When we were in Cinderella's neck of the woods, she was on break. Then it started to pour. We never did see her.

When I get to heaven, I'll get to meet Ruth and Boaz, and their great grandson, David, plus thousands of other people I'd like to see. All of them are real; they're not actors, paid to present an image of an imaginary character. Naw, these are real people who have followed God and made it home. They're all living happily ever after.

So will we. All we need to do is accept the gift of salvation Jesus offers us, and for all who are willing to follow Him home, He's prepared the happiest place (not) on earth. It beats the other one, hands down, especially in a downpour, with Cinderella on break. We're going to live happily ever after, with lots of company.

Meanwhile, life here can be a lot more fun than most of us make it. The key to a funner pre-heaven existence is deciding to be the kind of person who blesses others. Who are the happiest people we know? Those people. Right?

God loves to bless people through other people. Ruth and Boaz both chose to be a blessing to others, and succeeded. Naomi didn't need counseling; she needed a friend who would love her while she was still prickly. Boaz needed a woman as kind as he was. God used the kindness they showed others to bring them together. They became Mr. and Mrs. Blessing. We'll see 'em in heaven. Oh, and they made it into Jesus' genealogy. Just try and outbless God!

If we choose to be a blessing, we will be. A letter came today stuffed with encouragement, plus a generous check, both needed by me. It came from one who long ago determined to be a blessing, and succeeded. That's the way it always works. It's a no-fail plan for a lot better life. And that's just here.

The Bottom Line: If we choose to be a blessing, we will be.

DAY 21

Anything Big?

And Ruth the Moabite said to Naomi, "Let me go to the field and glean among the ears of grain after him in whose sight I shall find favor." And she said to her, "Go, my daughter." So she set out and went and gleaned in the field after the reapers, and she happened to come to the part of the field belonging to Boaz,... Ruth 2:2-3

The book of Ruth illustrates the tremendous influence of a godly businessman. In this story, Boaz is the "redeemer," his ministry more effective than any preacher when it comes to this family. He saves them. They didn't need a preacher, right then; they needed a savior and a protector and a provider.

Ruth could have stayed in Moab, helping fellow widows or something. She could have been a blessing in her homeland, maybe to many. But I don't know how she could have possibly been a bigger blessing than to commit to someone who had run out of hope, and promise a destitute, grieving lady that she would never leave her, no matter what. She traded off what she had of her own life, in order to bless someone else's. Rather than spending time in self-pity or commiseration, she went to work, doing the most humiliating, pitiful job there was—being a human seagull hoping to find a few grains of barley the harvesters had missed.

God used it to put her in contact with Boaz, a man of character holding out for a woman of character, someone like Ruth, willing to do whatever it took to be a blessing to people. Interestingly enough, Ruth didn't stay a gleaner for long. One season.

Boaz thought his time had passed, that he would never know the joy of a companion who was a woman of character, yet who loved him. God imported one from Moab. By the time it was all over, there were blessings all around.

It might have seemed like a pretty boring life, to them. Becoming a nobody in a foreign land, where the only person you know is a person no one can stand to be around, anymore. Then you start gleaning because you can't even get a real job where they pay you. Think "dumpster diving, B.C." Even when it all turns out nicely, and there is finally enough money, and a kid and the pleasantness has returned to life,.... still, what did they do? Anything big?

Is getting your love story put in the Bible big? Being King David's great grandparents? How about being ancestors of the Savior of the world? The choice two people made long before they met, of being a blessing to those around them, paid off handsomely. In Boaz and Ruth, blessing met blessing. It was a marriage made in heaven. We'll see them there.

The Bottom Line: When we determine to be a blessing to people, we will succeed.

DAY 22

Coyote Snacks

Two are better than one, because they have a good return for their work: If one falls down, his friend can help him up. Ecclesiastes 4:9

Do you know what they call animals that venture out alone in predator country? Snacks!

That's what the devil calls Christians who operate solo, and don't need anybody else: snacks. The "independent sheep" attitude—the one that scoffs at accountability and thinks groups are for sissies—is a very effective way to get yourself chomped. Satan knows there's nothing like the taste of a proud but lonely Christian who doesn't even think there is a devil.

The Buddy System or the Drowning System

In the days of swimming at the lake, our very first rule was the buddy rule—you had to have a buddy or you didn't swim. Your buddy didn't have to be a great swimmer, or even a good one—he just had to be your buddy. When the lifeguard blew the whistle, everyone grabbed hands with their buddy and thrust them in the air. All across the swimming area, hands were raised together, pair after pair. If the whistle blew, and you weren't hanging on to somebody, you were in trouble! Swim time was over for you. Why? It was just too dangerous, with splashing bodies everywhere, to assume that no one would get in trouble, or that if they did, the lifeguard would immediately spot them and respond in time. In order to be safe, we needed not only a lifeguard to rescue us if need be, but a buddy to keep track of us every minute. It was either the "buddy system" or the "drowning system"! Everybody needed a buddy. It was the law of the lake. Some of us were lousy swimmers, but no one ever drowned at our lake.

Would that the same could be said for the Church. Every few days it seems another one goes under. Often they're "strong swimmers," too often pastors or high-visibility leaders. Sometimes they even drown attempting to rescue another poor soul who was crying for help, so the gallant spiritual lifeguard dove in to save them, and never came back. Show me a church where there aren't any bodies floating around, and I'll show you a very small church—or a wonderfully unusual one!

None of these folks intended to go out and drown. Their intent was to grow in Christ, to minister to other people, to enjoy the "abundant life" promised in scripture. The reasons they were swimming alone are many: "It's easier, this way;" "Fewer restrictions;" "Church just wasn't meeting my needs;" "I wasn't getting 'fed';" "Not everyone is spiritually mature enough to handle this, but I've been a Christian a long time and I can;" "I didn't want to be hurt anymore, so I withdrew;" "My relationship with God is strong—I don't need anybody else."

I could go on and on, but you get the idea. People don't usually set out on their own because they prefer it that way—it's just easier, or less painful. And often, the initial feeling is one of freedom and excitement, kind of like running away from home when you're five. It takes longer for reality to bite you when it comes to spiritual stuff. Satan knows not to spook his prey by jumping out of the bushes while the rest of the crew are still within sight. He usually lets us get a long way down the road, plus make a few innocent wrong turns, prior to making any appearance at all. Even then, it will almost always be as an angel of light: a ministry "opportunity;" a new "friend" who brings us a mixture of excitement and danger, along with a rationalization for why that relationship is O.K.; a numbing fatigue brought on by ministry success. All I can say is "Watch out. There are a lot of dead bodies out there. I don't think it was 'natural causes.' "

Simon Peter (who ought to know) gives us an apt warning: *"Be self-controlled and alert. Your enemy the devil prowls around like a roaring lion, looking for someone to devour."* (1 Peter 5:8)

There you have it, from someone with bite marks. News flash! You have an enemy! And he's not kind!

What do we do, then, wait until our "number is up"? No. *We team up*. I'm tired of feeding the lion! Way too many of my friends have already been victims of his cowardly attacks. They've lost their ministries, their families, and even more; they got nothing in exchange except heartache. Those who managed to crawl home still bear many scars. They had thought they were pretty strong and capable. They had seen themselves as independent. What the enemy had seen was "snacks." Don't feed the lion. Get thee to a group. You don't want to end up on the lion's breath. And it looks like, long term, it's either the "buddy system" or the "drowning system."

The Bottom Line:
It's a jungle out there. Find a spiritual buddy!

DAY 23

A God-given Partner

"So, what kind of group? Isn't belonging to a church enough?"

In a word, "No." It's important to belong to a church, but you also need a buddy, and you need to be part of a group small enough that if you turned up "missing," they would look for you. Can't find one? Start one. It's that important.

I'm not asking you to be a small group guru; all I'm asking is that you find a buddy, and start with someone of your own gender, in growing together spiritually. A "group" of two is just fine. Like at the swimming hole, it's not necessary that you're a perfect match in terms of knowledge and experience; what's important is that you have someone. What's less important is who it is. (Please follow the safeguard of only teaming up with another person of the same sex—Satan does not overlook opportunities to turn what started out as innocent into mass destruction).

Is it really that important to have a partner? For some of us, time constraints have always made it next to impossible to maintain more than a casual acquaintance with anybody outside our immediate family—and some have gotten to the point where even the relationships within their family are almost on the "casual acquaintance" level, if we're talking about the amount of time spent together! I can hear a million pastors saying, "I don't have time for a buddy! (Plus, I don't really want one)."

Buddies can definitely crimp your style, take your time, and all that. Like college roommates, they're inconvenient, sometimes obnoxious, and the relationship can be quite one-sided. (And, like college roommates, a perfect stranger can rapidly turn into a lifelong friend).

Is the fellowship worth the dirty socks? Is having a buddy worth the time you know you'll have to wrestle away from other important things?

For someone who has traveled way too much of this journey solo, this is hard to say, but I think it's true: I need a buddy. I'm going to be as bold as to say I think you need one, too.

You'd have to know me to know how much it goes against my nature to need anybody. I grew up on a South Dakota farm, where our nearest neighbors lived a mile away. I didn't really know what it was to have a close friend until I was in college. On the farm, the attitude was always one of self-sufficiency—we didn't ask for help; we figured it out and did it ourselves. To say I grew up as a loner would be an understatement. Fortunately, this existence didn't even really feel that lonely, because I was constantly aware of God's presence. My growing up years were a non-stop stream of communication with God.

For the above reasons, and some more besides, I can identify with Elijah, the prophet. Months at a time with no one to talk to but God and the ravens—Elijah seemed a poor candidate for being anybody's "buddy," or needing or wanting one. Yet, in the aftermath of an astonishing victory on Mount Carmel, Elijah's self-proclaimed enemy, Jezebel, caused the prophet to run for his life. Then, in the midst of overwhelming fatigue and pressure, the prophet decided he was done with life. He was so tired and depressed he just wanted to die.

Step by step, God met each one of Elijah's needs. And one of the needs was for a buddy. God knew Elijah needed a partner. At the time of Elijah's greatest discouragement and depression, God gave him Elisha. If Elijah ever again experienced serious depression, we don't know about it. Coincidence? I doubt it.

Elisha didn't come to Elijah, asking to be mentored. Elijah went to him, not the other way around. Elisha was accepting of the relationship, but it began with the one needing the friend. When it comes to seeking out a partner, it will usually require us to take the initiative on our own. It's worth it to have a buddy—especially if it helps prevent something like the too-familiar story we'll revisit, tomorrow.

The Bottom Line: Find a spiritual partner.

DAY 24

Take Someone With You

Maybe it's because he's my namesake, but the story of David and Bathsheba in 2 Samuel 11 has always haunted me. I don't like it. I don't like to read it, yet I've read it dozens of times. The whole thing scares me, and I think it's meant to. If King David, "the man after God's own heart," can suddenly take this kind of spiritual dive, what does that say to people like me, who have no giant's shields on our walls and didn't even write the 23rd Psalm? If David can fall like that, what kind of chance do I stand, anyway?!

Ironically, some of the best advice I can find was written by a son born to David and Bathsheba, who himself became king of Israel:

Two are better than one, because they have a good return for their work: If one falls down, his friend can help him up.

But pity the man who falls and has no one to help him up!

Also, if two lie down together, they will keep warm. But how can one keep warm alone?

Though one may be overpowered, two can defend themselves. A cord of three strands is not quickly broken.

Ecclesiastes 4:9-12

Two are better than one... If one falls down, his friend can help him up. I'm trying to picture David with a buddy. At first it seems a little far-fetched, since it must be particularly hard to have buddies when you're king, considering the level of power you have over everyone, but I suddenly recall a buddy David actually *did* have, at a time when both of them already wielded considerable power: Jonathan.

On more than one occasion, Jonathan proved his friendship to David, even at great risk to his own life, not to mention displaying an astounding degree of humility, for someone in line for the throne. David and Jonathan's unlikely friendship set a kind of standard for friendships for all time.

Repeatedly, these two looked out for one another, honored each other. At one of the lowest points in David's life, Jonathan managed to find him and "helped him find strength in God" (1 Samuel 23:16). As long as Jonathan was around, David always had someone to whom he could turn. David always had God, but Jonathan was the man who helped David keep closer to God than he would have been without that special human friendship.

Tragically, David lost Jonathan, killed in battle. Not only did David lose his best friend, but he also lost his own vigor and youth. Now David is middle-aged.

When the army marches out to the battlefield in the spring, for the first time David watches them go, and remains behind at the palace.

One regrettable afternoon, what begins as a stroll on the roof triggers a chain of unbelievable events. It starts with lust, but quickly escalates from one sin to another. The king of Israel blows past all the warning signs and dives in to adultery. When it backfires, he summons all his power and wits to attempt a cover-up. By this time he is willing to arrange the death of one of his most loyal men in order to try to save his own reputation. In time, it all comes crashing down. How could this happen? How could a man so strong in his faith, so close to God, fall so fast and so far? David didn't *memorize* the 23rd Psalm; he *wrote* it! How do you get closer to God than that? How could he now be penning Psalm 51? Sitting in the wreck of his spiritual life, David truly repents. His relationship with God is restored; all the promises are still his. But the king's earthly existence will never again be the same. The direct after-effects of his departure from God's path haunt the rest of his days. Could this chapter in David's life have been somehow prevented, he would have been spared so much heartache and tragedy.

Could it have been prevented? A valid question! If I could keep what happened to my hero and namesake from happening to me, I'm interested!

This was a set-up, no doubt, but it certainly was not God who laid the trap. It takes no imagination at all to know who arranged all of this. The enemy of our souls seeks to kill and destroy. His trail is always covered with misery and blood.

So, do we sit around and hope it's not our turn to face Satan's planned destruction for us, or is there something useful we can do which might help us in escaping his snare? *"Pity the man who falls and has no one to help him up,"* wrote Solomon. Had his father's best friend, Jonathan, still been around, would David's sin with Bathsheba have ever occurred? It's still possible, but I can't help thinking it would have been much more unlikely. Jonathan was such a good influence on David. They seemed to bring out the best in one another.

I like to think that if Jonathan had still been living, even had he not been physically present, the mere existence of their strong bond would have been enough to help David somehow escape the temptation. And if the king had invited his great friend to go with him for a walk on the rooftop, I simply can't imagine David falling into Satan's trap, that afternoon. Friends don't let friends ruin their lives! Would they both have fallen? Hardly a chance. When it comes to Satan's attacks, *"Though one may be overpowered, two can defend themselves. A cord of three strands is not quickly broken."*

The Bottom Line: Find a spiritual partner!

DAY 25

Turn Us Again

Turn us again, O God; let your face shine, that we may be saved! Psalm 80:3

Turn us again. This is the literal Hebrew phrase in a request repeated several times in Psalm 80, with slight variations. Psalm 80 is a psalm of Asaph, written when times were tough—as in *really* tough. Israel had been overthrown. It seemed all was lost. They needed saving, and they knew it.

Why is it that people generally have to come to the end of themselves before they are willing to repent? Seldom do you find someone who just does it because it's the right thing to do; it usually takes a crisis. The Israelites had their crisis, if having your entire nation ravished by the enemy qualifies!

Asaph does the right thing. Repeatedly he cries out to God. Wisely, he doesn't just focus on "Why don't you come and save us?" "Don't you care?" etc., but three times in this psalm pleads, "Turn us again, O God." The idea is repentance, but it's also keyed in on the fact that repentance is a gift from God, not just something we decide to do whenever convenient. In order to turn around, we need God's help! We also need to respond to His help when it comes, but first, we'd better go to Him and ask for it. Have we done this, in America? The sad answer is, "No, we haven't." We haven't done much of any of it—the seeking God humbly and asking Him to turn us around, the repentance required to make the actual change, the acknowledgement that without the Lord we can't do anything at all.

I think the main reason America has not turned around, spiritually, is that we haven't wanted to. We haven't asked God to turn us around—we've sometimes asked Him to turn *others* around; not the same. When He has brought us to a point of personal repentance, we've been quick to refocus on someone else's more odious sin, and rationalized our own. When various crises have brought us low, we've looked to God just long enough to survive the situation, then gone back to self-dependence. We've waved off God's help so many times! We're like the person who tells their loved ones, "Now don't let me do this" (get fat, sleep in, start smoking again), yet snarls at them if they try to intervene as they were asked.

We're too much like the Chesapeake Bay Retriever I used to have. My dog, Cooper, was strong, stubborn and sometimes stupid. The first time he met up with a porcupine, it took four men to hold him down to get the quills out. Months later, a rustling sound in the trees got both our attention. I saw what it was, about the same time Cooper made a break toward it at full speed. Yelling "No! No! No!" at the top of my lungs, I tried to head him off, but he was determined to wreak vengeance on porcupines once and for all. He ran all the way around me in order to get to it, ignoring my warnings and my futile attempt to turn him around. Unsurprisingly, a crash and a series of yelps soon followed. I stalked off, muttering to myself, "Get your own quills out this time, you stupid dog!"(Somehow, he did).

We're just like Cooper. We rush headlong into sin, ignoring the shouted warnings of everyone who cares about us and knows better. When we get it into our heads that we want something, we won't let God Himself turn us! We'll run all the way around Him to dive into Satan's latest scam. Then, when the pain and humiliation hits, which it always does, we want God to remove the painful consequences, as if it were His fault we were hurting! This is when we hear lines like, "If God loves us, why would He let this happen?!" Free will has its downside.

For years I've been saying America was heading toward a cliff, and whether we went over it or not was going to be up to us. I think we'd better ask God to "turn us" before it's too late, both on a national level and an individual one. When He answers our prayer to turn us, we need to submit to Him. We need not ask for God's direction unless we're planning to go the way He directs. And the very idea of "turn us" means we'd better be willing to part with our own old plans, or we're not serious.

When He obliges and helps us avert the cliff, we need to stay turned toward Him. We need to stop the evil habit of charging around Him in order to get what we want, even while He is warning us of the danger.

What's the verse about not being stubborn like the horse or the mule? (Psalm 32:9) We need to be those who follow God even when we're not at the bottom, looking up, or sporting a nose full of quills.

The Bottom Line:
Only God can "turn us around." He will, if we're willing.

DAY 26

Letting Go Early

And as he was setting out on his journey, a man ran up and knelt before him and asked him, "Good Teacher, what must I do to inherit eternal life?" And Jesus said to him, "Why do you call me good? No one is good except God alone. You know the commandments: 'Do not murder, Do not commit adultery, Do not steal, Do not bear false witness, Do not defraud, Honor your father and mother.'" And he said to him, "Teacher, all these I have kept from my youth." And Jesus, looking at him, loved him, and said to him, "You lack one thing: go, sell all that you have and give to the poor, and you will have treasure in heaven; and come, follow me." Disheartened by the saying, he went away sorrowful, for he had great possessions.

And Jesus looked around and said to his disciples, "How difficult it will be for those who have wealth to enter the kingdom of God!" And the disciples were amazed at his words. But Jesus said to them again, "Children, how difficult it is to enter the kingdom of God! It is easier for a camel to go through the eye of a needle than for a rich person to enter the kingdom of God." And they were exceedingly astonished, and said to him, "Then who can be saved?" Jesus looked at them and said, "With man it is impossible, but not with God. For all things are possible with God." Peter began to say to him, "See, we have left everything and followed you." Jesus said, "Truly, I say to you, there is no one who has left house or brothers or sisters or mother or father or children or lands, for my sake and for the gospel, who will not receive a hundredfold now in this time, houses and brothers and sisters and mothers and children and lands, with persecutions, and in the age to come eternal life. But many who are first will be last, and the last first." Mark 10:17-31

"You're kidding. Right? Is this a reality TV show? All I asked was how to inherit eternal life, Lord—I wasn't talking about financial suicide! You can't be serious. I could see you asking me to fork over a pretty generous contribution to your ministry, or to maybe make a big pledge or something, but did I just hear you say 'Sell *all* that you have and give to the poor'?! That would make *me* poor! It's *one* thing to *give* to the poor; it's quite another to *become* poor. You're recalling that in our society there's no ladder that takes hardworking folks back up the social strata if they fall off (or jump). In our society, people born poor tend to stay that way, and people born rich *try* to stay that way. So, in asking me to sell everything and become a pauper in order to be a disciple, you're asking me to move into a different social class than I have ever known, with probably no way back. You're asking me to basically disregard the expectations of my family, who may well disown me if I follow you. You're asking me to exchange what is regarded in my culture as a bright future, in exchange for poverty and persecution, and the promise that you will reward my sacrifices, in this life and forever. What kind of a deal is this? I thought you loved me. Why would you ruin my life like this?"

And Jesus, looking at him, loved him, and said to him, "You lack one thing: go, sell all that you have and give to the poor, and you will have treasure in heaven; and come, follow me." (Mk 10:21)

How do you put "loved him" and "sell all that you have" in the same sentence? Which one is it? How does Someone who loves you ask you to not just go down the social ladder a few rungs, but to get completely off the ladder? How does a loving God ask a would-be disciple to trash financial security and be willing to become a social outcast, all the while acting as if He were doing us a favor?

He is.

I've presided over nearly a hundred funerals. Regardless of their age or how much they had, every single one of those people let go of everything they had. They didn't leave most of it behind; they left it all. It's a step we all take when making our exit from this life—letting go. Death is the final shakedown, but some find themselves bereft of cherished treasure earlier, like the millions mauled by the recent bear market. Israel had something a lot worse happen, about the time the rich young ruler would have been an old, established ruler. In A.D. 70, the torqued-off Romans reduced Jerusalem to rubble. Nothing was left. If the rich young ruler who bailed on the discipleship challenge because he couldn't let go of his stuff were still around in A.D. 71, he would have now been stuffless. If he didn't live to see the horrible end, then he had let go of his stuff, earlier. Either way, in retrospect, Jesus was doing him a favor that day, asking him to be a disciple, knowing this was a man who would pretty soon be giving it all up, anyway. Chained to his wealth, he plodded away, sad. He could have been a disciple.

Since we're all one day going to be separated from the treasures of this world, it makes sense to let go, early, if the Master requires it. We're going to let go, anyway—why not do it in time to receive not only the miracle and blessings of eternal life, but the miracle and blessings of a faith-filled life here on earth? When it comes to letting go of what we can't keep, anyway, I'm thinking that the earlier we let go, the better off we are. Since we're going to let go sometime, anyway, letting go early makes a lot of sense, almost as if a God who loves us really was doing us a favor.

The Bottom Line: If Jesus says "Let go," let go. He's doing us a favor.

DAY 27

Standing on a Wing and a Prayer

The man's name and face were all over the news; one morning, no one knew who he was, except his family and friends. What did he do to skyrocket to instant, worldwide fame? He saved the lives of 155 people (including his own) by landing an Airbus jetliner on the Hudson River. He did it coolly, perfectly, and thoroughly, without the loss of a single passenger. He gave one of them the shirt off his back—literally—so they would be warm. He walked the length of the aircraft, twice, checking to make sure nobody was left behind. No one was. They were all standing on the wings of the sinking aircraft. The first help arrived in three minutes; an alert ferry boat captain had already spotted them. He took on sixty people, as ferry passengers threw lifelines to complete strangers. Other boats arrived, including a fire boat which had completed an emergency drill that day! Emergency divers got there, and brought necessary help to a couple passengers who were in need of more immediate assistance.

They called it "Miracle on the Hudson." There were numerous miracles taking place at the same time; perhaps the biggest miracle of all was the simultaneous presence of all the right people—the ones who would respond immediately and correctly, in what could have been a horrific tragedy, but which instead was the sort of news story which made us proud, grateful and a little giddy.

Yes, Captain Chesley Sullenberger ("Sully") was the hero of the hour, but he didn't act alone. Bird strikes are common in aviation, but this was a double bird strike, taking out both his engines simultaneously, rendering the huge aircraft powerless, only moments after take-off. Instructions were given to land the plane in New Jersey, but the former F-4 fighter pilot quickly concluded that his Airbus turned glider wouldn't make the airport. The Hudson River? That he could make. And, wouldn't you know it? When Sully wasn't flying commercial airliners, he liked to fly glider planes. Oh, and he had a company that does safety consulting. They probably could have scoured the country, and not come up with a better person to have in the cockpit for this sort of emergency.

Preparation and training isn't everything, though; it still must all be properly executed. This was no drill, and there was no second chance. Everything would have to be done perfectly, or they would probably all perish. The impact of the huge Airbus hitting the water sheared off an engine, but the pilot had guided his craft at precisely the right angle and attitude to avoid serious injuries to anyone on board. They got out, without panic, wading through water up to their chests. The passengers made their way out onto the giant wings, already slightly submerged. It looked like a crowd of people standing on the water, on each side of the fuselage. Help was already on the way, from every direction. Had Sully attempted to make the New Jersey airport and failed, how many lives might have been lost, on the plane and on the ground? Sometimes, it just all goes right. So, a new hero was born, surrounded by a bunch of other heroes, just doing their job, being at the right place at the right time, using that training and knowledge in perfect teamwork, supported from underneath by the hand of a God who heard every one of those frantic prayers onboard and elsewhere. It could easily have been the greatest tragedy of the year; instead, it was one of the best stories. Thank you, God! Great job, Sully! Ditto to all the others who did their part.

Now, to the Church. What happened in 2009 on the Hudson should be happening, non-stop in the Church. What I'm talking about are people who have been trained by the Holy Spirit, responding to life as it comes at them, with grace and effectiveness, calm, thorough and loving. All we have to do to see what that looks like is to take a peek at Acts, any chapter. I especially like the last few chapters when Paul, bound for Rome as a prisoner, gets in a storm he predicted, then proceeds to take over the ship, not through force but by his relationship with God. He gets up, tells them what God told him, and the beleaguered shipmates let God rescue them from death by listening to the prisoner who knows God. Shipwrecked off Malta, Paul's helpfulness earns him a poisonous snakebite; he just shakes the thing off into the fire. He starts a healing ministry on the island, which doesn't hurt their PR any.

When the Church comes together, it's amazing. When we train ourselves in godliness, through constant obedience, when we keep our faith in practice, when we're ready and waiting for the slightest instructions from the Holy Spirit, God pulls off major rescues all the time. They're not all dramatic, like Sully's water landing on the Hudson, but some of the best ones are pulled off by praying parents, caring teachers, concerned pastors and a friend or two, who spend a couple decades investing in the life of someone whose life would otherwise have gone nowhere, but who, instead loves and follows Jesus Christ and is headed for heaven.

Teamwork is fun. It's exciting, inspirational, awe-inspiring. There's no greater rush than to know you have been used of God to pull off something life-changing, and you weren't alone. There's a world all around us who need the Church. Let's be ready, when the time comes. There will most likely be something we can do, tomorrow. Or today.

The Bottom Line: Be ready for God to use you.

DAY 28

Brace for Impact

Only three words were spoken to the passengers of Flight 1549 by their captain, Chesley B. Sullenberger, who quickly became known worldwide simply as "Sully." As the jetliner glided toward the Potomac, both engines silent and powerless due to a double bird strike, Sully was determined to land his aircraft safely on the surface of the river. One hundred fifty passengers were on board, in addition to the five crew members. It had never been done before successfully—ditching a jetliner in the water, but God had prepared this man for this task over the course of his whole life, including giving him the confidence to absolutely know he could do it. As the Airbus lined up perfectly with the river's surface, the passengers prayed rather than panicked, and obeyed the only instructions coming to them from the cockpit where a man held their lives in his two capable hands.

"Brace for impact."

They did. The force of the gigantic plane contacting the water was sufficient to shear an engine completely off. Sully kept the craft level and right side up, and God kept it floating. The passengers had time to deboard the aircraft onto the wings, looking for all the world like a crowd of people standing on water. Sully had time to walk the cabin twice, making sure his passengers were all out. In a matter of minutes they were surrounded by a flock of rescue boats, plucking people to warmth and safety. Everyone did what they were supposed to do. It all ended really well! No fatalities, not even very many injuries, new national heroes at a time of hero-deficiency. While Sully had to guide a powerless jetliner full of passengers into a safe, first-time-ever water landing, all the passengers needed to do was brace for landing, not panic, and get out of the plane. Guided by their captain's three calm words, and the heroic efficiency of crew and fellow passengers, *they all* made it.

Brace for Impact

Do you know what I think God is telling us in America, these days? I think He's telling us, "Brace for impact." The calm voice of God is telling us some things will get rough, and we need to prepare ourselves physically, mentally and spiritually, so we don't get hurt unnecessarily when what He's already seen coming makes contact with our lives.

We know we're in great hands, when God is at the controls. He will get us safely through. He promised that. Our job is to not panic, to be ready to take care of ourselves and our loved ones, to be ready to help others, to be ready to share Christ. Our confidence in the Captain will help others to keep from losing it. One other thing which I think applies: while every single person successfully got out of Flight 1549, their baggage didn't do so well, at least not on the first day. A lot of valuable stuff was still in the overhead bins, as shivering passengers saw their belongings sinking into the Potomac. Their luggage? Already gone. They got out with their lives, and that was about it.

We need to think about that. We're so stuck on our possessions, I'm afraid some of us might be willing to risk eternity just to hang onto earthly valuables a little longer. The morbid math reassures us that one day we'll be letting go, anyway, since trips to the next world don't involve carry-on's, luggage or real estate, but the thought of just walking off and leaving it while we're still breathing is still a tough one. At least, it is for me. Are we ready to let go of our belongings, if the impact of what God is doing in our world separates us from them?

Are we ready? Are we living so close to the edge that we have put ourselves in needless danger, and will need rescue if the least little thing goes wrong, or are we exercising restraint and wisdom in our finances and relationships? Are we ready not only to help ourselves and our loved ones, but to help others? Whatever happens in the next few months or years may present the best opportunities in our lifetime for genuine ministry. Last of all, are we ready to share Christ? This world doesn't make sense without Him, even in the good times. Not enough people know that. After we have helped people in practical ways, because we were prepared, would be an excellent time to gently tell them.

The Church in America needs to brace for impact. We need to listen to our Captain, stay calm, and lead the way, by following God's directions. This will have a calming effect on a nervous world around us, plus opening up myriad opportunities to witness. We need to loosen our grip on the things of this world, in case we must quickly leave them behind in order to obey God. We might as well; eventually, death will pry our fingers off, anyway (cheery thought!). If we get to keep our stuff 'til then, we'll enjoy it much more without the worry. Let go. Then the hard part is over and we can enjoy it until it really is time to leave the carry-on's behind and follow Jesus out onto the wing. Our Captain is in control. He will get us through whatever lies ahead. All we need to do is keep a very loose hold on the temporal things and a committed hold on the eternal, and the peace that comes with that package. Oh, and when they ask (and they will), don't forget to tell them about the Savior at the controls.

The Bottom Line: Brace for impact.

DAY 29

The Menu

The pastor sagged into the cushy seat offered him across the table from his wife, at the upscale restaurant. He painstakingly perused the eight-page menu by candlelight, as his bride did the same. So many choices. Some of them he didn't even understand, but they all looked good. Each entree seemed to call out his name. He was wishing he hadn't come to this place so hungry. Everything sounded wonderful. How could he choose? What if he ordered something and was disappointed? Afraid to make a wrong choice, he at last reached his decision.

The waiter checked with him three times to make sure he was hearing correctly: "You wish for *everything* on the menu, sir? Do you realize how much food this would be? Do you understand how long it will take to prepare it? Do you know there is very little difference between some of these entrees? Are you sure? This could get rather expensive, too." The waiter did a quick calculation of what his tip might be on this order, and decided to forego that last statement.

"I'm sure. I want one of everything. That's the only way to make sure I'm not disappointed. I want the very best."

Due to the special circumstances, they took the pastor's credit card at the time of the order rather than after the meal, as the head chef called for backup in the kitchen. More than an hour later, cart after cart of delicious food was wheeled out in the direction of the pastor's table. It all looked fabulous.

He got through one entree. No one remembers which one it was. He did sample a few others. There were a lot of doggie bags—more than would fit in their car on the way home, more than would fit in their chest freezer.

It was definitely a meal to remember! And though the pastor has been gone for years, now, his children still remember it each month, whenever the credit card bill comes. They hope to someday get it paid off. For some reason, none of them ever go to restaurants.

I made up this far-fetched, rather grotesque story because it represents painful reality for a lot of us–myself included. No, I've never gone into a restaurant and ordered the entire menu, but how many times when I've needed to make a choice, I've opted for "all of these" instead of choosing just one thing, only to find that the result of trying to minimize disappointment by saying "Yes" to everything is guaranteed disappointment.

All around us are those who thought it would be smarter to just order the whole menu than to have to confine themselves to one choice and live with it. We see it in finances, where wants and "needs" overwhelm reason, leaving people with no choice at all, now, and a crushing load of debt. Self-denial and self control would have been a better choice than self-indulgence, and, ironically, would have brought a great deal more pleasure in the end.

We see it in relationships, where the reluctance to commit to one person for life ("playing it safe") has resulted in a lifetime of failed relationships and heartache. Commitment-free, serial relationships have haunted their lives and resulted in indescribable pain, all in the name of avoiding it. Better to just choose one person, and commit to them for life. Who would have known that God's way would also turn out to be the safest?

For me, failure to "order off the menu" has most often shown up in ministry, where saying "Yes" is so easy, saying "No" so hard. It all looks so good! I like doing nearly all of these things. They all say they need me! How could I say "No" to such a worthy cause? Because if I don't, and I try to say "Yes" to everything, there's no way I can manage it, much less enjoy it, and the "bill" for ordering all of this is going to be something I'll still be trying to pay off, years from now. There are a lot of good reasons to just order something and choose to either enjoy it or learn from my mistake. If I don't order anything, I'll go hungry; if I order too many things, I can't pay for it all or enjoy it all.

I need to order off the menu. So what if it's not perfect? There's always next time. Enjoy what I've chosen, or take note and learn from my mistake. Not choosing anything at all, or ordering too many choices will both prove to be much more disappointing than any single choice I could make. In so many cases, the only wrong decision is the decision not to choose.

In ministry, "choose" usually means "focus." Concentrate energy and resources in one area, and pretty much ignore the rest for the time being. That's much easier said than done, especially in the position of pastor, which makes you fair game for every good idea anybody has ever casually mentioned to you. I think it was Pastor Rick Warren who said, "God loves you, and everybody else has a wonderful plan for your life!" How true.

In my years in pastoral ministry, if I could do one thing over, it would be to focus more. So much time, energy and resources were spilled in the vain pursuit of entire pages of the ministry menu, all at once. It just never worked well to go in too many directions, simultaneously. I guess a few multi-tasking ministers carry sufficient management skills to pull it off; I never did. If I had it all to do over again, I would pray and ask God to show me one area on which to focus, then devote as much time and energy as possible in that one direction. I would do that personally, and I would do that for the whole church. I've actually known the principle for years; it's applying it which gets to be the problem.

Part of maturity is learning from our past mistakes, instead of incessantly repeating them. Is it time to choose? Push aside the fear—of disappointment, of failure, of making a poor choice. Pray. There's a God who offers wisdom to all who seek it, no qualifications required (James 1:5). Then choose. Make a choice. Enjoy the results of that choice, or learn how to make a better choice next time. God help us to learn to choose.

The Bottom Line: Pray. Choose. Enjoy or learn, as the case may be.

DAY 30

Stop Global Whining!

Bless the LORD, O my soul,
and all that is within me,
bless his holy name!

Bless the LORD, O my soul,
and forget not all his benefits,
who forgives all your iniquity,
who heals all your diseases,
who redeems your life from the pit,
who crowns you with steadfast love and mercy,
who satisfies you with good
so that your youth is renewed like the eagle's.

Psalm 103:1-5

If God had a bumper sticker, I think it would say, "Stop global whining!" Psalm 103 is the opposite of whining; the psalm is so full of praise for God that it's actually difficult to stop reading it before coming to the end of its twenty-two verses. This is just one of the many psalms of praise David composed. No wonder he was considered "a man after God's own heart." If you want to feel the blessing of God, just praise Him!

From Wonders to Whiners

The Church in Acts was a Church of wonders and signs. Confronted with persecution, the Early Church went to prayer. Rather than asking God to remove the adversity, they asked God for courage and boldness—and got it. Signs and wonders often accompanied their witness, and so did evangelism.

When we flip ahead twenty centuries to the Church of today, particularly in America, what do we hear? Whining! About what? About everything! There is whining about the culture—the whole "The world is going to hell in a handbasket" thing, which is exactly why we need to convince the world to head for heaven instead of their currently programmed destination. There is whining about the state of the Church, sometimes even indirectly incriminating God in the process! And, what I consider most odious, there is whining—lots of it—about each other.

Stop the Whining!

Jesus made it clear that we are to love one another; why then is there so much complaining about each other? So many unresolved conflicts? So many divided "fellowships"? Then, after we've griped about the unbelievers, griped even more about fellow believers, and even muttered a little something about the raw deal we've been getting from God Himself, lately, we expect jaded non-believers to come flocking to our doors so we can tell them about this great way of life called Christianity?! The flow in the American Church right now is *out*, not *in*. Maybe this is why! Instead of blessing, there's a lot of blasting going on, and folks have gotten tired of it. Lighting up the welcome sign or throwing some money at advertising doesn't improve the atmosphere that much, when people who were merely a little curious about God head for the Church, only to hear what sounds like a domestic quarrel going on inside. They quietly turn around and head home, still Savior-less, but glad to at least have avoided having to listen to any more whining than they already had in their lives.

The solution? Stop the whining! About what? About everything! It does no good! Whatever the subject, whining is really poor evangelism! In fact, it drives people away from Christianity who might otherwise have been interested. If our complaining is helping to keep the people God loves out of His Kingdom, I would expect for Him to bring that up, someday! Remember the story of the Israelites in the desert? Of all their acts of disobedience, it was their lack of faith expressed by their complaining which seemed to tick Him off the most, with some pretty dire consequences for them! Let's not push Him like they did! Stop the whining!

What About Our Rights?

What about our rights? We're not in the Old Testament times, nor are we in the same situation as the people in the book of Acts, living in the Roman Empire. In the United States, we are living under a democratic system which includes numerous constitutional rights. At least in theory, our government belongs to "We, the people." We can vote to change things. We're in a different situation than Peter and Paul were. We're in a democracy; they weren't. Christianity is not officially the national religion, but in practice, nothing else comes remotely close to it, in terms of numbers. Roman money didn't say "In God we trust" on it. Ours does.

So, I don't think God expects us to let our civil rights be trampled when we have access to the law, and can save ourselves and our loved ones needless pain. Where I think we're making a big mistake is in our whining. It doesn't accomplish one thing, except to make people not want to be Christians! If we have a legitimate means of preserving our rights or the rights of others, I think it's fine to use those means, just like Paul did, on several occasions. But when Paul was on trial for his life, he didn't argue about his mistreatment, even though he had plenty of evidence to do so. Instead, he considered his trial an opportunity to give his testimony in front of governors and kings and even Caesar himself, and he did it boldly, yet respectfully, and without whining.

Whining—Poor Evangelism

I don't think we're to put our heads in the sand, the convent or the monastery and try to ignore the horrific problems in our sin-filled world. I do think we're a lot better off in pointing people toward a wonderful Savior than we are in "tsking" over their sin. John 3:17 reminds us that Christ didn't come to condemn an already condemned world, but to save it. He didn't save it by whining about how bad it had become; He saved it by laying down His life for it. Then He commanded His followers to do the same. Whining isn't part of the Great Commission.

America needs to turn toward God! Especially the Church! If the Church disciplined herself to bless God instead of blasting one another, the culture, and sometimes God Himself, the culture would have a new respect for our beliefs. As it is, they often see us as a bunch of whiners, and too often, they're right!

Not only do we need to discontinue the whining, but in its place we need to substitute "blessing." Blessing is a discipline of the mouth, traced back to the heart. Blessing comes from a mind and heart which have determined to find opportunities to build others up, not tear them down. This particularly involves the mouth, which is the best indicator of the attitude of a person's heart. Jesus said that out of the abundance of the heart, the mouth speaks (What's inside the vessel is what spills out, when you bump the vessel).

David had disciplined his attitude to be an attitude of blessing God. He then instructed his soul to do the same. He instructed his soul to bless God, knowing his mouth would follow suit, and also knowing that praise which comes from the mouth but not from the soul is empty. Again and again, David gives his soul this vital command: *Bless the LORD, O my soul!* Four times in this psalm alone he pounds in the instruction, which, if consistently obeyed, will result in lifetimes of blessing for the worshiper and his descendants. What a powerful way to live! Beats whining!

Set the Tone

The Early Church set the tone for Christianity. What the world saw in Christianity was a way of life which centered on worshiping and praising Jesus Christ. Is that what they see in the Church, today?

The world is listening to the Church, and we are sometimes setting the tone with whining, when it should be a tone of blessing and joy. I look around at the people in our community, whose spiritual gift seems to be complaining, and they don't need anyone getting them started! They need someone who is having such a great time serving Jesus they can't resist joining us. They don't need any more fuel for bitterness; they already have accumulated plenty! People around here lay up reasons for bitterness like some people store firewood! "Got enough bad stuff to dwell on to last you through the winter?" "Yep." "Need any more?" "No, I think I got plenty."

Discipline of the Soul

If we would just discipline our souls to bless the LORD, that one adjustment to our attitude would do wonders for the culture! It would help greatly in setting the tone. If we could reduce the whining and increase the blessing, toward God and toward others, the atmosphere of the Church would be changed for the better, and our witness would be much more powerful than it is, now.

How do we do it? It starts with concentrating on Jesus, not ourselves. Psalm 103 was written long before Jesus' earthly ministry, but look what happens when you take the statements about the LORD and turn them into questions:

Who forgives all your iniquities?
Who heals all your diseases?
Who redeems your life from the pit?
Who crowns you with steadfast love and mercy?
Who satisfies you with good so that your youth is renewed like the eagle's?

The answer is Jesus. There's no one else like Him. No one else can forgive our iniquities, redeem our life from the pit or promise us eternal life. As long as we have Jesus, what do we have to whine about?! If we will discipline our souls *to bless the LORD,...and forget not all his benefits,* we will set ourselves up for a lifetime of blessing which extends even to future generations (Ps 103:17). If we let God train us to bless others, rather than complaining to them or about them, we help to set the tone for all creation to realize what a wonderful, glorious God we have, who understands us, loves us, and is willing to redeem forever all who look to Him for help. We have the best job in the world, as followers of Jesus Christ. It is to tell the world what a glorious God we have, along with the Good News that He wants to be their God, too.

The Bottom Line: Whining isn't part of the Great Commission.

DAY 31

Promises the Hard Way

Then he brought out Israel with silver and gold,
and there was none among his tribes who stumbled.
Egypt was glad when they departed,
for dread of them had fallen upon it.

He spread a cloud for a covering,
and fire to give light by night.
They asked, and he brought quail,
and gave them bread from heaven in abundance.
He opened the rock, and water gushed out;
it flowed through the desert like a river.
For he remembered his holy promise,
and Abraham, his servant.

So he brought his people out with joy,
his chosen ones with singing.
And he gave them the lands of the nations,
and they took possession of the fruit of the peoples' toil,
that they might keep his statutes
and observe his laws.
Praise the Lord!

Psalm 105:37-45

God often does things "the hard way." But then, what's a "hard way," to God?!

If the end goal is for the descendants of Abraham, Isaac and Jacob to be in Canaan, isn't it easier to just leave them there?! After all, it took considerable sacrifice and effort for Abraham to leave every vestige of comfort and security behind in order to follow God's call into the unknown in the first place. After all the trouble of prying someone loose from his family in order to live by faith, and then promising him that his descendants would possess the land, wouldn't it be prudent to just let them stay in the Promised Land and multiply, and then you're done?

How God Keeps Promises

Not God. He wants His chosen people to appreciate what it is to have a land He has flat-out given to them, and He wants them to understand salvation, and divine leading, and obedience, and He wants them to know how awesomely strong He is. SO.....

He tells them, while they are still in Canaan, that they are going to end up in Egypt for 400 years.

He gives Joseph dreams, which irritates his brothers and they sell him into slavery, which lands him in Egypt. Now there's one Hebrew in Egypt.

He helps Joseph interpret dreams, when Joseph is in prison in Egypt as a result of doing the right thing.

He arranges the whole "Pharaoh's dream" thing, the Joseph solution, Joseph's promotion, the years of plenty, the years of famine... everything—in order to get 70 people to go to Egypt! That's a lot of trouble to go to, in order to move 70 people around!

God's just getting started, though. Now He's going to bring them back! First, He waits 400 years (which, I guess, is less than half a day, to Him). He prepares Moses, which takes 80 years; He does the burning bush thing; He does the ten plagues; then the Red Sea; manna; water coming out of rocks; quail storms; cloud by day; pillar of fire by night; the giving of the Ten Commandments and the Law; 40 years of time-out in the Wilderness for the disbelieving people; He leads their children across the Jordan River on dry land; He makes the walls fall down at Jericho; He helps them conquer the rest of Canaan; voila! They're back where they started.

But these are not the same people they would have been, had God left them to prosper and assimilate into the heathen culture of Canaan land for 400 years. These are people who know what it is to have a Savior, and who know what it is to follow God. This is a nation which crossed the river while God held the water back, who watched city walls simply fall down because God knocked them down with their praise. God knew what He was doing. I'll wager He still does.

An Uncomfortable Resemblance

We are so much like the Israelites that it hurts. The Pilgrims landing on Plymouth Rock in 1620 were refugees who had come to a new land seeking the freedom to worship God without hindrance. They were believers. God has done astounding things for this nation, from the very beginning. We haven't been perfect, but overall we have maintained a loyalty to God which has ratcheted us up to become the world's only remaining superpower. We are the people we are because of what we've come through, as a country.

And now what? We're like Rehoboam, the son of Solomon, who inherited one of the greatest kingdoms of the world. Asked how we are going to use our privileges, we confer among our equally spoiled peers, ignoring the sage advice of those who paid for our freedoms, and we retort that America will continue to be great because "we always have been." However, we're going to proceed into the future without the constraints of prudish Christianity. We'll still keep God on as a figurehead—kind of a national mascot—but we're certainly beyond any sense of allegiance to Him. We can take it from here—we're America! Like

Rehoboam, if we're even left with one tribe, it may be due to God's appreciation for our ancestors, and nothing more.

Repent and Relax

We're in trouble. But we can do two helpful things which seem in contradiction to one another: We can repent and we can relax.

First of all, "repent." It's a gift of God, repentance. We can't force ourselves to be genuinely sorry for our own sins or the aggregate sins of our nation; only God's grace even gives us the good sense to realize we're wrong. When the guilt hits, though, we can allow it to lead us into full-blown repentance or we can rationalize it away, searing our consciences to seal in the juices and firewall against the cleansing of the Holy Spirit. Opening the door to the Holy Spirit is like ushering a tornado into your living room. Don't expect to be able to recognize your life afterward—but it'll be clean. Repentance is yanking the door to our heart open and letting God's Spirit in. When He comes in, it's not to advise but to take over. That's a good thing.

Now that our old lives have been trashed by repentance, and God is in charge of the new Spirit He installed within us, we obey—but we also can relax.

What am I talking about? God will accomplish His purposes. He just will! He might do it "the hard way" and take 40 or 400 years, but if God promises something, it's already happened, at least from His perspective. We just have to wait around for evidence of the reality, 'cause we're on Earth.

Fateful Prophecy

Let me pose a few questions for us. Would it have done the Israelites any good to have toughed it out and stayed in Canaan during the famine? How about if they'd decided to do the same thing Joseph was doing in Egypt, and maybe saved up seven years' worth of food, in wise anticipation of a bad famine coming along? Would that have prevented the tribe of Israel from ending up in Egypt? Don't think so. They might have gone for a different reason, but they still would have gone! Why? God said they were going.

Had Moses been a more skillful negotiator instead of a hotheaded prince, would he have been able to cut a deal with Pharaoh and gotten the Israelites out of Egypt without having to resort to plagues? I don't think so. God was going to do plagues. The Pharaohs thought they were gods; God was going to show what a real God could do. And it wouldn't be until the 400 years was up, because that's how long He had said.

So, it wouldn't have done any good to have a slave rebellion after just 200 years in captivity, and it wouldn't have made any difference if Moses had played his cards right, earlier in life. Certain things were going to happen, simply because God had promised they would; all the sincerity, hard work or devotion in the world would not have ultimately changed it. This is not to say that we should forget about sincerity, devotion or hard work! But in the midst of it all, we might as well relax, too. God is in charge. If we're supposed to go to Egypt, we'll go, no matter how smart we are. And if He's getting us out of Egypt and it's time, the most powerful forces on earth won't prevent our leaving. Our job is to pay attention to the Lord, listen to Him and obey—and while we're at it, we might as well relax. This could take a while—especially if God said it would.

The Bottom Line: Repent and relax. God is in charge.

DAY 32

I Get It!

They made a calf in Horeb
and worshiped a metal image.
They exchanged the glory of God
for the image of an ox that eats grass.
They forgot God, their Savior,
who had done great things in Egypt,
wondrous works in the land of Ham,
and awesome deeds by the Red Sea.
Therefore he said he would destroy them–
had not Moses, his chosen one,
stood in the breach before him,
to turn away his wrath from destroying them.

Psalm 106:19-23

For many years the passages about God telling Moses He was going to kill the Israelites He had just delivered out of Egypt have confused me. God is love. Right? How does this jive with wiping out hundreds of thousands of people who are just acting rebellious, ungrateful, sinful and stupid? So Moses talks sense to Him, gets Him to change His mind, and the Israelites are spared. It's a good thing Moses was there, to help God not throw a tantrum and annihilate His own people.

The weirdness of that whole picture has been one of the many anomalies which has made me avoid that and other passages which I can't explain, and which I've feared would provide fodder for caustic God-haters looking for ways to discredit the God of Israel, whom they already see as neurotic, if they even believe He exists. So, it's been "on to the next passage"—and God goes back to normal, again—His old, loving self, who does miracles and forgives people and makes great promises which He then proceeds to keep.

It finally makes sense to me. This is not an aberration in God's character, but a really good display of it! In Exodus 32 and the recounting of it in Deuteronomy 9, God is multi-tasking, again—helping His people to understand His mercy and forgiveness; letting Moses do what He was born for—rescuing people; and all the while, setting the stage for Jesus, who would copy the actions of Moses, but do it perfectly and for all time. It's a real-life picture of salvation.

The Bottom Line: This is a picture of how salvation works.

DAY 33

Trinity Lessons

They forgot God, their Savior,
who had done great things in Egypt,...
Psalm 106:21

Certain groups are quick to point out that the word "trinity" isn't found in the Bible. Though the word is missing, the concept isn't. Even the Israelites got lessons on the Trinity, as they were led out of Egypt and across the wilderness.

First, they learned about a Father who can do anything. The old playground assertion of "My father can beat up your father!" was elevated to a contest of gods—Pharaoh vs. Yahweh. The Israelites saw for themselves: "My God is a lot stronger than your god!" Yahweh ("I am") is a wonderful Provider, Protector and a Maker and Keeper of Promises. He's a Father you can trust.

Then there's a savior. In this case, the savior was Moses, who came back to Egypt just to set the people free, at the command of God the Father. This "savior" is one who rescues; who intercedes; who risks everything for his people, when he wouldn't have to; one who is willing to die for them and try to stand in the way of God Himself in order to spare them. Deuteronomy ends with a statement about how there had so far never been another prophet like Moses. There wasn't—until Jesus. Moses was a very good example of what it's like to have a savior; Jesus came along later as a perfect, once-and-for-all Savior.

The Israelites also got a lesson on what it is to be led by the Holy Spirit. They were guided day by day on their journey by a physical manifestation which represented God's presence: A pillar of cloud by day; a pillar of fire by night. They didn't go anywhere except where the cloud led them. They were learning to follow God—literally. In the process, they were learning of the surpassing mystery of God—how He is uncontainable; beyond human understanding; not subject to man's control, regardless of how united or powerful mankind can esteem himself. When God's glory filled the tabernacle, even the priests couldn't enter. The Israelites knew what it was to witness God's power over and over again, yet never be able to see Him. It was a good primer on the Holy Spirit.

All-powerful Father, loving Savior, guiding Spirit. All there. Still is.

The Bottom Line: Throughout scripture, we see God the Father, Son and Spirit.

DAY 34

Intercession or Intervention?

Therefore he said he would destroy them–
had not Moses, his chosen one,
stood in the breach before him,
to turn away his wrath from destroying them.
Psalm 106:23

God saved the Israelites from Pharaoh; Moses saved the Israelites from God—or at least, His wrath. This was not a drill. Nor was God bluffing. I believe He really would have destroyed the Israelites and started over with Moses, had not Moses pleaded with God to spare them. God accepted Moses' intercession.

When Christians talk about "intercession," the implication is often that intercession is no more than just "praying for someone else." What Moses did for his people was far beyond that brand of "intercession"—it was, in fact, more like "intervention." Moses wasn't merely praying "God bless the Israelites;" he was willing to have his own name blotted out of the Book of Life if their names were going to be! There's a difference between encouragement from the sidelines and stepping in front of someone to take the hit intended for them. I'm thinking that true intercession is more like "intervention."

Know what Moses did? After the near-miss the Israelites experienced, Moses proceeded to go back up the mountain and lie on his face for 40 days, pleading with God not to destroy them! That's commitment! That's intervention.

It's what Christ did for us. With the wages of sin facing all of mankind, Jesus stood in the gap and turned away the wrath of God by taking upon Himself the punishment for all our sins, so we could go free. He intervened on our behalf.

Two things turn away God's wrath: Repentance and intercession. If we don't have one, we'd better have the other!

The Ninevites were stuck with a prophet, Jonah, who was actually disappointed that God didn't fry them like He'd said He would! Their repentance saved them, even though they had a prophet who refused to intercede for them.

Lot wasn't smart enough to repent, but he had an uncle, Abraham, who was willing to bargain with God on his behalf, and that did the trick. In both cases, God *wanted* to spare people, but either repentance or intercession was required.

Whom do we know who needs to repent but hasn't gotten there, yet? We should intercede for them. Intercession/intervention turns away His wrath.

The Bottom Line: True intercession is much like intervention.

DAY 35

Flashlight from God

Your word is a lamp to my feet
and a light to my path.

Psalm 119:105

The Word of God gives us wisdom and information others don't have. It helps keep us out of misery and trouble. It is sweet. It's one of God's greatest gifts to us. The Word is a light in a dark world.

The ancient Hebrews so appreciated the worth of scripture that the longest chapter in the Bible, Psalm 119, is completely devoted to the glories of the Word of God. The psalm is 176 verses long, arranged in acrostic form for ease in memorization. All 22 letters of the Hebrew alphabet are utilized, in order. Each letter has eight sentences which begin with that letter, followed by eight sentences beginning with the next letter, and so forth, all the way through the alphabet. The theme of the entire psalm is the importance and majesty of the Word of God.

The greatness of God's Word is expressed 176 different ways. Then they memorize it! That's dedication. I don't think I even want to compare the attitude of your average American Christian toward the Word of God.

I keep telling the young people I teach that "all the answers are in this Book." I say that because I believe it! In a dark world, wouldn't it be good to use a lamp if we have one? We do. But in order to be helpful, a lamp must be used. "Owning" one does not equal using one. The Word of God is glorious. It sheds unbelievable light on all of life. The scripture helps us to know things it would otherwise be impossible for us to know or understand. With the Bible, we outshine our enemies and even our humanistic, Bible-shunning teachers. Our Father wants us to know things, so He has told us in His Word. He wants us to understand the way to eternal life. He wants us to know Him. He has given us the Bible as a lamp for our feet. When we open our lives to the scriptures, we're opening our lives to the Light.

If we chose to, we could be people of the Book. We could learn and practice God's Law, and have an amazing effect on the society around us. Or we could continue to pay lip service to the Bible, but seldom read it or study it or follow its teaching. Then we would have.... well, what we have.

The Bottom Line: We have a light for our path.
Might as well use it!

DAY 36

Hell in a Handbasket

I have more understanding than all my teachers,
for your testimonies are my meditation.

Psalm 119:99

There was a day when nearly all of American society was somehow tied to the moral standards of the Bible. That day is not today. While it grieves me to see our country distancing itself more all the time from the God who has blessed us, what disturbs me even more is the ennoblement of sin. I saw it again last night.

If there has been one dominant, seemingly obligatory feature in TV series in recent years, it has been the presence of the noble gay. Invariably, the most sensible, strong, caring character is the one with the homosexual lifestyle. Christians are portrayed as crabby, judgmental and vicious. Oh, and hypocritical.

In last night's drama the writers had the homosexual character seize the moral high ground from her scripture-quoting father by countering with "Jesus" statements: "Love one another," "He that is without sin cast the first stone," etc. To those unfamiliar with the Bible the message was clear: The gay is the one truly living out the commands of Jesus. High ground goes to the homosexual. The bigoted father sheepishly concedes at the program's conclusion. End of sermon.

I used to just get angry when I saw something like this. More and more, I'm just getting sad. I'm seeing that writers, producers and actors are assuming the moral high ground *because they're convinced it's theirs*! Some must honestly think they are doing good by promoting the homosexual lifestyle. They style themselves moral warriors standing up against "bigotry and hatred"—in the name of Jesus. It's what happens when you don't read the whole Book. If all you've ever read or heard is "Love one another" and "Don't judge," and you haven't a clue about the Law or the awful consequences of sin—and what it cost Jesus to pay for our sin; if you don't understand, even as a Christian, that it's not just those who live out the homosexual lifestyle who are headed for hell and in need of a Savior, but every single one of us, including the nicest sinners we've ever met... Without a Savior, we're *all* headed for hell in a handbasket, not just Hitler and the people whose sins seem worse than ours.

Reading the Bible, accepting it as truth, will make us wiser than our teachers—even the clever but misguided Hollywood ones. We have the Book because God wants us to know the *real* answers—and avoid hell. And make heaven.

The Bottom Line: Without a Savior, we're *all* headed for hell!

DAY 37

Commanded Blessing

Behold, how good and pleasant it is
when brothers dwell in unity!
It is like the precious oil on the head,
running down on the beard,
on the beard of Aaron,
running down on the collar of his robes!
It is like the dew of Hermon,
which falls on the mountains of Zion!
For there the LORD has commanded the blessing,
life forevermore.

Psalm 133

Wouldn't it be nice if God ordered blessing to fall upon us and our friends? Actually, it's clear from the scriptures that He likes to do this! Whether He does or not is mostly left up to us.

What am I talking about? Unity. God loves unity. Where there is unity, God commands blessing. And when God commands stuff, it gets done! I can see Him in heaven pointing at a praying group of pastors from multiple traditions, gathered to intercede for their community, walking together in love and unity. The Lord says to His angels, "See those people? Bless them!" The angels immediately begin to follow orders, using their imagination to come up with all sorts of ways to bless believers who have chosen to live in unity.

God wants us to walk together with our brothers. Life will be more pleasant when we do. God wants to bless us, but first we need to get together.

I think He has made unity our responsibility. Instead of forcing it on us, He invites us to seek out our brothers. When we make that effort, when we take the first step and it succeeds, the result is a commanded blessing from God, and an indescribable joy which accompanies unity.

Right now, America is very short on unity. At all levels of society, including the Church, Americans are fractured and fractious. There seems to be little agreement on anything, with scant desire to even seek common ground. This would be a great time for Christ-followers to humble ourselves, build bridges to one another and discipline ourselves to walk as brothers instead of rivals. We could really use some of that commanded blessing. God is just waiting to say the word.

The Bottom Line: Unity brings God's commanded blessing.

DAY 38

Becoming Boring

The idols of the nations are silver and gold,
the work of human hands.
They have mouths, but do not speak;
they have eyes, but do not see;
they have ears, but do not hear,
nor is there any breath in their mouths.
Those who make them become like them,
so do all who trust in them!

Psalm 135:15-18

The pastor from the Philippines said it well, this morning. This first timer in America observed that recessions are not nearly as scary if you live in a country which is already poor. He also commented on how bored Americans seem to be.

He was right. We are rich and we are bored. It's because of the investment we've made in dumb idols. The trouble with dumb idols is they're so... dumb! They're also boring.

The idols of the nations are silver and gold, the work of human hands. Can anyone say, "America?" We are so self-reliant. Our economy is supposed to solve all our problems. We have conditioned ourselves (it's called advertising) to believe that materialism is the answer to all of life's questions. What materialism doesn't fix, education will. So we've been taught.

Here's the reality coming at us from the Bible concerning idol makers: *Those who make them become like them, so do all who trust in them!*

What does that make us? If the focus of our life is on money, possessions and the work of our hands, we're getting dumber by the minute, I guess. We're becoming boring! Each day we bear a closer likeness to a dumb idol. Smart, huh?

Meanwhile, our God does exciting stuff! He is good and He can do anything. This includes being able to do anything *through us*! Ponder that a minute. It has to be true, doesn't it? If God can do anything *without* us, I'll bet He could also do anything *through* us!

We could trust in a living God who can do anything! He's exciting, creative. Unlike the speechless idol, when God speaks, entire worlds spring into existence! He calls us to trust in Him, to be His disciples. It won't be boring.

The Bottom Line: Boring, dumb idols or wonderful, exciting God? Easy choice.

DAY 39

7-11 Scriptures

Give thanks to the LORD, for he is good,
for his steadfast love endures forever.

Psalm 136:1

It was humorous the first few times I heard it. Unfortunately, that was about a hundred times ago. The clever senior who first quipped, "Is that one of them 7-11 choruses?" with accompanying punch-line: "Seven words sung eleven times!" I rank right up there with whoever wrote "Father Abraham." Yeah, some of the choruses are repetitious, overly simple and even dumb, but then, so are some of the hymns! It's just that most loser hymns were weeded out decades ago, while fresh loser choruses are still fresh. And there's something to be said for songs one can sing without consulting a dictionary and a licensed theologian.

Who should be in the winner's circle, the connoisseur of fine hymns or the trendy chorus meister? If you ask God, I think He's like the father who doesn't care what you play on the radio—he's just wanting you to quit taunting each other in the back seat!

Back to repetition. Yes, it can get tedious, but is it wrong? Is it somehow an affront to God to sing, "Yes, Lord, yes, Lord, yes, yes, Lord" a couple dozen times, especially if we mean it? I would think He would accept that kind of praise better than some flowery verses telling Him "No," wouldn't you? And if God despises repetition in our worship, what do we do with Psalm 136? Stick that one up on the overhead and listen to the reaction! What?!

It starts out, *Give thanks to the LORD, for he is good, for his steadfast love endures forever.* Then there's another short phrase about the greatness of God, followed by *for his steadfast love endures forever.* Psalm 136 is 26 verses long—and *every verse* contains the words, *for his steadfast love endures forever.* Anybody want to grouse at God, "Is this one of them 7-11 scriptures?" His reply might be, "No, it's a 6-26 scripture—six words praising me, repeated 26 times. And I'd be offended at your comment, but my steadfast love endures forever."

Try, just try, to get through Psalm 136 without getting the point! *His steadfast love endures forever!* The repetition thing really works! And talk about easy scripture memorization! Oh, and one more thing. Let's lay off the 7-11 joke— and each other. Instead, let's keep our eyes on the One whose love endures forever. Hmm. Wonder why it says "endures."

The Bottom Line: *His steadfast love endures forever!* Imitate it endlessly.

DAY 40

God Repellent

For though the LORD is high, he regards the lowly,
but the haughty he knows from afar.

Psalm 138:6

Does God seem far away?

The attitude of our heart may have a lot to do with it. There's a principle which keeps popping up in scripture:

Humility attracts God; pride repels Him.

If you want to feel far from God, just try copping an attitude with Him! Pride is really repulsive to Him. It's no wonder—when you have all power and all knowledge, it must be hard to stomach having something you created spout off about their own personal grandeur. Add to that the audacity of denying your very existence or placing themselves on or above your level, and it must be difficult to refrain from just flicking them off the globe!

The counterpart of the haughty, "self-made" man is the lowly one. This is the appreciative individual who regards his God with respect and genuine, loving worship. He is ever-mindful of God's mercy and his own unworthiness. But rather than groveling or engaging in self-deprecation, he focuses on adoration of His Maker. Humility is not so much thinking little of ourselves, but thinking of someone *other* than ourselves. Humility seems to attract God's favor and presence like nothing else.

We get to choose—will we be haughty people or lowly people? Our choice will determine how close we feel to God. We can choose to adore God, humble ourselves before Him and enjoy His unmistakable favor. Or we can choose self adoration. That one gains a cold response from God. If we choose pride, God is going to feel distant—either that or He will be in our face, and not happy!

We need major humility in the U.S.! Even within the Church we are haughty people. No wonder God seems so far off, at times. Pride is like God repellent. Self adoration leads to God's disgust. What's the solution?

Become lowly.

The Bottom Line: Humility attracts God; pride repels Him. Go low.

DAY 41

Ridiculously Safe

Where shall I go from your Spirit?
Or where shall I flee from your presence?
If I ascend to heaven, you are there!
If I make my bed in Sheol, you are there!
If I take the wings of the morning,
and dwell in the uttermost parts of the sea,
even there your hand shall lead me,
and your right hand shall hold me.

Psalm 139:7-10

There's more, much more. These musings of David from Psalm 139 are just part of a grand worship poem which reminds me a lot of his most famous one, Psalm 23. Psalm 139 is, to me, sort of like a reprise of Psalm 23. The beautiful, poetic language, the intimacy, the wonder of considering God's majesty and love, it's all there, again (Read the whole thing). There is the focus on not only this present life, but God's creation— His role in creating each of us as individuals. And there is a beautiful, underlying theme of total security, of safety.

Do you suppose we're safe with a God like that? One who formed our body in the womb, One who not only knows our last day of earthly life, but has seen it? Do you think someone who knew the day of our death before the day of our birth could successfully thread us through the minefield of this life, should we ask Him to? We are unbelievably safe with God. We are ridiculously safe.

Unlike cell phones, there is no place—even Sheol, the place of the dead, where we are out of range of God's "coverage." His amazing love follows us all the days of our lives, then switches over to forever.

He knows us—everything about us. He knows our heart, our thoughts—He knows what we will say before we say it. He knows what we will do before we do it. He knows everything there is to know about us, and He has chosen to love us. He doesn't guarantee that we will avoid suffering, injury or death because we trust in Him, but He absolutely guarantees our spiritual safety. We will be with Him forever, if we want to be. He has chosen to keep spiritually safe those who love Him. Combine that with omniscience, omnipresence and omnipotence, and we are not "kinda safe"—we are ridiculously safe! Praise God!

The Bottom Line: We are ridiculously safe with God.

DAY 42

Doubtful Doubts

For you formed my inward parts;
you knitted me together in my mother's womb.
I praise you, for I am fearfully and wonderfully made.

Psalm 139:13-14

We could be the people who appreciate God—as Creator, Friend, Judge of all the Earth, Savior, Guide. We could be people of purity, who on a continuing basis allow God to search us, clean us up and lead us down the path He knows is best. Or we could swallow the lies of the world and try to convince ourselves that we are self-made humans, that we are the masters of the universe, and that somehow, relying on ourselves, our intellect, our strength, we'll make it and everything is going to be O.K. Yeah, right.

We need to decide who really is smart—us or God. Then we should live consistently with that choice, rather than hoping God will ignore the way we discard His truths in favor of more palatable manmade opinions. For instance, is God going to be O.K. when we plead ignorance to when human life begins, giving convenience the benefit of a (doubtful) "doubt," when it comes to the unborn? Especially when He has made it pretty clear from passages like this one and others that we don't suddenly become a real person when the doctor signs our birth certificate and announces, "I think it's a baby!"

When it comes to sin—such as the taking of innocent human life—God is *really* intolerant. We would do best to avoid sin in our own lives at all costs, repent of it when we mess up, and leave the judging of other people's sins to God.

Sometimes—for instance, in the voting booth—we do get to make a choice having to do with righteousness. Often, that choice is between "more righteous" and "less righteous," but at least it's a choice. We need to pray! Then choose according to God's truth, not the prevailing cultural wind (or bag of wind).

What should we pray? It's hard to top what David prayed in the final verses of Psalm 139. The way to a relationship with God is honesty before Him—and humility. This psalm is a splendid example of both, especially those last two verses, Psalm 139:23-24:

Search me, O God, and know my heart! Try me and know my thoughts! And see if there be any grievous way in me, and lead me in the way everlasting!

He will. There's a prayer God will answer!

The Bottom Line: God will lead us in the right way if we are interested.

DAY 43

God's GPS

Make me know the way I should go,
for to you I lift up my soul.

Teach me to do your will,
for you are my God!
Let your good Spirit lead me
on level ground!

Psalm 143:8,10

She saved our marriage. I'm talking about the traveling nag we now plug in to the cigarette lighter, who chirps out instructions right and left about where we are, where we're going and how soon we should be there. If we drive 150 miles past our exit, she doesn't even scold us or yank somebody's license—she just says "recalibrating" a lot and comes up with a new plan.

Of course, I'm talking about the GPS system we now have. It was purchased shortly after a cross-country family vacation two years ago, the lowlight of which was when one of us retorted to the other one who had just driven past the correct exit, "Fine! Read your own map!" Now, when the electronic guidance system steers us wrong (which sometimes happens), we both have someone to gripe at besides each other. Priceless. And if I were knowledgeable about GPS programming (which I'm not), I would customize a GPS with various accents and celebrity voices, plus insert sighs and comments like "You never listen to me!" Our GPS would have lots of personality, as well as a pretty good idea of where we were going.

David needed a GPS, too. I have the feeling when he wrote this psalm he was still stuck in the cave, hiding from Saul. In between pleas for mercy and protection, David asks God for guidance, expecting it. He gets it, too. My experience is that God always answers my prayers for guidance. When I ask Him to show me what to do, He always makes sure I know.

Men get the rap (often deserved) of refusing to stop and ask for directions, even when hopelessly lost (thus the invention of the GPS). We don't tend to like to ask for help! Help is available, though, for both male and female. We can plug into God's Positioning System, whereby we humble ourselves before Him, ask Him for directions and He shows us exactly what to do. God on board? Never lost.

The Bottom Line: The Holy Spirit is the ultimate GPS.

DAY 44

Marathon Praise

I will extol you, my God and King,
and bless your name forever and ever.
Every day I will bless you
and praise your name forever and ever.
Great is the LORD, and greatly to be praised,
and his greatness is unsearchable.

Psalm 145:1-3

I just spent four hours praising God publicly. I didn't mean to, and neither did Scott, my new friend, but that's how it ended up.

How did it happen? Scott, a local pastor whose church we have recently attended, wanted to get better acquainted with me, so he invited me to lunch at a restaurant. We started telling each other stories from our lives about the important stuff—family, friends, ministry. It turned out that in every single story God was the Hero. Another subject just brought on another God story. Some were funny. Some were emotional. In every single one of them, God came through. It turns out that for both of us, God is our ultimate Hero and best Friend. We praised Him publicly for four hours—and all we did was just talk about how good He is, how smart and loving He is, and what He has done for us, personally, in our lives. People came, ordered, ate and left, as we talked on and on about all the great stuff God has done for us. Behind us for the first couple hours was another pastor doing the same thing with his lunch guest. (Both these men are doing a fantastic job of shepherding their churches and touching the community, by the way).

We were in public, but I don't know if anyone else was listening or not. I don't really care. What mattered was that we were sharing out loud the stories of God's greatness. Just hitting a few of the highlights took us four hours; recounting all of God's blessings in our lives would have taken, well, *forever and ever.* And seeing as how the blessings never stop—such as a delightful afternoon of praising God in public with a new friend—that means we'll never get caught up. We'll never be done praising God. Hmm. Maybe that's the point. And if somebody at the teriyaki place ends up in heaven because they overheard people talking about how great God is, it's just one more blessing to add to an endless pile!

Every day I will bless you and praise your name forever and ever. That's a good plan. And we'll never run out of stories where God is the Hero.

The Bottom Line: *Every day I will bless you and praise your name forever and ever.*

DAY 45

Who Taught You to Fight?

Blessed be the LORD, my rock,
who trains my hands for war,
and my fingers for battle;
he is my steadfast love and my fortress,
my stronghold and my deliverer,
my shield and he in whom I take refuge,
who subdues peoples under me.

Psalm 144:1-2

When it comes to battles in the spiritual realm, Halloween is as in-your-face as it gets. The customary reaction of Christians to what is too often a celebration of all things ungodly is to cower, compromise or cringe. None of those responses feels very courageous. Aren't most of us just glad when it's over?

How about the rest of the year? When it comes to spiritual warfare, how many followers of Jesus "don't go in for that sort of thing," tending always to veer toward the sedate aspects of the Christian life? We won't even pray for patience, fearing God might answer our prayer and give us some, then make us use it!

I've heard people try to apologize for God's violent past, as if it were something He had to outgrow, like a tribal deity herded into anger management.

David, author of Psalm 144, thanks God for some things. One of them is for teaching him to fight. Talk about a politically incorrect passage! But think who this is—this is the psalm-writing harp player with a bear skin rug and Goliath's sword over the mantle before he was full-grown. Who taught David to fight? God did. The same One taught him to make music and write the grandest psalms in the history of mankind.

Are we being trained for anything? If not, why not? Does God "not do that sort of thing anymore"? I'm *not* advocating some sort of physical violence against anyone in the name of Christ. I'm talking about spiritual warfare, when we stand up to Satan and rescue people in Jesus' name. I'm talking about prayer, tearing down spiritual strongholds we can't even see, by talking to a God we can't see, either. I think God wants us to submit to Him for training. What would He do with us?

In a world where the devil is trashing lives with cruel abandon everywhere we look, I just can't see God training us to sit, and nothing more. If we let Him teach us spiritual warfare, I'll bet we'll have our chance to actually use those skills.

The Bottom Line: If we are willing, God will teach us to fight spiritual battles.

DAY 46

What Pleases God

His delight is not in the strength of the horse,
nor his pleasure in the legs of a man,
but the LORD takes pleasure in those who fear him,
in those who hope in his steadfast love.

Psalm 147:10-11

I know people who delight in horses. Some delight in dogs or cats. Some delight in cars. People collect all sorts of things, from antiques to faceless dolls. Many delight in sports. Or the latest technology. Everyone with grandchildren seems to delight in them. The list is endless. So, is there anything in which God delights? As a matter of fact, there is, according to Psalm 147:11: *but the LORD takes pleasure in those who fear him, in those who hope in his steadfast love.*

There is a delight which comes to God's heart when people respect and honor Him. When people depend on Him and accept His love for them, it gives God pleasure. It's not really that hard to please God! All we need to do is love Him back. When we delight in Him, we can be sure He delights in us.

Is that so difficult? What is not to like about God?! Yet, the tendency is to be more preoccupied with things like cars or houses than with the God who made the Universe! It's quite easy to transfer the attention which ought to be focused on our Creator to something else. Remember the end of the book of Jonah? The prophet is unceremoniously delivered to his assigned destination by being wretched up on the beach by a giant fish. Having now learned the lesson that obedience to God is inevitable, Jonah still hadn't learned the attitude part. He preaches repentance to Nineveh, and is so successful in his endeavors that God gladly changes His mind about destroying the city.

Instead of being happy about it and writing a best-selling book for prophets on revival techniques, Jonah sulks outside the city, despondent because God spared his enemies. God provides a fast-growing gourd plant to furnish Jonah shade for his pity party. Instead of delighting in God, who is kind to both prophets and pagans, Jonah's delight is only in the gourd. It's his new best friend.

God takes it away; Jonah bitterly complains. The book ends with God's gentle rebuke for a prophet who cares more about a shade plant than for an entire city of people. What pleases God? People who hope in Him, delight in Him, and have His heart. If we try to please God, we will. It's that simple.

The Bottom Line: What pleases God?
Obedience, with a good attitude.

DAY 47

Make My Day

The fear of the LORD is the beginning of knowledge;
fools despise wisdom and instruction.

Proverbs 1:7

The tide of information keeps growing higher. We're drowning in it. But what about wisdom? Not so much.

Man's knowledge has gotten us to the moon and back. God should be impressed. After all, He only created the moon; we landed some people on it. Isn't it obvious which one of us is smarter? We can accomplish anything we want.

"Just like at the Tower of Babel."

"That was different. Those were primitive people who didn't know any better. Now we have computer technology so once again, almost everyone in the world can understand each other. We can do anything we want. This time you wouldn't be able to stop us."

"So you're going to try to beat me with knowledge, something I created in the first place? Is that right? As one of your own poets has said, 'Go ahead. Make my day.'"

"What could you do?"

"I think the right question is, 'What can't I do?'

All of your knowledge is based on things you've learned about a Universe I created. I gave you that knowledge in the first place. I gave you the ability to think. You think you're smart because you learned the rules I put in force! If I made the rules in the first place, how hard would it be for me to change the rules? Make new ones? Eliminate any or all of the rules? Eliminate any or all of Creation? I'm not bound by 'knowledge.' Had I wanted to destroy your space program, or anything else, it wouldn't have been very hard, for me!

Do you think that somehow, because I've allowed you to accumulate a little pile of knowledge, I am subject to your knowledge? That's the oldest lie ever told, isn't it? Who was it that said that if you just got enough knowledge—if you knew about not only good, but also evil, then you'd be like Me? The serpent. Do you recall where believing that lie led?

Meanwhile, for all who are interested, I offer more than just information. I offer wisdom. There will always be fools who think they are smarter than Me. But for those seeking true wisdom who submit to my instruction and follow Me, the learning will never stop. Knowledge is a creation of mine. It begins with Me. It will never rule Me. If someone wants to try to defeat Me using knowledge, that's up to them. But a wise person would never do that. It's why they're wise.

The Bottom Line: Real wisdom begins with a respect for God.

DAY 48

Children of Privilege

The true light, which enlightens everyone, was coming into the world. He was in the world, and the world was made through him, yet the world did not know him. He came to his own, and his own people did not receive him. But to all who did receive him, who believed in his name, he gave the right to become children of God, who were born, not of blood nor of the will of the flesh nor of the will of man, but of God.

And the Word became flesh and dwelt among us, and we have seen his glory, glory as of the only Son from the Father, full of grace and truth. John 1:9-14

The world looks different for children of privilege. While some kids in poor countries patrol garbage dumps looking for lunch, children of privilege know which fork to use and have never been to a garbage dump. A child born into a wealthy home doesn't think about whether or not they will eat, but only about what. They don't fret over finances for things like food and shelter. When holidays roll around, hopes are justifiably high.

The attitude of the rest of society toward children of privilege is usually, "Lucky kid! They'll never have to do without." More than a bit of class envy lurks in our society. Never mind that so many rich kids grow up to be decadent, spoiled brats, completely lacking in wisdom, relationship skills and privacy. A lot of them don't look "lucky" at all. Better to be raised by God-fearing, hardworking parents who "encouraged" us to mimic their values and work ethic upon pain of whatever it took. Praise God for lack of "privilege," when it comes to some stuff!

But speaking of God, did you catch the "privilege clause" in this first chapter of John? The part that said that whoever wanted to had the right to become a child of God, and all we have to do is believe it's a genuine offer and accept it? Talk about lucky kids! Can you see God's child doing without? (Actually, we can. Christmas is coming up. Doesn't every first-time mother dream of giving birth in a barn and not having so much as a clean place to lay her new baby, born without benefit of a doctor?) So, the "child of God" part doesn't always equal luxury accommodations, at least, not here. (After here, we'll not be disappointed).

Think of the things we don't have to stress over since we're children of God. He doesn't wish for us to become decadent, spoiled brats, so He'll probably allow us to earn our own way, make our own choices, face our own consequences. In addition, the sin-strewn world we inhabit hasn't been remodeled for our enjoyment, yet. But the day is coming when we receive our inheritance. Meanwhile, our Father can do anything. His kids have a whole lot of stuff to not worry about.

The Bottom Line: We have a lot to not worry about.

DAY 49

Formula for a Miracle

On the third day there was a wedding at Cana in Galilee, and the mother of Jesus was there. Jesus also was invited to the wedding with his disciples. When the wine ran out, the mother of Jesus said to him, "They have no wine." And Jesus said to her, "Woman, what does this have to do with me? My hour has not yet come." His mother said to the servants, "Do whatever he tells you."

Now there were six stone water jars there for the Jewish rites of purification, each holding twenty or thirty gallons. Jesus said to the servants, "Fill the jars with water." And they filled them up to the brim. And he said to them, "Now draw some out and take it to the master of the feast." So they took it. When the master of the feast tasted the water now become wine, and did not know where it came from (though the servants who had drawn the water knew), the master of the feast called the bridegroom and said to him, "Everyone serves the good wine first, and when people have drunk freely, then the poor wine. But you have kept the good wine until now." This, the first of his signs, Jesus did at Cana in Galilee, and manifested his glory. And his disciples believed in him. John 2:1-11

What's the formula for a miracle from God? Take a genuine need, then add faith and obedience. The bridegroom needed a miracle. He was out of wine and money, with days left to go in the wedding feast, and few options. Jesus' mother didn't have any money, either, but she'd given birth to the Son of God. She barged past His reluctance to get involved. Her faith in Him prompted His first miracle. Sometimes, that's what it takes. God hardly ever comes up to people saying, "Wanta see a miracle?" First, there's need. Then, there's faith.

I love the way she involves Jesus by involving the servants. *"Do whatever he tells you."* Always good advice, when it comes to God! With a parting "Tag, you're it" motherly move, suddenly it's all up to Jesus. The servants will obey; if He says nothing, they're off the hook. He says two sentences, they obey, and the Messiah's first miracle is in the books. Need. Faith. Obedience. Miracle. Easy!

If it's so easy, why don't we see more miracles? Little need, for one thing. Miracles are for people with no other option. Little faith, for another. How many of us take our needs directly to Jesus, instead of hatching our own plan? Then there's obedience. Is it hard to follow instructions which don't make sense, like carting water to your boss, who is expecting wine? Yes, but obedience is the final ingredient for a miracle. The formula is there in the Book: Need. Faith. Obedience. Miracle. Easy.

The Bottom Line: Formula for a miracle:
Need. Faith. Obedience. Miracle.

DAY 50

Praising God in an Empty Barn

Though the fig tree should not blossom,
nor fruit be on the vines,
the produce of the olive fail
and the fields yield no food,
the flock be cut off from the fold
and there be no herd in the stalls,
yet I will rejoice in the LORD;
I will take joy in the God of my salvation.
GOD, the Lord, is my strength;
he makes my feet like the deer's;
he makes me tread on my high places.

Habakkuk 3:17-19

Thanksgiving Day in a land of plenty. Even in a deep recession, we have much for which to be grateful. Sadly, many aren't thankful at all. The fact is, gratitude is a choice, not something which happens to people with full tummies. If we don't learn to choose thanksgiving, contentment will always be elusive.

Habakkuk the prophet had learned contentment. In this passage he shows how effective it can be. Rather than praising God for a year of bounty, he is praising God in an empty barn. He speaks of a situation where every crop has failed, no food is available and there are no livestock in any of the pens. Starvation is a definite possibility. No hope is on the horizon. Yet he is rejoicing in the Lord. What can you do to someone like that? Satan knows the answer: Not much.

Though for a lot of us the barns aren't exactly bulging with abundance, at least compared to times past, we're still a long ways from Habakkuk's situation. If he could praise God in an empty barn, we could at least do it sitting down to a Thanksgiving feast! Sure, we have bills to pay. There are uncertainties in our economy. There are things we might like which we cannot afford. So what? We have a great God who, when we trust Him, makes our steps as surefooted as a mountain goat's. He'll come through for us. We need to trust Him and loosen up.

We don't have to wait for things to get better before we thank God. It's a choice we can make, whether the pens are full or empty. The enemy of our souls finds it unsettling: "If they praise God in an empty barn, what would they do in a full one?!" If we want great acoustics for praise, it's hard to beat an empty barn. Let 'er rip.

The Bottom Line: We don't need full barns in order to praise God.

DAY 51

Too Much to be a Disciple

And Jesus, looking at him, loved him, and said to him, "You lack one thing: go, sell all that you have and give to the poor, and you will have treasure in heaven; and come, follow me." Disheartened by the saying, he went away sorrowful, for he had great possessions. Mark 10:21-22

The rich young ruler had a lot to leave behind: the family inheritance, the wealth, the privileges that went along with it, the expectations of his family. Jesus made it clear, though: *So therefore, any one of you who does not renounce all that he has cannot be my disciple.* (Lk 14:33) He meant everyone, not just people on the "rich and famous" list.

In our mind, we reason, "That's not fair! I can't leave all of this! I have too much, to just walk away from it!"

The Lord, reading our minds, answers, "Precisely. That's why you must leave it. You can't follow me and manage an estate at the same time. You can't obey my orders and fulfill your family's dreams at the same time. It's one or the other.*"Any one of you who does not renounce all that he has cannot be my disciple.*

What do you mean, I can't be Your disciple?! All of this is Yours!

Good. Then leave it, and come follow me alone, without any of this. You can't follow me and manage all this stuff at the same time.

But...

I thought you said it was all mine, that you were doing it all for me. Did I misunderstand?

No, but... Why are you making this so hard for me? I just asked you to bless what I'm doing for you; I didn't ask you to take it all away!

Fine, then. I'll be going, now.

Where are you going?

I have blessings to deliver to some people who call me "Master" and mean it.

We'll have revival when we want it more than we want our wealth. Man, I hate to say that, but I'm afraid it's true. Like the young ruler, as long as we love our wealth more than we love following Jesus, we're going to be stuck watching the Lord work in other people's lives and in other countries, while we ride herd on the inheritance. Revival may not actually cost us our wealth, but then again, it probably will. And for those of us who have a hard time walking away from the riches, God may just do us a tremendous favor and send along a natural, economic or political disaster to free us up to follow Him.

The Bottom Line: If I'm not willing to give up everything, I can't be a disciple.

DAY 52

Houston? Gotta Problem

If anyone thinks the Church in America is firing on all cylinders, I don't know whom it might be. If we were a sports team, we'd be something like 1-16 at this point in the season. Reflecting on the glories of our solitary win won't make the rest of the season less painful. We need a pretty big turnaround. Meanwhile, our competition grows more confident.

What's our problem? It's not God. It's not the Bible nor the plan of salvation. No updates needed there. So, what are the key factors which have put the Church in America in such a mournful condition? These are a few of the observations I've made, in no particular order:

Lack of Focus

We just want it all, in America. Most churches try to do everything, afraid to neglect anyone's good idea. The energy is diffused all over the place, like someone attempting to put out a fire by opening the fire hydrant prior to the truck getting there. A lot of water shoots out, but it just goes down the drain.

Lack of Purpose

Churches have mission statements, but people generally don't pay much attention to them or even know what they are. Instead, they bring their own agenda for the purpose of the church. Finding others with the same agenda is like finding a blood donor match—difficult. It's also tough to find people willing to lay aside their personal agenda in order to participate in someone else's larger plan.

Lack of Love

I hate to even talk about this one. Where's the deep-seated love for Jesus in the American Church? Where's the committed love for one another, even for our spouses? Until love reigns in the Church, we will be frustrated and floundering.

Lack of Holiness

This goes with the lack of love. If we don't really love Jesus, why would it bother us if we're not becoming more like Him? As long as Christianity is presented to the world as a 2-minute prayer, a 2-second dunk, then you're in the church directory waiting for the bus to heaven, there won't be much difference between believers and non-believers. If no real change is even expected, we ought to quit calling it "conversion." God's standard has always been holiness. It hasn't changed. We need to get back on His standard and ditch ours.

The Bottom Line: Problems in the Church?
Lack of focus, purpose, love, holiness.

DAY 53

Houston? More Problems

Not only are we facing severe *lack* in the Church in America in several areas; we're also dealing with *too much*. How so?

Too Many Resources!

We're drowning in resources. Much of the time, all it does is keep us from ever needing God for anything. Sure, a personal tragedy or a national scare temporarily drives us to our knees, but as soon as the danger is past and things are back under our control, we resume spending our lives in the endless accumulation of possessions, each of them exacting its own tax on our time. Refusing to deprive ourselves (or our churches) of the basic niceties of life, we trudge on, managing our resources and pleading for more, neglecting our souls. Spiritually, we'd be better off with less. The kind of whining "less" would generate is something I'd rather not consider. We already have too much, and we want more.

In the Old Testament book of Judges (ch. 7), God required Gideon to pare down his army from 32,000 to 300. God knew if He granted the Israelites victory with a real army, they would take credit, themselves. With 300, there was no question who had helped them win. Are we willing to let God do *decreases* in our lives in order to free us from burdens or to simplify things, or will we only allow Him to *add*? What would have happened to Gideon had he decided to say "Thanks, but no thanks" to God's direct instruction? Would he have just won with 32,000 instead? In the Church in America, time after time, we're stuck with our resources and another loss, when we could have had a win if we'd done it God's way. Does that mean we need to shed our stuff? We do, if God said. Either way, we'd better get with His plan if we hope to see victory.

Too Many Choices

Jesus gave His disciples one choice: "Follow me," or not. Caught up in the spirit of our age, we've managed to make discipleship—obedience to Jesus—optional, rather than a core requirement of Christianity! In its place has arisen the consumer mentality which customizes the Christian faith to align with our own personal preferences, in everything from worship styles to doctrinal beliefs. If we don't get what we want, we just go elsewhere. The Almighty does not take dictation well. True disciples take orders from their master; they don't give them. If we follow the Lord, He will get us home. If we try to lead God through a maze of requirements to satisfy us, we'll find ourselves making a journey to nowhere, all alone. Disciples get one choice: Follow Jesus. Or not. Only one choice leads home.

The Bottom Line: Don't let anything keep you from following Jesus.

DAY 54

Starting Over

Now there was a man of the Pharisees named Nicodemus, a ruler of the Jews. This man came to Jesus by night and said to him, "Rabbi, we know that you are a teacher come from God, for no one can do these signs that you do unless God is with him. Jesus answered him, "Truly, truly, I say to you, unless one is born again he cannot see the kingdom of God." Nicodemus said to him, "How can a man be born when he is old? Can he enter a second time into his mother's womb and be born?" Jesus answered, "Truly, truly, I say to you, unless one is born of water and the Spirit, he cannot enter the kingdom of God. That which is born of the flesh is flesh, and that which is born of the Spirit is spirit. Do not marvel that I said to you, 'You must be born again.'" John 3:1-7

Nicodemus was in a bind. He realized Jesus had to be from God, yet to acknowledge this would be to lose his position in the Sanhedrin, the Jewish ruling council. He wanted to know more, but didn't dare make his inquiry in public. He came to Jesus by night, thinking this was a safe way to gain information without losing his spot in society. What he didn't realize was that a person can never gain the Kingdom of God and keep their place in the world. We have to start over.

The principle of spiritual transformation is STARTING OVER. That's it. Instead of taking a society of fleshly human beings and educating them or prospering them into some sort of positive change, the only real answer is in them being born again, and starting over, this time as people born of God's Spirit. We *start over*, or there's no change. The only one who can transform lives is Jesus.

That's why we need to lift up Jesus. We need to look to Him as our ONLY hope! We need to stop calling it "conversion" when people haven't been born again, they haven't started over, and they haven't even been asked to. We must be born again, this time of the Spirit, rather than the flesh. And we need to learn to operate by the Spirit, instead of starting out with the flesh, then trying to make it spiritual. Only the Spirit gives birth to spirit.

So we start over. We relinquish all our fleshly gains, humble ourselves before God, and begin anew with Him. This time, instead of the self-made man or woman, we are born of Him, and belong to Him. We're spiritual, not because we logged so many hours in religious instruction, but because we're born of the Spirit. The rub is being willing to start over! Nicodemus had a lot to lose: Great political influence, reputation, economic status. As a Pharisee, he had made a career out of keeping the Law. He knew the scriptures like few others. But to even get into God's Kingdom, he still had to start over. So do we. We must be born again.

The Bottom Line: Salvation is about starting over, being born again.

DAY 55

A New Old Model

Where can we find a model which would point us in the right direction for the Church of today? It's pretty hard to top the Early Church. What was unique about them? Here are just a few observations:

- The Early Church were servants of Jesus Christ, and not much else.
- Christianity was not something they practiced on rainy weekends, or where allowed by law. When they became believers, it changed everything in their lives— and sometimes ended their lives! Death-defying commitment was considered normal, for them.
- They were exclusive, yet inclusive. The Gospel and the love were for everyone–even their enemies, but the fellowship was reserved for those who were committed believers, and *"none of the rest dared join them."* (Acts 5:13)
- They focused on making disciples instead of "converts."

The contrast to the Church in America is painful. It's obvious that we need something "new," yet "old,"where:

- Lives are actually changed, and everyone can see the difference.
- People have a deep-seated commitment to God and a mutual commitment to one another.
- Discipleship is an expectation.
- The focus is on the Lord, rather than the organization or the pastor.

The Church in America is not doing very well, these days. There's a lot of dissatisfaction and hurt. Much of it has to do with how far removed we are from the focus and the mentality of our forebears in the Early Church. They had problems, too. They faced incredible obstacles, yet God used them to transform their society. Our current ineffectiveness is directly tied to our lack of commitment and discipline. The more we move in the direction of the old model of Christianity, the more our results will resemble theirs. This new idea of part-time Christian commitment isn't working. We can throw all the money, advertising, church growth techniques and technology we want at our society, but they won't budge, spiritually, until they witness lives which have been shockingly changed by Jesus, forever. When luke-warm, gripy Christianity is replaced with death-defying commitment, not only to God but to one another, it will shake things up. Until then, we'll just have to read about it in Acts. Lesser plans are not going to help us.

The Bottom Line: Death-defying commitment to Christ and one another–normal.

DAY 56

Free Range Hearts

Keep your heart with all vigilance,
for from it flow the springs of life.
Proverbs 4:23

Headlines shouted to the world the news of sins thought secret. The richest athlete in the world dived into seclusion, struggling to repair self-inflicted damage to his family, reputation and finances. I prayed for him and his family. It's a reminder to us all that if you let your heart run free, it will probably take you over a cliff. The point is, knowing the right thing to do and doing it are two entirely different things. How many times have we been shocked to find that the very person exposing someone else's immorality was later discovered to have been engaged in the same sin?

Where does stupid and tragic sin begin? In the heart. Logic is dislodged in favor of lust. Offenses are left lying around, unforgiven, and pretty soon there's a crop of baby bitterness plants sprouting. Bitterness takes root, then takes over. It grows and becomes justification for deeds which would never have withstood the least bit of objective scrutiny. Shielded in the heart from the ravages of reality, the monster mutates. Sin is conceived. It grows and gives birth—to death (James 1:15).

But sin can never survive God's light. Everything we bring before Him is quickly burned clean. In order for sin to grow, it needs the welcoming shelter of an unguarded heart, a heart turned away from God's light. If we neglect to keep a vigilant watch over what we allow to enter our heart, it soon becomes a greenhouse for sin. When it comes to that, it's like my pastor, Paul Cunningham, used to say: "Sin always takes you further than you intended to go."

The place where sin must be stopped is at the heart level. A clean heart harbors no sin. We do best when we follow the apostle Paul's prescription and drag every thought into the light and make it submit to God (2 Corinthians 10:5). If we give solace in our heart to sinful desires, they are like a ticking time bomb—it's only a matter of time and opportunity before wrong desires will turn into wrong actions. It's only a matter of time before every single one of those wrong actions will be made known to all (Luke 12:2-3).Then, what?

The smart plan is to guard our heart with all vigilance. God will help us. It's a battle worth fighting, because everything depends on it. What is in our heart will one day be revealed to all. Meanwhile, all of life springs from what we let in to our heart, and more importantly, what we allow to stay.

The Bottom Line: We dare not leave our heart unguarded.

DAY 57

Beyond John 3:16

Whoever believes in the Son has eternal life; whoever does not obey the Son shall not see life, but the wrath of God remains on him. John 3:36

In the past several decades we've heard a lot about "belief" in Jesus in the Church, but not as much about obedience to Him, and hardly anything at all about the "wrath of God." I realize there have been periods in our country when "hellfire and brimstone" preaching may have been overdone, but the reality of God's wrath and a final Judgment for all didn't suddenly disappear because it no longer made such a popular sermon topic. The only way to avoid "the wrath of God" is through believing in *and obeying* Jesus, the Son of God. That's not a statement based upon a current fad or pet doctrine, but merely the truth of the Bible. We don't have to like it or be comfortable with it in order for it to be true.

Too many people have stopped at John 3:16: *For God so loved the world, that he gave his only Son, that whoever believes in him should not perish but have eternal life.* Great promises! Eternal life! All we have to do is "believe" in him and it's ours. There's not a word about obedience to Him or repentance or following Him, so that means it's only about "belief," right?

Then why is it that 20 verses later, in the same chapter, belief and obedience are used interchangeably, as if they were basically the same thing? Whoever believes in the Son has eternal life; whoever does not obey the Son shall not see life, but the wrath of God remains on him (John 3:36). Also in the same chapter, why is Nicodemus, the Jewish ruler who came to Jesus at night admitting his "belief" that Jesus had to have come from God, told he must be born again, seeing as he already believed Jesus was from God?

How could we think that saying we believed in Jesus was the only thing which counted, but obedience to Him was optional? If we believe in the Son, we'll obey Him. If we choose not to obey Him, it means we don't really believe He is the Son of God, in which case, God's wrath remains on us. We dare not stop at "belief," especially if that "belief" is nothing more than a weak acknowledgment of Jesus' existence and maybe deity, but includes no submission on our part to His will. True belief and obedience are so closely linked we'll not find one without the other.

There's not a thing wrong with John 3:16. Millions have found Christ through this verse. What is wrong is stopping at "belief," when the expectation is clear that with belief in Christ comes obedience to Christ. If we choose not to obey the Son of God, we'll deal instead with the very real wrath of God, regardless of what we say we believe. John 3:16 is a great beginning. But keep going.

The Bottom Line: Don't stop at John 3:16. Go on to obedience.

DAY 58

The Sin for Stupid People

For the lips of a forbidden woman drip honey,
and her speech is smoother than oil,
but in the end she is bitter as wormwood,
sharp as a two-edged sword.
Her feet go down to death;
her steps follow the path to Sheol;

Proverbs 5:3-5

Even in a nation awash in immorality, adultery still bears a price tag. It always has. It's just that in cultures which have chosen to distance themselves from God's laws, the real price tag is concealed. It's a classic bait-and-switch technique. What is offered are the glories of adventure, romance and intrigue. "True love," (crow the songs, movies, romance novels and TV dramas) ignores the restraints of "a piece of paper" (i.e., marriage license) and roams where it wants, with a happy ending for all involved. Reality plays out differently. Reality is, well, like the saga of the world's greatest golfer and his now fractured perfect family. You mean adultery is a sin which can blow up your whole life, and you can basically lose it all? Yup. Cool, huh? Who wouldn't want to toss away a marriage to a supermodel, two beautiful children and $100 million in endorsements based on your reputation for a little extra excitement in life? Such a deal! Not only that, but you get to face God after it's all over and answer to Him for your actions, even if you manage to slide through life without getting caught. Adultery! Sounds like the sin for stupid people.

Our God longs for us to be wise. Proverbs 5 is a full-chapter expose on adultery, which should be read in its entirety. The scripture pleads with sons to avoid this sin at all costs and instead "rejoice in the wife of your youth." We're reminded that God sees all we do. There is mournful, true-to-life testimony which applied to the adulterer in 1,000 B.C. and still applies in the 21st century. Listen!

I did not listen to the voice of my teachers
or incline my ear to my instructors.
I am at the brink of utter ruin
in the assembled congregation. (Prov. 5:13-14)

Does this sound like someone glad he chose the exciting route of unfaithfulness? Was the passion worth the price? The answer is a resounding "No!" In our owner's manual for life are some pretty strong warnings. One of them is that adultery is a sin for stupid people.

The Bottom Line: Adultery is stupid!
Always has been. Always will be.

DAY 59

Jump on the Bed Verse

How long will you lie there, O sluggard?
When will you arise from your sleep?
A little sleep, a little slumber,
a little folding of the hands to rest,
and poverty will come upon you like a robber,
and want like an armed man.

Proverbs 6:9-10

This was my brother's jump on the bed verse. He would quote it to me as he pounced, sent from Mom or Dad to wake me so I could do morning chores on our farm before going off to school. Being a sound, sleep-loving sleeper, it was not one of my favorite scripture passages, particularly considering the source of the gleeful recitation and the manner of its delivery. Who doesn't want a scripture-quoting, pouncing kid brother for an alarm clock? Everyone, that's who.

It was effective, though. It got me up, even if it was to try to pound him. Maybe that's what woke me up prematurely this morning, on a Christmas vacation day when I didn't need to rise early, but couldn't go back to sleep. My brother is a couple thousand miles away, so it wasn't him, and nobody jumped on my bed quoting this or any other scripture. I think what woke me was a combination of worry and unfinished business. Mulling over numerous projects and errands in need of completion, worrying over the sufficiency of resources, financial and otherwise, it was hard to relax and go back to sleep, even though my wife and I had worked past midnight.

I find that worry makes me tired, all by itself. It need not be accompanied by any work at all—just thinking about the what if's and what if not's brings on a sensation of weariness that makes me want to go to bed and forget it all in sleep. It also makes me want to stay there. Roll over and catch a few more winks, instead of getting up to face unpleasant responsibilities! It's like the adage I recently heard: "Why procrastinate today when you can procrastinate tomorrow?"

But procrastination has a way of multiplying problems. Changing the engine is harder and more expensive than changing the oil, but if we ignore the oil long enough, we get to do the engine. A lot of life is like that, including relationships. The best way to deal with responsibility is to get up and deal with it. If we try to sleep it away or lose ourselves in other mind-numbing diversions, we shouldn't be surprised if poverty and want show up to break down the door. I'd rather get jumped on by my brother. *How long will you lie there, O sluggard?* O.K., I'm up.

The Bottom Line: Get up. Do something constructive, instead of worrying about it.

DAY 60

At the Well

A woman from Samaria came to draw water. Jesus said to her, "Give me a drink." John 4:7

How do we influence people toward faith? John 4 reads like a textbook on the subject. It was Jesus who initiated the conversation with a Samaritan woman. He's the one who wouldn't let her just brush Him off, though she tried. He's the one who piqued her appetite for spiritual things. And He's the one she told about when she went back to her village and became an evangelist, herself. Jesus spent two days with the people of her village, and poured Himself out among them. It started at the well, the place where everyone must go.

And what happens in our churches in America? We too often gather to hide and divide. We hide from the scary people of the world who don't want anything to do with us, who wonder why we even would talk to them, who remind us of our scandals and our prejudices and faults every time the subject comes up, but who would be very interested in living water, if we ever pushed through to that subject, instead of getting stuck on non-essential details. And when we gather, there seems to be too little burden for the world of weary people outside our doors. We become fixated on our traditions and trends. All the world knows of us is "You don't think we do it right; you say we have to worship in your church and in your way or it's not really worship." Too often, they're right! That is what we think. Until we're willing to meet them at the well, the public place where everyone is forced to go, like it or not, we will *never* see the harvest, because the harvest doesn't go stampeding into the barn or the granary. We have to go out and get it.

First we have to see it. We're sitting in our churches, wringing our hands over programs and building payments, trying to find just the right minister for our church to keep everyone satisfied and fed, and maybe make the church grow enough to give us a sense of pride and accomplishment, but not enough to significantly alter our lifestyle or intrude on our comfort zone. Meanwhile, the fields are "white" with harvest, meaning if we don't get with it, we're going to lose the whole thing!

People are looking for *something*. They're looking for living water, because they're tired of the tedium of trying to scratch out a reason for existence, every day, in lives which are unfulfilled and crammed with sin. If the Church in America regained a vision of the harvest, and allowed the Holy Spirit to launch us out of our buildings, big things could happen very quickly. We could let the harvest go, or we could choose to love and engage the lost He died for. We'll find them at the well.

The Bottom Line: Those we need to reach are at "the well." Let's go to them.

DAY 61

The New Year's Kit

For by grace you have been saved through faith. And this is not your own doing; it is the gift of God, not a result of works, so that no one may boast. For we are his workmanship, created in Christ Jesus for good works, which God prepared beforehand, that we should walk in them. Ephesians 2:8-10

That's the scripture reference the world saw, emblazoned below the eyes of one of the most talented, most disciplined and most godly quarterbacks ever to play college football, Tim Tebow, as he played his final college game for the Florida Gators. To say he did well in it would be an understatement. He set five Sugar Bowl records and snagged MVP honors on the way to a win over previously undefeated Cincinnati. His passing and rushing for the game added up to 533 yards. Good grief! The scripture references on the cheekbones have been standard fare for a long time. So has the lifestyle to match the scripture. Even his critics haven't found holes in Tebow's witness. There are high hopes for an NFL career, but whatever happens, if Tim Tebow keeps living for the Lord, his future is really, really bright.

But then, so is ours. I haven't noticed any NFL recruiters lurking around, lately (or ever), and I seriously doubt if painting Bible references on my face would help, seeing as I wasn't even draft material for grade school recess, back in my prime. Now if they had a reverse draft where you paid someone not to be on your team, I might have qualified for that one! No matter. God has a plan for each of us, including the athletically challenged.

It's like a kit, individually prepared for us, with this year's date on it. What's in it? All the resources we will need. Specific instructions. Technical support. Good works, prepared in advance for us to do, with our individual talents in mind. Some assembly is required, so we'll get to use our imagination and faith and stuff, but it's all there—everything we'll need to have a really great year. It's not "one-size-fits-all," but custom-made for us. We can always trust God for a perfect fit.

This whole year is lined out for us. There are good works prepared with our name on them. Resources wait in the wings. Someone created us for what lies just ahead. He's the One who will guide and strengthen us as we go forward in His name. It's all there, everything we need.

For we are his workmanship, created in Christ Jesus for good works, which God prepared beforehand, that we should walk in them.

Pick up your kit and walk.

The Bottom Line: God has a "good works" kit prepared for each of us.

DAY 62

Pick a Duck and Shoot It

"You miss 100% of the shots you never take." Wayne Gretzky

Years ago, as a high school kid, one of my favorite sports was duck hunting. Growing up on a South Dakota farm with five lakes, fifteen minutes was all I needed to go hunting. When it came to bagging ducks, I had ample access, plus the time and equipment, but two problems kept me from consistent success.

The first was poor marksmanship. Ducks fly fast, presenting a difficult target, and I was still a novice with a shotgun. I missed a lot.

The second problem was mental. Ducks not only fly fast; they also tend to fly together. The usual scenario was to be surprised by a flock zipping overhead, barely in range, and moving out in a hurry. I often had only a second or two to get my gun up and fire, from first sighting to last chance. Therein lay my problem.

I've never been one to make decisions easily, or quickly. I like to ponder stuff, consider all the possibilities, procrastinate a little to avoid making hasty mistakes. This tendency was making our farm a safe place for ducks. When a flock of mallards buzzed by, unannounced, I had to figure out what to shoot at. Should I aim at the one in front? The biggest one? Should I try to make sure I shot at only drakes? Sometimes I would start aiming at one, then change my mind and switch to another. Sometimes I would get greedy and start plotting how to get more than one. Sometimes I would just point toward the flock, trying to bring them all down!

I usually did actually fire my gun, but seldom did anything fall. While I was deciding, they were flying. I never did bring one down with a confused look.

Eventually, I nagged myself into a concept that made my 20 gauge a bit more intimidating to waterfowl. First of all, I kept at it and gradually improved some in shooting ability. Even more importantly, I learned to *pick a duck and shoot it* (or at least *at it*). Rather than gazing at a big flock with a bewildered stare, trying to compute the angles and attributes of each possibility, I forced myself to just *pick one(!)*, and totally ignore the rest. When the flock had passed, I couldn't tell you how many there had been. All I knew was that I had chosen one, aimed, fired, and followed through. It was all I could manage in two second's time.

Once I got the knack, I started making a few connections! Even when I missed, I at least knew what my target had been, and I tried to apply whatever I learned to "next time." There were a lot of next times, until I became successful enough at it to realize how little I liked to eat the ducks I had risen at 4 A.M. to shoot, and went on to other rewarding hobbies, like sleep.

In life, as in duck hunting, one of my persistent mistakes has been to not make a decision. I've been so afraid of making a wrong choice that I made no choice at all. I've fired parting shots at so many good ideas! More often than not, I've either deliberated on the wise choice sufficiently long that there were no choices left by the time I was ready to pull the trigger, or I've "flock-shot" at a whole host of ideas, determined to not let a single one get away, and managing not to hit any at all.

Time and time again, I've dragged home, empty-handed, muttering to myself, "Pick a duck and shoot it!" It doesn't have to be the biggest idea or the most attractive or the most popular or the most cost-effective or the latest idea—just *pick one, please!*

I've tried all the different ways of not choosing: analysis, followed by more analysis. I've even tried prayer, followed by more prayer (careful to never commit to making a *decision* after prayer). I've often gone the route of not wanting to leave anyone or their idea out in the cold, so we've just all stayed inside together, doing nothing but occasionally further brainstorming to add to the compost pile of good ideas fermenting in the board room.

A lot of times, I've shot up my ammunition at ideas going over the horizon. At least I came home with a warm barrel, like everybody else.

I've tried it all, and if there was one single theme I would try to follow, if I had to do it all over again, it could be summed up in the phrase, "Pick a duck and shoot it!"

Yes, pray. But then, *pick*!

Analyze? Do research? O.K., but don't make a career out of it (We get an exemption if God *has* told us to make a career out of it). Set a deadline and at that point, stop doing research and gathering information, and pull the trigger at something!

Quit trying to bring down the whole flock, this year, and just pray, pick a duck, and shoot it! Who knows? There may be time for more than one shot. But we don't have forever to decide. Ducks and ideas fly fast. Kids grow up at 60 mph, or better. If we don't figure out what to do with our time and energy, it will be decided for us, by someone with less than our best interests in mind.

Focus! Ask God's help in selecting one thing which will happen, regardless of what else happens, and concentrate on it like a laser beam. Quit looking for bigger flocks or happier hunting grounds. Pick one and bring it down! If we focus, even in failure there is success. Focusing is its own reward. Success is a nice byproduct.

It really is O.K. to concentrate on something to the point of action. Check the Book. Faith shouldn't even be called "faith" if it never results in action. Faith with no accompanying works is in reality just disobedience, covered up with religious-sounding excuses. Not only is it O.K. to pick a duck, to focus on just one need or ministry; it's vital to seeing anything happen! There are way more good causes than there is time, energy or resources for them—all the more reason to focus on just one good cause and make a difference, since we can't possibly accommodate all the available options, anyway. Pick one!

The Bottom Line: I believe my Lord would have me focus on:________. Good shot.

DAY 63

God's Alarm System

Can a man carry fire next to his chest and his clothes not be burned?

Proverbs 6:27

I like the story of a pastor and parishioner outside a small country church, pounding a hand-lettered sign into the ground. A motorist in a gleaming sports car pulls up to read the sign, which states, "The end is near. Turn yourself around before it's too late!" The man in the car yells at the pair, "You religious nuts! Why can't you just mind your own business and leave everybody alone?" as he peels out, scattering gravel behind him. Seconds later, the pastor and his helper hear more screeching of tires, followed by a big splash. The layman turns to his minister and says, "Pastor, do you think maybe we oughta just have the sign say, "Bridge Out"?

Warnings come in many varieties, some of them a little unclear. The greater dangers earn the most urgent, most oft-repeated warnings. So what would it say to us when God would warn us of something over and over and over? Do you know how many times the Bible warns of the dangers of the same thing in the first seven chapters of Proverbs? Seventy times. What is the deadly danger which would merit 70 warnings from God in just seven chapters? Adultery. Entire chapters (5 & 7) are devoted to the dangers and tragedy of adultery. Seventy warning verses are issued. Hmm. Must be serious. Reading through Proverbs 5-7 will confirm what could easily be guessed: This sin is a ticket to absolute disaster.

I like the way God doesn't just post a bunch of warning signs and leave it at that, though. He breaks down this sin, telling us how it works as well as the outcome, gives revealing information as to what to look for. He's trying to save us from tragedy. We would do well to pay attention, particularly if we think this is one temptation we'd never fall for.

God, in His wisdom, starts with prevention: Scripture knowledge. Familiarizing ourselves thoroughly with the scripture is like setting up a temptation alarm system. For the person who has immersed himself in God's truth, anything contradictory is pretty easily discerned. It just doesn't look or sound right, because it isn't. Scripture knowledge stored in the mind and heart has a way of kicking out and identifying temptations as they arrive, tipping off the person wise enough to equip himself with God's alarm system.

Two more great preventive tools? Guarding our hearts (keeping our affections under control) and guarding our relationships (being careful to nurture our marriage). The enemy of our souls has a hard time penetrating a three-part defense system composed of Bible knowledge, guarded heart, thriving marriage.

The Bottom Line: Are 70 warnings in seven chapters enough? Avoid adultery!

DAY 64

Caught By an Eyelash

Do not desire her beauty in your heart,
and do not let her capture you with her eyelashes;

Proverbs 6:25

"Her" is an aspiring adulteress, usually not all that beautiful, who makes effective use of smooth speech, boldness and, oh yes, eyelashes (not even real) to bag her prey. Not only are the eyelashes not real; neither is the professed love or the promised ability to keep everything discreet. It turns out none of it is real except the pain. Sigh. Another family ruined. Caught by an eyelash? Pathetic.

The target of Satan's adultery attack is the man who thinks he's smart, and who would like to think he's attractive to women. An outline of the method used provides some really helpful warning signs, should we choose to note them for our own safety. A whole chapter of "pickup lines to look out for" is Proverbs 7. Read the chapter carefully, but here's the basic script:

This is safe. The bold approach of the adulteress lays his greatest fear– rejection, to rest. She grabs him and kisses him in public! She describes her boudoir and her husband's itinerary (won't be back for weeks). We don't even have to do anything wrong. I just want you to see my room. No one will know. It's safe.

I am attracted to you. It's the attraction of attraction. She says she came out to find not just anyone, but him! How amazing. Somehow she can see how special he is. She is almost uncontrollably attracted to him. She openly admires him. It may be the most admiration he's received in years. He's still got it! This person sees him as he wants to see himself: Smart, strong, attractive to women.

I'm a spiritual person, so this is O.K. The woman reports she is returning from offering sacrifice, which means two things: (1) She's spiritual. (2) Leftover steak. Steak plus spirituality must mean this whole thing is O.K. with God, too!

I am totally available. Once again, fear of rejection is neutralized. She talks of "love till morning" and there's no mistaking what she means, she uses plenty of smooth speech to prepare the way, then she finally just blurts out a raw proposition, in case he's so dense he has missed all the more subtle clues.

What will a smart, strong, married man do?

The Bottom Line: Don't fall for Satan's well-used pick-up lines.

DAY 65

All At Once

With much seductive speech she persuades him;
with her smooth talk she compels him.
All at once he follows her,
as an ox goes to the slaughter,
or as a stag is caught fast
till an arrow pierces its liver,
as a bird rushes into a snare;
he does not know that it will cost him his life.

Proverbs 7:21-23

How bad could this be? What could be the harm? After all, her husband is gone for a long time, so he'll never know. I don't have to fear rejection, because it's obvious she's already crazy about me. She has leftover steak and I really would like to see that bedroom she's talking about. It all sounds interesting and exciting, plus she likes me for me! She finds me attractive—irresistible, in fact. She's been looking for me all day. It's like this is meant to be! I won't do anything wrong. I'll stop before I cross the line and do something immoral. I won't do anything stupid. Right now, I'm just enjoying the attention. It's nice to be sincerely admired. It's been a long time since I felt that way. Here is this beautiful woman who thinks I'm smart and handsome! And since I'm a mature, spiritual person, I won't do anything I'll regret—but even if I did, we wouldn't get caught, because she said it's safe and I know she would never tell. Nice eyelashes. And the way she talks! Especially when she says my name. She thinks I'm great. She's a spiritual person, too, but she's also kind of wild and exciting. She's crazy about me. She needs me. She wants me to see her bedroom and smell the perfume. In order to do that, I'd have to be there. She just said she's ready for a night of real love. She just kissed me.

I'll just humor her, go have a look at her place, and then head home.

Snap.

Didn't see that coming.

The idea of a trap is that the prey will be totally unaware of its presence until it's too late. *All at once he follows her, as an ox goes to the slaughter,... He does not know that it will cost him his life.*

By the time he saw the sign, it was too late. Why would there be 70 warnings in Proverbs 1-7 about a sin smart, spiritual people would never fall for?

The Bottom Line: Of course it doesn't look like a trap. Because it is.

DAY 66

What's Behind the Signs

With much seductive speech she persuades him;
with her smooth talk she compels him.

Proverbs 7:21

Once again the subject is avoiding adultery. These warnings are straight out of God's Word, not my personal experience. The reason they are in the scripture is because if we heed them, it need never *become* our personal experience! Just like reviewing the signs is a good idea before taking the driver's test, we would do well to look again at the warning signs in Proverbs 6-7. But we have to pay close attention! The signs are presented from Satan's angle—what he promises—wonderful opportunities—but lead to disaster, instead. When we realize what's behind the signs, Satan's invitations become our warnings.

Don't forget the delivery system: Seductive speech, smooth words. It doesn't sound like temptation at all, just an invitation to real love. The longer we listen, the harder it is to see what's behind the signs. Here are three signs we need to heed—by going the opposite direction! These may not look like warning signs, but we could use them to stop adultery from ruining our lives.

Warning Sign #1: Dangerous Attraction Ahead. We don't have the ability to prevent temptations, but we get to choose where our mind will dwell. Inappropriate attractions, coming and going, need to be starved in the mind. Guard the heart by disciplining the mind. Flattery does not dissolve wedding bands. Gushing admiration for you does not make you a better person. Avoiding forbidden attractions does.

Warning Sign #2: Nothing to Fear. The sign says you need not fear rejection or discovery, and there will be no ill consequences. Behind the sign lurks reality, and every one of the things you weren't supposed to have to fear.

Warning Sign #3: Chance of a Lifetime. All the doors are open. Maybe this was meant to be. It was—by Satan. None of this is "chance"—it's pre-arranged, the beautiful person is the bait, and it's a battle for your soul. Who will win?

If you're ignoring the signs, here's one last warning before the cliff: What if this was the absolute last thing you ever did and tomorrow you face God? Still a good idea?

The Bottom Line: Learn to recognize the warning signs God provides for our good.

DAY 67

Boot Camp: The Movie

And calling the crowd to him with his disciples, he said to them, "If anyone would come after me, let him deny himself and take up his cross and follow me." Mark 8:34

Boot camp is one of those experiences in life which has passed me by. But I've heard about it. Most of what I've heard about this long-held military tradition is that (A) It's not fun, and (B) It's not optional.

What if they did boot camp differently? What if, instead of having to participate in midnight marches, obstacle courses, etc., recruits could substitute "exposure" to the various unpleasantries? For example, instead of having to endure crawling through the mud with a full pack and a rifle as a drill sergeant screamed at us, what if we could just listen to lectures about how bad boot camp is, or maybe pop in a DVD about what we were supposed to learn? Who would choose the real thing, if we got to pick between the mud and the mud movie? We could watch other people's experiences at boot camp, try to identify with them, then come back next week and view another boot camp message or testimony.

But then, suppose we got shipped off to Afghanistan. Our lives might often depend on the soldiering qualities of the person next to us. If we had our choice, would we rather be teamed up with the guy who had gone through the rugged weeks of actual training, or the one who had just watched the instructional video? And how happy is he going to be to find that we are his new partner?

Boot camp will never be fun; that's not the idea. Neither will it ever do its job if boot camp is relegated to just the over-achievers, and everyone else can skip it or listen to a lecture, instead. The idea of boot camp is that everyone in an army will have gone through the same training, training which gives them the best chance at survival and victory, in an arena where the bullets are real and mistakes are fatal. In a battle, unprepared soldiers are more of a hazard to their own side than they are to the enemy. That's why boot camp is not optional. If you're going to be in the army, you do the training. Period.

So how did boot camp become optional, in the Church in America? By "boot camp," I'm referring to the kind of discipleship of which Jesus spoke when addressing would-be followers. He gave them the low-down: Self-denial is expected. Discipleship is not an option, but a requirement. There is no part-time discipleship. If you're signing up to be a disciple, you're issued a cross, if that tells you anything. It won't all be fun. But you can't be useful in the Kingdom unless you're a disciple. Disciples pick up their cross and follow Jesus. All of them.

The Bottom Line: Boot camp is required in the army; discipleship, in God's army.

DAY 68

Is This a Test?

Lifting up his eyes, then, and seeing that a large crowd was coming toward him, Jesus said to Philip, "Where are we to buy bread, so that these people may eat?" He said this to test him, for he himself knew what he would do. Philip answered him, "Two hundred denarii would not buy enough bread for each of them to get a little." One of his disciples, Andrew, Simon Peter's brother, said to him, "There is a boy here who has five barley loaves and two fish, but what are they for so many?" Jesus said, "Have the people sit down." Now there was much grass in the place. So the men sat down, about five thousand in number. John 6:5-10

It didn't sound like a test to Philip, just a bad idea. He tried to help Jesus by reasoning Him back to reality. "Even if we had the money, which we don't, it wouldn't be enough to make a difference. Forget it." Case closed.

Philip's approach is mimicked by the Church in America, often: "We don't have enough." "We can't do it. Why try?" The Church in America peers out across a global landscape littered with human need, counts up resources and concludes, "Not our problem. We could put everything we had toward it, and it wouldn't even make a dent. We don't even have enough to take care of our own. Forget it."

The world goes on, Christless. Churches await sufficient resources to supply internal needs and wants, assuming the someday excess will be used to do outreach or save for a rainy day. The harvest rots, along with the Church's reputation. My friend Carl Cady says, "Vision precedes provision." He ought to know. Years ago, he founded a relief organization meeting the needs of thousands in Indonesia. International Friends of Compassion (ifcus.org) continues to accomplish amazing things, because people caught the vision. Vision precedes provision.

Many churches in America aim no higher than keeping the doors open. Interest is confined to the church membership. Other people's needs? "Not our problem." The vision never extends to what can be done to serve the community, or lead people to Christ, or even to adequately address the needs of the congregation; the "ministry" is a position to be filled, the church is a building, and the "vision" is to maintain the building, support the pastor (kinda) and run some programs to make people think it's all important. It's sad!

What if hundreds of churches across America had a vision that said, "God is making it our responsibility to see that these people get fed! Sure, we don't have the resources or the money, but we're going to take what we do have and bring it to Jesus, then just serve, and make sure we don't waste any of His provision.

Our current situation. Is this another one of God's bad ideas? Or a test?

The Bottom Line: Our current situation may be a test. Let's trust God.

DAY 69

Jesus and the Highway Patrol

When I look in the Bible, every time someone checks with God about something, they get it right—God makes sure they do! I've also found that to be true in my own life. Every single time I've checked with God about something—anything—I've found what I needed, in the way of guidance. I've never been disappointed in the path I've taken, if I checked with God, first. Nearly every time I've made a major error in judgment or in attitude, that error was based on an assumption, which I later found to be erroneous. There have been many times in my life when I didn't know what to do, but God showed me because I asked; the times when I've gotten off the path were usually when I felt I didn't need to consult God, because I thought I already knew the answer to that one.

Assumptions generally start with truth, then keep going even after the truth runs out. It's like those cartoons where the coyote chases the roadrunner from solid ground out off the cliff, then looks down to find he's once again standing on thin air. We start out with solid ground—stuff like "God loves me." But then we keep going: "God loves me" (solid); "therefore, He wants me to be happy" (not so solid—He seems to be more concerned about me being good than being happy); "therefore, this thing I really want to do has to be His will, since it makes me happy" (There's now a lot of fresh air under our feet).

By the time we've stepped out onto the clear blue sky, we're able to do the mental gymnastics to justify pretty much anything. For instance, this is how it works with adultery: "God loves me, He wants me to be happy, she makes me happy and my wife doesn't, so this must be O.K. with God." See how easy that is? We look down and get that weird look on our face a split second before the gravity of sin kicks in, and we find ourselves in freefall. Unlike Wile E. Coyote, we don't just get up after we splat against the canyon floor. It takes Jesus to begin to put the pieces back together, again.

That was a more extreme example of the hazards of assumption; most of the time, we'll be dealing with more mundane scenarios. However, it's the routine assumptions which cause us to drop our guard and not recognize that we've passed the point of solid ground. Remember another cartoon character, Mr. MaGoo? The guy always drove around with his eyes closed, oblivious to near-disasters every second or so. When he somehow made it through, the line was always the same. He'd chuckle and say, "Mr. MaGoo, you've done it, again!" Some of us treat God's grace the same way. Our guardian angels drop to their faces in exhaustion, and we proudly announce, "Mr. MaGoo, you've done it, again!"

Jesus and the Highway Patrol would like us to drive with our eyes open.

The Bottom Line: Stick with the solid ground of God's leading, not assumptions.

DAY 70

A Long Way from the Cliff

Everyday assumptions we make?

-"God really does want me to be happy, so that justifies..."

-"It's an open door, so it must be from God!" (Question: Is God the only one who knows how to open doors?")

-"Since this worked well the last time I did it, God must want me to do the same thing, again."

-"I'm valuable to God, so of course, He would never put me on the bench, or tell me to wait. He wants me in the game!"

-"This doesn't make sense to me, so it can't be from God."

See the subtleness of assumptions? Years ago, a minister friend informed me I was throwing my life away to remain in a small town, pastoring a small church. Someone I respected appreciated my abilities! In my mind, I built on the assumptions. Watch the progression from solid ground to nothing:

"God has given me a calling and spiritual gifts."(Solid)

"God doesn't waste anything."(Solid)

(My friend thinks) "I'm wasting my life in this town."(Not-so-solid. It wasn't my friend who called me to the town; it was God, in a wonderful answer to prayer).

"Since God doesn't waste anything, and my talents are being wasted in this town, that means that God will move me to a place where I can shine for Him!" (Thin air. God got off, back at "doesn't waste anything.")

Within a year's time, I had myself basically asking God, "O.K., God, where do you want me in the limelight?"

How did limelight get in there? Assumption. After all, what else would God do with a rising star He would never waste?! My Heavenly Father made it pretty clear to me that it was He who had called me into ministry, He who had placed me in that small town, and He who had the right to leave me there for the rest of my life if He wanted, seeing as how this whole thing had nothing to do with my "career," "limelight," or anything else but His will! He graciously put me in my place, and I got down to work, instead of peering over the fence. Within several years, God placed me in a church over twice the size of the one I was pastoring, in a much larger city. There was no question who had done the moving.

Obedience is what counts. If God wants us on the bench for forty years, it wouldn't be the first time He's done it! We need to drop the assumptions. They get us into trouble. Let's build a long way from the cliff.

The Bottom Line: Assumptions get us into trouble. Following God keeps us out.

DAY 71

Hell's Best Commercials

The woman Folly is loud;
she is seductive and knows nothing.
She sits at the door of her house;
she takes a seat on the highest places of the town,
calling to those who pass by,
who are going straight on their way,
"Whoever is simple, let him turn in here!"
And to him who lacks sense she says,
"Stolen water is sweet,
and bread eaten in secret is pleasant."
But he does not know that the dead are there,
that her guests are in the depths of Sheol.

Proverbs 9:13-18

The Superbowl features not only the top teams in the NFL for the year, but also the best commercials—or at least, the most expensive. Corporations cough up millions for a few seconds' worth of product face time. The hope is for a clever, well-done commercial to capture the interest of would-be customers, the end result being sales in the stratosphere. Sometimes it works that way.

Evil advertises, too. Satan continually campaigns to lure the simple off the straight path and into an eternal pit. For those who don't believe in his existence, it just makes it that much easier—the message comes across as enlightened and sincere, when it's nothing but a string of loudly proclaimed falsehoods.

Satan's aggressive ad campaign targets those who lack sense but wish to be smart. He appeals to basic desires with empty promises, going on the assumption that if one says something long enough and loud enough, it will be believed by the simple, even if it defies all logic. Unfortunately, this strategy works. Think of how it works with beer commercials. Show beer, athletes and beautiful women together long enough, and the connection is made: Drink beer, you'll be a better athlete and beautiful women will be attracted to you. Prove that one!

"Stolen water is sweet, and bread eaten in secret is pleasant." "Sweet." "Pleasant." Well, if he says so!... How would a person know that what really lies behind Door Number Two are the stacked body bags of suckers who believed this garbage? When we swallow the devil's assumptions and let him lure us off the straight path onto one of his shortcuts, we shouldn't be surprised to drop through a trapdoor to hell. It's advertising, baby. Buyer beware.

The Bottom Line: Watch out for Satan's lies. They're lies.

DAY 72

What Causes Poverty

A wise son makes a glad father,
but a foolish son is a sorrow to his mother.
Treasures gained by wickedness do not profit,
but righteousness delivers from death.
The LORD does not let the righteous go hungry,
but he thwarts the craving of the wicked.
A slack hand causes poverty,
but the hand of the diligent makes rich.
He who gathers in summer is a prudent son,
but he who sleeps in harvest is a son who brings shame.

Proverbs 10:1-5

What causes poverty? Oh, there have been and are plenty of theories, but at least one major cause of poverty is spelled out in Proverbs 10:4: *A slack hand causes poverty,...* A slack hand? Laziness. Laziness causes poverty. Wickedness and foolishness are big contributors, too.

Do you mean that government aid or charity will not stamp out poverty among people who are lazy, wicked and foolish? Um, yeah. The way out, according to the Bible, is for people to turn toward God, seek His wisdom and work hard. It's a simple plan: righteousness, wisdom and diligence, one which can't be forced upon unwilling citizens by a government. It works pretty well for parents, though, which is why the difference between sorrow and gladness for parents is how wise their offspring turned out to be.

Teaching those young ones diligence and righteousness pays off big-time. Letting them sleep through harvest and learn to be lazy is not showing them love! The loving thing to do is teach them to work and to have a healthy fear for the Lord. In doing so, we're preventing entire generations of poverty!

Sorry to burst anyone's bubble in an election year, but parents have a great deal more to do with stamping out poverty than any government official ever could. Parents are able not only to provide for their children through diligent labor; they are able to guide their children into being the kind of members of society who bounce to the top like basketballs held underwater. How? By training those hands to not be slack, by overruling the excuses for why they need the sleep when it's time to work or to attend worship services. (There aren't many "born workers;" they are instead "shaped.") If you want "rich" kids, just teach them to work hard and love and serve God. They'll become "rich" kids, with proud parents.

The Bottom Line: Raising kids who know how to work prevents poverty.

DAY 73

Nervous Salvation

Jesus said to them, "I am the bread of life; whoever comes to me shall not hunger, and whoever believes in me shall never thirst. But I said to you that you have seen me and yet do not believe. All that the Father gives me will come to me, and whoever comes to me I will never cast out. For I have come down from heaven, not to do my own will but the will of him who sent me. And this is the will of him who sent me, that I should lose nothing of all that he has given me, but raise it up on the last day. For this is the will of my Father, that everyone who looks on the Son and believes in him should have eternal life, and I will raise him up on the last day." John 6:35-40

As a young kid striving to be a Christian, I was really nervous about my salvation. The good part was that it kept me on a pretty short leash with God. I couldn't go to sleep with unconfessed sin in my life! What if Jesus sneaked back and grabbed His Church while I was snoozing and I awakened as a lonely 10-year-old on a post-Rapture planet? What then? Better go get Mom to pray with me. I needed to make sure I was a real Christian, forgiven and everything, before I could relax and go to sleep. After multiple late-night episodes of getting her son saved all over again, she finally told me to quit listening to the devil after ten o'clock. It worked. I don't think I ever bugged her again about my salvation.

The cool thing I learned about salvation security was in 1 John 1:7:*But if we walk in the light, as he is in the light, we have fellowship with one another, and the blood of Jesus his Son cleanses us from all sin.* I don't need to itemize and process sins before bed? No. All I have to do is come into the Light, open and honest before Him. He deals with all my sin. He makes clear what I am to do, if anything, and I obey. There is constant peace in the Light. We're free from Rapture anxiety and all its cousins. Mom gets more sleep.

Whoever comes to me I will never cast out. Now, there's a promise! If you want to be saved, you will be! The only way to "lose" such a great salvation is to never accept it in the first place or to change our mind about serving God and consistently and insistently reject Him and His commands. Even then, God's hand is extended toward us for as long as we live. It's not too late to look to the Son! *God's will is that everyone who looks on the Son and believes in him should have eternal life.* Everyone who looks to Jesus and who wants to be saved, will be. This includes nervous 10-yr-olds. If we put our trust in Him, we are absolutely secure. Jesus has never lost one, yet. Nervous salvation is still salvation, but salvation with peace is even better. One more thing: This offer still applies after 10 P.M.

The Bottom Line: *Whoever comes to me, I will never cast out.*

DAY 74

A Tongue Out of Control

The wise lay up knowledge,
but the mouth of a fool brings ruin near.

Proverbs 10:14

Tongue control is a difficult feat. It always has been. Why else would there be so many proverbs regarding the proper use of the tongue, and so many warnings about its misuse? If you want to know what direction someone's life is heading, all you have to do is listen to them for a few minutes—their tongue is an accurate indicator. The righteous, disciplined, controlled tongue leads to life and lots of blessings; the foolish tongue is headed for disaster, usually with plenty of pain to show for it, already.

We must keep our tongues under control. If we don't exercise discipline over our speech, we will suffer the consequences of an unrestrained, wicked tongue, and have only ourselves to blame.

Freedom of speech is like driving on a winding, mountain road. Along with the feeling of freedom and exhilaration, there's also danger. We don't release the steering wheel and let the car go wherever it wants—it's really, really important to keep it between those lines on the road! While we need the freedom to steer the car, we need the control to stay in our lane and on the road.

An unrestrained tongue is like an unrestrained car on a mountain road. Disaster is certain! What kind of disaster? Let's see. Here are just a few of the ill consequences of wicked speech and behavior listed in Proverbs 10: a rod for the back; transgression and sin; leading others astray; being labeled a fool; death by stupidity; having what you dread come upon you; being swept away by the storms of life; having a short life; dead dreams and unfulfilled expectations. Wow! Sounds like a great deal! All of this from just one out-of-control life, led by the tongue? Yup.

Then there's God's way, which is, of course, righteousness. Wisdom, especially in speech, brings: life; riches without sorrow; God's blessings; joy; a prolonged life; desires granted; getting to be a blessing to others; the pleasure of wisdom; an established, secure life, which will never be removed; the knowledge of God's approval and acceptance. Oh, and yes, more wisdom—all you want.

Once again, the choice is before us. We can allow our tongue to roam free, and suffer the inevitable disastrous consequences, or pick the righteous route, control our tongue, and live to see another day, then another and another, all under the blessing of God. Hmm. I wonder which path I should choose!

The Bottom Line: Controlling the tongue is a very vital part of discipleship.

DAY 75

Improv at the Judgment

Doing wrong is like a joke to a fool,
but wisdom is pleasure to a man of understanding.

Proverbs 10:23

The mere mention of the word "sin" is supposed to produce laughs in America, these days, if you queried media executives and the like. Too often, it does. Instead of being upheld as noble, moral standards are mocked in movies and television shows. "'Doing wrong'? What's that? What do you mean by 'wrong'? You must be kidding." Solomon wrote, "*Doing wrong is like a joke to a fool.*" You mean making fun of sin is not the invention of late-night television comedians? I guess not. Fools have been at it for a very long time.

The problem is that fools don't take sin seriously. The idea of consequences for "doing wrong" actually can strike them as funny. It's just one more of Satan's tricks to assure the unwitting that his path is the safe and pleasurable one, while God's is restrictive, unpleasant and sometimes ridiculous. The more the devil can get people to laugh off sin, hell or his existence, the easier it is to herd them toward the Abyss, chuckling all the way. Never mind the faint cries from beyond the grave coming from the residents of places like Sodom and Gomorrah. They laughed off sin, too. No matter. We'll be fine.

Wise men know differently. They understand not just the reality of God, but the importance of obedience to Him, and the consequences of doing otherwise. Sin is no joke to the wise man—what he fears most is damaging his relationship with God through disobedience. The healthy fear of God is the foundation of his wisdom. It serves him well. As a result, the greatest pleasure in the wise man's life is in his relationship with God. Forgiveness through Jesus Christ makes him free of sin and its consequences; contemplating the cost his Savior paid to free him from sin makes doing those things again no joke. *Wisdom is pleasure to a man of understanding.* That wisdom is found in God. Satan's advertisement of sin being so pleasant and satisfying is known to be false by the individual who has been redeemed by the blood of Jesus.

Sadly, there are still millions who find sin a joke, and some who make millions by portraying those who follow God's commands as fools. Scripture reveals the true fool. It's not the one who takes pleasure in learning from and loving God; it is the man who refuses to take seriously the Creator or His commands. There won't be improv at the Judgment.

The Bottom Line: Sin is not a joke.
Our only hope is in Jesus Christ!

DAY 76

Always Broke

And while he was at Bethany in the house of Simon the leper, as he was reclining at table, a woman came with an alabaster flask of ointment of pure nard, very costly, and she broke the flask and poured it over his head. There were some who said to themselves indignantly, "Why was the ointment wasted like that? For this ointment could have been sold for more than three hundred denarii and given to the poor." And they scolded her. But Jesus said, "Leave her alone. Why do you trouble her? She has done a beautiful thing to me. For you always have the poor with you, and whenever you want, you can do good for them. But you will not always have me. She has done what she could; she has anointed my body beforehand for burial. And truly, I say to you wherever the gospel is proclaimed in the whole world, what she has done will be told in memory of her." Mark 14:3-9

People in love are almost always broke. Why? Some of it is the manipulation of our society—how is it that roses mysteriously double in price on Valentine's weekend, each year? They get away with stuff like that because people in love tend to ignore the price and keep their attention focused fully on one another, to the detriment of most rational thinking and particularly their bank account. Married folks come to realize that it's not very loving to spend the family senselessly into oblivion with lavish gifts for one another, so reason usually returns to financial decisions even though they're still in love; those in love but not yet married usually don't fare so well. It seems they're always broke. Measured, practical actions don't seem to fit with true love. When it comes to giving, true love has a hard time stopping at "practical." Lavish, extravagant is the rule.

The disciples, who had themselves received so much from Jesus, stood around embarrassed as a woman came to Him with the most precious thing she owned, a bottle of perfume worth a year's wages, then proceeded to break it open and empty the contents on the head of Jesus in worship and love. It would have been a big deal to have squeezed out a few drops of the stuff, but she gave it all—and was criticized for it. "Why this waste?" All of a sudden, practicality and "the poor" are dragged into the discussion. Funny. They weren't talking about the poor a minute ago, before she made them all look bad. Now she's broke, her perfume is gone, and she is labeled a selfish idiot because she wasn't practical and sensible in expressing her love for Jesus. The Lord springs to her defense, and immortalizes her and her gift, then dies for us all, days later, the smell of perfume still clinging to His body. Completely, absolutely "broke." That's true love.

The Bottom Line: When it comes to giving, true love doesn't stop at "practical."

DAY 77

What Follows Pride

When pride comes, then comes disgrace,
but with the humble is wisdom.

Proverbs 11:2

This proverb has always been popular, because it applies to other people. After all, who among us reading through the scripture would label ourselves "proud," and thus destined for disgrace? We, of course, know people who are proud; this proverb applies to them. Meanwhile, those of us blessed with humility are told by scripture that we are wise. No wonder people like this verse. We all come out on the right end of it, plus it promises a comeuppance for the obnoxious folks in our lives. Such a deal!

Unless maybe we mis-labeled ourselves. Could it possibly be that we are prouder than we think? Here's a quick self-test which might help indicate whether we lean to the proud side or the humble: How easy is it for someone else to teach us anything? Are we the sort of individual who can only learn alone or from a very short list of people we respect? Or are we so easy to teach we can learn from practically anybody?

What does that have to do with anything? This: You can't teach a proud person much of anything; a humble one is like a sponge for true wisdom. If we find we can only learn from very few people, we are probably packing a good-sized amount of pride. According to Proverbs, some kind of disgrace won't be far behind. We might want to lighten the load before it's too late.

This Bible principle applies not only to individuals but to entire nations, which is a scary fact. Take a quick glance across history, look for proud empires and rulers, and find the ones which continue without disgrace. Good luck. You might find one or two, but it won't be easy. What does that say to us living in the world's current superpower? No pride here, right?! A little humility would buy us time, I'm thinking. Disgrace will show up, eventually, but it wouldn't take that many humble, God-loving people stationed in America to postpone disgrace for a few more decades. I'd like that. I'm sure God would, too. It's up to us.

How does it work, again? Proud? We're headed for disgrace. Humble? Getting wiser by the minute.

Pride and wisdom don't go together. Humility and wisdom do. Proud people and nations have difficulty in learning because they think they already know; the humble are willing and successful learners. They are also willing to hang around and clean up the inevitable mess the proud leave behind them when disgrace comes.

The Bottom Line: Humility gains us wisdom; pride leads to our downfall.

DAY 78

A Really Dumb Plan

Where there is no guidance, a people falls,
but in an abundance of counselors there is safety.

Proverbs 11:14

Want to hear a really dumb plan? Let's just all do what we think is good for us. That way no one has to submit to anyone else's leadership or rules. We'll all be free. No one will be safe. But this is precisely the world view espoused by some in our nation, these days. The Founding Fathers warned that democracy would not work without a just and moral people, which means we aren't our own authority; God is. In the early days of the Republic, the Bible was the underlying foundation for nearly all laws and many of the principles of society. The Word of God is currently in disfavor among many in our country. Their agenda is to move on without the restrictions of the Bible or Christianity, or any moral code, for that matter. Puffed up with their own knowledge, guidance from any corner is disdained, be it from a God in whom they don't believe or an electorate to whom they won't listen. The most vain will only listen to those who admire and echo their thoughts. All other opinions are cast aside and demonized. It's a recipe for disaster. Listen again to how it works: *Where there is no guidance, a people falls, but in an abundance of counselors there is safety.*

Guidance from where? From whom? The best guidance we'll ever receive is from a God who loves us, and from the sacred scriptures He has given us. There is guidance which will never steer us wrong.

Along with divine guidance, we've also been offered the wisdom of men. If we gather around us numerous counselors who are truly wise, who are given opportunity to freely express their opinions without fear of reprisal, who are focusing on solutions to problems rather than coaxing along someone's agenda or getting themselves re-elected, the chances of making serious errors go down to about zero. Get a bunch of wise people together, let them think through the situation, and someone will catch the mistakes and come up with a good plan, if that's really the goal.

Or, we could just all do whatever we think best. We could throw off the restraints of biblical morals and Bible guidance and find our own truth. We could ignore the wisdom of the sages and the ages and proceed with what we know is best. We could wreck an entire nation in a brief span of time. It's what happens to peoples who don't need guidance. They fall. They take their kids with them. Let's not.

The Bottom Line: We desperately need God's counsel and wisdom.

DAY 79

A Stone's Throw from Judgment

They went each to his own house, but Jesus went to the Mount of Olives. Early in the morning he came again to the temple. All the people came to him, and he sat down and taught them. The scribes and the Pharisees brought a woman who had been caught in adultery, and placing her in the midst they said to him, "Teacher, this woman has been caught in the act of adultery. Now in the Law Moses commanded us to stone such women. So what do you say?" This they said to test him, that they might have some charge to bring against him. Jesus bent down and wrote with his finger on the ground. And as they continued to ask him, he stood up and said to them, "Let him who is without sin among you be the first to throw a stone at her." And once more he bent down and wrote on the ground. But when they heard it, they went away one by one, beginning with the older ones, and Jesus was left alone with the woman standing before him. Jesus stood up and said to her, "Woman, where are they? Has no one condemned you?" She said, "No one, Lord." And Jesus said, "Neither do I condemn you; go, and from now on sin no more." John 8:1-11

It was a setup, designed to tag Jesus as either a heartless executioner or someone who spoke of the Law but didn't really uphold it. The whole thing was just a trap, set for Jesus. He caught the whole gang in it.

He catches us, too. How many people have we dragged before Him, asking Him to zap them for their sins? Like the woman, Jesus proceeds to forgive them and let them go. It's not condemnation which transforms people. It's forgiveness.

The woman caught in adultery was not changed because she was caught by men. Neither was society, except to maybe make it a little more frightening to engage in adultery. The woman was changed forever when she was facing death as a result of her own sin, and the Savior stepped in between her and judgment. He forgave her sin, then told her to take a new direction in life. It wasn't condemnation or enforcing the rules which changed her life; it was an encounter with a Savior who, instead of condemning sinners, forgives them and gives them a brand new start in life. He sets them free from judgment, sin and condemnation.

We're to lift others up, so they can reach Jesus' hand, instead of shoving them away from Him. We need to lose the entire condemnation routine, even while we rush back toward the Word of God as our only standard for faith and practice.

We need to avoid the role of the Pharisee. Pharisees don't convert anyone to Christ. They only once in a while convert someone to Phariseeism. Jesus has clearly marked out our role: Love these people in my name. Leave the stones alone.

The Bottom Line: Our role is to love people in Jesus' name, not play the judge.

DAY 80

Days of Delight

Delight yourself in the Lord, and he will give you the desires of your heart.
Psalm 37:4

Do you know how to improve a relationship? Delight in that person. Those of us who are married can remember when our partner was perfect. Flaws were unnoticed and irrelevant. To be with the object of our love was pure enjoyment. We adored them, and it was mutual. Somewhere along the line, reality crowded in, as glaring imperfections forced delight to give way to acceptance. Instead of euphoria, the marriage motors along on committed love, grace and forgiveness. As it should be, but wouldn't it be nice to have the kind of delight back we once knew? (And to anyone married more than a couple years whose euphoric delight is still completely intact, congratulations! You're an example to us all).

I have a suggestion for all of us who would like to get more of the delight back in our most important relationships: Change from a noun to a verb.

What do I mean? Usually, we use "delight" as a noun—it's a "thing" we experience. "That was a delight." Something good happened to us that triggered really positive emotions, so we call it a "delight."

Have we ever thought of delight as a choice, something we do? In this scripture, it's used as a verb: *"Delight yourself in the Lord,..."* So the Bible is saying we have a choice in the matter? Guess so. Delighting is something we can choose to do, not just a passive experience.

What would happen in our marriage relationship if we recalled something that attracted us to them in the first place and chose to once again delight in that, ignoring all quirks and faults, like we used to? What would happen? "But they're not the same..." Like we are! The embers of delight are still there. Blow on them a little, and see what happens. Will it make our marriage worse?

And if choosing to delight in our partner would help our marriage, would choosing to delight in God make things better, spiritually? It's pretty plain: *Delight yourself in the Lord, and he will give you the desires of your heart.*

How do we delight in the Lord? Once again, delight is a verb, this time, not a noun. But the verb leads to the noun—if we delight in the Lord, we get the delight of our heart's desires being fulfilled. Think of something wonderful about God— there's an endless list! Now we delight in Him. We think about how great He is, what He has done, what He has promised, what He has given us and just how amazing it is to know His presence, and the delight we choose becomes the delight we experience. Choosing to delight leads to delight, and starts a delightful cycle.

The Bottom Line: Choosing to delight leads to delight, and starts a delightful cycle.

DAY 81

Swine Accessories

Like a gold ring in a pig's snout
is a beautiful woman without discretion.

Proverbs 11:22

My friends used to show their pigs at the fair. They would wash them spotlessly clean, then herd them around in front of the judge in hopes of snagging a purple ribbon. I never once saw a pig sporting jewelry. I have a feeling that even if my friends had added a big string of pearls, diamond earrings and a solid gold nose ring, their pigs would have still looked like pigs. Rich pigs.

A gold ring in a pig's snout would be a waste. So is *"a beautiful woman without discretion,"* according to the Bible. It would be a pity to stick several thousand dollars worth of jewelry into a pig's snout in the hopes of making it something other than a pig. It wouldn't change a thing. Likewise, the woman who convinces herself she is not good enough for a man of character, who settles for less. A prostitute might start out beautiful, but her beauty and character quickly decline. Promiscuity decimates character. Beauty soon follows. It's a waste.

Our society seems bent on promoting promiscuity, though. Consider the lifestyles exalted these days, and those disdained. What is the reaction of much of the culture when an attractive, virtuous, godly woman lives out her faith and hangs onto her purity? "What a waste." Meanwhile, the most decadent, godless females grace the covers of magazines as poster children for glamour. Immoral behavior is assumed as a prerequisite for fame. Check back in 20 years in the trash bin of society and see how it went with them. Usually, not very well. They are so quickly replaced with new material to be exploited in the name of fashion, love and "cool."

Would that we would all quit playing this game! Sin is not cool at all; it ends in death, every time. Jesus, the Righteous One, purchased our salvation with His own blood, so we could escape judgment.

Purity is not to be pitied, but honored, respected and treasured. Immorality ends badly every time. We needn't market it in size zero dresses stuck on people with zero character. True beauty has as its foundation true character. A gold ring doesn't change the heart, but Jesus does.

I can think of nothing more attractive than a beautiful woman with Jesus in her heart, who has committed herself to Him and saved herself for one man. Give that lady a gold ring! Put it on her hand. It won't be a waste. Thank God for a beautiful, committed woman. And a gold ring in the right place.

The Bottom Line: Sin spoils everything!
Save yourself for God and His plan.

DAY 82

The Key to Stupidity

Whoever loves discipline loves knowledge,
but he who hates reproof is stupid.
A good man obtains favor from the LORD,
but a man of evil devices he condemns.
No one is established by wickedness,
but the root of the righteous will never be moved.

Proverbs 12:1-3

You know, it's probably not a good thing when even God is calling you stupid. That's the gist of this passage, though: *He who hates reproof is stupid* (and will stay stupid). As usual, it comes down to choices. We can ignore correction, despise discipline and march down the road toward stupidity with the crowd, or we can practice lonely discipline, humble ourselves to receive reproof and learn from it, and wind up on the winner's podium under the blessing of God.

The key to knowledge is discipline and humility. The willingness to accept correction matters. Disciplined study gains more knowledge than undisciplined whining. Laziness leads to stupidity, while the disciplined never stop learning.

Yet it seems we take pride in our lack of discipline! Our pride is a source of national pride. Self-esteem is taught to young and old, apart from character. We are raising proud, arrogant, undisciplined people with no concept of self-control.

A showcase for misplaced pride is American Idol's tryout sessions, where numerous singers have lots of self-esteem, but zero talent or humility. They defy the world to contradict their self-assessed grandeur. Everyone else is wrong; they are right. Contrast that with disciplined young people who have spent thousands of lonely hours practicing figure skating or whatever, who perform brilliantly and with great grace, yet exhibit such humility when recognized for their achievements.

We love the results of discipline, but as a whole, we don't love discipline in America, these days. That needs to change. If we began to discipline ourselves more in all areas of life (but particularly spiritually), we would experience a revolution of knowledge, and much, much more. It could be incredible. Or we could continue to blame the ref, whine about the unfairness of the competition, trust in political leaders to rescue us from our own sloth while maintaining our national pride, and keep bouncing downhill toward national stupidity (and bankruptcy).

How does it get turned around? When we choose to love discipline. When we choose to learn from correction. When we take God's way, with no shortcuts. We could be filled with knowledge from God. Or, there's always the stupid route.

The Bottom Line: Love discipline. Learn from correction.
Or...well, you know.

DAY 83

Trophy Wife

An excellent wife is the crown of her husband,
but she who brings shame is like rottenness in his bones.

Proverbs 12:4

Today I'd like to pay tribute to my trophy wife. Nearly three decades ago, we fell in love. We still are. The day she became my bride I count as the happiest day of my life, among some pretty stiff competition.

I had always wanted a true partner for life, but had begun to wonder if my standards weren't set too high to ever become reality. I was looking for a woman of character who loved God with all her heart. I wanted a friend with whom I could share life. I needed someone who would love me, whom I could trust and love with my whole heart. I found her.

Actually, I didn't really find her; God sent her to me in answer to about a million prayers, and used a prank phone call from a teen camp in Nebraska to get the ball rolling! It was a wonderful and bizarre courtship, engagement and first-time meeting, in that order, but when our eyes met for the first time at the Anchorage International Airport, I was meeting someone I already loved and knew as if I had always known her. She is my special gift from God. She is the crown of her husband. I love her. I'll never stop loving her.

Yes, I know. Very, very few people are that fortunate in love. I wish there were a lot more "happily ever after" stories out there. Two things, if you are married to someone who has brought more pain to your life than comfort: (1) Some of the greatest men in history have succeeded despite a lack of support from their wives. (2)Things might get better if you treated her like a queen. Give her tenderness and honor, regardless of her response. It couldn't hurt, could it?

There are exceptions, but generally speaking, the wife can make or break the man. It's the power of the position. Most of the time, the man with an excellent wife will go much further in life than he otherwise would have, and a man whose wife is not supportive of him or who brings him shame in some way will have many, many more struggles in life. If you have been blessed with an excellent wife, don't forget to thank God for her every single day. Treat her with the tenderness and gratitude she well deserves. She is a gift to you from God.

If you're not yet married, hold out for one you know will still stand with you on the worst days of your life and hers. How deep is her character? Does she bring out the best in you? An excellent wife in a God-blessed relationship is like a crown to your whole life. Don't settle for anything less. I'm glad I didn't!

The Bottom Line: Wait for someone with true character; treat her like a queen.

20/20 Blindness

"Never since the world began has it been heard that anyone opened the eyes of a man born blind. If this man were not from God, he could do nothing." They answered him, "You were born in utter sin, and would you teach us?" And they cast him out.

Jesus heard that they had cast him out, and having found him he said, "Do you believe in the Son of Man?" He answered, "And who is he, sir, that I may believe in him?" Jesus said to him, "You have seen him, and it is he who is speaking to you." He said, "Lord, I believe," and he worshiped him. Jesus said, "For judgment I came into this world, that those who do not see may see, and those who see may become blind." Some of the Pharisees near him heard these things, and said to him, "Are we also blind?" Jesus said to them, "If you were blind, you would have no guilt, but now that you say, 'We see,' your guilt remains. John 9:32-41

I *love* this story! I never get through it without laughing. Our amazing Lord shows mercy to a man born blind. He heals him by spitting on the ground, making mud and placing it on the man's eyes, then sending him to wash at a nearby pool. The healing attracts the attention of the Pharisees, who grill the guy on who did this and how, once they've checked his I.D. They liked him better blind. John chapter nine is an entertaining exchange between a great witness and the irritable religious leaders whose main concern was that Jesus broke the Sabbath according to them. How? By "working"—making tiny mudballs of spit and dirt, then using them to heal a man born blind!

We need to quit trying to make God fit our rules! Consider it: The Pharisees were criticizing the Son of God for doing a wonderful miracle of healing, telling Him He couldn't be from God, because He spit on the ground and made a little ball of mud on the Sabbath! Man, it bugs me when we make up rules about God that He is supposed to follow; when we try to command Him to do things; when we think we have Him all figured out and can predict what He will do in some situation. It also bugs me that just because we saw Him spit on the ground and make mud in order to heal a blind man, we assume that the next blind man will likewise get the mud treatment, too. We American Christians spend way too much time making up rules, assigning blame, charting trends and trying to box up God, and not nearly enough time just working in the harvest field! God, help us!

If we want revival, our best bet is a blind man who can now see because of Jesus, not a Pharisee whose only interests are self-righteousness and power. There's no one more blind than a Pharisee with 20/20 vision who refuses to see.

The Bottom Line: There's no one more blind than the one who refuses to see.

DAY 85

Back to the Beginning

Some of us have longed for a lifetime to see revival in America. We have endured many prophecies and fads. We've held onto hope through recessions, wars, political and church scandals, etc., etc., etc. We have "claimed" verses which someone said would do the trick, then been left to turn out the lights. The pursuit of true revival (and not just an emotional sideshow) has been too much like snipe hunting. So, do we just forget the whole thing, shrug our shoulders and throw ourselves into something where our batting average isn't so dismal?

How about if we start at the beginning?

What, and go all the way back there? No, I think our problem is that we haven't ever spent a lot of time "there" in the first place. Our sights have usually been a lot further down the revival road. We've wanted to start at the end instead of the beginning.

What do I mean? Take a look at this hypothetical progression and see what you think.

It starts with prayer—prayers of repentance, which leads to a renewed love for Jesus, which leads to more prayer, which leads to holiness, which leads to the fruits of the Spirit, which leads to transformation, which leads to compassion, which leads to intercession, which leads to kindness, which leads to more repentance, which leads to new Christians, which leads to the need for nurseries, which leads to disciples organizing into teams, which leads to missionaries, which leads to more conversions, which leads to societal transformation, which leads to political victories (which can easily lead to corruption and abuses).

Way too much of the time, we've focused on the very last thing on the list, and put that first! No wonder we're still back at square one. We need to start at the beginning, in terms of revival, instead of wishing for the top and never getting to it.

What is it at the beginning, again? Prayer, starting with prayers of repentance. It's a lonely, inglorious spot, kind of like army boot camp. Who wants to start there?! We want victories! We want big change! But if we don't start with prayer and build with prayer, even the political and societal victories we do see turn out to be hollow and fleeting. History doesn't paint a pretty picture of what happens when political power is handed to the church prior to a heart-changing spiritual revival.

Should we pay attention to politics? You bet! Let's steer society in godly directions at every opportunity, but always with a Christ-like spirit. We want revival. But the end result will be better for all if we start at the beginning.

The Bottom Line: Revival? It begins with prayer. Always.

DAY 86

Fools' Rights

The way of a fool is right in his own eyes,
but a wise man listens to advice.
The vexation of a fool is known at once,
but the prudent ignores an insult.

Proverbs 12:15-16

Fools have a lot in common. Maybe they should start their own union and negotiate for fools' rights. Maybe they already have. They do seem to be out in force, these days.

It's easy to pick out card-carrying fools: They are always right. Not "most of the time;" absolutely always. Even the past is revised to reflect their "rightness." Someone is always at fault, but it never happens to be them.

Wise men listen when people offer advice, but fools don't have time for such nonsense. Talking to a fool is like talking to a Pop Tart, except less satisfying. The Pop Tart may not acknowledge your wisdom, but neither will it interrupt you or cuss you out. It leaves a much better taste in your mouth, too.

Meanwhile, a wise man will listen to and even seek advice, something fools rarely trouble themselves to do, since then they might be expected to heed it. Why ask someone when you already know your way is right?

Besides always being right and not listening to advice, another characteristic of fools is the ease at which they are provoked. It doesn't take much. Sometimes just occupying the space in front of them is sufficient to irritate them into unkind behavior. A fool will always let you know you have upset them. Neglecting to cater to their demands may mean encountering their attorney.

The uniform of a fool sports a chip on each shoulder. The rapid response, should a fool feel offended, ranges from hand gestures to lawsuits, sometimes including more violent retribution when convenient. Like I said, we never have to wonder if we've upset a fool.

Here's the contrast: *A wise man listens to advice;* a fool only listens to himself. *A fool ignores advice; the prudent ignores an insult.*

God's will is that we would not be foolish. That means we'll be ignoring some insults, rather than stupidly defending the honor of our every opinion, in the assumption that because we think it, it must be correct. That means admitting when we are wrong, rather than reassigning blame to everyone else. It means operating with grace and humility, overlooking things unworthy of a fight. That attitude might get us kicked out of the fools' union. That would be a good thing.

The Bottom Line: We don't need to act like fools.
God has a better way.

DAY 87

The Tongue of the Wise

There is one whose rash words are like sword thrusts,
but the tongue of the wise brings healing.

Lying lips are an abomination to the LORD,
but those who act faithfully are his delight.

Anxiety in a man's heart weighs him down,
but a good word makes him glad.

Proverbs 12:18,22,25

Ever been laid open by a razor tongue? *Rash words are like sword thrusts.* What an appropriate comparison! Who hasn't been pierced to the soul by words spoken without aforethought? Lies are an abomination to God, but also to the one deceived. Anxiety is an unwelcome visitor we can't get to leave. Here are three things which make life harder than it already is. Would there be a remedy?

God's prescription for someone wounded by words is "the tongue of the wise." *The tongue of the wise brings healing.* How does that happen? It just does. The wise person knows what to say (or not say). In complete contrast to rash words delivered without thinking, the words coming from the wise are formed by prayer and delivered tenderly. Wise people speak to others with the caution exercised by medical personnel in a hospital burn unit. They bring healing. Thank God for "the tongue of the wise"!

Proverbs 12:22 is a not-so-subtle reminder that "lying lips" make God's "abominable" list, the same as things we might considerable more abominable, *but those who act faithfully are his delight.*

Proverbs 12:25 reminds us of the weight of anxiety, and what helps: "A good word." A good word? Think "encouraging." Uplifting. Positive truth, cutting through the lies, complaints and assorted anxiety-inducing verbiage. There's nothing like "a good word," delivered by an honest, faithful, wise person.

When the unbelieving world listens to us, what do they hear? Does it sound like "Good news"? Or does it feel like a sword thrust to people already hurting and anxious? Rash words only increase defiance. *The tongue of the wise brings healing.* That could be us. We could choose words which honor God and lift up people. The Good News is too often hidden in harsh language, delivered in a way that makes hurting sinners feel humiliated, rather than relieved. It ought to sound and feel like good news. Our words should bring healing, and delight God.

The Bottom Line: God wishes for us to have "the tongue of the wise."

DAY 88

The Soul of the Sluggard

The soul of the sluggard craves and gets nothing,
while the soul of the diligent is richly supplied.

Wealth gained hastily will dwindle,
but whoever gathers little by little will increase it.

Proverbs 13:4,11

We're becoming "Sluggard America." An increasing number of Americans see everything as an entitlement, work as an evil option. The Protestant Work Ethic is not dead, but it's dinged up.

Many have fallen into the habit of craving, but not working. It doesn't help when sloth is rewarded by the government, due to our system's inability to distinguish between the truly helpless and the truly lazy. We should care for the helpless; the rub comes when people expend more energy trying to be "helpless" than they do trying to work. Meanwhile, the diligent can expect to be penalized for their trouble by those whose main concern is equity, regardless of effort. Sigh.

But wait! The Bible is talking about not the government grants denied to the saver who needs a boost and doled out to the profligate, but the soul. The sluggard may get financial aid for being "needy," but self-respect doesn't come with those monthly checks. The pride of a job well done, of financial independence—those things are missing in the life of a sluggard. There is a hole in the soul which can't be backfilled by self-esteem teaching or welfare. The person with the satisfied soul is the one who has learned to work. Of course, this is a separate issue from the free gift of salvation, but God made the soul with a need for purposeful labor. It's not just a financial issue, but a spiritual one, too.

Another place we're hurting as a nation is in the craving for "rapid wealth." What's one of the worst things which could happen to someone? They could win the lottery. Check the stats. People inept at handling money (or relationships) prior to their winning ticket aren't suddenly awarded financial wisdom, too.

How should we grow wealth? *Little by little*. "But that's so boring!" Not once we discover the satisfaction of saving and self-restraint.

Don't be a sluggard. It's O.K. to want stuff, but if we're not willing to work for it, that's not O.K. Be diligent. Keep at it. Don't be silly and keep focusing on "get-rich-quick" schemes. Work hard and save little by little. It's not only a good way—it seems to be God's way.

The Bottom Line: Work produces good results and is satisfying to the soul, too.

DAY 89

When God Shows Up Late

Now when Jesus came, he found that Lazarus had already been in the tomb four days. John 11:17

To get the power of this chapter, one should read the whole thing. The synopsis is that someone very close to Jesus had taken ill, and the sisters, Mary and Martha, frantically get word to Jesus. What a good time to know the Son of God on a personal basis! They waited for Him to come rushing in to save His beloved friend. They'd seen His stuff before—they knew that whatever ailed their brother could be taken care of by just a word or a touch from Jesus.

Nothing.

Lazarus up and died, and Jesus didn't so much as head their way. The baffled disciples with Jesus couldn't figure out His response, either. He stayed put for two whole days, then announced they were returning to Judea, in order to wake up Lazarus, whom He assured them was dead.

Everybody was confused: The disciples, Mary and Martha, everybody but Jesus. Like usual, He knew exactly what He was doing. Outside the village, He was met by a disappointed Martha, then Mary, both saying the painfully obvious thing: *"Lord, if you had been here, my brother would not have died."* The message behind their words was clear: God, you're late. You didn't even try to make it in time. How could you wait two more days after you heard?! Don't you even care about us? We thought you loved us. If you had only been here, or at least come in time, none of this would have happened. You're late, Lord.

Too late for the healing. Right on time for the resurrection. Read the account in John 11 of the Son of God standing before the tomb of a loved one already decaying, shouting his name, Lazarus emerging alive. It was quite a show. They'd seen healing's, but never this. The sisters had sent a desperate plea to Jesus, asking for a healing. Instead, they got a resurrection.

A lot of us will go through that same pattern. We'll plead with God to come through with yet another of His great healing miracles, then sit in disappointment when He doesn't show up in time, this time. Because this one isn't a healing, it's a resurrection. Just as the Lord called Lazarus from the dead by name, so He will do with each one who belongs to Him. Except this resurrection is forever.

In those times when it seems that God shows up late, or not at all, we can be sure it's not because He stopped caring or has forgotten about us. Just before they took away the stone, Jesus said it: *"Did I not tell you that if you believed you would see the glory of God?"* (Jn 11:40) Believers can't miss it.

The Bottom Line: If we believe, we will see the glory of God. Every time. On time.

DAY 90

Things Which Hold Us Back

What's holding us back from spiritual growth, these days?

First of all, busyness. People think of their spiritual needs much like they think of their waist-lines. "Yeah, I should really be doing something about this, but who has time to exercise? And it's not easy."

If it's not a priority, not much happens. That's true of all areas of life.

And what happens to those who make spiritual life a priority? Too often, they end up chained to a merry-go-round of church obligations and activities which seem to have extracted most of the joy from their lives! They're tired, they're burned out, they're frustrated, and the idea of serving Jesus being joyful has been gone for a long time! Oooh! That hurts, but I think it's true for way too many!

When church activity crowds out relationship with God, it's a very unsatisfying replacement! The work of ministry needs to be carried out, but if it's not based on an underlying love relationship with Christ, it can become nothing more than an obligation. The love relationship takes time; all love relationships do. Are we offering the Lord *time*? Or are we merely offering Him activity?

There is a current trend away from church attendance, even among those attempting to follow Jesus. I can appreciate the longing for freedom from the expectations and obligations of association with the organized church, in order to get beyond activity and feel closer to God. From what I've observed, though, that's not usually the end result when people bolt from the fellowship of other believers in a church, in order to further their spiritual growth. They often shrivel, instead. Alone.

It's like that exercise thing. We do better in discipline when we join with others pursuing the same goal. Who has more likelihood of jogging on a regular basis, the solo resolver or the person who has promised to meet with a friend at a specific place and time to do it together? And if you're really serious about getting in shape, sign up for the military. You supply the signature; they'll supply the discipline.

Spiritual disciplines are like that, too. Without commitment to others heading the same direction, without consistent fellowship with other believers, most spiritual disciplines never get beyond wishful thinking. Prayer, Bible study, worship, ministry.... all of these things and more should be part of our walk with God. We ought not to let busyness bump our relationship with Jesus down the priority list, even "church" busyness. Neither should we forego the fellowship of other believers just because it can be a hassle. Hang in there. Grow *together*.

The Bottom Line: Excessive busyness holds us back from spiritual growth.

DAY 91

When God Calls an Audible

I'm no football player, nor ever have been, but I'm familiar enough with the game to know what an "audible" is. It's when the quarterback calls a play from the line of scrimmage. Only seconds ago, in the huddle, the players were informed of the play they were about to run. Everyone knows their assignment. There is a clear plan. But something happens when the quarterback steps up to the line and surveys the situation. There is something about the way the defense has lined up that indicates the play given in the huddle is not the best play, now. Things have changed, in a matter of seconds. A new play is needed. So, he just calls out a new play from the line. It's in some sort of code, of course, hopefully meaningless to the opposition, who now have no time to adjust before the ball is snapped. That's the beauty of the "audible"—it gives the opponent no time to adjust.

The key is in the willingness and the ability of the quarterback's team to adjust. Suppose a few players grump, "I'm going with the play he just gave us back in the huddle! He said that's what we were supposed to do, and that's what I'm doing!" The result would be a disaster, if half the team ran the old play and the other half ran the audible. The success of the audible is based on the team's readiness to immediately adjust to a new plan.

You probably already know where I'm going with this. Some of us spend a lot of time seeking the will of God. We pray and sometimes fast, trying to be open to God's plan. It happens! We hear from God! Somehow, some way, He communicates to us the plan. We're all excited to have received the "vision" from God. We might print up brochures on the grand vision, as we venture forward together on God's team. It was a huddle to remember!

Then it happens. Somebody gets an audible from God. It seems He is completely ignoring what He previously made clear was His will, and now He is telling us (or someone) that we are going in a new direction. Wait a second! Shouldn't we go with what we clearly knew to be His will for us a short while ago? What's the deal, here? Why the new plan? And which one is right?

What's going on is that God is calling an audible. We're not the only ones who heard the plan in the huddle. The opposition picked up on it, too—and adjusted. We *did* hear from God back then, but He's changing the plan, now, for our good. If we are willing to adjust, we're the kind of people who are willing to go with it when God calls an audible.

Do you know what the Lord is saying to me, these days? He wants me to be ready to go with an audible. That means paying attention. That means being willing to forego earlier plans, in order to immediately obey when God calls out a new one.

The Bottom Line: Be ready to respond when God calls an audible.

DAY 92

Rods, Early or Late

Whoever spares the rod hates his son,
but he who loves him is diligent to discipline him.

By the mouth of a fool comes a rod for his back,
but the lips of the wise will preserve them.

Proverbs 13:24, 14:3

It seems we are destined for the "rod" of discipline, either early or late, especially if we're male. The alternate translation of verse 24 is, *Whoever spares the rod hates his son, but he who loves him disciplines him early.* We're not talking babies here, but children old enough to learn right from wrong. It's important that they be guided toward right, with just enough discipline to help them get there. It's important that the love being shown is love for the son, not the rod! Brutality masquerading as discipline helps no one. There is a line between discipline and child abuse. One is motivated by love for the child, the other by frustration. True discipline often doesn't even require physical force, but merely diligence in following through on promised actions. The end result of loving discipline is a child who learns self-control. Child abuse, however, crosses the lines of good sense, comes out of frustration or anger and results in resentment, not self-control.

If we really love our children, why would we ever dare resort to physical discipline in order to alter their behavior? How could "love" and "spanking" go together? I've never met a kid yet (including me) who was "pro-spanking." If children universally don't like this, why would anyone do it to a child they loved?

Because of what happens if we don't. Sure, some kids are naturally compliant; all it takes is a stern look to steer them wherever you want them to go. But for most, a kid who has not faced much in terms of parental correction is a kid you don't want to face! Unrestrained, out-of-control children with zero self-control are the sort who drive teachers to early retirement. If they are unfortunate enough to go through their growing-up years without encountering the discipline necessary to learn self-control, they must then learn it in adulthood, a far more painful process. The rods get bigger as we go along, and are wielded by folks with no love for us at all.

Here are our choices: We can apply the "rod" of discipline with love, and shape self-disciplined lives who will never again need the "rod." Or we can ignore discipline, allow children to grow to adulthood without self-control, and watch as they encounter the "rod" for the rest of their days. Which choice is more loving?

The Bottom Line: Ignoring the discipline of our children sets them up for failure.

DAY 93

Thinking—and the Alternative

The simple believes everything,
but the prudent gives thought to his steps.
One who is wise is cautious and turns away from evil,
but a fool is reckless and careless.
A man of quick temper acts foolishly,
and a man of evil devices is hated.
The simple inherit folly,
but the prudent are crowned with knowledge.

Proverbs 14:15-18

Thinking things through is not bad! In fact, those who choose to be reckless, those who choose to believe everything, and those who act rashly because of a quick temper are all folks destined for "folly." Meanwhile, *the prudent are crowned with knowledge.*

One who is wise is cautious and turns away from evil. This would be in contrast to the fool who leaps into every temptation strewn in his path, and believes each lie Satan trots in front of him.

In the Information Age, we all have to continually dog paddle just to keep from drowning in information. Not very much of it can be taken at face value as truth. Most days I receive one or two plaintive appeals from Africa to hold someone's inheritance for them, since they know I can be trusted. Delete. Delete. Anyone who believes everything they get in an unsolicited email or see on the internet is simple, indeed! We all have a constant need to discern.

Don't believe everything you hear or read, especially if it's what you wanted to hear, anyway. Not every email forwarded to you is God's truth. In fact, few are! Not every conspiracy theory you hear is valid. (Nor are all of them invalid)! Only the simple believe everything. They pay for it, dearly. We need to think! (And pray). Think things through. If we do it prayerfully, God will help us get to the right answer.

We could be people of discernment, if we did the work. Some folks don't like to think, so they let others do their thinking for them. Not a good plan! Look at the end results for those who have chosen to believe whatever they wanted to believe, without exercising any discernment. P.T. Barnum, the original circus man, used to say, "There's a sucker born every minute." That might be true, but we don't have to stay that way. Think! Pray! Those two things are an unbeatable combination.

The Bottom Line: Think! Pray! Or pay the price.

DAY 94

Servant Leadership Illustrated

When he had washed their feet and put on his outer garments and resumed his place, he said to them, "Do you understand what I have done to you? You call me Teacher and Lord, and you are right, for so I am. If I then, your Lord and Teacher, have washed your feet, you also ought to wash one another's feet. For I have given you an example, that you also should do just as I have done to you.

A new commandment I give to you, that you love one another: just as I have loved you, you also are to love one another. By this all people will know that you are my disciples, if you have love for one another. John 13:12-15,34-35

When you think of Christians in America, what comes to mind? I'm guessing it may not have been "servant leadership." If we insiders don't automatically associate the Church with love for one another and humble service to all, is it any wonder outsiders would not often label the Church as loving or compassionate?

Jesus illustrated servant leadership in the most uncomfortable way possible, just before He was betrayed. He washed the feet of His disciples. The footwasher was the one at the bottom of the simple hierarchy of slaves. It was the least desirable of jobs. Jesus took it upon Himself, willingly and on purpose, then instructed His followers to do likewise for one another. Point? If we choose not to serve one another, we're being disobedient to Christ.

The Church in America needs to begin to practice service toward one another and toward the rest of the world in ways we have not even attempted, before. For many of our churches and denominations, the only thing the world knows of us is what we are against.

Do we want to know how to influence the world, so they believe? It's not even just a matter of loving the world; it's loving one another that really convinces them we belong to Jesus. This may be our greatest evangelistic tool! And show me a church reaching their community where there isn't love for one another.

Wouldn't you love to see the churches in America honoring one another, instead of rudely competing with one another? Within the Church, wouldn't you love to see Christians serving each other, instead of condemning each other? So would our Lord!

What do we do? We follow the example of our Teacher and Lord, and we wash feet—we do the things no one else wants to do, which need to be done. We serve one another in the name of Jesus. We follow the Master in service.

Servant leaders. In the Church, that's basically the only kind.

The Bottom Line: Serving one another is how we serve Jesus.

DAY 95

Church Rollovers

There's nothing quite like getting that license. You are now officially a driver! Other folks would be smart to get out of your way, especially for the first few days. Months. Maybe years. There's nothing like a Buick rising up to meet us or the sound of crumpling metal and glass to take the euphoria out of driving and settle us down into less spirited and enthusiastic driving habits. Would there be a reason insurance rates for young drivers are sky high, especially for boys? You bet. Reality just doesn't seem that real, until we've been in a real accident. Quick reflexes aren't always enough to compensate for lack of judgment or caution. The most enduring lessons in physics are often learned in terrifying split seconds. If they can be learned without tragedy, that's a really good thing!

It isn't just new driver's licenses that can make folks go a little crazy. I've seen the same thing with preacher's licenses. "Finally, a green light to go do something great for God! And these uneducated laymen have hired me to be their leader!" Armed with a shiny preacher's license and a matching diploma, I can finally get this thing turned around, so it's no longer an embarrassment to God. "First, we need to get the thing into the current century! It's this way—follow me!"

"One question. Well, two. #1: What happened? #2: How come the gas pedal is on the ceiling?"

"Dispatch? Yeah. Another church rollover."

"I'll be right there."

With a young pastor at the wheel, the impulse to make sudden, drastic changes too quickly often proves irresistible, and another church rollover occurs. It's not just the young who are prone to aggressive church driving. Especially with a top-heavy church, laden with tradition and lots of aged experience, quick maneuvers usually wind up with people flying off everywhere and what's left of the church in the ditch. There's a reason why they no longer want to sell 15-passenger vans to churches. It doesn't take much to flip one over. Fill it up with people, try to change directions drastically and suddenly, and it may well go over. Cautious drivers arrive a little later than erratic ones, but at least they arrive.

There's a reason why alarms go off when a traditional congregation is interviewing a pastoral candidate under 40. "What's this kid going to do to us? Did you hear about what happened over in _____, when they got a young guy? That used to be a good church. He just wrecked everything. It's sad." A friend of mine says making changes in his large church is like turning an oil tanker at sea.

Changes in direction are part of "driving," be it church van or church board. Changes are necessary, rollovers not. No one has a steadier hand than God. Please?

The Bottom Line: Changes are necessary, but rollovers are not. God's way is steady.

DAY 96

Poor Procrastinators

In all toil there is profit,
but mere talk tends only to poverty.

Proverbs 14:23

Hmm. I'm not sure a world-class procrastinator like me is going to enjoy this one. I'm the kind of person who needs to make a list and figure out which of the many important things I need to do should be at the top of that list, then number the other items in order of importance. Meanwhile, my industrious wife didn't even make a list but has already accomplished seven tasks without even figuring out which one was most important! I was at least two days into our marriage before I figured out I was never going to be able to keep up with her, when it came to work.

Talk vs. toil—that can be a hard one for some of us. If we don't talk at all, our relationships suffer. If we don't toil at all, relationships suffer even more! It doesn't take long, working beside a lazy braggart, to wish for a new work partner, one who would toil more and talk less. It doesn't matter what kind of work, either. Proverbs says that *in all toil there is profit.* People who work will get things done. People who only talk and never work, mostly just aggravate people, particularly their employer. *Mere talk tends only to poverty*. In our current system, labor unions provide some protection for those who seldom confuse employment with actually working, but outside of an artificial environment, being lazy is the quick way to being poor. Which is a good thing!

So, here's to non-procrastinators, whose idea of a bad day is one in which they didn't accomplish anything. Here's to non-list makers, who work circles around the rest of us and do what needs to be done, without much analysis. My hat's off to those, especially in my family, who could be rationed to 100 words a day and have rollover words left most of the time, but who have seldom, if ever, been outworked by anyone within twenty years of their age.

It's spring break, and I'm sorting through what I need to do this week. But there's already a cloud of dust in our house. It represents what my wife has already accomplished while I'm working on getting my list straightened out. *Mere talk* (or mere writing) *tends only to poverty.* Ain't it the truth! There are lots of things I need to do, some of them important, some, not so much. But I could probably start practically anywhere and have something to show for my effort. Or, I could blow half the week making plans and wrestling priorities. "Toil" sounds like the more profitable way to go! "Talk" is fun, but poverty isn't, particularly. And procrastination is not next to godliness, but uncomfortably close to poverty.

The Bottom Line: How about *doing* something on the list, instead of just making it?

DAY 97

Slow Fuses and Long Relationships

Whoever is slow to anger has great understanding,
but he who has a hasty temper exalts folly.
A tranquil heart gives life to the flesh, but envy makes the bones rot.

Proverbs 14:29-30

Slow fuses lead to long relationships. Tranquil hearts beat longer. I don't know if either statement is backed by human research, but I believe them both.

The person who tries to understand before giving vent to frustration will almost never say or do things in anger which they regret. Understanding kicks in and saves everyone another mess. It makes for long-lasting relationships when we listen first, get angry later, or not at all. Great understanding is a great result.

But instead of condemning quick tempers, we have moved, in America, toward enshrining them. Picture chair-throwing coaches on the sidelines who are revered for their anger, as long as it produces wins. Think of guitar-smashing rock stars. Rambo. The Incredible Hulk. Riots disguised as "protests." Folly exalted.

Don't be part of exalting folly. Uncontrolled anger is not very admirable. We should quit admiring it, or allowing ourselves to be impressed.

We should pay attention to not only our outward response to frustration, but our inward one. While it's good to quit popping off in public, it need not stop there. If we don't allow ourselves to be envious, even our body will be better off. We'll deal with much less anger. Bitterness won't get a foothold. We'll live longer!

We need to be careful of being manipulated by society, too. Class warfare is being stirred up, these days. Envy has become a national pastime. As we teeter toward a socialist mindset, anyone with something we want becomes a target of envy. "We should have what they have! If we need to take it away from them and force them to 'share,' so be it!" The sad thing is, even if the jealous don't get what they desire, they get the ill effects of lusting after what doesn't belong to them. Envy rots the bones. It rots democracy, too. It can take out an entire society.

Those preoccupied with the possessions and power of others are setting themselves up for a lot of misery. *Envy makes the bones rot.* That doesn't sound like a good thing. *A hasty temper exalts folly.* That's not good, either! The people of understanding are those who have chosen to try to understand, rather than get even. The person who has better health, as a whole, and the person with the long-lasting relationships and the enduring admiration is the one slow to anger, the one with the healing heart. That's the person I want to be.

The Bottom Line: Listen first; skip or delay the anger.

DAY 98

A Wonderful Replacement for Worry

Let not your hearts be troubled.

John 14:1

This is only the first sentence. John's gospel goes on for four chapters with Jesus' promises and comfort to His disciples on that night, culminating in His prayer for them. But the first sentence is a beauty. The strong implication is that we have at least a degree of control over our own worry.

Some of us were born fretting over pretty much everything. Had we been able to speak as infants, we would have expressed our concern that we weren't sure there would be enough food. A few seem to have had the worry gene removed somewhere along the line, which has meant a more joyous life for them and has meant parents, spouses and others have gotten to "worry for two." They didn't actually have to, but for those of us with the worry gene in place, people who don't worry worry us, so we feel the need to do it for them as a way of showing we care. If you didn't understand that last line, be thankful.

It's not as if the disciples were enjoying a carefree evening, either! This was not a tropical vacation, enjoying a meal with the Son of God, far away from rabid Pharisees. This was within a few hours of His betrayal, crucifixion and death. I know the effect of the word "cancer" on my spirit; I can't imagine what "crucifixion" must have done to theirs. And they're supposed to be calm?!

At least they remembered what He had said, and wrote it down, years after the horrible and wonderful events of His passion, resurrection and ascension. I'm glad they did, because I need what He said: *Let not your hearts be troubled.* Rather than just commanding us to stifle our worries, He offers a wonderful replacement for them: *Believe in God; believe also in me.*

These days, there's plenty of worry-worthy material available to each one of us. If we run out at home, the plight of our extended family and friends will quickly fill in any gaps. We haven't even gotten to the festering local, national and international situations stealing what's left of our inner peace. Who can get through life with an untroubled heart?! *Believe in God; believe also in me.*

Let not your hearts be troubled. That's one tall order! That's one beautiful option. To let go of our need to worry and fret over our own problems, plus those we've borrowed from the neighbors, to actually live in peace in the most troubling of situations? That's possible? It's not just possible. It's a command. How do we pull it off? Let go of worry (and the responsibility of needing to worry to show you care). Grab hold of God. When we let go of worry, we can see the promises.

The Bottom Line: God offers a wonderful replacement for worry: peace.

DAY 99

What Kind of Unity?

I do not ask for these only, but also for those who will believe in me through their word, that they may all be one, just as you, Father, are in me, and I in you, that they also may be in us, so that the world may believe that you have sent me. The glory that you have given me I have given to them, that they may be one even as we are one, I in them and you in me, that they may become perfectly one, so that the world may know that you sent me and loved them even as you loved me. John 17:20-23

Jesus prayed for unity between His followers. But what kind? Would His desire be for modern-day believers to all be scrunched into the biggest sanctuary in town, so we could all be "one Church," instead of meeting in dozens of cross-laden buildings throughout the city, some with no instrumental music, some you can hear from the parking lot?

Does God desire that every church become a mega-church, with a large staff, large facilities, large everything? Is God into large and nothing else, when it comes to church? That seems pretty limiting for a God who made both mosquitoes and blue whales, atoms and galaxies.

So, when Jesus was asking the Father for "unity," what would the answer to His prayer look like in my neck of the woods?

In the military, there are several branches of the service, each with their own distinctive terminology, traditions and methods, but all with the same purpose—defending the United States, and all with the same commander-in-chief, the president. The Navy Seals do one thing, the Air Force another, but they are not "divided" in their allegiance. They all serve the same country.

It just makes sense to be able to divide forces, assign different missions to different branches, corresponding to their resources, and have an over-all battle plan, rather than assuming that in the interests of "unity," everybody should be all together, doing exactly the same thing!

It's unity of purpose, and it's unity of loyalty that count, in a war. We're in a war with Satan. If our purpose is to be disciples of Jesus Christ and we recognize Him as Commander-in-Chief, if we know whose side we're on and that we're all on the same side, we are probably a lot more united than it seems.

The unity for which Jesus prayed was the unity which results when Christ lives in us and we all have the same God living in us. Differences become irrelevant when we all joyfully serve the same Master. The more diverse we are, the more the true unity shows up. Christ in us, the hope of glory. That's the unity we need.

The Bottom Line: Joyfully serving Jesus produces the kind of unity God wants.

DAY 100

What Exalts a Nation

Righteousness exalts a nation, but sin is a reproach to any people.

Proverbs 14:34

What exalts a nation? It depends on whom we ask. Some would claim that a strong military is most important in exalting a nation. Probably more would argue for the economy as key. "Democracy" and "freedom" would be the cry for many. Minor factions would root for their preferred flavor of political correctness.

When a country is exalted above others, what do they call it? "Superpower." Since the collapse of the U.S.S.R., the United States of America has regarded herself as the world's only remaining "superpower." Military might? Dominant. Economy? Dominant. Influence? Dominant, particularly in all things entertainment. Another indicator of a dominant superpower is the flow of traffic: Are people trying to get into the country or out? No question. They still want in, even to the point of breaking the law in order to come here.

We could add other ingredients to the argument for the U.S. being a great superpower, based on the opinions of generals, economists, politicians and others.

What about God?

Would the Almighty consider the U.S.A. a force with which to be reckoned? Do we intimidate Him with our might or money? When it comes to "exalted" status, which nations might rise to that level in the Lord's eyes? What impresses Him, if anything? Let's put it this way: Is America a spiritual superpower?

I don't like thinking of the answer to that question. There are those who would argue that because we *have been* a spiritual superpower, it means we still are. Others might say that because we're still predominately religious, we're still a spiritual superpower.

Let's use the Bible as a measuring stick instead of our own opinions: *Righteousness exalts a nation, but sin is a reproach to any people.*

Oh. Is the U.S. becoming more righteous (right with God) or more sinful? *Sin is a reproach to* any *people.* I'm pretty sure that would include us.

Which is being exalted more in our land, these days, sin or righteousness? Sin (as defined by God, not us) is a reproach, not a right. Righteousness is how we got to superpower status in the first place. It is the *only* way we'll keep it for long.

What is the answer? Let go of the sin which destroys us, as individuals and a people. Embrace the righteousness which only comes from a holy God. That's what exalts a nation.

The Bottom Line: Sin tears up a nation; righteousness exalts it.

DAY 101

The Wrath Whisperer

A soft answer turns away wrath, but a harsh word stirs up anger.

Proverbs 15:1

There are many times when a wrath extinguisher would come in handy. Proverbs tells us "a soft answer" does the best job of defusing anger. And in the unlikely event that we would ever need some way to stir things up, one harsh word will generally suffice.

Note the difference in the predicted results of soft answers and harsh words, despite the fact no mention is made as to whether the answers are right or wrong. It's because it doesn't matter!

Huh?

When it comes to putting out the fire of an already angry person, "being right" doesn't get you any farther than being wrong, unless your response is "soft."

Soft in what way?

Every way.

Soft in volume. Soft in approach. Soft in body language. A good friend of mine pastors a church where their bulletin urges people to respond to one another with "soft eyes." I've never heard the term elsewhere, but I like it. It's self-explanatory. And it works.

Soft speech. Soft approach. Soft body language. Soft eyes. Anger deflected or defused. Maybe not immediately, but wrath doesn't stand up well to a soft answer. Meanwhile, returning harshness for harshness may keep the thing going for a generation or two, even if the responder is "right"!

Soft answers divert anger, while the least bit of harshness provokes it, even if the message is accurate, logically sound and all that. "Harsh" drowns out all logic. When we're already upset, it's all we hear.

Praise God for "wrath whisperers," those souls who have a way with angry people. When folks are yowling mad, the wrath whisperer doesn't outyell anyone into submission or mount an impassioned logical counter-offensive. Mostly, they listen. If they say anything at all, it's soft—in every way. Someone has been dishing out anger at volume ten. They look into soft eyes which refuse to condemn, or even reflect anger. They feel their anger being absorbed by someone strong enough to stay vulnerable. No matter what comes their way, the wrath whisperer responds softly, gently, calmly. Anger dies down with the volume. Rage is reduced. A little logic returns. Good job, wrath whisperer. The Father is proud of you.

The Bottom Line: A soft answer works like an air bag on wrath.

DAY 102

Pop-up Commandment

This is my commandment, that you love one another as I have loved you. Greater love has no one than this, that someone lay down his life for his friends. You are my friends if you do what I command you. No longer do I call you servants, for the servant does not know what his master is doing; but I have called you friends, for all that I have heard from my Father I have made known to you. You did not choose me, but I chose you and appointed you that you should go and bear fruit and that your fruit should abide, so that whatever you ask the Father in my name, he may give it to you. These things I command you, so that you will love one another. John 15:12-17

The commandment is as persistent as internet pop-up ads. Just about the time we think we're safely past the reminder, here it comes again—the pop-up commandment. *Love one another.* We can't sneak very far through the New Testament without being confronted by Jesus' favorite commandment. In books like 1 John it shows up in nearly every paragraph, just so we won't forget.

How could such a great commandment feel so confrontational? I guess it's meant to be. The commandment to love one another is not like Weight Watchers, where you can substitute some other commandments in place of this one, if you don't like it. It's the glaring dividing line between light and darkness. In 1 John, the apostle explains it bluntly, in way too many ways to miss: If you don't love your brother, you don't love God, either. You're fooling yourself. Case closed.

This might be a frustrating, sometimes annoying commandment, but it's not an optional one. Loving our brother is not in the list of spiritual gifts; it's in the list of requirements to even be a disciple. We can't beg off on this commandment because "it's harder for us than it is for some people." God isn't accepting excuses of why we "can't" love one another. It's expected of all disciples. Trying to get through the New Testament without being confronted by the requirement is futile. It's everywhere, and God is not kidding.

The best approach to the pop-up commandment is to not waste time trying to avoid it, but to obey it. When we once set our sights on loving God through loving the people He has placed in our lives, the whole Gospel begins to make sense, not to mention becoming immeasurably more fun. I'm glad God cares so much about helping us "get" this commandment. If we don't learn another thing in this life, He wants us to learn to love. It's what the Gospel is all about. There's no use hiding from the commandment. There's no use missing out on all the fun, either.

The Bottom Line: It keeps popping up again and again: Love one another!

DAY 103

The Pursuit of Righteousness

The sacrifice of the wicked is an abomination to the LORD,
but the prayer of the upright is acceptable to him.
The way of the wicked is an abomination to the LORD,
but he loves him who pursues righteousness.

Proverbs 15:8-9

It's not just the "sacrifice" that counts; it's the heart. Going through the motions without any real interest in righteousness is an abomination to God. Everything the wicked do is detestable to Him. Why? Because of the heart. He doesn't detest *them*; He detests what they *do*. God loves us, but He doesn't necessarily love everything we do. And until there is a change of heart, even our sacrifices are rejected.

There is a lot of the philosophy going around that it doesn't particularly matter about the heart, so long as people contribute. And the religion of tolerance has such a grip on our country that some consider righteousness to be whatever they jolly well want it to be, in total rejection of any kind of higher authority than themselves. It's not hard to see where that would be detestable to God! The prayers of the wicked aren't getting through—unless they are prayers of repentance. Their "sacrifices" don't matter. They may help in keeping the church organization running, but they don't impress God in the least. On the contrary, they are counted an "abomination" to Him. The way of the wicked is disgusting to Him. A little money or service thrown His way doesn't change His mind.

What I think we're missing is the pursuit of righteousness. We have "the pursuit of happiness"—usually a fruitless pursuit when that's the main goal—but where is the pursuit of righteousness?

The pursuit of righteousness indicates a willingness to allow God to do anything He wants in our lives, in order that we might be free from sin and in a right relationship with Him. That means everything surrendered to Him, nothing held back. How many Christians do we know who are living with this mindset?

He loves the people who pursue righteousness. Why not be those people? Pursue righteousness. Pray. He would use us to change the world. We could live under the favor of God. Or we could pretend He doesn't care about our heart, so long as He gets the cash. We would be so wrong.

We could place "the pursuit of happiness" as first place in our lives—and be miserable. Or we could pursue righteousness—and be happy.

The Bottom Line: The pursuit of righteousness is the pursuit which honors God.

DAY 104

Bovine Alert

Seek good, and not evil,
that you may live;
and so the LORD, the God of hosts, will be with you,
as you have said.
Hate evil, and love good,
and establish justice in the gate;
it may be that the LORD, the God of hosts,
will be gracious to the remnant of Joseph.

Amos 5:14-15

Amos had one tough job. (Prophets have never been too popular). Amos got to tell his countrymen they were headed for disaster or repentance.

God holds His own people to a higher standard, just as families apply corrective measures to themselves, not wandering strangers, as a rule. There are exceptions: I clearly remember the worst spanking of my life, which came from a woman who had just disciplined her child, my cousin, then heard his accomplice state, "You can't spank me! I'm company!" I was wrong about that.

The nation of Israel had convinced themselves they were beyond any kind of discipline from God. After all, they were His "chosen people." Amos blew past their pedigree and addressed the upperclass women of Samaria as "cows of Bashan." (Amos 4:1) I'm sure they were flattered! He pronounced judgment on them for their oppression of the poor, telling them they would be led out by fishhooks through the breaches in the city wall. Sure enough, later Assyrian illustrations seem to show prisoners being led away by rings in their noses, like cattle. No wonder the prophets weren't popular.

Not only did Amos give warnings from God; he also pointed out warnings already given, ranging from drought and famine to defeat in war. Nothing yet had moved them toward repentance. Those were warnings from God? Guess so.

God always sends warnings. He sends trembling prophets to tell us the bad news ahead of time, and He sends disasters in stages, hoping we'll get the hint and come to our senses before it's too late. If we reject the prophets and ignore all the warnings, then eventually we'll get the whole thing—because we asked for it and refused to repent. It doesn't have to be that way. We could repent, while there's still time and grace.

"God would never discipline us—we're America!" Wrong. But a little repentance and a little righteousness could make an incredibly big difference.

The Bottom Line: We could repent, while there's still time.

DAY 105

Gone Fishing

Simon Peter said to them, "I am going fishing." They said to him, "We will go with you." They went out and got into the boat, but that night they caught nothing. John 21:3

When we don't know what else to do, we instinctively resort to what we think we're good at, to the familiar. Peter announced, "I'm going fishing." Six others went with him. The result was a fruitless night. Jesus appeared on shore, and with simply a word, repeated His original miracle among the disciples. They caught 153 fish, and all they had to do was follow Jesus' instructions to put the net down on the right side of the boat.

In the Church, we're always going back to what we think we're good at, especially if Jesus doesn't seem to be anywhere near. If we've always relied on programs or business sense or talent or determination, we go back to those things. Often, it's fruitless, and we don't even know why. Then Jesus shows up, gives us new instructions, and miracles occur.

Did Jesus scold the disciples for going fishing and catching nothing? No. He helped them, He fed them, He reinstated Peter.

So, what's the lesson for us?

Jesus already told us earlier in John, *"Apart from me you can do nothing."* (Jn 15:5) He meant it. Without Jesus, we won't really be successful in anything. That includes things we think we're good at. Without Jesus, there is no fruit. We might as well wait for His instructions, rather than just drumming up a program or borrowing a business technique, and hoping she'll go.

For Peter, the lesson on the water was followed by two more on the beach. The first was a painful reinstatement, where each time Peter affirmed his love for Jesus, he was given the command: "Feed my sheep." That's the way we show our love for Christ—by loving one another, by caring for the weak, in Jesus' name.

The final lesson was one caused by Peter's propensity to worry over the affairs of others. "What about him?" was the question tossed out concerning John. The Lord gently refocused Peter's attention on minding his own business. Our job is not to police our brothers. Our job is, "Follow me." We need to follow Jesus, and quit worrying about what others are doing, or what others are getting. It will save us much grief and even more bitterness.

Peter thought he was going fishing, but really, he was going to school. The end result was another Jesus encounter, 153 fish and three lessons: *Apart from me you can do nothing. Feed my sheep. Follow me.* Not a bad night at all.

The Bottom Line: *Apart from me, you can do nothing.*

DAY 106

White-water Pastor

I've never been on one of those white-water rafting trips, but it looks like fun, particularly if you don't die.

When I look at pastoring, I see some similarities. The white-water raft guide would be the pastor. It's his job to safely get a boatload of people through the rapids on the way to heaven, without dumping everyone out.

It's important that he prepare himself and these people for the rapids. (There doesn't look to be much time for instruction during the actual white-water experience. That's not to say that while everyone else is paddling for their lives, there won't be someone patiently raising their hand in the air with a question.)

Preparation, skill—it takes that and a lot more to get a group through the rapids and safely over to the calm water. While in the rapids, this is not a good time to be thinking about other rafts, or even about what one is going to do once back on dry land; this looks to me like a focus time, where keeping your own boat right side up is pretty much at the top of the list.

Guiding through the white-water is not the only part of the job, though. There is this thing of recruiting—giving off an air of warmth, competence and quiet confidence which would entice people to sign their life off into your hands for a few hours, plus pay you for the privilege of scaring them half to death, confident that it'll in fact only be "halfway," and not the real deal that activates wills and stuff.

Sound political? Yeah, maybe. But every pastor knows that "being right" or having a diploma on your wall doesn't mean people will come flocking toward you like mosquitos in a nudist colony. If those folks don't like being in your raft, they'll find themselves another raft, or stay home with the people who prefer their excitement to come with commercial breaks and a remote. You have to be able to convince people they can entrust to you what's important to them (their lives, the lives of their loved ones), and the only way to consistently do that is to be that— trustworthy, disciplined, calm, competent. Most of those things come through experience, and experience comes through...experience. You have to be willing to float with a pretty much empty boat, especially at first. The happy survivors will be your best recruiters for future trips.

For the critical times of life—the rapids, it's good to have a white-water pastor on board, trained in the Word and prayer, devoted to God and the people. It's nice if they've seen white-water and survived, nicer if they have developed grace and not lost the thrill.

"If it's you, Lord, tell me to come to you on the water." "Come."

The Bottom Line: God is looking for white-water pastors to help guide His people.

DAY 107

Bleacher Calls

Sheol and Abaddon lie open before the LORD;
how much more the hearts of the children of man!

Proverbs 15:11

Nobody knows hearts like God. Our God, who sees and knows all, is never fooled by the sales pitch or the spin. He sees through talented actors playing "sincere." His gaze penetrates to the core of man's being. He sees the things of which even the person himself is not aware.

That's why it's a waste of time and attitude to be dragging things before God's attention. When we tattle on folks to God, it's better than tattling on them to other humans, but it's pretty pointless in the end, since we're not telling God anything He doesn't already know. The good part of telling God instead of telling others is that when we tell God, He doesn't pass it along to others, so at least the gossip chain is dead-ended with the Lord.

But there's an aspect of even telling God that I haven't considered much, before. For those of us who are parents, how much do we enjoy having people tell us how bad our children have been? If there's correction which needs to be made, yes, we need to be made aware of the offense, so sometimes the information is helpful. But what about those times when someone is basically just telling us they don't like our kid? They might justify it with petty little things, or even big ones, but the bottom line is, they don't like our kid. How does it make us feel? Not warm and fuzzy, anyway. More like Mother Bear.

We're all God's children, right? So, what is God's response to us going to be if we are constantly griping to Him about His children, tattling on them incessantly when He already knows their hearts better than they themselves know them, whining about their faults and peculiarities as if we wanted Him to rid the earth of them? God's grace and patience are great, but I think one thing that ticks Him off is when we attack His children. (It makes me feel better to know He doesn't like people attacking me, either. He's a really good Defender.)

He knows our hearts! Really knows them! That disqualifies us for the position of judge, just as the person in the nosebleed section of the auditorium really shouldn't be reprimanding the ref on those close calls he got wrong. God can see it all; we're lucky if we see even a small portion of the total picture. He will make the right calls. God sees the heart. Mine, too. Unless He gives me a striped shirt and a whistle, there are a lot of things I see which I need to keep to myself, and leave to the One who sees everything.

The Bottom Line: God doesn't need us to inform Him of the sins of others.

DAY 108

Calling Shots

"And on that day," declares the LORD GOD,
I will make the sun go down at noon
and darken the earth in broad daylight.
I will turn your feasts into mourning
and all your songs into lamentation;
I will bring sackcloth on every waist
and baldness on every head;
I will make it like the mourning for an only son
and the end of it like a bitter day.

Amos 8:9-10

Amos was prophesying. Prior to God calling him to be the first of the writing prophets, Amos had occupied himself picking figs and herding sheep. Nobody taught him to write a sermon. So, where is he getting all this?

God. God told Amos what to say; Amos said it. Then he wrote it down. Why would God tell Amos these things? So people would know—not just Amos' generation who would see much of the fulfillment in their lifetime, but later generations as well, including ours.

An example is the scripture above. Read it again. Remind you of anyone?

Fast forward several hundred years to an eyewitness account of the day the only-begotten Son of God died: *Now from the sixth hour there was darkness over all the land until the ninth hour.* (Mt 27:45)

The sixth hour? Noon. Oh. *"And on that day," declares the LORD GOD, I will make the sun go down at noon and darken the earth in broad daylight.*

There wasn't even a solar eclipse to help out. Solar eclipses only occur during a new moon, and commentators point out that Passover feast is always at the full moon. God made it dark, just like He made it light in the first place. Passover feasting became mourning on the day they buried God's only Son.

Why did Amos write this prophecy, one of so many meticulously fulfilled hundreds of years after its writing? Because God told him to. It needed to be written down, it needed to be impossible for man to predict.

God calls His shots. From over 700 years out, He predicts darkness at noon on the day His only Son will die. Though it will be during a feast, people will mourn, bitterly. That's merely *one* of the dozens of prophecies about Jesus' death and resurrection, made from hundreds of years out, fulfilled precisely. When God calls His shots, we'd better believe.

The Bottom Line: When God says something, we'd better believe it!

DAY 109

Left Holding the World

Do not love the world or the things in the world. If anyone loves the world, the love of the Father is not in him. For all that is in the world—the desires of the flesh and the desires of the eyes and pride in possessions—is not from the Father but is from the world. And the world is passing away along with its desires, but whoever does the will of God abides forever. I John 2:15-17

We love what we choose to love. That's why it's so important to place our deepest attachments to things eternal, rather than the temporal. It's hard to do, seeing as how, to the naked eye, the temporal appears permanent and the eternal appears to be imaginary. How many times have believers in an eternal God had to endure the stares of pity coming from worldly and "reasonable" atheists, who only cling to things which are "permanent," like Mother Earth?

One day Mother Earth will kick the bucket. There may be a RIP sign over it. The earth will pass away, along with everything in it, including pride. Even all those worldly desires will be gone. Imagine that! None of it will mean anything, anymore.

And the world is passing away along with its desires, but whoever does the will of God abides forever. In light of this, how much sense does it make to become overly attached to worldly pursuits and possessions, seeing as how one day they will be torn from our grip?

In place of the baubles of this world, God offers eternal life. He warns us not to love the world or its things. Devotion to worldly pleasures takes away from devotion to God. In fact, *if anyone loves the world, the love of the Father is not in him.* That's a pretty strong statement! I'm glad God made it, not me.

Are we to hate our life here, just because we want to go to heaven? A very famous verse reminds us that "God so loved the world,"... so I don't think it's about hating life here, despising our surroundings or trying to live a Spartan existence which shrugs off human needs. God, as usual, is talking about the heart. We need to realize that if we allow our heart to chase the desires of this world—*the desires of the flesh and the desires of the eyes and pride in possessions*—those desires didn't come from God, and they certainly won't lead us closer to God.

If we love the world more than we love God, in the end we may get our wish—and be left holding the world, when those more interested in God are receiving their reward.

It's not about trying to hate the world more; it's about choosing to love God more. The more we love Him, the weaker the grip of worldly desires, possessions, pride. The way to live forever is to choose to love a God we can't see. Yet.

The Bottom Line: Let go of the world. Hang onto God.

DAY 110

The Proper Use of Volkswagens

Remember an ancient practice whereby college students would try to see how many human beings could be stuffed into a Volkswagen? I guess the goal was the Guinness Book of World Records and all the accompanying pride. Beyond that, I never was sure about the ultimate reward in it, other than feeling really close to some people, and maybe a life-long case of claustrophobia.

I had a family in the church I began in Alaska who really knew how to use a Volkswagen. Each Sunday the Roemhildt's would pile their own six kids into their Volkswagen van to make the six-mile trip to church, stopping along the way to cram in others. Every Roemhildt with a driver's license and a vehicle brought people, young and old, to church. The van or pickup would pull up and deliver its priceless cargo at the church steps, often heading back for more. After church was a reverse procedure, requiring multiple vehicles and sometimes multiple trips. A Roemhildt child with a restroom need after church became the inspiration for "No Child Left Behind." Twice. "Not again!"

Why would a family with plenty of needs of their own pay so much attention to the needs of others? God's love. It took something like thirty seconds to be around the Roemhildt family before one would sense God's love or hear about it. Whatever they had in their family was used for God's service, including a Volkswagen van they packed with kids in order to bring them to church. For some of those little people, church represented the only sensible, normal thing in their lives, and this family represented the only people who knew them, who loved them enough to be involved in their lives and invite and bring them to church.

So how did it all turn out? The Roemhildt's are still a mainstay in the church and the community. For some reason, in one of the toughest spiritual environments anywhere, the whole tribe of Roemhildt kids grew up to serve God. A new generation has joined their parents and grandparents in making a difference for Christ, wherever they are. Wouldn't you know, the eldest daughter, Jennifer, is now engaged in worldwide ministry reaching out to victims of human trafficking. (http://Preventrestore.wordpress.com) Jennifer was chosen Northwest Nazarene University's 2009 Alumnus of the Year. (We're proud of you, Jennifer)! She has a ministry of helping frightened, desperate people find safety and Christ. I think I know where she picked up that mindset about a purpose in life. The proper use of Volkswagens leaves a very lasting impression. So does a family who serves God.

You don't get in the Guinness Book of World Records for using your Volkswagen as a church bus. But you do get your friends and neighbors into the Book of Life. Which, over the long haul, is a far better use of Volkswagens.

The Bottom Line: We have what we have so we can use it to serve Jesus.

DAY 111

The First Theologian

Now the serpent was more crafty than any other beast of the field that the LORD God had made.

He said to the woman, "Did God really say, 'You shall not eat of any tree in the garden?" And the woman said to the serpent, "We may eat of the fruit of the trees in the garden, but God said, "You shall not eat of the fruit of the tree that is in the midst of the garden, neither shall you touch it, lest you die." But the serpent said to the woman, "You will not surely die. For God knows that when you eat of it your eyes will be opened, and you will be like God, knowing good and evil." So when the woman saw that the tree was good for food, and that it was a delight to the eyes, and that the tree was to be desired to make one wise, she took of its fruit and ate, and she also gave some to her husband who was with her, and he ate. Then the eyes of both were opened, and they knew that they were naked. And they sewed fig leaves together and made themselves loincloths.

And they heard the sound of the LORD God walking in the garden in the cool of the day, and the man and his wife hid themselves from the presence of the LORD God among the trees of the garden. Genesis 3:1-8

He was the first theologian. Adam and Eve were quite well acquainted with the LORD God, and didn't really need anyone to explain His true intentions, but the serpent (a.k.a. Satan) was more than willing to help. *Did God really say?...* The question was knowingly followed by a huge exaggeration—but there is something about saying it, even when the listener knows it's not true, which begins to turn the tide in the speaker's favor. Eve corrects the serpent, but now she's listening.

"You will not surely die." Interpreted: "God is a liar. He's just trying to scare you. In fact, you should call His bluff, because if you just partake of this tree, not only will nothing bad happen to you, but you will be as wise as God, because you will no longer know just about good; you will also know about evil." Two of Satan's favorite tricks: telling people "what God really means by what He said," and convincing the innocent and naive that a firsthand knowledge of sin is somehow a good thing—wisdom, even. Both tricks worked on Eve. Adam first looked passively on, then stupidly followed his wife into death.

Their perfect bodies eventually died; they were expelled from their perfect world. All creation fell with them. The very first casualty was their innocence. So this is what it is to "know" evil. The serpent said that was a good thing. He seemed so smart. He was telling us all about what God was really like. The first theologian turned out to be a snake. If we want to know what God meant, ask God.

The Bottom Line: If we want to know what God meant, start with asking God.

DAY 112

Children of a Greater God

See what kind of love the Father has given to us, that we should be called children of God; and so we are. The reason why the world does not know us is that it did not know him. Beloved, we are God's children now, and what we will be has not yet appeared; but we know that when he appears we shall be like him, because we shall see him as he is. And everyone who thus hopes in him purifies himself as he is pure. 1 John 3:1-3

God's adopted children are very, very rich kids. It's not just the money or resources which God could, and sometimes does, make available to us. It's everything. The common childhood concept of "My Dad can do anything" becomes reality: My Dad can do *anything!* And the fact that the God who spoke the Universe into existence *wants* to call me His child!

We're not bums hanging around in search of a hand-out and some pity. We're children of the Most High God, with our own bedroom with our name on the door. The Book of Life contains our name, too. We're not illegal immigrants who decided to try to crash heaven; we are not even "invited guests." We're citizens of heaven! (Philippians 3:20) We're family! Heaven is not "a place I hope to go, someday"—it's home! My home!

Meanwhile, we're in the waiting area called Earth, being called names just like they did to Jesus. We haven't grown into our heavenly body, yet, because it isn't time.

One of these days...

One of these days, He'll be back. Jesus is coming for His Church. He will appear, He will gather His brothers and sisters to Himself, and we're all going home! Somewhere in that process we'll be perfected at last—not "perfect" as we imagine, but something that will knock the walls out of our best imagination efforts. *We shall be like him, because we shall see him as he is.* Sounds worth it.

And everyone who thus hopes in him purifies himself as he is pure. The reality of being God's child and the hope of eternity with our Dad is enough to make us want to be cleaned up and ready to go when the bus arrives to take us home.

God's child, huh? What are the implications of that? Who is richer than we are? Who has a stronger Father than God's children? We're children of a greater God—greater than anyone, anything, all of them put together. And He is the One who chose us, rather than it being the other way around. Man, do we have it made!

The Bottom Line: We are adopted children of the Most High God.

DAY 113

Happy Hearts and Homes

A glad heart makes a cheerful face,
but by sorrow of heart the spirit is crushed.
The heart of him who has understanding seeks knowledge,
but the mouths of fools feed on folly.
All the days of the afflicted are evil,
but the cheerful of heart has a continual feast.
Better is a little with the fear of the LORD
than great treasure and trouble with it.
Better is a dinner of herbs where love is
than a fattened ox and hatred with it.

Proverbs 15:13-17

What's on the face starts in the heart. And we get to choose what's in the heart. Those who choose a cheerful heart have "a continual feast." Those who choose victim status spend their days feeling "afflicted." There aren't any good days for victims. There is only one bad, unfair thing after another. *All the days of the afflicted are evil, but the cheerful of heart has a continual feast.*

The person who has chosen to be cheerful, the one who refuses victim status, regardless of what happened, has a continual feast of one good day after another. Why? It doesn't depend on circumstances. It depends on the heart. A cheerful heart always has good days—some are better than others.

What applies to the heart applies to the home. When the choice is made to have strife, where hatred is harbored, fancy food or expensive possessions don't counteract the poisonous atmosphere of that home. Far better is the person barely getting by, financially, but who enjoys rich relationships, hatred-free.

We get to choose. If we're applying for victim status, we all qualify, at least in our minds. Anyone who has been on this planet a week has already suffered some humiliation and injustice. Newborns are welcomed into the world by people who make them cry on purpose. It's a wonder they don't sue. It doesn't get easier.

We can choose a cheerful heart or we can grant ourselves victim status and consider ourselves "afflicted." Poor, pitiful victims. It turns all our days evil.

We get to choose the atmosphere of our home. Will it be tarnished by hatred and envy? Or wallowing in peace and contentment, even as the Jones' leave us behind and sprint into yet another tax bracket?

A cheerful face, a home where love is—these are not accidents of fate, but the direct results of choices of the heart: "Non-victim." "Forgiveness." Joy.

The Bottom Line: A cheerful heart always has good days–some better than others.

DAY 114

The First Victims

In the course of time Cain brought to the LORD an offering of the fruit of the ground, and Abel also brought of the firstborn of his flock and of their fat portions. And the LORD had regard for Abel and his offering, but for Cain and his offering he had no regard. So Cain was very angry, and his face fell. The LORD said to Cain, "Why are you angry, and why has your face fallen? If you do well, will you not be accepted? And if you do not do well, sin is crouching at the door. Its desire is for you, but you must rule over it.

Cain spoke to Abel his brother. And when they were in the field, Cain rose up against his brother Abel and killed him. Then the LORD said to Cain, "Where is your brother?" He said, "I do not know; am I my brother's keeper?" And the LORD said, "What have you done? The voice of your brother's blood is crying to me from the ground." Genesis 4:3-10

It started with Adam and Eve, perfect people in a perfect setting who suddenly are convinced they are victims in need of liberation through knowledge. The prescription given them by the serpent becomes the first sin, and The Fall.

Their first son determines to take the same route which cost his parents the Garden. When his brother Abel's sacrifice to God is accepted and his is not, rather than repentance and a change of heart, Cain just has a hardening of heart. He tells himself it's unfair. Shouldn't God treat everyone the same? Why would God show favoritism and accept one person's offering, but not another's? Cain let his anger roam free. He told himself he was a victim of unfair treatment from God, and he took it out on the one who pleased God.

The first murder victim in history was a result of a brother who painted himself as a victim, when in reality he was just a sinner who needed to repent. Victims have "rights"—lots of them. They have a right to be angry; they have a right to all privileges and rewards, regardless of their actions; they have the right to do whatever they want, and feel justified in doing it. They have the right to smart off to God and think they'll get away with it. The problem with victim's rights is that they exist only in the mind of the self-appointed victim. The most harmful right of all is the right to be a victim. Once that one is claimed, all the rest follows. It leaves a trail of genuine victims in its path.

Ah, the apple doesn't fall far from the tree of the knowledge of good and evil, does it? God, spare us from victim status. It's an ugly, downhill plunge. Sin desires to rule over us all. We must master it. If we refuse victim status and do what's right, we'll be accepted by a God who doesn't make victims or mistakes.

**The Bottom Line: Refuse victim status.
Do what's right. Find acceptance by God.**

DAY 115

Love Before First Sight

When our eyes first met, it was like coming home. Not only were we already in love; we were also engaged to be married. My long-distance call across the 4,000 miles which separated us had been intended to let her know my feelings, without any pressure for an answer, but her immediate response had been, "Yes, without reservations." We got engaged over the phone. Twelve days later, we met, face to face, for the first time.

The funny thing is, I already knew her better than anyone I had ever dated. The letters and phone calls had effectively opened our souls to one another. The bizarre and wonderful courtship which originated with a God-ordained prank phone call from Nebraska teen camp and culminated in a meeting at Anchorage International Airport was so obviously an answer to both of our prayers. Was this beautiful lady God's answer to my prayers for a partner for life? I've never been more sure of anything.

I'm still sure. Always have been. She is still beautiful and wonderful. She has been at my side through it all, for nearly three decades, since the October day we wed. I have thanked God for His gift countless times through the years.

In the weeks leading up to our engagement, I told myself again and again, "This thing is rigged!" I just knew God was behind it all, orchestrating the whole thing. Today, as I was thanking Him again, I felt Him say to me, "If you think that was rigged, wait until you see what I have for you in heaven!"

What a God we serve! He can do anything! We can trust Him, absolutely, and if we know for sure that something is from Him, faith is not that hard, especially if God has treated you like He's treated me!

I love God. I haven't seen Him, face to face, yet, but that doesn't matter. I know Him and He knows me. I love Him and He loves me. One day, I'll meet Him, face to face. I'll be home in heaven, where things are definitely "rigged"! And once again, I'll know it was love before first sight.

The Bottom Line: We can absolutely trust God, with anything.

DAY 116

Options Which Aren't

By this it is evident who are the children of God, and who are the children of the devil: whoever does not practice righteousness is not of God, nor is the one who does not love his brother.

For this is the message that you have heard from the beginning, that we should love one another. We should not be like Cain, who was of the evil one and murdered his brother. And why did he murder him? Because his own deeds were evil and his brother's righteous. Do not be surprised, brothers, that the world hates you. We know that we have passed out of death into life, because we love the brothers. Whoever does not love abides in death. Everyone who hates his brother is a murderer, and you know that no murderer has eternal life abiding in him. 1 John 3:10-15

Some options aren't. For example, how many times have we heard fellow Christians discount righteousness—living in a right relationship with God instead of following the old, sinful path—as unreachable and irrelevant? In other words, "God doesn't truly expect His children to pay any real heed to standards of holiness. They are just there to remind us of how hopelessly lost we are without Christ."

Really? Then why is the standard of holiness used in books like 1 John as a dividing line which tells you who belongs to God and who belongs to the devil? It's not just in an isolated place or two, either. Again and again and again in 1 John, the apostle beats the same drum: You can't serve God and ignore righteousness.

Throughout the whole Bible, holiness is never portrayed as just an "option," for Christians seeking extra credit with God. It has, and always will be, God's standard. What else would a holy God expect of His people, but holiness? Righteousness is not optional, for followers of a holy God. Righteousness through Jesus is available to all, but like a kid with a coat, we must "put it on" in order for it to do us any good. Throw away the sin; put on the righteousness of God.

The same thing applies to love for our brothers. Interesting, how many Christ-followers try to beg off on this one, but the scripture is relentless when it comes to love. Thirteen times in 1 John alone, the call comes through: Love your brother! If you don't love your brother, don't bother trying to tell God you love Him, because you're lying!

Living a holy life before God. Loving our brothers. Those are a couple of options which aren't. Instead, they are life-changing requirements which show very clearly on whose side we are. No more excuses. We get to follow Jesus, but we don't get to do it without holiness and love.

The Bottom Line: Love is not optional; it's a command.

DAY 117

Hot-tempered Self-control

A hot-tempered man stirs up strife,
but he who is slow to anger quiets contention.

Proverbs 15:18

Hot-tempered Christian. That sounds like an oxymoron to me. I think it's supposed to. James advises Christ-followers to be *"slow to anger, for the anger of man does not produce the righteousness of God."* (James 1:19-20)

So what does produce the righteousness of God? The Holy Spirit. When we invite Him to assume total control of our lives, we can expect the fruit of the Spirit to begin to grow in us (if we want it). The fruit? *But the fruit of the Spirit is love, joy, peace, patience, kindness, goodness, faithfulness, gentleness, self-control...* (Galatians 5:22-23)

All the fruits of the Spirit are in contrast to out-of-control anger. Put "hot-tempered" next to any of them and it sounds like an oxymoron: Hot-tempered joy? Hot-tempered patience? Hot-tempered kindness? Hot-tempered goodness? Hot-tempered faithfulness? Hot-tempered gentleness? Hot-tempered self-control? Hmm. Something is wrong with the picture of the self-proclaimed Christ-follower, filled with the Spirit, who always grants himself exemption when it comes to controlling his anger. Something is wrong, indeed. The fruit of the Spirit doesn't look like out-of-control anger. Maybe we aren't to excuse ourselves for our impatience and lack of self-control just because "that's the way we are."

How do quick-tempered people do a better job of keeping their cool?

-We quit making excuses for our behavior and let the Spirit mold us.

-We choose peace and patience (fruits of the Spirit) instead of anger.

-We hang around a calm God.

-We assign more value to being patient and less value to being comfortable. If getting our way is a priority but learning patience isn't, the years will roll by as our temper only gets edgier, when God's will is that we would be acting more like Him than we used to. Anger doesn't just happen—we decide to get angry. Anger is set up in advance when we assign great value where it doesn't belong, and not enough value when it comes to our character development. If having the fruit of the Spirit called patience in our life is important to us, we will continually grow in that direction. If all we care about is getting our way and we'd just as soon not ever have to use patience, anger will increase its control over our lives.

What will grow in our lives, a hot temper or the fruit of the Spirit? Whichever we want. But one grows at the expense of the other.

The Bottom Line: We will see the Fruit of the Spirit in our lives, if we want it.

DAY 118

Geezers and God-pleasers

The LORD saw that the wickedness of man was great in the earth, and that every intention of the thoughts of his heart was only evil continually. And the LORD was sorry that he had made man on the earth, and it grieved him to his heart. So the LORD said, "I will blot out man whom I have created from the face of the land, man and animals and creeping things and birds of the heavens, for I am sorry that I have made them." But Noah found favor in the eyes of the LORD. Genesis 6:5-8

Genesis 5 details the life-spans of Adam's descendants. Those guys lived a long time! Had Hallmark been around then, they would have had cards saying, "Happy 900th Birthday!"; "Congratulations on your 450th wedding anniversary"; etc. Methuselah took the prize. He made it to 969 years before breathing his last.

With age comes wisdom. Right? Well, it depends. It seems that for those who choose to be as bad as they want to be, all advanced age gets them is an ever-bigger pile of accumulated sins. People who wise up by turning toward God seem to grow kinder and wiser as the decades roll by, but not so those who choose sin as a career path. I'm thinking just about people who hang around on earth for the better part of a hundred years. What would happen to those bent on evil if their life span was multiplied by nine or ten times? They would just have that much more time to sin! It would be like ornery to the tenth power!

That's what God was looking at, in the days leading up to the Flood. The long life spans only gave people more time to do evil! There were some really old geezers hanging around, with no other purpose in life than exploring new ways of sinning. There was one exception, and only one: Noah. Only one person was even attempting to please God. The story of Noah is confirmation of a true cliche' I have often heard: "If you were the only person on Earth, God would have done all this just to save you." Noah was the only person on Earth who was trying to please God. God provided a plan of salvation when only one person was interested.

After the Flood, human life spans were drastically shortened. Less time to get in trouble. We have maybe ten decades to do what we're going to do. If we choose sin as our lifestyle, 100 years is more than enough time to do the damage we're going to do to ourselves and the world, and be out of the picture. If we're not seeking God, the longer we live, the worse we'll get (and the harder to live with). On the other hand, if we choose to please God, however long we live doesn't seem long enough to our fellow man, because we bring blessing on Earth. And for those who follow God, we don't just get long life. We get eternal life.

The Bottom Line: Following God gets us a better life here, an eternal life to follow.

DAY 119

Anything But Prayer

If revival came just because we needed it, we'd already have it! We also have to want it, including the change that accompanies revival. There is a personal cost, as God's Holy Spirit renovates areas of our lives which we thought were fine. There is a big cost for those in ministry, who are called upon to help restore broken and messy relationships and lives. There is also a cost in prayer, and not just for a handful of ministers. Revival comes through prayer.

Winston Churchill used to say of Americans, "Americans always do what's right—after they've tried everything else." That's quite true of the American church as well. We've tried it all, haven't we? If there were a way to have life-changing renewal in our land without prayer, we'd have found it by now. We haven't. Each cute new "trend" turns out to not quite do the trick, unless one counts forming a new mega-something out of the disemboweled remains of a bunch of littler churches as "life-changing renewal" (I don't).

Meanwhile, the best way I know for a pastor to have time alone is to announce a prayer meeting which will consist only of talking to God for about an hour!

There just has to be another way to get revival without prayer, isn't there? We're wasting time if we're looking for it.

How about committing to join with some other believers in spending at least an hour a week in praying for a spiritual awakening, and repenting for the sins of our nation?

Do we really need to spend that much time in prayer, when there is so much else to do? Let's put it this way. Would we ever have fallen in love with our spouse if we hadn't cared to focus our attention directly on them for even an hour a week? So, a spiritual awakening, the experience of falling in love with Jesus all over again, is going to happen when it's not even worth an hour of anybody's time?

Let's pray. We've already tried everything else.

Commit yourself to at least one other person, to pray on a regular basis for a spiritual awakening. Open your heart to fall in love anew with Jesus Christ, and undergo whatever changes that brings about. Pray for yourself. Pray for others, by name. If we want revival, we'd better talk to the only One who can send it. Pray.

The Bottom Line: We've tried everything else; let's try prayer.

DAY 120

When God Shuts the Door

In the six hundredth year of Noah's life, in the second month, on the seventeenth day of the month, on that day all the fountains of the great deep burst forth, and the windows of the heavens were opened. And rain fell upon the earth forty days and forty nights. On the very same day Noah and his sons, Shem and Ham and Japheth, and Noah's wife and the three wives of his sons with them entered the ark, they and every beast, according to its kind, and all the livestock according to their kinds, and every creeping thing that creeps on the earth, according to its kind, and every bird, according to its kind, every winged creature. They went into the ark with Noah, two and two of all flesh in which there was the breath of life. And those that entered, male and female of all flesh, went in as God had commanded him. And the LORD shut him in. Genesis 7:11-16

For as were the days of Noah, so will be the coming of the Son of Man. For as in those days before the flood they were eating and drinking, marrying and giving in marriage, until the day when Noah entered the ark, and they were unaware until the flood came and swept them all away, so will be the coming of the Son of Man. Matthew 24:37-39

Sin matters. But God saves. That's the message I get from the account of the Flood. When it came time to destroy all flesh because of their sin, God was willing to take anyone who wanted to be saved. It turned out there was only one, but God saved him and his family, anyway, plus the animals.

The Flood caught mankind by surprise, but not Noah. God had told him far in advance, giving him time to build an immense boat for salvation. But when the man, his family and the seed stock for the animal kingdom were all safely inside, Noah didn't shut the door. God did. And for the first time, it started to rain.

When Jesus spoke of His Second Coming, He spoke of it being like "the days of Noah." People assumed things would go on as they always had, until suddenly everything changed. Jesus' return will take everyone by surprise. For those who are ready, it will be a glorious surprise. For those who chose not to believe, it will be suddenly too late. When God shuts the door, it's shut. No one opens it.

Right now, the door to salvation is wide open. It's available for anyone and everyone. All we need to do is climb in the ark of safety which is Jesus Christ. Believe on Him and you're in! The time to get in the Ark is now—today. If we find ourselves one day staring at a closed door when it starts to rain, it will be no one's fault but our own. Get in the Ark, please?! And live ready for our moment.

The Bottom Line: Sin matters. But God saves. Get in the Ark.

DAY 121

Better Lawns and Lives

I remember the feeling of pride I had when I had completed my first underground sprinkler system. Being at least smart enough to try it out before I buried the thing, with great anticipation I turned the water on and waited for my nine new sprinkler heads to pop up and begin watering the back yard. None did.

I didn't suspect trouble with the new equipment, plus I had individually tested parts of the system before gluing together the plastic pipe. What could it be? All the heads just sat gurgling. This was no way to water a lawn.

At last, I discovered the source of my problem. It was lack of pressure, caused by trying to use too many sprinkler heads, simultaneously. The answer? Zones. I wasted some connections and pipe, and had to put out some money for valves. I found my system would only support three sprinklers at a time. More than that, and there was insufficient pressure for the sprinkler heads to pop up. Once I reconfigured the system, everything worked perfectly.

God has frequently reminded me why I struggle to get things done: I try to concentrate on too many things at the same time. There's usually nothing wrong with the tasks—there are just too many of them. I'm more of a one-or-two tasks at a time person; when someone cons me into nine at a time, nothing much happens, except frustration.

I've said it before. If I had it to do over again, the biggest thing I would change in pastoral ministry is one word: *Focus!*

Through the years I've spent too much time collecting good ideas to never implement; going to conferences, then looking for a place to store another plastic notebook. And not saying "No" nearly enough. The wise realize that saying "Yes" to everything is basically saying "No" to everything, since the promises quickly overwhelm the resources and we're left with sputtering sprinkler heads. If we would put all our resources toward just one or two good, prayer-driven ideas and politely decline the rest, we'd have better results.

Pray, then focus. Pray, then decide. Pray, then actually do something besides formulating yet another lifeless plan or resolution that'll never see the light of day. I find plans all the time that I don't remember writing. Nobody else knew about them, either, because nothing happened!

Does the whole lawn need watering? Yes. That's precisely why we must focus on one or two things at a time, instead of everything at once. Not all good ideas require our attention. Pray, then pick one. My lawn's life improved once my focus did. That same principle applies in ministry and most everything else. Prayer, then focus. It makes for better lawns and lives.

The Bottom Line: Pray, then focus. Result? Better lawns and lives.

DAY 122

Him Who is True

We know that everyone who has been born of God does not keep on sinning, but he who was born of God protects him, and the evil one does not touch him.

We know that we are from God, and the whole world lies in the power of the evil one.

And we know that the Son of God has come and has given us understanding, so that we may know him who is true; and we are in him who is true, in his Son Jesus Christ. He is the true God and eternal life. Little children, keep yourselves from idols. I John 5:18-21

The world is under Satan's control, but we're not. That's the message I'm hearing from these final verses of 1 John.

It's good to know we don't have to trudge along in the old ruts of sin and idolatry—it's not God's plan at all for us to continue to sin after we've found the Savior. We're not talking perfection, here, but we are talking about living under God's grace and protection, instead of blithely continuing to disgrace the name of Christ under the guise of grace. Just because all our sins are forgiven doesn't mean we have to try all the flavors! We are offered protection from the evil one, if we will take it. It's part of what it means to be *"in him who is true."* When we take refuge in the Son of God, there isn't a thing Satan can do about it.

Him who is true. I love that phrase because it is such a wonderful and accurate description of God. He is true. He is totally trustworthy. Meanwhile, there's the reminder that when we see the unfair and the disgusting, it's because this world is presently under the control of the evil one, which makes those living for Jesus Christ feel unwanted and unloved by the world, but cherished and protected by our great God. After all, we are His children. I would not want to mess with God's kids!

Him who is true. We not only get to know Him and trust Him, we get to be *in Him!* We are absorbed into the life of a true and living God who can do anything. One day the Son of God will reclaim the earth He made, the evil one will be gone, and the rejoicing will kick up to a level never seen before. *He is the true God and eternal life.* He doesn't just *offer* eternal life—He is eternal life! It's a good reason to keep ourselves from idols. Anything short of Jesus Christ is by no means worthy of our worship. *He is the true God and eternal life.* Accept no substitutes.

The Bottom Line: When we find refuge in God's Son, we are totally safe.

DAY 123

The Best Father's Day Gift

A wise son makes a glad father,
but a foolish man despises his mother.

Proverbs 15:20

Father's Day is notorious for its awkwardness. With Mother's Day, most offspring can fall back on flowers or plants and a nice card, chosen from among rows and rows of sentimental offerings, and they will be just fine. Father's Day? Finding a card that isn't dorky or an outright lie is tougher, and figuring out a gift is often downright painful. What does a father want? If you ask him, the answer is either "I don't know" or "a new truck," or something in a similar price range.

What will make Dad glad? Probably not a new tie or whatever the store was pushing as a "can't miss" idea. The new truck would make him smile, until he found out how much you paid for it and what a lousy bargainer you are, not to mention you didn't even get the right one. Plus, it was actually his money you used. Not a good plan.

This is the sure-fire plan for making Dad happy, and not just for a day or two—are we ready?

A wise son makes a glad father.

When it comes to fatherhood, cards and gifts are not the pay-off that bring joy. (That's not what really brings joy to mothers, either). What makes Dad (and Mom) glad is a wise son or daughter. If you have the great fortune to have a child or two who follows God, uses their head and exhibits wisdom and grace, you already have the best gift they could give you, and it's year-round. Whatever they stick in a box and hand you on "special" days is just extra.

The all-time favorite Father's Day gift I've ever received was a few years back, when our daughter, then in middle school, bought me a hose nozzle (which quickly broke). The gift, while thoughtful and purchased with her own money, wasn't much. What brought me to tears was the homemade label she had attached to the wrapped gift.

The most similar features between my daughter and I have always been our hands. Palm to palm, the match makes us smile. For a label, our young daughter had traced her hand on a folded piece of blue paper, then cut out a hand-shaped outline which opened to reveal the message inside. On the outside of the label she had written, "I know I have your hands..." Inside, it read, "I hope I inherited your heart."

What makes me glad? Two children like that, a beautiful wife, a great God.

The Bottom Line: What does Dad really want?
Wise, good children.

DAY 124

Major Changes

So Noah went out, and his sons and his wife, and his sons' wives with him. Every beast, every creeping thing, and every bird, everything that moves on the earth, went out by families from the ark. Genesis 8:18-19

They emerged into a new world, one very different from the one they had known a year before, when they had entered the ark. The changes were enormous.

For one thing, they were alone. Not another human or animal was anywhere to be seen. It must have been like landing on a new, uninhabited planet.

In some ways, it *was* a new planet. Now it rained; before, a mist had come up from the ground to water the earth. Noah and his family must have been terrified the first few times it rained. Would the phenomenon which had wiped out all living things now destroy them, too? Did they need to get back in the ark? They needed assurance. God gave it to them in the form of another new marvel, the rainbow, along with His solemn promise to never again flood the whole earth.

In this new world, the animal kingdom was subject to man, and food for man. Prior to the Flood, this had apparently not been the case.

Given another chance at a perfect world with no sin since all the wicked people are gone, the survivors quickly fall back into sinful behavior, anyway. The next time God provides a Savior, He will be one who saves from sin, not just from water.

Noah and crew emerged into a world so different from the one previously known. Talk about major adjustments! They had to cope with a whole new system. It wasn't just a different climate—it was a different kind of world. And they were alone. Everything was up to them. What were they going to do, now?

Noah's first action was to make a sacrifice to the God who had saved them. He worshiped God. With all the adjustments they would have to make, the first priority for Noah was to worship his God.

Noah wasn't a perfect man; his family, even less. But God's grace doesn't require perfection; only attention and belief. Noah tried to please God when no one else cared. He believed God's word to him about how to save himself and his family, enough to act on it. Though he was imperfect and probably very confused, the Lord got him through everything, including the huge adjustments of starting over on what had become basically a new earth.

What adjustments are we facing? If we kept worshiping God as our first priority and righteousness as our goal, is there some sort of major change too big for us, when our faith is in God? I don't think so.

The Bottom Line: God can get us through anything.
We only have to trust Him.

DAY 125

Gray World

I have written to the church, but Diotrephes, who likes to put himself first, does not acknowledge our authority. So if I come, I will bring up what he is doing, talking wicked nonsense against us. And not content with that, he refuses to welcome the brothers, and also stops those who want to and puts them out of the church.

Beloved, do not imitate evil but imitate good. Whoever does good is from God; whoever does evil has not seen God. Demetrius has received a good testimony from everyone, and from the truth itself. We also add our testimony, and you know that our testimony is true. 3 John :9-12

We're living in a gray world. I'm not just talking about the Pacific Northwest, where the startling appearance of the unclouded sun causes us to scramble for our sunglasses, our eyes being unaccustomed to so much light. I'm talking about a world where black and white, right and wrong, righteousness and depravity are seldom-used labels. It's all gray. We are constantly crowded toward a philosophy without absolutes of any kind. "It's supposed to be gray," we're told.

That's not what the Book of Truth says. The Bible declares things—and people—to be either righteous or sinful, good or evil. There are dividing lines everywhere, the main one being, "What did you do with Jesus?" In John's former letter, he writes, *And this is the testimony, that God gave us eternal life, and this life is in his Son. Whoever has the Son has life; whoever does not have the Son of God does not have life.* (I John 5:11-12) Not a lot of gray there! There isn't supposed to be.

"But what about 'Don't judge'? Didn't Jesus teach tolerance?" It depends on whether we're referring to the sins of others or our own sin. With others, we get to leave the judging to God, while we are commanded to love. With ourselves, it's different. We *need* to distinguish between good and evil, repenting for the evil and imitating the good. We need to walk in the Light, not in the darkness, not in the gray. We *need* to quit excusing ourselves for sin, painting it gray. We need to come into the Light.

God is light, and in him is no darkness at all. (I John 1:5)

It's not a gray world, to God. It's His world, and He's a God of Light. Darkness will never please Him. Neither will gray. Good and evil are both realities; we are on one side or the other. We should imitate the good. We should avoid the evil. We should not try to blur lines meant to be clear. We should choose Light, not darkness, not gray.

**The Bottom Line: Our God is Light.
We need to walk in His light.**

DAY 126

When God Was Welcome

We are the spiritual descendants of people who came to this land in search of the freedom to worship God as they chose. It is hard to overstate the determination and sacrifice of people like the pilgrims who landed at Plymouth Rock, Massachusetts, in 1620. Only half their party survived the first brutal winter. Freedom bore a high price.

When our new nation was established, one of its characteristics was not only freedom of religion, but a respect for God at all levels of society. The evidence is found in government documents, monuments emblazoned with scripture, colleges established primarily to educate the clergy. Prayer was a vital part of daily life.

The point is, with few exceptions, God was honored and welcomed in American life, from our earliest days on this continent. Our forefathers sought not only His blessing and help; they sought to please Him. Even those with slight religious inclinations tried to appear spiritual, if only to gain respect among the truly God-fearing populace. God was welcome in America.

That was then, this is now. What is becoming the attitude toward God in America, in these days? Oh, there are still millions who love Him with all their heart, but there are also millions who have come to resent Him and, particularly, His followers. The resentful contingency has come to occupy many positions of power in the U.S. Under the guise of "separation of church and state," these people have determined to crowd God from the public square, entirely, a concept which would have astonished our Founding Fathers. At one time, God was welcome in every way, in America: His name, His laws, the Bible, His blessings. Now there are many, even within the established church, who continue to welcome and expect His blessings, while rejecting His influence and His commandments.

Will we serve the God of our fathers? There is a reason America has prospered. Throughout history, there has been a direct connection between a people wishing to be godly and good, and manifold blessings. At the same time, nations which have served God but later forsaken Him have all met the same fate.

For centuries, God has been welcome in America. Our national track record, while not spotless, has been good. God's continued blessing on America is up to us. If we welcome not only His blessings but His presence, we will have both. If we sincerely worship God and welcome His influence and His Word, we will continue to enjoy His protection. If, as a nation, we want Him to leave us alone, He will. Anyone desiring that fate should read a little history to discover what happens to nations who go from honoring God to resenting Him.

Lord? Please stay.

The Bottom Line: We get to choose whether God will continue to bless America.

DAY 127

You're On, Martha

Now as they went on their way, Jesus entered a village. And a woman named Martha welcomed him into her house. And she had a sister called Mary, who sat at the Lord's feet and listened to his teaching. But Martha was distracted with much serving. And she went up to him and said, "Lord, do you not care that my sister has left me to serve alone? Tell her then to help me." But the Lord answered her, "Martha, Martha, you are anxious and troubled about many things, but one thing is necessary. Mary has chosen the good portion, which will not be taken away from her." Luke 10:38-42

Martha's of the world, rejoice! Your time has come.

For years, you've squirmed at the story of Mary and Martha, the triumph of the "worshiper" over the worker, the humiliation of trying to level the playing field and having the Referee call foul on *you*, of all people!

Worship, as they call it, has always been hard for you: People weeping, dancing, carrying on, looking ridiculous. Maybe there's something to do in the kitchen. Your comfort zone has always been in the area of preparation, of work. It's not that you don't know how to love—it's just that your love comes with the smell of fresh-baked bread or fresh-changed oil. Your love has always been in overalls, not some outfit that cost a small fortune. Your love is the kind that doesn't require Kleenex or a second mortgage to express itself; yours is the kind that thinks of every last detail, prepares lovingly and extensively, then picks up the check, funded out of your own hard-earned savings. And when it's all over, it's not really the praise you were after; it's the thrill of having done the right thing, especially when nobody else had even thought of it.

Jesus understands you, Martha. Better than that, He likes you, every bit as much as Mary. Sure, you skipped the sermon to make pot roast. It doesn't mean you're not a Christian; pot roast is how you love.

I have a message for you, Martha. You're on. There is a world around you which very soon will be in desperate need of the way you love Jesus: by being good at what you do, then doing good with it. They won't even put a microphone in your face. But when they ask "Why?"—and they will—all you'll need to say is "Jesus," and they will understand. You love Him, too.

Be ready, Martha. The time has come for you to show the world that you love Jesus. The fragrant aroma of that love will draw people to the arms of the Lord. It's time for you to do what you're good at. Be ready. You're on.

The Bottom Line: We can show Jesus we love Him through our work, too.

DAY 128

Straight Ahead for Jesus

Folly is a joy to him who lacks sense,
but a man of understanding walks straight ahead.

Proverbs 15:21

I can't read this verse without thinking of my former district superintendent, Dr. Hugh Smith, who ends nearly all correspondence with the admonition, "Straight ahead for Jesus." Not only has he prescribed this path in life; he has lived it. His life and ministry have been an encouragement and an inspiration to thousands. He is a man who understands the importance of an unwavering commitment to Jesus Christ.

There are plenty of diversions available which would pull us off track, *but a man of understanding walks straight ahead.* I have been blessed to have had men and women of understanding in my life, who chose the best course and stayed on it. There is something very inspirational about a person who is focused on an all-consuming mission, who refuses to be detained or distracted.

Then there are the others. Around each of us are also people who lack sense. They are often the sort of people who scoff at the straight and narrow path. Anyone choosing to follow the rules or do what is expected is slapped with a disparaging label by this crowd.

Among those lacking sense there is an attraction to danger. Rebellion is considered "cool." Individuality is prized far above common sense. Conventionality is despised. "Why would anyone be content to plod along on a boring path of conformity to someone else's standards? I've gotta be me!" "Me" is generally pretty stupid. What energizes idiots? Folly. Idiotic schemes, pranks, crimes, geared toward veering as far as possible off the straight road and into the exciting wilderness of individuality and fun. *Folly is a joy to him who lacks sense.* These are the folks who give the press something to write about.

But it's the "straight ahead" people who keep society functioning. Those who look toward heaven, grab onto a Savior and keep walking are the only ones who understand what true joy is, and we're only getting started! Meanwhile, those without good sense will continue to pursue the path of idiots, strewn with false joys mixed with misery.

Ignoring the allure of folly, there will be those of us who have chosen the good path. Name-callers on the sidelines don't stop us. We don't fall for the traps of the tempter. We won't fizzle out, get discouraged or quit. We understand that those who reach the finish line are those who live "straight ahead for Jesus."

The Bottom Line: The best way to get through life?
Straight ahead for Jesus.

DAY 129

The Joy Label

Count it all joy, my brothers, when you meet trials of various kinds, for you know that the testing of your faith produces steadfastness. And let steadfastness have its full effect, that you may be perfect and complete, lacking in nothing. James 1:2-4

It's always interesting to see how people label an event."How was church today?" "Fine." "Fantastic!" "Boring." (The three were seated side by side.)

When difficulties strike (which seems to be every few minutes), some brush it off and proceed as if nothing happened, while some will stall out and refuse to go on until everything is to their liking. One person calls the situation "disastrous;" another calls it "opportunity." The labels we use are very important, because it sets the tone for our general response to life. Satan is quick to note that with some people all it takes to stop them is a bit of frustration, and they're done for the day/week/month. Well, that's easy. On to the next victim. Much more of a challenge to him is the person who insists on counting everything that happens as just one more reason to praise God. What can the devil do to someone like that?! The answer is, "Not much." It's why *"count it all joy"* is such a good plan.

We all have enough griping material laid in to get us through a lifetime. There are plenty of things which bug us—many of them encountered on a frustrating, daily basis. There are also people, some of them permanent fixtures in our lives, who fit the category of *"trials of various kinds,"* in the effect they have on our spirit. It really matters what label we assign to these trials. If we regard each aggravation in our lives as another unfair imposition, we will never run out of frustration. Not only that, but as we age, it takes less and less to irritate us, since we live on the edge of anger. The slightest nudge sets us off.

There's a better way to respond to difficulties: Label it all "joy." If the frustration is purposely looked upon as an opportunity to strengthen faith, develop perseverance and just one more reason to praise God, the power leaks out of the frustration and is diverted into spiritual maturity. Cool. The result is a joyful, indomitable spirit and a steadfastness which only grows steadier. The list of things which can knock us off balance gets to be really, really short, and continues to decline. God smiles. So do those around us, particularly those who haven't learned the trick of the "Joy Label" yet, who continue to get pounded by Satan on a daily basis, using just routine trials and irritations. They see that maybe there's hope—a better way to cope with the junk of life than considering it all disaster. When we *count it all joy*, we take a big leap forward. God helps us land on our feet.

The Bottom Line: When we "count it all joy," disaster is defused. We forge ahead.

DAY 130

Don't Do the Math

"Do the math." This phrase has been used countless times in an attempt to provoke people to thought, instead of mindless action. It means to do the research, figure it out, think it through. When we "do the math," we'll reach a much better conclusion than if we just proceed without considering all the pertinent information. Unless we're talking about faith in God, and obedience to Him.

I'm not advocating laziness, here—a refusal to do the hard work of facing reality. I'm just saying that, in a whole lot of cases, when it comes to trusting and obeying God, if we detour into human logic and the opinion of experts above the expressed orders of God, God will detour around us and His miracles will happen in the lives of people whose faith in God exceeds their faith in reason or themselves.

Consider just how many times in the Bible God chose to use the individual who would trust Him for the absolutely impossible. Nearly always, the God-follower had to make a choice: Reason or faith? Rarely could reason get them to where God wanted them to be. In some cases, God insisted on making it harder, eliminating the no-man's-land of "maybe" and forcing it into sheer impossibility just to prove His point. The Lord wanted there to be no question who was making it all happen. This wasn't probability and statistics; it was God.

In one of my favorite Bible stories, Gideon is chosen by God to deliver the Israelites from an enormous army which fills a valley. Gideon has zero military experience, and not much more confidence, but he has sufficient faith to obey God, even as Jehovah whittles his army of 32,000 semi-brave Israelites down to 300 certified water-lappers (Judges 7). It would have been a bad time for Gideon to do the math. He didn't. The impossible happened, the Israelites won, and everyone knew it was God. Those relying strictly on logic would have never gotten to the first step.

Over and over in scripture, God shows Himself strong through the lives of people who choose to trust Him without the benefit of scientific proof or logic. In routine, everyday life, He wants us to do the math! Figure it out. Use your head. But when it comes to faith and obedience, what is required is a head and heart willing to disengage from everything except trust in the Father. People willing to do that get to see miracles, just like the twelve disciples who organized 5,000 into groups of 50, in order to feed them five loaves and two fish, then picked up twelve baskets of leftovers! (Do the math on that one! :))

If we're stuck on math, we miss the miracles, because we won't trust God for what doesn't make sense, or even ask. What do we want, math or miracles?

The Bottom Line: When God instructs us to take faith over reason, it's O.K.

DAY 131

Planning Which Succeeds

Without counsel plans fail,
but with many advisers they succeed.

Proverbs 15:22

"Many advisers" are a pain in the neck! Which is exactly why they have a way of helping plans to succeed.

Plans made without counsel take on a life of their own. Beautiful assumptions give way to grandiose, magnificent scenarios. On paper, the plan is so great. With no one to burst the bubble, the planner exults in things which will never take place, because faulty assumptions and wishful thinking don't survive long in the real world. Someone should shoot the thing down before it hurts somebody.

The place to root out wrong conclusions is in the planning stages. We need visionaries and dreamers or nothing new will ever be attempted; we need realistic people around to make visionary ideas run the gauntlet of "what if's?" If an idea can survive the scrutiny of nay sayers in the planning process, it might have a chance. The job of the nay sayers is not to kill ideas but to avoid disaster. "What if?" people can't help but see pitfalls. This is not a bad thing. It keeps people who listen out of pits. Just *try* to get a pitfall-strewn program approved by a team peppered with nay sayers! It's not happening. They're not about to sign on to stupidity, and they can see it coming a mile away. If a plan can survive a gang of honest realists, reality itself probably won't faze it.

But we're also in trouble if we lack dreamers on the planning team. Without them, the committee will meet, share gripes about the general state of everything, knock down a few feeble ideas, and wonder why anyone should even try to do anything about the messes caused by (fill in the blank). The realists will never propose any stupid new ideas. Come to think of it, they will probably not propose any new ideas, since they can see folly in all of them. If change of any kind is needed, better get some dreamers on board.

Get enough advisers looking at an idea (that a dreamer proposed) and something is going to happen. Bad plans simply will not survive. Some good ones will also be shot down. Plans firmly entrenched in the heart of a dreamer will be carried forward by the determination of the author. With a bunch of advisers around to knock all the rough edges off, the plan will actually succeed. Not to mention, there's a committed team, ready and able to answer tough questions.

It's easier to plan alone. It's also easier to fail alone. For plans which succeed, we'd better find ourselves some advisers.

The Bottom Line: Many counselors make for better, hardier plans.

DAY 132

He Chose Pain

Dear Jesus,

I understand, more than I ever did before, and it makes me weep. For a while this morning, prior to getting in to the dentist, I was sobbing—and it wasn't because of the extreme pain I've had for the past several days which resulted in me losing a tooth which had become badly infected. It was because of the realization that, wimp that I am when it comes to pain—even a little of it—you had volunteered for the most agonizing pain known to man, plus much more which could never be understood by mortals. And for what purpose? To save me. To save me!

I'm sobbing again. You are so brave and so kind and so strong! I was thinking this morning of each part of your suffering on the way to the cross: The whipping; the spitting; when so-called religious leaders slugged you in the face in the name of your Father as they mocked you, mercilessly. They pulled your beard out by the roots. They stripped you naked, then beat you with a "cat of nine tails." They jammed a crown of thorns onto your head. Hired liars publicly accused you of blasphemy and treason. Sold by one of your disciples for the price of a slave, denied three times by one who had promised faithfulness no matter what, deserted by all. And for one moment, even your Father turned His back on the sin you bore for us all.

Then there was the crucifixion itself. The agony was unimaginable, indescribable. You refused the pain-deadening potion offered and went through it with a clear mind. To know you were facing the cruelest death devised by mankind, to know you would soon be in Satan's power because of our sins you carried, to know that not one of those sins was your own... You suffered for the sins of the entire world. The pure, spotless Lamb of God took away my sin, and not only mine, but the sins of all mankind. It is finished.

All of these things I've mentally understood until this morning. I've wept over your sacrifice for me many times. But it was this morning, when I was struggling with the pain of a mere infected tooth which had numbed half my face—it was when I was trying to do anything I could think of to avoid more pain, that the realization hit me harder than ever before: You chose the pain. You volunteered for it. Why? It was the only way I could be saved. You took all my sin upon yourself. You conquered death so I could live forever with you. Instead of avoiding the suffering, which could have been done with a nod of your head, you heroically endured it all. You took my pain. You did it because you love me. How could I heartlessly continue to commit the sins which put you on the cross? You are my Lord and my God. I will serve you forever. I will praise you forever.

The Bottom Line: Jesus chose the pain, and saved the world.

DAY 133

When God Says "Go"

Terah took Abram his son and Lot the son of Haran, his grandson, and Sarai his daughter-in-law, his son Abram's wife, and they went forth together from Ur of the Chaldeans to go into the land of Canaan, but when they came to Haran, they settled there. The days of Terah were 205 years, and Terah died in Haran.

Now the LORD said to Abram, "Go from your country and your kindred and your father's house to the land that I will show you. And I will make of you a great nation, and I will bless you and make your name great, so that you will be a blessing. I will bless those who bless you, and him who dishonors you I will curse, and in you all the families of the earth shall be blessed." Genesis 11:31-12:3

It's always been this way. Those who would follow God are asked to leave behind their old life in order to follow Him into a new future. Not only are the sins of the past to be left behind—many times the call is also to leave behind the comforts of home and family. It seems it's hard for most of us to live anything like a new life in an old, familiar setting, particularly if we have helpful family hovering nearby to talk us out of God's plans for us. Family is great, but when it comes to things like extreme faith or obedience, family represents a pretty heavy undertow. That's why the first call of God is often to leave behind the relatives and just follow Him. God's first word to Abram? "Go."

The very first step of obedience brings blessing, though. Abram had not yet left Haran when God's incredible promise was revealed to him. There would be more steps of obedience, more promises from God, and more blessings. In fact, the blessings have never stopped, and never will.

It was all new to Abram. He wasn't continuing some great spiritual heritage, but discovering God for the first time. God wanted to get him out of earshot of the relatives. So God's first word and command to Abram was "Go." It meant being willing to leave behind what little security existed to become an adventurer for God. The next requirement of Abram was to believe. He was on the receiving end of some of the most outlandish promises in the history of the world, yet he believed. In God's eyes, it was righteousness. Last, and certainly not least, there was obedience. It would be the key which unlocked many lifetimes worth of blessings and launched the nation of Israel.

We have reached a point in America where most in the younger generations don't know God. They need an Abram experience, an encounter with a God who says "Go, leave your old, unsatisfying life of selfishness and sin, and follow me into a life of promise and blessing." His first word to us is, "Go."

**The Bottom Line: God is still calling people.
Usually the first word is "Go."**

DAY 134

Dangerous Beauty

Now there was a famine in the land. So Abram went down to Egypt to sojourn there, for the famine was severe in the land. When he was about to enter Egypt, he said to Sarai his wife, "I know that you are a woman beautiful in appearance, and when the Egyptians see you, they will say, 'This is his wife.' Then they will kill me, but they will let you live. Say you are my sister, that it may go well with me because of you, and that my life may be spared for your sake." When Abram entered Egypt, the Egyptians saw that the woman was very beautiful. And when the princes of Pharaoh saw her, they praised her to Pharaoh. And the woman was taken into Pharaoh's house. And for her sake he dealt well with Abram; and he had sheep, oxen, male donkeys, male servants, female servants, female donkeys, and camels.

But the LORD afflicted Pharaoh and his house with great plagues because of Sarai, Abram's wife. So Pharaoh called Abram and said, "What is this you have done to me? Why did you not tell me that she was your wife? Why did you say, 'She is my sister,' so that I took her for my wife? Now then, here is your wife; take her, and go." And Pharaoh gave men orders concerning him, and they sent him away with his wife and all that he had. Genesis 12:10-20

Sarai was so beautiful it was hazardous. Abram, who just wanted to live, accurately predicted Sarai's beauty would attract the attention of people powerful enough to take her from him, so he asked a favor of his wife: Lie. It was only part-fabrication, since Sarai was, in fact, Abram's half-sister as well as his wife. Sarai ended up in the palace.

This is where God steps in. Although Abram hadn't particularly been trusting God to protect him, God does it, anyway. Pharaoh figures out the connection between Abram and Sarai and the plagues which have befallen him. He's not pleased, but he's savvy enough to know not to mess with someone God has chosen to bless. And Abram and Sarai leave Egypt, rich.

Huh? How does that work, anyway? You get blessed even when you didn't trust God? You do when God has promised to bless you, and you believe Him. That's what set Abram apart—he believed God. It was an imperfect, enduring faith, and God is still rewarding it. Abram had a dangerous faith to match Sarai's dangerous beauty. Both were long-lasting. The woman Pharaoh coveted was maybe 70. The same couple repeated the ruse with a different king when Sarai was—get this—90 (Gen 20)! The way to survive a rough world is to have dangerous faith. Staying dangerously beautiful until you're 90? I think the Hebrew word is "Botox."

The Bottom Line: When we believe God, our faith is dangerous—to our enemies.

DAY 135

Rich Relatives

When Abram heard that his kinsman had been taken captive, he led forth his trained men, born in his house, 318 of them, and went in pursuit as far as Dan. And he divided his forces against them by night, he and his servants, and defeated them and pursued them to Hobah, north of Damascus. Then he bought back all the possessions, and also brought back his kinsman Lot with his possessions, and the women and the people. Genesis 14:14-16

Without Abram, Lot would have been just another vision-less dude hanging around Mesopotamia. Had it not been for his uncle Abram, Lot might have died as a captive slave. Without Abram, Lot would have perished along with the other inhabitants of Sodom. Who gave his nephew first choice of the land when the herds they had acquired made it so they needed to separate? Abram. Who gathered his own small army and took on five kings and their forces to rescue his none-too-smart nephew? Abram. Who pleaded with God Himself to make a bargain in the hopes of sparing the city of Sodom, when it became apparent that the day of reckoning for wanton wickedness had come to the city? Abram. Was there anyone else willing to go to bat for Lot, after making selfish and foolish choices consistently for years? Abram's bold intercession on Lot's behalf elicited a promise from the Lord that if Sodom contained even ten righteous people, the city would be spared. (Abram had started at 50 and worked his way down)!

As it was, not even ten people qualified as righteous in Sodom, and Lot himself only slid into that category through God's grace and Abram's prayers. In the end, Lot was literally led out of Sodom by the hand, the angels explaining to him that they had orders not to destroy the city until Lot was clear of it. Does intercessory prayer matter?! You'd better believe it!

Lot's life was spared on more than one occasion by the intervention of his uncle, Abram. Lot's life was incredibly enriched by the faith, vision, generosity and courage of his relative. It pays to have rich relatives. Abram was rich in many ways, but most of all in his relationship with God. When it came down to it, the best thing Lot had going for him was a relative who knew God.

And as I get to spend time among family this week, I'm reminded of how many rich relatives I have, and what a blessing it is to be related to people like this—so rich in courage, generosity and especially faith in God. They share their vision with you, give you first pick, come to your rescue even when you deserved what you got, and go to God on your behalf again and again and again. Rich relatives. One of God's greatest blessings. Thank you, Lord.

The Bottom Line: Relatives who are rich in faith are a tremendous blessing.

DAY 136

The Humiliation of Wealth

Let the lowly brother boast in his exaltation, and the rich in his humiliation, because like a flower of the grass, he will pass away. For the sun rises with its scorching heat and withers the grass; its flower falls, and its beauty perishes. So also will the rich man fade away in the midst of his pursuits. James 1:9-11

It's sort of like delayed gratification. Can this person handle lowly circumstances on earth and still serve God faithfully, or must he be coddled with a certain amount of possessions or he will become bitter and envious? Think of the examples of people in the Bible who were saddled with riches which ruined them. Their lives were devoted to the maintenance of their earthly wealth, which they inconveniently left behind at death, anyway. Great importance was placed upon the achievement of wealth, to the detriment of their spiritual life. They made somewhat of a splash here on earth, then were gone. It must have seemed to them that there was no choice; to onlookers from subsequent centuries, it appears a pretty abysmal trade for the one life granted to us—something on the level with Esau forking over his birthright for a bowl of stew.

Not all rich folks have been spiritual failures. In fact, the rare person able to maintain a humble, faithful walk with God while controlling great wealth is the sort of blessing who can affect an entire nation. But it is a challenge requiring a huge amount of self-discipline and humility, two things which often slide off people with each increasing level of prosperity.

It's why James' advice is so good: Rather than the poor man bemoaning his fate or focusing all his energies on trying to become a rich man, the lowly servant of God can choose to exult in the confidence God has put in him, that he will faithfully serve his Heavenly Father in lowly circumstances, patiently awaiting the day when he is welcomed into a Kingdom with no want.

And rather than the rich person being tied to his wealth, expending so much of his attention on trying not to lose it or in being proud of what will so soon be gone, if he can choose the attitude of holding it all loosely, remembering how fleeting is the responsibility and privilege of earthly wealth, and choosing to consider it a sort of concession to weakness, rather than a badge of superior intelligence, it will help him in being the sort of individual to whom God can safely entrust much wealth without that wealth ruining him.

Consider lowly circumstances as exaltation; consider riches as humiliation. Isn't it like God to make it so whatever we have, we can be content, we can be humble, we can be useful to others and a blessing for eternity? We all get to win.

The Bottom Line: Can God trust us to serve Him in lowly circumstances?

DAY 137

Bone Refreshment

The light of the eyes rejoices the heart,
and good news refreshes the bones.

Proverbs 15:30

When people love something or someone, you can see it in their eyes. There is a "spark" present. Mention that subject or that person and their eyes light up. The more they talk about the object of their affection, the more animated they become. It's hard to shut them down when the subject is what they really love.

What lights up our eyes also lights up our heart. Seeing the person we can't wait to see thrills us down to our soul. Our entire being is encouraged and energized by the presence and the pursuit of what or whom we love.

I think the connections go beyond what we might assume. For someone suffering from some sort of bone disease, what would be the effect of some good news? Would it help or hurt? *"Good news refreshes the bones."* Such is the impact of good news, of hope—it affects us all the way down to our bones. The same with "the light of the eyes"—everything about us rejoices when we're in contact with what we truly love.

Let's talk heaven for a minute. Most people want to go there, particularly when approached with only two choices, heaven or the alternative. And what is the main feature of heaven? The presence of God. It's sort of confusing to me when I see people who claim to be headed for heaven who have very little time or patience for anything spiritual, now. Church is an oft-neglected drag for them; they have absolutely no interest in the Bible or participation in worship; prayer is a fearful thing. But they're one day going to be transported to a place where worship and praise are the principal activities forever, and they will suddenly like it?! If the worship of God brings no light to our eyes now, no sense of refreshment and joy to our being, will death suddenly make us fall in love with Him?

The Gospel is the best news ever—Jesus came to save us. But what if we regard the "Good News" as not all that good? We'll miss out on the refreshment for ourselves which good news brings to every part of our being. Those around us will also miss out. If there is no light in our eyes when it comes to Jesus, if the Gospel is ho-hum to us, we won't be very interested or effective in sharing it. There are those around us whose hearts desperately need what only Jesus can bring. There is a world lunging for hope or good news. Let's bring encouragement every chance we get. And let's be sure not to forget the best news of all: Jesus loves you and He came to save you.

The Bottom Line: If we have little love,
we have little interest in sharing about it.

DAY 138

Sanitized Sin

Now the men of Sodom were wicked, great sinners against the LORD. Genesis 13:13

Then the LORD said, "Because the outcry against Sodom and Gomorrah is great and their sin is very grave, I will go down to see whether they have done altogether according to the outcry that has come to me. And if not, I will know." Genesis 18:21

Sodom had developed a well-earned reputation. Genesis 19 is a sad chapter which only confirms the degree of depravity to which Sodom had sunk, and how widespread was their sin. Abraham had boldly bargained with God on his nephew Lot's behalf; God had agreed to what Abraham thought must be a safe quorum: Only ten righteous people in Sodom and God would spare the city. Sodom didn't even come close. "Righteousness" and Sodom had little to do with each other.

Sodom's wickedness is still being referenced in the New Testament, when Peter (2 Peter 2) talks about Sodom and Gomorrah's wickedness and Lot's rescue, as an example of what happens to the ungodly and how determined God is to save the righteous. Leviticus 18:22-30 makes it clear that God sees homosexual acts as an "abomination;" sexual immorality causes even the land to become "unclean."

Here's the point. What the men of Sodom were doing was sin. It was wicked, it was depraved. Not many people are described in the Bible as *"great sinners against the LORD;"* the Sodomites were. Sodom's namesake sin wasn't their only one, but I honestly can't see how any Bible scholar can conclude that homosexual practices are O.K. with God, after His purposeful judgment on Sodom. All we need to do is read Genesis 19 to get a God's eye perspective on what some today insist is noble and normal, but what God has always termed "sin."

So, are homosexual practices a "gay" lifestyle, deserving of honor and special rights and total acceptance? Or do homosexual practices deserve the label "sin," regardless of how many times we've seen them purposely portrayed as anything but that?

But what if public opinion has changed? What if the majority think it's O.K.? Like all but one person in the whole city? Like Lot? Wouldn't that change God's opinion, if it's an accepted practice within that community? Apparently not. Men may try to sanitize and sanctify this sin or others as much as they want; it remains sin. Sin always bears ugly consequences. And when it comes to determining whether or not something is sin, I'm going with what God says, not man.

The Bottom Line: Sin is still sin, regardless of public opinion. God makes the rules.

DAY 139

A Deadly Philosophy

Let no one say when he is tempted, "I am being tempted by God," for God cannot be tempted with evil, and he himself tempts no one. But each person is tempted when he is lured and enticed by his own desire. Then desire, when it has conceived gives birth to sin, and sin when it is fully grown brings forth death. James 1:13-15

A deadly philosophy grips much of our world, today. This philosophy ignores the reality of sin, or if sin is acknowledged, always defers the blame to someone or something else. In other words, there either is no such thing as sin, or if there is, it's always someone else's fault, never mine. The result of this philosophy is death. Every time.

James, ever practical, gives us the mechanics of sin in this passage. Here's how it works. It never starts with God, because God can't be tempted by evil, nor does He ever tempt anyone. It doesn't even start with the devil, the convenient scapegoat: "The debbil made me do it!" The debbil can't make us do anything; he can only make suggestions. Since those suggestions are evil, it's called temptation.

The hard truth is that sin begins with us. Satan can't make us sin, nor can he tag us with his own sin and make it stick. Sin begins with our own desire. We wish to do something we know to be wrong. We desire to have something which belongs to someone else. Et cetera. The desire is there, we know it's wrong, but instead of expelling the desire and replacing it with something we know is noble and right, we coddle the thought and let it stay. Desire hangs around, waiting for opportunity. Pretty soon opportunity knocks. Sinful desire opens the door. Sin is conceived. Death always follows.

The philosophy of "no sin" or "no responsibility" is killing us. Until we acknowledge that there is, indeed, such a thing as sin, that it produces death and that it is our own personal problem requiring God's grace and forgiveness, we are headed for spiritual death. Until we own up to our personal responsibility for sin, we can't be free from it. Until we deal with desires—what we allow to stay, what we boot out—we are only one opportunity away from devastating sin. Sin starts with us. It's never God's fault. Sin begins when we make a home for wrong desire. Then it's only a matter of time. Where sinful desire is not welcome, temptation bounces off, too. If we deal with desires, we deal with temptation in the process. If we accept responsibility for not only our own sins, but also our own desires, God will make sure we win the battle. He is the Righteous One. His desire is that we also would be righteous. If that's our desire, too, we'll get our wish.

The Bottom Line: Sin is not God's fault; it's ours. But Jesus saves.

Lousy Listeners

The ear that listens to life-giving reproof
will dwell among the wise.
Whoever ignores instruction despises himself,
but he who listens to reproof gains intelligence.
The fear of the LORD is instruction in wisdom,
and humility comes before honor.

Proverbs 15:31-33

We have this big thing in America about education, the power of knowledge, etc. As a nation, we think we're pretty smart. After all, we're leaders in the "Information Age." When it comes down to it, though, as a nation we are lousy listeners! We don't listen very well, or even try, especially when it comes to our elders or to God. There seems to be little interest in listening, whether it's politicians listening to their constituents or husbands listening to their wives. And if what is being said ranks as "reproof"—constructive criticism, we're really not interested in hearing it! How dare anyone approach us with the information that we are doing something wrong! We'll sue!

The person willing to listen to reproof, especially from God, will grow ever wiser and more intelligent. The person not willing to receive correction from anyone, who always has to be right, won't learn much, no matter how many degrees they plaster on their wall or how much money they make. Wisdom doesn't start with wanting to be smart; it starts with listening.

In our nation we'd rather be thought smart than to be smart. That's a generalization, of course, but unfortunately, truer than we'd like. The same goes for honor and humility. We crave honor but disdain humility. Not only do we not seek to be humble, ourselves; we sometimes even despise it in others, considering it weakness, instead. We tend to lump honor, self-esteem and outright pride together as something of a birthright, while the Bible counters that until we learn some humility and decide to listen, we ought to forget about being honored.

One of the best ways to honor someone is to listen to them. How many of us don't stink at listening? We seek our own honor, but the more we seek it, the more elusive it becomes. *Humility comes before honor.* Humility begins, not by trying to be humble, but by focusing my attention on someone besides me. When we listen, especially to God, when we get our minds off ourselves and focus on other people, listening to them, learning from them, loving them, something happens: Wisdom and honor show up when we're not looking.

**The Bottom Line: The person who listens—
especially to God—becomes wise.**

DAY 141

It's Complicated

And the child grew and was weaned. And Abraham made a great feast on the day that Isaac was weaned. But Sarah saw the son of Hagar the Egyptian, whom she had borne to Abraham, laughing. So she said to Abraham, "Cast out this slave woman with her son, for the son of this slave woman shall not be heir with my son Isaac." And the thing was very displeasing to Abraham on account of his son. But God said to Abraham, "Be not displeased because of the boy and because of your slave woman. Whatever Sarah says to you, do as she tells you, for through Isaac shall your offspring be named. And I will make a nation of the son of the slave woman also, because he is your offspring." Genesis 21:8-13

It's complicated. Ishmael's story begins in Genesis 16 and continues to this day, where many of Abraham's descendants through Ishmael hate nothing on earth quite as much as Abraham's descendants through Isaac and Jacob, the nation of Israel. It's still complicated. Very. It started out that way, too.

Abraham had received promises from God which included having a son. He believed God, but after still being childless some years after the promise, Sarah, a practical, take-charge kind of person, came up with the idea of using her servant as a surrogate wife. Abraham agreed to it. The plan worked out, biologically. Relationally? Not so much. Abraham finally had a son, the slave girl had an attitude and Sarah felt even worse than before. She took it out on everyone.

The person happiest about the whole situation was Abraham, who was perfectly fine to let Ishmael be the promised son and call it good. God was insistent, though. The promised child would be born to Sarah. Isaac's arrival was evidence that God was willing and able to keep His own promises.

But now what about Ishmael? Abraham and Sarah's attempt to help God fulfill His promise had created a sticky situation. Ishmael's juvenile mocking was the last straw for Sarah. She wanted him and his mother gone. Abraham wondered how it had gotten this complicated. And God told him to listen to Sarah! Funny. God hadn't told him to listen to Sarah when she suggested the surrogate deal in the first place, but now, when Sarah wants to send them away, He does!

When Abraham dutifully sent his son Ishmael away, God took over, establishing nations through Ishmael, too. But back at home, it was finally now according to God's plan, not man's.

God always gets His way. If we make His plan our first choice, our path will be straight and studded with miracles. If we supply our own plans or borrow the plans of others, it quickly gets complicated. That's O.K. God still gets His way.

The Bottom Line: The way to a less complicated path is to just go God's way.

DAY 142

Fake Presents

Do not be deceived, my beloved brothers. Every good gift and every perfect gift is from above, coming down from the Father of lights with whom there is no variation or shadow due to change. Of his own will he brought us forth by the word of truth, that we should be a kind of firstfruits of his creatures. James 1:16-18

The offers keep coming. The sender calls them "presents," "free gifts." They are always supposed to be offers too good to pass up. In reality, all they are is temptation. And something weird about temptation is that every single time, the temptation is to accept a fake in place of what God offers for real!

Here's how it works. *Every good gift and every perfect gift is from above, coming down from the Father of lights...* Got that? If it's good, it came from God. If it's perfect, it came from Him. Now, here comes temptation. What is the devil's line? "This is good." His advertising is over the top. What he's pushing is always going to make you feel good, look good, etc. The label is always that this is "good," except for when "bad" is more desirable, making it, in effect, the new "good." Either way it's a fake. It's a lie. From the Garden of Eden through this afternoon, all he's ever offered were poor substitutes for real joy, real love, real riches. It's all he has, just fakes, poor imitations of what is offered by a real God.

If it's truly good, it came from God. Period. If it's truly perfect, it came from Him. If we believe that, it will save us worlds of trouble! It will give us the good sense to reject every offer by Satan of something supposedly superior, which is, in fact, a poor substitute for what God offers. God is good. What He has for us is good. Accept no substitutes!

Do not be deceived, my beloved brothers. Who? Us? We would never believe that what Satan has stamped "perfect" actually is perfect, instead of being an absolute and evil forgery which will only keep us from the genuine, perfect gift God had for us. We immediately recognize that every image the devil throws up on the screen is a forgery, all his promises are lies, and that every single truly good thing comes from God. I wish we were that smart. I wish I was that smart.

If it's good, it came from God. If it didn't come from God—if this is temptation—it's not really good; it's a fake, no matter how good or perfect it looks. If we could just camp out on this truth, we would be like a kind of firstfruits of God's Creation, the truly smart people, the ones Satan couldn't fool. What was the first lie he told the first humans? "Eat this. It will make you wise." No. Really smart people believe God and ignore Satan. God is good. Satan is not. Ever.

The Bottom Line: If it's good, it came from God.
If it didn't come from God, run!

Prayers and Plans

The plans of the heart belong to man,
but the answer of the tongue is from the LORD.
All the ways of a man are pure in his own eyes,
but the LORD weighs the spirit.
Commit your work to the LORD,
and your plans will be established.

Proverbs 16:1-3

I still remember pawing through the Bible, searching desperately for guidance in regard to the first big decision of our soon-to-be-married life: What to do about a vehicle. I had an hour in which to make the decision; my fiancé, already gone, had left it to me. It was hard enough for me to make decisions which only affected me—now I was faced with trying to do the best thing for the two of us, when I honestly didn't know what that was. It was my introduction to the responsibilities of a husband.

I don't remember all the different passages I hastily consulted. The only one which sticks in my mind is the one which sealed it for me, Proverbs 16:3, which in my New International Version read like this: *Commit to the LORD whatever you do, and your plans will succeed.*

Ah! The sweet relief which comes with a promise from God! Lord, do you mean that if I'm checking with you, listening to you, trying my best to be obedient, I can just go ahead and make plans and not have to worry too much about if I've drifted out of your will? And that there will be times when you don't specify some great divine plan for my life, but instead just give me the green light to go ahead and plan, but keep listening for your guidance and you'll bless whatever I do? Yep.

The decision I made that day was a good one, one I still feel good about 25 years later. (I still have the vehicle)! Had I chosen to go with the other option, I think I would have been satisfied with that decision, too. When we start out with committing stuff to the LORD, our plans have a way of succeeding, even if we didn't get any voice from heaven and we basically just thought it through and did what we thought best. Prayer is such an integral part of good planning. If we start with prayer, and we *commit* our plans, our work, to the LORD, meaning He can do absolutely anything to our plans that He wants, we enter a safety zone where our intentions (to please God) are what is honored. If we begin with a commitment to try to please God and a readiness to go whatever direction He indicates, then maintain that attitude, our plans will succeed. He makes sure of it.

The Bottom Line: For plans which succeed,
start out with God, then obey.

DAY 144

A Willing Sacrifice

And Abraham took the wood of the burnt offering and laid it on Isaac his son. And he took in his hand the fire and the knife. So they went both of them together. And Isaac said to his father Abraham, "My father!" And he said, "Here am I, my son." He said, "Behold, the fire and the wood, but where is the lamb for a burn offering?" Abraham said, "God will provide for himself the lamb for a burnt offering, my son." So they went both of them together.

When they came to the place of which God had told him, Abraham built the altar there and laid the wood in order and bound Isaac his son and laid him on the altar, on top of the wood. Genesis 22:6-9

An angel's voice stops the upraised knife on its way down. A ram in the thicket replaces Abraham's only son on the altar. God will provide. Yes, He will. More than any other event in his life, this one marked Abraham for all time as a man of faith and obedience.

But what about Isaac? How much faith would it take to submit to this scenario? After all, how hard would it be to get away from a winded centenarian trying to kill you?! But instead, you carry the wood for your own sacrifice, then allow this living fossil to tie you to it without protest? Abraham isn't the only one on the mountain who has faith!

The theme of Isaac's life seems to be submission. It wasn't out of weakness; it seems to have been his calling. Isaac wasn't the visionary, nor was he the strong-willed rebel. He was a man of faith, and his faith is what caused him to submit to God's plan, even when it looked like God's plan would kill him.

Where do we fit? Sometimes all God is requiring of us is enough faith in Him to submit to His plan. He's not asking us to be visionaries or leaders. He's not asking us to come up with a plan. He's asking us to submit to His. He is asking us to be willing to be a sacrifice—usually a living one—and submit to His plan.

It takes faith to submit. Sometimes that's all that's required of us. We might want to do all kinds of impressive stuff and be used of God. We want to dazzle people, change the world, plus have a great family, too. And sometimes, all God is asking of us is that we allow someone to tie us down on the altar of whatever, and be willing to give our lives for the cause, one day at a time. Instead of martyrdom, our calling will usually be more along the lines of marriage, parenthood, unheeded servanthood. The headlines will probably go to another. But we and God will know that the whole thing wouldn't have happened without a willing sacrifice.

The Bottom Line: A big part of obedience is simply submission to God's plan.

DAY 145

What Helps

Know this, my beloved brothers: let every person be quick to hear, slow to speak, slow to anger, for the anger of man does not produce the righteousness of God. Therefore put away all filthiness and rampant wickedness and receive with meekness the implanted word, which is able to save your souls. James 1:19-21

Some people seem to believe that if they get mad enough, it will make them more righteous. This might be true if they got mad at sin and filthiness enough to get rid of it in their lives, but instead they tend to get mad at the church, their family, the government or themselves. Man's anger doesn't result in righteousness. What does? The "implanted word," which is able to save our souls. How does that happen? Instead of railing at ourselves or God or the world in general, we accept what God says about us, then do what He says. He gives us instructions— practical ones—about what to do to live a righteous life. It starts with coming clean before God, admitting our sins, asking forgiveness. An important next step is to distance ourselves from wickedness and whatever mars our relationship with God, and purposely accept His Word, not just in acknowledgment but in action. As the Holy Spirit leads us, we learn to reverse the bad habits we've accumulated and develop new ones—like listening first, then speaking; like choosing not to be offended over every little thing. The fruit of the Spirit begins to sprout in our lives. Our friends, and especially the people we live with, notice a change for the better.

This instructional passage in James needs to come alive in the Church, these days! When we look at the culture at large, we often find exactly the opposite of what is prescribed here. That means that if Christians would live out this scripture, we would *really* stand out! We should at least try. I hear too many excuses from Christians for why they can't live the way the Bible tells us to: "I''m just this way." "I can't control it." There are all sorts of excuses for why sin seems to be unavoidable, often coming from people who have surrounded themselves with temptation and sin, on purpose. Relationships are routinely discarded, when all that would need to happen to reverse everything would be to listen more, talk less, and refuse to get offended and fuel the anger which not only doesn't help in the righteousness category; it also doesn't help relationships.

If we just followed this passage we would stand out pretty significantly, even in the Church. We could either take God's direction or we could be like everybody else, with our excuses and our anger and no righteousness to show for it, plus lousy relationships. Our choice.

The Bottom Line: *Quick to hear, slow to speak, slow to anger.* Good plan.

DAY 146

Simple, But Hard

The LORD has made everything for its purpose,
even the wicked for the day of trouble.
Everyone who is arrogant in heart is an abomination to the LORD;
be assured he will not go unpunished.
By steadfast love and faithfulness iniquity is atoned for,
and by the fear of the LORD one turns away from evil.
When a man's ways please the LORD,
he makes even his enemies to be at peace with him.
Better is a little with righteousness
than great revenues with injustice.
The heart of man plans his way,
but the LORD establishes his steps.

Proverbs 16:4-9

We get pretty upset about the wicked. (The wicked are never "us"). We wonder if justice will ever be served, and we fret about how much stuff they get away with. But right here in scripture is the reminder that the arrogant in heart are neither unnoticed by God nor unpunished by Him; He'll take care of it. We don't have to. That's a relief. Kind of. It does seem that God might need a little help, maybe some suggestions on what might constitute a just punishment for the arrogant people who tramp around in our lives. And there are times when we feel God has a right to be told about the injustices and wickedness we observe in others, just in case He forgot to be omniscient that day.

The fact is, when it comes to dealing with arrogance and wickedness in other people, our duties are usually very limited. Our main duty concerning the arrogant is to not be one of them. And it's not our problem to punish the wicked. It's our job to not be wicked. It's all quite simple, really. Sometimes annoyingly simple.

This whole passage is a gentle reminder that our responsibilities lie in monitoring our own attitudes and actions, not those of others. There are some roles where we are responsible to correct the behavior of other people (parenting, for example), but those roles aren't where the problem lies; the problem is when we are distracted by the misdeeds of those over whom we have no control.

In the alternate path God lays before us, we focus on pleasing Him, rather than correcting others. We mind our own business, live to please God, avoid wickedness, pursue righteousness and find life to be simpler, happier and blessed, to the point where even our enemies co-exist peacefully with us. Simple, but hard.

The Bottom Line: God doesn't overlook arrogance.
Neither should we—in ourselves.

DAY 147

Playing With Matches

At a pastor's gathering the fare was the usual: Inspirational talks, prayer, testimonies, practical instruction, plus some housekeeping items, lunch. During the session, we were challenged to get alone with God for a few minutes and seriously examine our personal spiritual lives, particularly the level of our commitment to Christ. I looked around at people standing alone under trees like children counting down for hide-and-seek, and I wondered what God might be telling any of the others. What He told me surprised me.

You don't expect to make a difference, anymore.

Huh? I realized He wasn't addressing just me but our whole group and beyond: You don't expect to make a difference, anymore.

With a few exceptions, I thought of how many in the group were in their assignments as place-holders, trying not to make a mess of things, hoping for enough money and parishioners to not look bad or lose the building, hoping to survive and maybe even show a little attendance growth. Impacting the entire region for Christ? I wonder if that was even on any of our minds, much less the expectation that it would occur.

It's easy to become like the Israelites who had endured Goliath's taunts for forty days, coming to consider it normal for each morning to begin by listening to someone trash talk them and their God, then going on with life in a paralyzed army. It took David coming in fresh from God's presence to put the thing in perspective, again. "No, this is not O.K., and it's not normal. God wants me to do something that will make a difference." The other Israelite braves had resorted to dreaming of tax exemptions for the guy who could somehow make Goliath go away. They'd stopped expecting to make a difference, themselves, even the king.

The Early Church wasn't perfect, but they did tend to live in anticipation. Once in a while their faith ran low, such as when they were trying to pray Peter out of jail and Peter practically had to beat the door down to convince them their prayers had actually been answered, but mostly they expected something to happen when they prayed. They prayed a lot.

When Paul set out for Corinth, he didn't expect Corinth to be the same when he left. It wasn't. Paul expected Christ to make a difference everywhere he went. He audaciously approached a Christ-less landscape with his tiny team and expected to leave a string of churches in his wake. That's what happened, time and again.

There's a difference between occupying a spot for a few years, trying not to fail, and setting the place on fire for Christ. It's the difference between building a fire and playing with matches.

The Bottom Line: God wants to make a difference through us, if we're willing.

DAY 148

Paths to Choose

How much better to get wisdom than gold!
To get understanding is to be chosen rather than silver.
The highway of the upright turns aside from evil;
whoever guards his way preserves his life.
Pride goes before destruction,
and a haughty spirit before a fall.
It is better to be of a lowly spirit with the poor
than to divide the spoil with the proud.
Whoever gives thought to the word will discover good,
and blessed is he who trusts in the LORD.

Proverbs 16:16-20

These are daily choices with eternal consequences. Will we seek wisdom or gold? Will we choose the highway of the upright, not stopping for evil, or will we live an unguarded life with a haughty spirit to match? *Pride goes before destruction, and a haughty spirit before a fall.* I've heard that. According to God, pride's a bad choice; according to the world, it's a requirement, particularly if we want our share of life's goodies. What to choose? The world promises riches; God, blessing. We know God delivers on His promises. The world? Not so much.

If we could just make a good choice once and for all and be done with it, that would be nice, but we don't have that privilege. (We also fortunately aren't locked into an entire lifetime of bad choices, either, no matter how rotten our track record—we get to change our mind and change our direction and find peace and forgiveness in Jesus if we ask for it. Praise God!) Whether good choices or bad, it comes back to "daily." We all make daily choices as to which path we will pursue—walking in humility with a righteous God or flaunting our freedom to make stupid decisions and not have to pay for them, at least not today.

Back to that once-for-all decision thing. In one way, it's like that. When we come to Christ in humility, repenting of our sins, we get the eternal life He wanted us to have all along, born again as a new person. It's a one-time choice, good for eternity! But each day we are faced with all sorts of decisions. Will I stay on the highway of the upright or try a little adventure, assuming it will be O.K. with God and everybody? Righteousness doesn't work on auto-pilot. We daily choose to continue on God's path or veer off on our own (very expensive). Better think this through. Which path leads to blessing here, eternal life there? Pick that one, again, today. It's better than riches, pride and being lost.

The Bottom Line: We have a daily choice: Continue with God or go our own way?

DAY 149

Fun Faith

The man bowed his head and worshiped the LORD and said, "Blessed be the LORD, the God of my master Abraham, who has not forsaken his steadfast love and his faithfulness toward my master. As for me, the LORD has led me in the way to the house of my master's kinsmen..."

Then Laban and Bethuel answered and said, "The thing has come from the LORD; we cannot speak to you bad or good. Behold, Rebekah is before you; take her and go, and let her be the wife of your master's son, as the LORD has spoken."...

And they called Rebekah and said to her, "Will you go with this man?" She said, "I will go." Genesis 24:26-27,50-51,58

This whole story is packed with faith. There is the faith of Abraham, who commissions his head servant to make the journey back to his homeland, to try to get a wife for his son Isaac. Abraham is adamant that Isaac himself not go there.

The unnamed servant is a faith hero who prays expectantly and sees God's answers before he is finished praying.

There is the faith of Isaac, who is willing to commit himself for life, sight unseen, to whomever the servant brought home!

And there is the faith of Rebekah. All she did was water a stranger's camels, and the next day she is leaving home forever to go marry someone she's never met!

Because it's from God, it all works out, beautifully. Faith is fun! There is nothing quite like looking at a situation and knowing, "This is from God." There's no experience quite like answered prayer, so specific, so perfectly timed that there is no question about it being mere coincidence. Living by faith is the best way to live.

This is not to say that we discard logic, planning, hard work or common sense. It is to say that when we put our trust in the LORD and we know it's Him saying, "Jump," we can make the leap and never regret it.

This story has a lot of meaning to me. Years ago, a beautiful young woman responded in faith to a single pastor waiting on God, and our lives were brought together by God in a wonderful and bizarre long-distance courtship. She had the faith to say she would go with this man, whom, like Rebekah, she had never met face to face. We got engaged over the phone. Twelve days later, we met for the first time. We're still together, still in love, still living by faith. When we're sure it's God who is doing the arranging, it's not only O.K. to take a leap of faith; it's fun.

The Bottom Line: Faith is fun, when we're sure God is leading the way.

DAY 150

Bible Implants and Memory Chips

Therefore put away all filthiness and rampant wickedness and receive with meekness the implanted word, which is able to save your souls.

But be doers of the word, and not hearers only, deceiving yourselves. For if anyone is a hearer of the word and not a doer, he is like a man who looks intently at his natural face in a mirror. For he looks at himself and goes away and at once forgets what he was like. But the one who looks into the perfect law, the law of liberty, and perseveres, being no hearer who forgets but a doer who acts, he will be blessed in his doing. James 1:21-25

What are we planting in our lives? Is it God's Word? In the past couple years I have re-memorized the book of Philippians, memorized 1 John and am now working on James. It's not particularly easy, but it's rewarding. Having implants of a couple books of the Bible makes it lots easier to remember what it is we're supposed to do. Plus, there's no more effective deterrent to Satan's lies and temptations than knowing what God said without having to even look it up.

Contrast this to the steady diet of filthiness and wickedness available to us through various technologies, with practically no effort. How much of this stuff are we planting in our lives, to come back and haunt us? It's hard to live a holy, God-pleasing life when we're continually, on purpose, imbibing junk we can't forget even if we want to. It's difficult to repeatedly wallow in moral crud, then try to wash it all off and be pure and holy. The memories linger. And we have to try to reprogram our minds to line up with God's Word again, when everything we just planted in our brains led the opposite direction. It's tough. That's why it would be a good idea if we planted more of the Word and less of the world in our minds. Our minds are directly connected to our hearts.

Nor does it stop with mind and heart. Unless our faith results in action, it's not worth much. James says it's like someone looking in a mirror, then forgetting what he looks like. God's Word, like a mirror, reveals the truth about us. When God speaks to us through the Bible, we know exactly what to do. Here's the rub: We can either do what the Word says, or forget it and go back to our own way. It's our choice, but it's also our bacon. Action-less faith reveals lack of faith. We alone are deceived when we try to have faith without obedience.

The implanted Word can save our souls, if we act on it. We're saved by faith, but true faith is always accompanied by action.

The Bottom Line: We need to plant God's Word in our mind, then do what it says.

DAY 151

Whoa, There!

If anyone thinks he is religious and does not bridle his tongue but deceives his heart, this person's religious is worthless. Religion that is pure and undefiled before God, the Father, is this: to visit orphans and widows in their affliction, and to keep oneself unstained from the world. James 1:26-27

I love the way James just blurts it out: If you don't control that stupid tongue of yours, your religion is worthless! And by the way, if you really loved God you'd stop playing around in sin, and you'd look after the helpless, needy people God has put all around you. End of lecture. Now get out of here and go live for God!   He could easily have gotten a whole chapter out of that, but for James, two sentences was plenty. That way we can't so easily wreck it by analyzing what he really meant.

We've all known plenty of folks with a free-range tongue. The thing just did whatever it pleased, regardless of whom it hurt or how many times someone tried to reprimand its owner. Mustang tongues that roam the range at will, nipping at rivals, refusing restraint...what can be done with them? Not much.

The tongue and heart are closely linked. If we claim to have a heart for God but our mouth is continually ungodly, we're deceiving ourselves. That kind of religion is worthless. That tongue needs a bridle, and an owner willing to use it!

The purpose of a bridle is to give the rider of a horse control over the animal, so the horse obeys the directions of the rider, rather than being free to do whatever it likes. We must take control of our tongue if we want to live a life pleasing to God. Excuses about not being able to control our own tongue are merely that: excuses. Real disciples rein in their tongues. For some it's not that hard. Others are in for a rodeo ride where controlling it for eight seconds at a time is pretty good! No matter. It's part of being a Christian. If you fall off, get back on. This is a battle you'd better win, unless you want a worthless, godless tongue flopping around in your mouth the rest of your days, undoing any possible good the rest of your body might accomplish for God. Do whatever it takes to control it.

A gentle, halter-broke tongue—it's a great starting point for self-control. If we keep our tongue out of mischief, often the rest of the body is easy. Now we have more time for widows, orphans and lonely family members. Everybody is easier to get close to when we no longer spook them with a biting tongue. In all God's Kingdom, there are fewer things more impressive than a well-trained tongue.

The Bottom Line: Bridle that tongue.
Keep yourself clean. Look out for the needy.

DAY 152

One Person Under God

When Abram was ninety-nine years old the LORD appeared to Abram and said to him, "I am God Almighty; walk before me, and be blameless, that I may make my covenant between me and you, and may multiply you greatly." Then Abram fell on his face. And God said to him, "Behold, my covenant is with you, and you shall be the father of a multitude of nations. No longer shall your name be called Abram, but your name shall be Abraham, for I have made you the father of a multitude of nations. I will make you exceedingly fruitful, and I will make you into nations, and kings shall come from you. And I will establish my covenant between me and you and your offspring after you throughout their generations for an everlasting covenant, to be God to you and to your offspring after you. And I will give to you and to your offspring after you the land of your sojournings, all the land of Canaan, for an everlasting possession, and I will be their God. Genesis 17:1-8

In the past years I have striven to find keys to the spiritual transformation of America, scouring the scriptures for clues, looking for patterns in history which might indicate what we could do to make a difference resulting in revival in our land. Fellow disciples have been on similar pursuits, although most of them didn't quit their jobs in order to focus on it.

What we yearn for is "one nation under God." It doesn't have to be perfect, nor do we expect it to be, and we're not talking about forcing our religion upon unwilling fellow citizens. We're talking about a nation where the great majority of people live for God because they want to, not because they have no choice. How do we get there? How do we get to "one nation under God," again?

The answer is not to be found in political or legislative victories, which are generally the *result* of spiritual transformation, not the cause. When God forms or transforms a nation, He does it by transforming individuals, sometimes even to the point of changing their name. How did God form the nation of Israel? He challenged one man to, *"Walk before me and be blameless."* A nation was formed as the result of God's call to one man, and that man's faith and obedience.

For those of us longing for national revival—spiritual transformation, here's our answer, and it's something we can do which is more profitable than hand-wringing through elections: *"I am God Almighty; walk before me and be blameless."* One nation under God begins with one person under God.

The Bottom Line: One nation under God begins with one person under God.

DAY 153

Why He Doesn't Tell Us

So David and Abishai went to the army by night. And there lay Saul sleeping within the encampment, with his spear stuck in the ground at his head, and Abner and the army lay around him. Then said Abishai to David, "God has given your enemy into your hand this day. Now please let me pin him to the earth with one stroke of the spear, and I will not strike him twice." But David said to Abishai, "Do not destroy him, for who can put out his hand against the LORD's anointed and be guiltless?" And David said, "As the LORD lives, the LORD will strike him, or his day will come to die, or he will go down into battle and perish. The LORD forbid that I should put out my hand against the LORD's anointed. But take now the spear that is at his head and the jar of water, and let us go." So David took the spear and the jar of water from Saul's head, and they went away. No man saw it or knew it, nor did any awake, for they were all asleep, because a deep sleep from the LORD had fallen upon them. 1 Samuel 26:7-12

David was just a boy when the prophet Samuel visited his home and anointed him as the next king. The trouble was, Saul was still king at the time, and not wishing to give up his kingdom anytime soon. (Kings are like that). Fortunately, few even knew of the event, but Saul's jealousy goaded him into making a career out of pursuing David instead of pursuing Philistines. David had already spared Saul's life once before when Saul, hunting for David, stopped for a restroom break and picked the cave in which David and his men were hiding. David's men deemed it divine providence, but David settled for cutting off a piece of Saul's robe and shaming him into stopping the deadly pursuit—for a while. Now Saul was back.

What kind of courage does it take to sneak into the center of an army of 3,000 men whose mission is to kill you, stand over the person who has devoted his life to your destruction, have your comrade say, "Just give me the nod and I'll end this for you—God has given him into your hands!" and walk away with nothing but the proof you were there? God had promised David the throne, but David refused to take it on his own. He was determined to let God fulfill His own promise. David was repeatedly given the opportunity to fulfill God's promise for him with nothing but a nod. He repeatedly refused. It was outrageous courage. It was rewarded.

Why doesn't God tell us stuff ahead of time? Because there are so few who can be trusted with that knowledge, who refuse to try to make God's promises come true for Him. The more we trust God, the more He can trust us.

The Bottom Line: The more we trust God, the more He can trust us.

DAY 154

Burn Permit

When the days drew near for him to be taken up, he set his face to go to Jerusalem. And he sent messengers ahead of him, who went and entered a village of the Samaritans, to make preparations for him. But the people did not receive him, because his face was set toward Jerusalem. And when his disciples James and John saw it, they said, "Lord, do you want us to tell fire to come down from heaven and consume them?" But he turned and rebuked them. And they went on to another village. Luke 9:51-56

I'm sorry, but I can't help but laugh out loud when I read this passage. James and John had gotten a taste of spiritual power and authority. Jesus had authorized them, sent them to cast out demons and cure diseases. Their recent field trip had gone awfully well, but they'd not had the opportunity to see what this power would do when applied to Jesus' enemies—so far everything had just been about *helping* people. Here was their big chance! Here were Samaritans—easy people for a pure-blood Jew to not like in the first place—who had acted offensively toward Jesus. Their solution? Fire from heaven! The two disciples wanted to toast a few Samaritans and turn them into crispy critters. After all, these idiots had insulted the Son of God! Time for a little vengeance. *"Lord, do you want us to tell fire to come down from heaven and consume them?"* Jesus' response: *What?!!!!* Well, it doesn't say that—it says He "rebuked them,"but I'm trying to picture the look on His face. I think the disciples tried to forget it. Whatever of God's power we get is to love people, not fry them.

It wasn't the only time He had to corral His followers for trying to operate by the worldly methods of vengeance and violence. In the Garden of Gethsemane, Peter pulled out a sword he wasn't very good with, and tried to stand off the army. All he got was one ear, and a rebuke from Jesus. "Put that thing away before you hurt somebody with it. This is not how we do things." Something like that.

It isn't how we do things. We're Christians. Our "weapons" are spiritual. We're commanded to love everyone—even our enemies. I'm glad the pastor in Florida agreed to at least suspend his plan to publicly burn the Koran. It was never a good idea in the first place.

Jesus commanded us to love our enemies, not get even with them, not try to humiliate or enrage them. The One who forgave those nailing Him to a cross gave His followers an example, and a license to love, not a burn permit.

The Bottom Line: God's power in us is to love people, not fry them–or their books.

DAY 155

Spirit-led People

God has always looked for people willing to be led by His Spirit. Some have always struggled with this concept, even some who truly love God but can't let go of their own logic long enough to trust Him in things which don't make sense to them. It's O.K. There's a spot for everyone in God's Kingdom, including those chained to their calculators and spreadsheets.

But when it's time to move out into new territory, the pioneers are nearly always people of faith, led by the Spirit. Sometimes, God insists on doing it with entire nations, such as when He taught the Israelites to be led by His Spirit in the form of a cloud for forty years in the Wilderness. Mostly, it's individuals, though, the rare bird who is willing to listen to God's guiding voice and actually obey it, despite being misunderstood and maligned.

Jesus' brothers were bewildered when He wouldn't take their political advice. He seemed to be on a different track than everyone else. He was. He told His disciples that He didn't even say anything except what was given Him from the Father. That's "Spirit-led."

Jesus said that flesh gives birth to flesh, but the Spirit gives birth to Spirit. Does that mean that the stuff born of the flesh and not the Spirit doesn't automatically turn spiritual just because we dragged it into a church or a church service? Yep. The flesh-born systems of the world don't become spiritual just because we tried to Christianize them and call them Christian. Unless it's born of the Holy Spirit, it's still flesh, regardless of the label. What's the goal? That His followers would be led by His Spirit.

In the prayer Jesus taught His disciples, there's the part about "Thy will be done on earth, as it is in heaven." Are things done according to the flesh, in heaven? Of course not. In heaven, everything would be done according to the Spirit. Therefore, if we really mean that prayer, we should be moving more and more in the direction of being led by God's Holy Spirit, while still on earth. We can choose to be calculator-led or Spirit-led, but not both. But check it out. The people God uses greatly are people who are taking their orders from Him, not from the world, not from their own minds. Spirit-led looks a lot more fun, to me. And a lot more productive.

The Bottom Line: God wants us to be Spirit-led people.

DAY 156

Jesus, Take the Wheel

I know and love the song, but before I ever heard it, I'd already heard a first-hand account in which a young lady, now a friend, had lost control of her car on ice and found herself sideways in the crowded freeway, in front of a truck so close she could see the driver's horrified face. She knew she was going to die, so she closed her eyes, shouted "Jesus!" and took her hands off the steering wheel. When she opened her eyes, her car was stopped on the shoulder, facing the right direction. Not one vehicle had even made contact with another.

Well, I just had the coolest dream. Maybe it was the extra piece of pizza, but I doubt it. This was from God.

In the dream, some acquaintances and I were traveling down a winding mountain road in what seemed to be a Greyhound-type bus, when something went wrong. The driver couldn't stop it or control it very well, so he went outside the bus, apparently to try to fix it (as if one can fix the brakes on a moving bus).

I found myself in the driver's seat of this thing, with the driver outside (too many action films), and we're tearing down the mountainside. Oh. And I can't see. It's like night for me, because I can't see a thing, but everyone else apparently can, so I'm guiding the bus by following the orders of the people who are screaming.

I can't see what I'm doing, but neither can I see the danger, for the most part. I'm driving blind. After going sideways and straightening out the bus in time to miss a car coming uphill, and some other stuff that I only hear about since I can't see it, I finally just let go of the wheel and the bus is driving itself, and rather well. We're all praying, calling on Jesus to help us, and when I start singing a praise song to Jesus, I'm joined by the others. We have this concert going on. I'm still behind the wheel of the bus but it's been a long time since I touched the wheel, which keeps doing cool things like managing to keep us on the road. I close my eyes and praise God, since I can't see anything, anyway.

We finally roll to a safe stop at the foot of the mountain. Still no bus driver to be seen. My fellow passengers excitedly compliment me on my superior driving skills, and I tell them I couldn't see a thing, didn't know how to do it even if I could, and that a lot of the time, I wasn't even touching the steering wheel. This information gets a pretty remarkable response from my already pale passengers.

All I did was trust God. I couldn't see a thing, including Who got us through. There's nothing quite like hurtling down a mountain with Jesus at the wheel. This is us. This is our country. We can scream, or praise God. Jesus, take the wheel.

The Bottom Line: Enjoy the ride. Jesus, take the wheel.

DAY 157

Weary Faith

Now there was a famine in the land, besides the former famine that was in the days of Abraham. And Isaac went to Gerar to Abimelech king of the Philistines. And the LORD appeared to him and said, "Do not go down to Egypt; dwell in the land of which I shall tell you. Sojourn in this land, and I will be with you and will bless you, for to you and to your offspring I will give all these lands, and I will establish the oath that I swore to Abraham your father. I will multiply your offspring as the stars of heaven and will give to your offspring all these lands. And in your offspring all the nations of earth shall be blessed, because Abraham obeyed my voice and kept my charge, my commandments, my statutes and my laws."

So Isaac settled in Gerar. When the men of the place asked him about his wife, he said, "She is my sister," for he feared to say, "My wife," thinking, "lest the men of the place should kill me because of Rebekah," because she was attractive in appearance. Genesis 26:1-7

Why is this in here? Why stick something unflattering in the Bible about one of the patriarchs? Isaac, a vulnerable stranger with a beautiful wife, was only lying to protect himself, and following the example of his own father, who (twice!) relied on white lies instead of God to get out of similar circumstances.

God had given Isaac the same amazing promises given Abraham. Strongly implied in all of this was protection for Isaac and his loved ones. After all, it's tough to have buco descendants if you're dead, so God seemed to think Isaac and Rebekah would be around at least long enough to have a kid or two. Why the fear?

Ask any junior high kid. The fears may make little sense to a parent or other seasoned adult, but they are all too real to the kid. It's fine to trust God for some things, and then there's the reality of true bullies and others committed to your destruction. Fear is pretty hard to beat off, no matter how spiritually grounded we are. Particularly when we get weary.

I'm glad this is in here. It's a reminder to me that even the super-faith people get weary in faith at times, or they're able to trust God really well in some areas, not so well in others, but God insists on blessing them, anyway, despite a spotty track record.

I love the promise in 2 Timothy 2:13 that *"if we are faithless, he remains faithful."* You mean it's not all up to me, to maintain flawless faith? Naw. He has enough faith for both of us.

The Bottom Line: *If we are faithless, he remains faithful...* (2 Timothy 2:13)

DAY 158

Caesar Jokes

Those who stood by said, "Would you revile God's high priest?" And Paul said, "I did not know, brothers, that he was the high priest, for it is written, 'You shall not speak evil of a ruler of your people.'" Acts 23:4-5

I just thought of a presidential joke that would have been a zinger. I wasn't even going to share it, just preserve it to remind myself of my cleverness, when I felt checked by the Holy Spirit. I deleted it. Sigh. I thought it was funny, Lord.

The thought occurred to me that the Apostle Paul, genius that he was, had the brainpower to humiliate people at will. In pre-conversion days, Saul was like a heat-seeking missile, systematically destroying everyone he considered fair game. Jesus turned him into a different guy (a very familiar story in real conversions).

The ability still had to linger, though. In off-hours, wouldn't the world's first Christian missionary have been entitled to poke some good-natured fun at the corrupt, blow-hard aristocracy who seemed so intent on making life miserable for so many? After all, when you're sitting in prison for such crimes as healing people and helping them find eternal life in Christ, a person ought to at least have the right to tell a few Caesar jokes! Right?!

If he told them, he didn't write them down. The letters to the churches, which Paul had no idea would ever become "scripture," contain no Caesar jokes. On the contrary, there are admonitions to pray for all leaders, including the very ones jailing and mistreating Christians! True, Free Speech rights were in the distant future—stand-up comics would have had extremely short lives in the First Century—but still... No Caesar jokes?

Guess not. The threat to Caesar's empire and the religious strongholds of the time were not witticisms muttered under someone's breath and passed along; it was in lives so totally changed that even those incredibly skilled in vengeance could now be trusted to not even malign evil people who tossed them in jail or cut off their heads, but who would, instead, pray for them and urge others to do the same, then die forgiving their tormentors, just like Jesus. It's not very funny, but it seemed to be very, very effective. Sigh (again). I need to pray for somebody.

The Bottom Line: Instead of thinking up jokes, I need to pray for the president.

DAY 159

Favored Families

My brothers, show no partiality as you hold the faith in our Lord Jesus Christ, the Lord of glory. For if a man wearing a gold ring and fine clothing comes into your assembly, and a poor man in shabby clothing also comes in, and if you pay attention to the one who wears the fine clothing and say, "You sit here in a good place," while you say to the poor man, "You stand over there," or "Sit down at my feet," have you not then made distinctions among yourselves and become judges with evil thoughts? Listen, my beloved brothers, has not God chosen those who are poor in the world to be rich in faith and heirs of the kingdom, which he has promised to those who love him? But you have dishonored the poor man. Are not the rich the ones who oppress you, and the ones who drag you into court? Are they not the ones who blaspheme the honorable name by which you were called?

If you really fulfill the royal law according to the Scripture, "You shall love your neighbor as yourself," you are doing well. But if you show partiality, you are committing sin and are convicted by the law as transgressors. James 2:1-9

The consumer mentality gripping the Church in America works both ways. Not only are people "shopping" for a church which meets their needs; the church folks, too, especially the pastor, tend to be on the lookout for those who will bring benefit to the group, while shying away from those who look to be a drain.

A shabbily-dressed man hung around church one morning, waiting for a welcome. Of a crowd of 300, only one approached him. I, the pastor, arrived to have seniors tell me about the "scary" guy, who was my friend and the guest speaker. He'd been testing our church to see how accepting we were. We failed.

The new people most welcomed by churches and pastors are families with children, people with good income and potential *children's workers!!!* Established church folks who know how to act in church, possible committee volunteers, committed tithers, attractive people with good social skills, nice cars and homes... these are the people who can expect a warm reception from most any church.

Then there are those who need love the most: people with issues, people with no money and no job, high-maintenance seniors with health problems, homeless people with zero social skills... it's a rare church where they will be greeted with the same level of warmth and acceptance as the BMW family, out church-shopping.

The favoritism game has been played for a long time. That doesn't make it right.

The Bottom Line: Love is right; favoritism is wrong, pure and simple.

DAY 160

Ir-retractable Words

His father Isaac said to him, "Who are you?" He answered, "I am your son, your firstborn, Esau." Then Isaac trembled very violently and said, "Who was it then that hunted game and brought it to me, and I ate it all before you came, and I have blessed him? Yes, and he shall be blessed." As soon as Esau heard the words of his father, he cried out with an exceedingly great and bitter cry and said to his father, "Bless me, even me also, O my father!" But he said, "Your brother came deceitfully, and he has taken away your blessing."...

Then he said, "Have you not reserved a blessing for me?" Isaac answered and said to Esau, "Behold, I have made him lord over you, and all his brothers I have given to him for servants, and with grain and wine I have sustained him. What then can I do for you, my son?" Genesis 27:32-37

After arguing with both spell-check and the dictionary, I finally stuck a hyphen in "ir-retractable" and got relief. It makes sense to me that the word should exist, particularly since words are, well, ir-retractable. Once we launch 'em off our tongues, we can't get them back. All we can get is credit or forgiveness. Man has the ability to speak but not to un-speak. Ask Richard Nixon.

No, ask anybody. Which dumb things have we ever said that we were able to retrieve and un-say? Mis-speaking is different, like saying, "Go left," when we meant our other left. For stuff like that, we can get an annulment from our words; for what we obviously meant at the time, it's a marriage. "I hate you!" "I never loved you in the first place!" Try getting that one back. There's only forgiveness.

I've smiled at the episode of Isaac being deceived into giving a blessing to the wrong son, then thinking he couldn't just do it over. Come on! Now that you know what's what, give the big pronouncement to the right kid, revoke the previous blessing, curse or at least rebuke the deceiver, and get on with life! Right?

Isaac couldn't do that. Why? Because words are ir-retractable, especially words spoken in faith. Isaac blessed a deceiver wearing goat hair, but it didn't cancel the blessing spoken in faith. When he spoke, he was creating a future, and he knew it. He could no more get the future back than the words used to create it. For folks like me who dabble in faith but live in "reality," it doesn't make sense; it sounds simplistic, foolish. It also may explain why we experience so little of the extraordinary, and how quick we are to say things we can never retract.

Lord, may this tongue be used to serve and bless you.

The Bottom Line: Our words are ir-retractable.
Use that tongue to bless.

DAY 161

Lifeboat Bouncers

They brought to the Pharisees the man who had formerly been blind. Now it was a Sabbath day when Jesus made the mud and opened his eyes. So the Pharisees again asked him how he had received his sight. And he said to them, "He put mud on my eyes, and I washed, and I see." Some of the Pharisees said, "This man is not from God, for he does not keep the Sabbath." But others said, "How can a man who is a sinner do such signs?" And there was a division among them...

So for the second time they called the man who had been blind and said to him, "Give glory to God. We know that this man is a sinner." He answered, "Whether he is a sinner I do not know. One thing I do know, that though I was blind, now I see."... "Never since the world began has it been heard that anyone opened the eyes of a man born blind. If this man were not from God, he could do nothing." They answered him, "You were born in utter sin, and would you teach us?" And they cast him out. John 9;13-16,24-25,32-34

The picture told a story all too true. The painting was of a large lifeboat in choppy seas, surrounded by desperate souls, reaching for safety. Onboard was a small group of bored-looking people having a church service, complete with preacher and pulpit, paying no heed to those drowning within reach. A man in the safety of the boat gazed dejectedly into the face of a man reaching for him.

I would add something to that sad picture. I would add a Pharisee, tossing others out of the lifeboat, smugly thinking he's doing God a favor. What matters to him is not saving folks drowning in sin, but keeping a tidy lifeboat, where everyone is in synch with his theology, traditions and personal preferences. Only the few, the pure, the real Christians. And we wonder why so many people these days can't stand Christians! If there was anything like that sort of passion toward loving the world into faith, instead of condemning not only the world but fellow believers as well, we might get somewhere.

A writer I like recently penned a fair and gentle article regarding a non-orthodox person who is urging our nation to prayer. She was quickly pitched overboard by lifeboat bouncers obsessed with exposing heresy right and left according to their own perceptions and keeping the lifeboat of Christianity pure and even less crowded than before. So that's what Jesus sent us to do?

We need your help, Lord! Help the Church to be both righteous and loving. If we're missing one or the other, we are in real trouble.

The Bottom Line: Our job is to help people get in the lifeboat, not toss them out.

DAY 162

Fishing with Dynamite

The wise of heart is called discerning,
and sweetness of speech increases persuasiveness.
Good sense is a fountain of life to him who has it,
but the instruction of fools is folly.
The heart of the wise makes his speech judicious
and adds persuasiveness to his lips.
Gracious words are like a honeycomb,
sweetness to the soul and health to the body.

Proverbs 16:21-24

Harsh speech doesn't convince anybody. It just makes them defensive. If we truly want to persuade someone to see things our way, sweetness is the way to go. They want to go our way when we build them up; they want to get away when we tear them down.

Is what the world hears coming from Christians "sweetness of speech"? "Gracious words"? Wisdom of the heart, not just hurled scripture quotations? We would be a lot more persuasive that we were actually right if we spoke with more grace and less condescension. We need to practice sweetness of speech. Much of the anger of the world toward the Church is not due to our association with Jesus, but our harsh tone. The attempt to nag people toward Christ only pushes them away. Critical fault-finding and condemnation, then inviting people to become like us so they, too, can be right, is about as ineffective a form of evangelism as could be imagined. If we want to persuade folks that following Jesus beats the way they're headed, sweet, gracious speech would convince many more than trying to win theological arguments.

Jesus said that out of the overflow of the heart the mouth speaks. If we humble ourselves before the Lord and allow Him to change our hearts, our speech will follow.

What are some of the tools in our bag which actually help us to change society? Wisdom of the heart. Sweetness of speech. Good sense. Gracious words. All these tools are available to us if we want them. Too often, they go unused while someone is, once again, fishing for men with dynamite.

It's not harshness which persuades people, but honey. If we really want our friends to love Jesus, we need to sound—and taste, more like Him.

The Bottom Line: It's sweetness of speech which persuades people, not criticism.

DAY 163

God on the Ladder

Jacob left Beersheba and went toward Haran. And he came to a certain place and stayed there that night, because the sun had set. Taking one of the stones of the place, he put it under his head and lay down in that place to sleep. And he dreamed, and behold, there was a ladder set up on the earth, and the top of it reached to heaven. And behold, the angels of God were ascending and descending on it! And behold, the LORD stood above it and said, "I am the LORD, the God of Abraham your father and the God of Isaac. The land on which you lie I will give to you and to your offspring. Your offspring shall be like the dust of the earth, and you shall spread abroad to the west and to the east and to the north and to the south, and in you and your offspring shall all the families of the earth be blessed. Behold, I am with you and will keep you wherever you go, and will bring you back to this land. For I will not leave you until I have done what I have promised you." Then Jacob awoke from his sleep and said, "Surely the LORD is in this place, and I did not know it." And he was afraid and said, "How awesome is this place! This is none other than the house of God, and this is the gate of heaven." Genesis 28:10-17

Jacob had been a jerk and he knew it. At his mother's insistence, Jacob had duped his father and stolen his brother's blessing. Now he's paying the consequences. He's basically running for his life. Under the auspices of finding a wife from non-Hittite stock, Jacob is sent off to his mother's relatives back in Haran, interestingly enough, with his father's blessing. Jacob is already changing. Esau was the outdoorsman; now it's Jacob using rocks for pillows.

It was "just a dream," but it was a life-changing one. In the dream, God's promise to the patriarchs is passed on to yet another unlikely recipient, a childless, lying fugitive who doesn't even own a pillow. God's promises must have sounded unbelievably good to a weary man who had messed up his life.

It wasn't just the promises; it was the presence of God. Jacob's eyes were opened to this magnificent God, the same One who had guided his father and grandfather, who now promised to guide him.

Jacob had nothing to offer God except his sin. These outlandish promises were completely undeserved. Jacob wasn't even looking for God; God was looking for him! At the lowest point of Jacob's life, God came down the ladder to give new life to a weary, lost soul. It's what God always does.

The Bottom Line: God has made it so we can get to heaven. He came to us.

DAY 164

The Mercy Standard

If you really fulfill the royal law according to the Scripture, "You shall love your neighbor as yourself," you are doing well. But if you show partiality, you are committing sin and are convicted by the law as transgressors. For whoever keeps the whole law but fails in one point has become accountable for all of it. For he who said, "Do not commit adultery," also said, "Do not murder." If you do not commit adultery but do murder, you have become a transgressor of the law. So speak and act as those who are to be judged under the law of liberty. For judgment is without mercy to one who has shown no mercy. Mercy triumphs over judgment. James 2:8-13

Oh, man. I don't think I've ever heard a sermon on this passage—and I've been in church my whole life! I don't think I've ever preached on it, either. Some passages just "happen" to get overlooked. A lot. Apparently, this is one of them.

I think I know why. Most of us—even semi-notorious sinners—have at least a couple sins we don't like. I've heard scathing condemnation of smoking come from preachers so obese they could barely stagger across the platform. Did they ever preach on the sin of gluttony? Neither did anyone else I can remember. Over-eating is somehow sanctified by thanksgiving—either the holiday or the attitude. "Bless this gluttony we are about to receive..." Mercy! Unless they're smoking.

It's a lot easier for people who can't stand smoke to condemn those who stand in the chill with an after-dinner cigarette, than to condemn ourselves for scarfing 3,000 calories at one sitting. It's easier to judge those with obvious faults in their theology than it is to grant them mercy. After all, we know what "those" people are like! Meanwhile, all our beliefs are justified—and correct.

Then there are certain sins—and certain kinds of sinners—which are so odious to us we're pretty sure no one we know is even tempted by that sin. Time to pile on! We can all get into judging those folks! Lawbreakers! Ungodly sinners!

And what's this? Where are they taking us? Out to be condemned! What do you mean, I'm a lawbreaker, too? I never did that, never even wanted to. Oh, you're talking about this other thing. That's a sin? Yeah, but it's not the same kind of sin as his. Mine's better. A lawbreaker is a lawbreaker? Well, could I at least be in a different cell than these people? No? You're applying the exact same standard to my life as I have applied to theirs? Oh. I get it. The standard of judgment you're using on my life is the one I've been using on theirs. Mercy!

The Bottom Line: The one who shows no mercy gets no mercy. Show mercy!

DAY 165

A Working Appetite

A worker's appetite works for him;
his mouth urges him on.

Proverbs 16:26

Hunger is a powerful cure for laziness. When it comes to motivating people to work, when they realize they are in a situation where if they don't work, they and their family don't eat, hunger can be a gift which produces the incentive to get out of bed, when the body is declaring that it's not worth the trouble. A healthy appetite helps make for better self-discipline.

Self-preservation is a great motivator, too. I like the joke about the hiker in tennis shoes, "in case a bear is after us." "You can't outrun a bear!" his partner snorts. The reply? "I don't have to outrun the bear. I just have to outrun you."

On my first Alaskan backpacking trip, we awoke to windblown rain and snow on a treeless mountain pass. A teen boy came up to our trail leader and announced, "Mr. Hellenga, we have to go back! We have to turn back! I can't go another step!" Dean calmly looked around and said, "It's twenty miles to go ahead, eighteen miles to go back. I think I saw grizzly tracks nearby. You can stay here if you like, or you can go back by yourself. The rest of us are going through the pass."

I didn't see the kid the rest of the day. He was ahead of me. The boy who "couldn't go another step" wanted to climb a mountain after he got to camp.

It's a firm grip on reality which boosts the farmer out of bed to plant crops which won't produce food for months. He knows sleeping through the planting season will result in no harvest. Better get up and work.

The college student staggers out of bed and heads to class because she wants the degree badly enough to ignore her body's complaints and excuses. She gets a degree—and self-discipline. Good deal.

Nothing promotes self-control quite like a good appetite and a system which rewards hard work, not sloth. Nothing de-motivates folks more quickly than being rewarded for laziness and penalized for achievement. Don't kill good appetites.

If we repent and serve God just to avoid hell, that's not bad. Fear is a favor if it helps us get on the right track.

Whether we're talking eternity or the practical, mundane things of life like getting out of bed to go to work or school, a healthy appetite and a system which rewards work and penalizes laziness are both working for us, not against us.

The Bottom Line: Appetites which motivate us to do the right thing are a gift.

DAY 166

Seven Years to Life

Jacob loved Rachel. And he said, "I will serve you seven years for your younger daughter Rachel." Laban said, "It is better that I give her to you than that I should give her to any other man; stay with me." So Jacob served seven years for Rachel, and they seemed to him but a few days because of the love he had for her. Genesis 29:18-20

Asking my wife to marry me is one of the wisest decisions I ever made, and one of the few decisions I have not second-guessed. Nearly three decades have flown by, and we're still in love. *So Jacob served seven years for Rachel, and they seemed to him but a few days because of the love he had for her.* I get that. And though seven years of shepherd duty were not required of me in order to get my wife's hand, I did take on a second job in order to pay for my phone bill when we were separated by thousands of miles, which was all but 21 days of our pre-wedding lives. Would you believe over $2,000 in long distance bills? That's what you get for falling in love before email, Facebook, texting and free long distance.

At least Jacob got to be around Rachel during the seven years he was paying down her dowry. That's why it seemed like a few days. Had he been thousands of miles apart like my fiancé and me, seven years would have bordered on eternity. Jacob was satisfied, because when we truly love someone, we don't have to possess them in order to be fulfilled. True love delights in their mere presence.

Seven years was nothing to Jacob, when it came to loving Rachel. He never stopped. My parents are like that. As a young man, my father tucked my mom's high school photo in his wallet and never took it out. It's still there. It'll never come out while he's alive. They've clocked more than 65 years as husband and wife. Not only are they still together; they're still in love, and act like it. It's a joyful, willing life sentence. I know that feeling. I'm doing 25 to life. I'd do it again in a heartbeat.

The same thing goes for my relationship with Jesus. One of these days, we'll be summoned home, forever. Meanwhile, we get to experience the joy of a daily relationship with a God we can't see. Someday it will be different, better. When these few days on earth are over, we will be with our Lord. The Bible describes it as a wedding feast, the Church as His bride. It will be worth it! Whatever we endure on this earth will quickly be forgotten, once we see our Lord, face to face. True love makes the years fly by, and the trials seem as nothing.

**The Bottom Line: When we are with Jesus,
Earth's trials will seem as nothing.**

DAY 167

Working Faith

What good is it, my brothers, if someone says he has faith but does not have works? Can that faith save him? If a brother or sister is poorly clothed and lacking in daily food, and one of you says to them, "Go in peace, be warmed and filled," without giving them the things needed for the body, what good is that? So also faith by itself, if it does not have works, is dead.

But someone will say, "You have faith and I have works." Show me your faith apart from your works, and I will show you my faith by my works. You believe that God is one; you do well. Even the demons believe—and shudder! Do you want to be shown, you foolish person, that faith apart from works is useless? Was not Abraham our father justified by works when he offered up his son Isaac on the altar? You see that faith was active along with his works, and faith was completed by his works; and the Scripture was fulfilled that says, "Abraham believed God, and it was counted to him as righteousness"—and he was called a friend of God. You see that a person is justified by works and not by faith alone. And in the same way was not also Rahab the prostitute justified by works when she received the messengers and sent them out by another way? For as the body apart from the spirit is dead, so also faith apart from works is dead. James 2:14-26

Whoa, baby! I'm reminded of why this passage is customarily skipped over by so many people, particularly pastors looking for sermon passages. It's "confusing," "controversial." No, it's not. It's all too plain, despite the seeming contradiction to some more popular scripture passages and a whole lot of popular theology.

I've met a whole lot of workless Christians who prided themselves on their faith and disdained even the suggestion that works might have something to do with righteousness. "We're not justified by works! The only thing that counts is faith!" they scream, then proceed to live like the world, all the while clinging to the belief that a professed faith is all that matters. It reminds me of co-habiting couples who profess true love and commitment because "marriage is just a piece of paper," but it's a piece of paper they don't choose to sign. A little legal commitment would make their love seem more convincing.

Works—actions motivated by faith—show that faith is alive. According to James, a workless faith is a worthless faith. Thought we might still call it "faith," if it never moves, it's dead. Sorry. Hey, I didn't write it.

The Bottom Line: Works show our faith to be alive. Workless faith is dead faith.

DAY 168

Bad Boys of the Bible

A worthless man plots evil,
and his speech is like a scorching fire.
A dishonest man spreads strife,
and a whisperer separates close friends.
A man of violence entices his neighbor
and leads him in a way that is not good.
Whoever winks his eyes plans dishonest things;
he who purses his lips brings evil to pass.

Proverbs 16:27-30

This is the message we have heard from him and proclaim to you, that God is light, and in him is no darkness at all. (1 John 1:5) Contrast this verse to the passage in Proverbs which describes those who don't choose to walk in the light, but instead prefer subterfuge and darkness. These are the bad boys (and girls) who spread discord and evil like a farmer spreads seeds.

One of the most refreshing things about God is that He is Light—as in, all the way through. There is no "dark side" to the Lord. He is pure, holy. He is Light. Those who wish to follow Him need to take that same path, because the road to ruin is one where we think we're smart enough to get away with evil and not get caught. Proverbs has a name for those who plot evil: Worthless. It's what worthless people do—plan more bad stuff to do.

It's interesting what is labeled as bad stuff, too: Speech that scorches people like fire; spreading strife; dishonesty; whispering?! Yeah, it goes back to that "God is Light" thing—where if we're saying something we don't want everyone to hear, it's probably not helpful, most of the time. What separates close friends? Not direct attacks; that only brings them closer to each other. What kills friendships are whispered lies spoken as truth. It's hard to defend ourselves against what we can't hear. How sad when beautiful friendships die with a whisper.
Trouble follows bad behavior. It doesn't have to be illegal to be evil. All it takes to leave a ruinous trail is an unrestrained temper or tongue. We might not go to jail over it, but sowing strife and dishonesty have their own "reward"—not good.

There are plenty of bad boys in our world who could care less about the suffering they cause. They will answer to a God of Light. So will we. We need to choose our path and our companions carefully.

The Bottom Line: Watch out for bad boys.
More importantly, don't be one.

DAY 169

Anything but Disappointed

So Jacob served seven years for Rachel, and they seemed to him but a few days because of the love he had for her.

Then Jacob said to Laban, "Give me my wife that I may go in to her, for my time is completed." So Laban gathered together all the people of the place and made a feast. But in the evening he took his daughter Leah and brought her to Jacob, and he went in to her... And in the morning, behold, it was Leah! And Jacob said to Laban, "What is this you have done to me? Did I not serve you for Rachel? Why then have you deceived me?" Genesis 29:20-23,25

Jacob loved Rachel, but married Leah by mistake. Except it wasn't a mistake. It was deliberate deceit which turned the couple's first day of marriage into a nightmare and gave Jacob an extra wife. The trickster had been tricked. Shortly afterward, Jacob was given Rachel as well—in exchange for seven years' more work. Laban's deception resulted in a sadness and envy in this family which haunted them for generations. When we think we're smart, we're probably not.

When my wife and I celebrate a wedding anniversary, I can't help but think of the contrast between Jacob and me. I've been anything but disappointed in my wife!

But for two sisters married to the same man, life was disappointing. Leah felt very unloved. Why couldn't she be like Rachel? Meanwhile, Rachel was long childless, while her sister bore seven children! Why couldn't she be like Leah?

Aren't most of our disappointments in life because we feel unloved, or we think we don't measure up?

Tests have shown that I don't have the "personality" of a leader. "See, God? I told you!" It didn't stop Him from calling me to be a pastor. When I quit trying to fit someone else's leadership mold and just obeyed God, it got easier. It seems God often calls people to lead who aren't leaders. Sometimes they follow Him better when they don't have so many leadership strengths to overcome.

The point is, we don't have to be a certain personality type in order for God to use us or love us. We don't need to be miserable because of what we're not. We get to serve a God who loves all kinds of people and uses all who are interested.

God loves us all: mousy introverts and used car salesmen, televangelists, prison inmates, hunters and vegans. God loves people of all hair colors, and those who formerly had hair. He recruits all personality types. Serving God is anything but a disappointment.

The Bottom Line: God loves us all, and works through all kinds of people.

DAY 170

The Untamable Tongue

Not many of you should become teachers, my brothers, for you know that we who teach will be judged with greater strictness. For we all stumble in many ways. And if anyone does not stumble in what he says, he is a perfect man, able also to bridle his whole body. If we put bits into the mouths of horses so that they obey us, we guide their whole bodies as well. Look at the ships also: though they are so large and are driven by strong winds, they are guided by a very small rudder wherever the will of the pilot directs. So also the tongue is a small member, yet it boasts of great things.

How great a forest is set ablaze by such a small fire! And the tongue is a fire, a world of unrighteousness. The tongue is set among our members, staining the whole body, setting on fire the entire course of life, and set on fire by hell. For every kind of beast and bird, of reptile and sea creature, can be tamed and has been tamed by mankind, but no human being can tame the tongue. It is a restless evil, full of deadly poison. With it we bless our Lord and Father, and with it we curse people who are made in the likeness of God. From the same mouth come blessing and cursing. My brothers, these things ought not to be so. Does a spring pour forth from the same opening both fresh and salt water? Can a fig tree, my brothers, bear olives, or a grapevine produce figs? Neither can a salt pond yield fresh water. James 3:1-12

Try to imagine a ship plowing through the ocean waves, arriving at a far-off, tiny destination, when all the while the rudder has been under the control of someone who doesn't wish to go there. Whoever controls the rudder controls the ship. It will only arrive at the destination if he wishes. Whoever holds the reins controls the horse. Whoever controls the tongue controls the person.

We've all known plenty of out-of-control Christians, when it comes to the tongue. Some even seem to think it doesn't matter, that their good works or excuses will make up for the lack of self-discipline in the mouth. Not so. We are accountable for what we do with our tongue, especially if we claim Christ.

When it comes to starting fires, the tongue is the usual culprit. The autopsy of charred relationships nearly always reveals arson, the work an undisciplined, poisonous tongue, probably a whole nest of them. It shouldn't be that way, but is.

No human being can tame the tongue. But God can. He will, if we surrender it to Him. He can take "a restless evil" and turn it into a spring of blessing.

The Bottom Line: No human being can tame the tongue. But God can.

DAY 171

Prayer Apnea

Rejoice always, pray without ceasing, give thanks in all circumstances; for this is the will of God in Christ Jesus for you. 1 Thessalonians 5:16-18

If we're stuck on what God's will is for us, this scripture is a strong hint. Some have misunderstood the part about *"pray without ceasing,"* assuming it to be just another impossible demand placed on us by a God who keeps forgetting we're only mortals. "In other words, all I'm supposed to do is pray, and nothing else?! That's your will for my life?! Thanks a lot, God!"

For too many Christians, prayer is a chore, a guilt-ridden obligation both scary and boring. They have a hard time doing it even in 15 second occasional bursts in private—and God wants them to do it all the time?!

I like to think of prayer like I think of breathing, which is a pretty essential habit. If our body forgets to breathe for a while when we're asleep, they call it "apnea." Obviously, it's only a short while that we quit breathing before we resume it; otherwise, they call it "death."

How often do we think about breathing? Usually, the only times we focus on it are when something makes breathing difficult. Otherwise, rarely.

Prayer can be as natural as breathing. We get to the point where we don't even think about doing it—we just do it. God wants our relationship with Him to be so close, so natural, that we live in a constant state of contact with Him. I look at *"Pray without ceasing"* like I do, "Don't stop breathing!" Prayer apnea is tough on our spiritual lives, particularly if it's deliberate.

So, what is God saying when He tells us to *"pray without ceasing"?* Is He expecting marathon prayer sessions where we don't shut up for days? Jesus commented on the uselessness of wordy prayers done for show, and the model prayer He taught His disciples only takes seconds to repeat. No, I don't think God is after filibuster-style prayers.

What I think He's saying is quite simple: "Don't *quit* praying." That's like "Don't quit speaking to your friend." Keep the relationship open all the time. Don't relegate prayer to a conversation you have with God, and then you're done for the week or the day or whatever. Prayer is a continuing, two-way conversation with God; you're never "done," any more than you're "done" talking to your spouse. We know our prayer life is improving when we routinely enjoy God's presence, it's so natural we don't always realize we're doing it, and we never quit doing it on purpose.

The Bottom Line: Don't quit praying.

DAY 172

33 Below

I called on your name, O LORD,
from the depths of the pit;
you heard my plea, 'Do not close
your ear to my cry for help!'
You came near when I called on you;
you said, 'Do not fear!'

You have taken up my cause, O Lord;
you have redeemed my life.

Lamentations 3:55-58

The world was transfixed as, one by one, 33 Chilean miners emerged from over 2,000 feet underground to be reunited with loved ones and the world. They had been trapped for three months! It took 69 days to drill the hole which would provide a way of escape. Each miner squeezed into the tiny escape capsule to begin the long journey skyward, until finally none were left behind. The rescue was complete. The joy was shared around the world.

What if some of the miners had refused rescue? What if some had stubbornly adopted the attitude, "There has to be another way out of here. I'll find my own way out. I don't want to be obligated to anyone. Just leave me alone."
They'd had plenty of time to know there was only one way out. They wisely took it.

I wish the world would be so wise when it comes to spiritual rescue. We're all in trouble and we know it. We're trapped in sin, the wages are death, there is no escape. But wait! There is a Savior! He came all the way from heaven to this earth, His only purpose to rescue us and provide a way to escape hell and gain heaven. There is only one way out of here—it's through Jesus Christ. He said it Himself, and the whole Bible agrees. We can wave off His salvation, claim that we'll find our own way, complain about the hypocrites in the Church or the stupidity we've observed in others who are being rescued, or we can quit whining and get in the capsule, thankful that Someone loved us enough to provide a way out, even at the cost of His own life.

I'm so grateful that we have a Savior. There's only one way to heaven, but at least there's one way! We'd better take it. When it comes to eternal life in heaven, the only ones to be left behind will be those who have chosen to be fools.

The Bottom Line: There is only one way to heaven: Jesus Christ. Accept salvation.

DAY 173

A Crown of Glory

Gray hair is a crown of glory;
it is gained in a righteous life.

Proverbs 16:31

My hair has been turning glorious since I was 21, same as my Mom. I was 35 when they first started asking me if I wanted the seniors discount at Sizzler. Now people ask what color my hair used to be. Like I told them at the church board interview when I got the question about premature graying, "I'd rather have my hair turn gray than turn loose!"

So here's my very own verse in Proverbs, announcing that *"Gray hair is a crown of glory; it is gained in a righteous life."* Cool. I guess. What exactly is it saying, though? Gray hair is something rarely coveted in my culture. On the other hand, how many of the things which *are* sought after in my culture are things which gain God's approval? Not many. There seems to be pitifully little effort made toward gaining righteousness in our society—even among believers—and huge effort which is made toward preventing aging, or even the appearance of it.

Once again, we have it backwards. What if, on an individual basis, we pursued righteousness with the kind of fervor with which we pursue youthful appearance? What if we proudly displayed our affection for God, as if our relationship with Him were the absolute best thing about us? What if we didn't even try to hide how much we love Jesus? And what if we didn't worry quite so much about looking older? As in, accepting the signs of aging as a crown of glory, instead of a curse of heredity or the indicator of too many birthdays.

I have no problem with hair dye, although when I tried it once, people from my own church didn't recognize me. I don't think God minds at all if we apply Lady Clairol or whatever and buy a few more years worth of youthful appearance. But one of the best ways to live long enough to turn gray is by living a righteous life, day after day. And the way to live a righteous life is to go hard after the things God likes, and avoid the things God hates. This will generally find us at cross purposes to the world. Not to worry. The world looks at us and sees a bunch of gray-haired, religious old fogies. God looks at us and sees a crown of glory that He put there. One day He'll add a crown of life. The world looks at us and just sees gray hair; God looks at us and sees a righteous life. Youthful appearance is O.K., but a life lived for God—now that's attractive!

The Bottom Line: Righteousness is even more attractive than youthfulness.

DAY 174

Faith in the Real World

Then Jacob took fresh sticks of poplar and almond and plane trees, and peeled white streaks in them, exposing the white of the sticks. He set the sticks that he had peeled in front of the flocks in the troughs, that is, the watering places, where the flocks came to drink. And since they bred when they came to drink, the flocks bred in front of the sticks and so the flocks brought forth striped, speckled, and spotted... Whenever the stronger of the flock were breeding, Jacob would lay the sticks in the troughs before the eyes of the flock, that they might breed among the sticks, but for the feebler of the flock he would not lay them there. So the feebler would be Laban's, and the stronger Jacob's. Thus the man increased greatly and had large flocks, female servants and male servants, and camels and donkeys. Genesis 30:37-39,41-43

What's with the striped sticks? Well, Jacob, having finally paid off the wedding dowry on two wives, now is trying to acquire some sheep. He makes a deal with Laban: Jacob's share of the flock will be only whatever is speckled, spotted or black; everything else will be Laban's. Fair enough. Laban immediately sends his sons to sort out all animals fitting that description and hide them from Jacob, leaving him with nothing. (Their relationship has always been like this).

Jacob, undeterred, simply resorts to what seems to be a completely bizarre superstition—making a bunch of striped sticks to lay in the watering troughs—as if this is going to change the laws of genetics. But it does. Well, something does, because before long, Jacob has much, Laban has little.

The ESV Study Bible assures me that "The text should not be understood to imply any causal relationship between the sticks and the newborn animals." Yeah? Well, Jacob sure thought there was! And, lo and behold, the flocks of Laban started producing striped, speckled and spotted animals! Was it the sticks or was it the faith? Or was it just God's blessing? Or maybe some ancient, long-forgotten shepherd's trick, so there really was a causal relationship, somehow?

I have a problem with the philosophy which discards things just because they don't make sense to us. Things happen when people pray in faith. Things happen when people do stuff like peel the bark off of sticks and trust God to make a difference in things we can't see and don't understand. When it comes to Jacob and his sticks, what counted is that he had faith in a God who doesn't need sticks to do miracles, but sometimes uses them, anyway. Right, Moses?

The Bottom Line: Faith goes beyond "reality."
It's what makes it faith.

DAY 175

The Meekness of Wisdom

Who is wise and understanding among you? By his good conduct let him show his works in the meekness of wisdom. But if you have bitter jealousy and selfish ambition in your hearts, do not boast and be false to the truth. This is not the wisdom that comes down from above, but is earthly, unspiritual, demonic. For where jealousy and selfish ambition exist, there will be disorder and every vile practice. But the wisdom from above is first pure, then peaceable, gentle, open to reason, full of mercy and good fruits, impartial and sincere. And a harvest of righteousness is sown in peace by those who make peace. James 3:13-18

The book of James is so pure I feel I'm spoiling it to add anything to such profound truth. The truth in this passage is about wisdom—real wisdom, not the kind which boasts incessantly of itself, particularly at this point in an election year. If there is any meekness in election year politics, I've missed it. The boasting and mud-slinging continue. It's supposed to be "wisdom" for the benefit of discerning voters. Hmm.

"The meekness of wisdom"? Again and again I've been hearing, "I'll fight for you!" which I've come to know usually means, "I'll fight to keep my job!" Any sort of genuine meekness is pounced upon by the opposition as weakness.

It makes me wonder if an election could be won in America if a person focused on what God calls wisdom, instead of falling back on the baser instincts which seem to define politics. Think of a candidate for political office who presented these qualities: *Pure, peaceable, gentle, open to reason, full of mercy and good fruits, impartial and sincere.* Think of a candidate who pursued peace over getting elected, and especially after getting elected.

My candidates usually get clobbered, anyway. I'm a conservative in a liberal state. I long for godliness, or at least honesty and decency, in the political candidates I support, and seldom see anyone even close to that succeed.

When the campaign signs come down and the exhausted airwaves return to regular commercials instead of the barrage of trumped-up lies lobbed every which way, wouldn't it be nice to be able to say we had actually gained some wisdom from a campaign? That at least one candidate had treated the opposition with fairness, mercy and grace, had not told multiple lies or made ridiculous promises, and instead of sowing discord for years to come, had even planted some peace in a weary nation? It seems to me that a person who ran a godly campaign would win, either way.

The Bottom Line: Why not try more godly wisdom in the election process?!

DAY 176

The Power of Kindness

While he was still speaking, there came a crowd, and the man called Judas, one of the twelve, was leading them. He drew near to Jesus to kiss him, but Jesus said to him, "Judas, would you betray the Son of Man with a kiss?" And when those who were around him saw what would follow, they said, "Lord, shall we strike with the sword?" And one of them struck the servant of the high priest and cut off his right ear. But Jesus said, "No more of this!" And he touched his ear and healed him. Then Jesus said to the chief priests and officers of the temple and elders, who had come out against him, "Have you come out as against a robber, with swords and clubs? When I was with you day after day in the temple, you did not lay hands on me. But this is your hour, and the power of darkness." Luke 22:47-53

I'm trying to imagine how palpable the spirit of evil must have been on that hillside. It's all there: Betrayal, rage, hatred, fear, open hostility. It's all focused upon the Son of God, and it will only intensify in the hours to come. *"But this is your hour, and the power of darkness."* Even as darkness seemingly overpowered everything in its path, I'm struck by an act of amazing kindness on the part of the Savior. The servant's ear.

Correlating accounts fill in the details: The servant's name? Malchus. The guy with the sword? Peter (Who else?). Hadn't Jesus asked about swords just a short time ago? If they weren't supposed to use them, why bring them? Peter's one-man Rambo act didn't last long. Jesus called him off after one ear. But the Lord didn't stop there. It's as if everything is put on "pause" while Jesus not only stops the violence on both sides, but goes over to the wounded bondservant, touches his ear and heals him!

Look at the scene. The combined forces of evil—Satan's finest—are arrayed against the Son of Man. Nothing is being held back. Every bit of evil which can be mustered is pitted against Him. And He breaks the grip of evil with one act of kindness. It is so obvious in this situation who really is in charge: It's Jesus. The Lamb of God will go to the Cross, but only because that's why He came in the first place. Evil has some fierce power, but a single act of kindness is more powerful.

In these rancorous times, the airwaves and streets abound with harsh jabs. It's considered a good deal to cost your opponent an ear. And then today I met a kindly Christian doctor who gave me free treatment and meds, and was reminded again of the wonderful power of kindness. Thank you. Kindness rules.

The Bottom Line: Kindness will always be more powerful than evil.

DAY 177

No Chance

The lot is cast into the lap,
but its every decision is from the LORD.

Proverbs 16:33

Maybe this explains why my brother could beat me at Risk when he was three years old! The kid could roll sixes with annoying consistency. Maybe he was getting divine help all along. It's no shame to get beat when you're playing against God.

I don't know if games with dice are really equivalent to casting lots or not, but the Old Testament surely has some prime examples of using the "lot" to get information from God. It was God Himself who came up with the Urim and Thummim, engraved stones bearing the names of each of the twelve tribes, to be carried by the high priest (Exodus 28). They were used for decision making. The first Israelite king was chosen by lot (1 Samuel 10). The fact that the lot ultimately fell on the person the prophet Samuel had previously anointed only confirmed that God was highly involved in this business.

Our God seems to have very little interest in chance. His Creation is orderly, incredibly complicated, amazing, but not random. Planets and galaxies are carefully arranged. With the Earth's rotation, the sun "comes up" every single day, not two out of three.

Years ago, in a book, I saw a checklist of conditions necessary in order for a church to grow. I went through the list, noting that the church I pastored did not meet a single condition! I complained to God about my predicament. "My church can't grow! The odds are all against us!" I whined. The immediate reply I received was an encouraging rebuke: "I don't do 'odds'; just miracles."

The church grew. My God doesn't do "odds"; He just does miracles.

I'm often amused when I hear of fellow Christians putting hope in something like the lottery. Even the advertisements promoting it dutifully warn that this is supposed to be for "entertainment purposes only," not "investment." I like the bumper sticker that says, "The lottery is a tax on people who are bad at math."

I would suggest that we can do a lot better than that! Instead of throwing money away in a system which seems to be hardest of all on its "winners," how about just putting our trust in a God who loves us, who can do anything, and who never leaves anything to chance?

The Bottom Line: Our God can do anything,
and He leaves nothing to chance.

DAY 178

Starter Material

What causes quarrels and what causes fights among you? Is it not this, that your passions are at war within you? You desire and do not have, so you murder. You covet and cannot obtain, so you fight and quarrel. You do not have, because you do not ask. You ask, and do not receive, because you ask wrongly, to spend it on your passions. You adulterous people! Do you not know that friendship with the world is enmity with God? Therefore whoever wishes to be a friend of the world makes himself an enemy of God. Or do you suppose it is to no purpose that the Scripture says, "He yearns jealously over the spirit that he has made to dwell in us?" But he gives more grace. Therefore it says, "God opposes the proud, but gives grace to the humble." Submit yourselves therefore to God. Resist the devil, and he will flee from you. Draw near to God, and he will draw near to you. Cleanse your hands, you sinners, and purify your hearts, you double-minded. Be wretched and mourn and weep. Let your laughter be turned to mourning and your joy to gloom. Humble yourselves before the Lord, and he will exalt you. James 4:1-10

Once again, I'm suitably speechless when I get done reading this passage. It's so blunt. It's also so true. I can't help but think of how somehow I've never heard this particular portion of the Bible even referred to on the religious programming which aims for the wallet, not a changed or humbled heart.

This call to repentance doesn't fit with a self-centered philosophy which pretends God's only goal is to make us happy. "*Be wretched and mourn and weep. Let your laughter be turned to mourning and your joy to gloom. Humble yourselves before the Lord, and he will exalt you.*" How does that fit with the well-known verse, "God wants me to be happy"? Guess which passage is really in the Bible.

If we're wondering what starts fights, it's easy: Unrepentant hearts. Everywhere you find a human being who has not humbled himself before God, you will find conflict, within and without. Each human being who refuses the Spirit of God and insists on yielding to the spirit of sin will be a constant fountain of evil attitudes and actions. That person will leave a trail of conflict, sin, hurt feelings, disappointment. That person is trapped in pride. Part of the pride is in wanting to have it all—the pleasures and friendship of the world, and heaven, too; the freedom to do whatever we want and the blessing of God.

No, we have to choose. Which will it be? Pride or repentance? Humility and obedience to God, or our own way? The conflict continues until we surrender.

The Bottom Line: The source of conflict is an unrepentant heart. God can fix that.

DAY 179

Peace and Quiet

Better is a dry morsel with quiet
than a house full of feasting with strife.

Proverbs 17:1

Feasting is over-rated, if it comes with a house full of strife. The same could be said of fame, of money, of various sorts of power. If the money, notoriety or whatever is going to wreck your relationships and ruin your life, who needs it?! Better to be a nobody living in peace than a "somebody" in divorce court. Better a dry bowl of Wheaties in peaceful circumstances than an extravagant, expensive meal, facing off with a mean adversary.

Our bodies know the difference. It doesn't take much strife to take all the fun out of food, particularly digestion. It's difficult to enjoy a great meal and a big argument with someone we love, at the same time.

The problem is, some folks rather enjoy strife. They get a kick out of arguing. They make it a point to not agree with anyone if they can help it. For some people, it's only interesting if there is conflict. For others of us, conflict avoidance is a high-priority goal in life. We don't enjoy arguing, nor do we care to hear others arguing. When in stressful, tense situations, we look for a solution or we look for the door. We don't like it stirred up. We like it calm.

For those Christians who are more comfortable with conflict, an effort needs to be made to contain and control it. If a person enjoys a good verbal debate like some enjoy a good steak, what is needed is to find another willing participant who is able to easily separate thoughts and ideas from self-worth and dignity. (For some people, if you attack their idea, you just attacked them. For others, ideas are like baseballs—they are made to be batted around!)

We need to keep "debate" from becoming "strife." Debate is a verbal contest between people who treat each other with respect, even after they win or lose. Strife indicates a lack of peace, a lack of civility, a lack of respect. Debate is noble and often productive; strife is humiliating and often harmful. Those who routinely sow strife just for the fun of it will one day answer for the discomfort they cause, particularly if they claim to be Christ-followers.

There's much to be said for peace and quiet. For one thing, it's when we have a quiet spirit and we are at peace with our brothers that we most often hear God. The Spirit of God is a Spirit of peace, not strife. Come to the quiet.

The Bottom Line: We're better off to pursue peace, worse off if we pursue strife.

DAY 180

Who Needs Salvation?

Then Midianite traders passed by. And they drew Joseph up and lifted him up out of the pit, and sold him to the Ishmaelites for twenty shekels of silver. They took Joseph to Egypt. Genesis 37:28

God's relocation project has begun. One Hebrew is now in Egypt. The rest will eventually follow, after Joseph becomes second-in-charge of Egypt.

What's going on, here?

God is teaching His people, and He takes generations to do it. The Israelites are a called people and they know it. Abraham left Ur of the Chaldeans to follow God to a Promised Land, never went back, and insisted that his son not go back. Abraham's grandson, Jacob, ran to relatives while he was in exile, but God led him back to Canaan. The family was now growing large. Given a little time, they could achieve enough critical mass to no longer be considered aliens. They had already been present in the land for decades. But now this.

Skipping ahead to the end of Genesis and the story of the Exodus, God will allow the entire family to be forced to relocate to Egypt. Joseph, using his gift for dreams, has prepared the way for them to survive the severe famine. Things go well for the Israelites for a while. Then come the hard times and slavery.

Four centuries will pass, with the promises made to Abraham all but forgotten, though God had informed Abraham that his posterity would spend 400 years in a land not their own, before returning. Moses arrives on the scene, gets his desert education, then his divine commission, and leads the Israelites out of the grip of slavery in Egypt to be ready to enter the Promised Land, once more, but this time as a nation of hundreds of thousands.

What in the world was God doing? If He wanted them in Canaan, they were already there! Why drag them to Egypt, then bring them back?

They didn't know what salvation was, back in Jacob's day. They didn't know what it was to be hopelessly enslaved, powerless, then see the mighty hand of God humiliate the most powerful man on earth, then hold the waters of the Red Sea back for them. They didn't know what it was to be saved, back then, or to need a Savior. The generation God brought back to Canaan knew what it was to be saved. That's what it was all about.

When God doesn't move things in a straight line in our lives or in our nation, what is He doing? Probably teaching us. There's a lesson in here, somewhere.

The Bottom Line: Not only does God teach individuals; He instructs entire nations.

DAY 181

Speak No Evil

Do not speak evil against one another, brothers. The one who speaks against a brother or judges his brother, speaks against the law and judges the law. But if you judge the law, you are not a doer of the law but a judge. There is only one lawgiver and judge, he who is able to save and to destroy. But who are you to judge your neighbor? James 4:11-12

They're pulling up the political campaign signs today, all across the country. Yesterday's election marked a seismic political shift, proving voter anger to not be fictitious. Unfortunately, neither was the degree of negativity in this campaign cycle. Hundreds of television ads honed in on the "evils" of opponents, often distorting the truth or spouting out-right lies. Suffice it to say there was a whole lot of evil spoken against one another over the past few months. Maybe that's just "the way it has to be," in politics, but I'd like to believe differently.

It's definitely not "the way it has to be" in the Church. Yes, many veteran Christians have witnessed stuff as nasty on church property as they've ever seen in a political slugfest, but we're called to a lot higher standard, aren't we?

Do not speak evil against one another, brothers. Some verses leave wiggle room, or we can pull out the "in the original language it meant this"excuse so we can do what we want and stay biblical, but this one is too plain: Don't do it, at least if you want to act like a Christian.

I have great admiration for folks I know, so disciplined in their speech that you can't even trick them into speaking evil of another person. They just won't do it! They're not biting. God bless 'em! I'm not in that league, but it's so nice to have friends who are, because around them you always know you're safe. They don't even judge their enemies; why would they ever start with their friends? And if they ever ran for a political office, I'd vote for them in a heartbeat, for the simple reason that I can trust them!

When it comes to voting for candidates, we need to be skeptical, we need wisdom, we need to make judgments based on the best information we can get, which may have nothing to do with what is being said on TV! When it comes to our neighbor and our brother, though, judging is not our job, at all. That's up to the only One who knows the whole story about them, and it's not us. When it comes to speaking evil of another person, it's never the Christlike thing to do. When it comes to our neighbor, we have a much better job than judging them: Love them.

The Bottom Line: Our assignment is to love our neighbor, not judge them.

DAY 182

You Might Not Want to Do That

Whoever mocks the poor insults his Maker;
he who is glad at calamity will not go unpunished.

Proverbs 17:5

Do you mean God takes it personally when we mock poor people? It looks like it. God loves people. Those who are glad to see evil befall folks are not going to get off unpunished, according to the scripture. That includes our enemies.

Mocking the poor? I'm thinking middle school kids mocked by the fashion police; high school and college kids put down for their lack of money. I'm thinking addicts and alcoholics not given the dignity normally granted to dogs.

Why would God care? Because He's our Father. When you insult one of our kids, we are insulted—it doesn't matter what they did or whose fault it was—it reflects on us. If you hurt them, you just hurt us, their parents. Period.

When God's Son came to Earth, He came poor, grew up poor, stayed poor. When we start thinking we deserve to own a home, that we deserve all kinds of extravagant possessions as a kind of birthright, we should think about Jesus. No wife or children. Never owned a house. Supported by women. They buried Him in a borrowed tomb. During Jesus' ministry years, He didn't even have an address!

The poor are God's children, too. When we choose to mock them, we are insulting God. When we choose to rejoice in awful things happening to people we don't like, we are going to have to answer to their Father—and ours. Better not.

The way to earn the permanent gratitude of parents is easy: Be nice to their kids. Show kindness, respect and love to their children. They'll never forget it.

If you want to impress your enemy, show up after a calamity without a hint of gloating. Silently administer kindness and mercy to everyone, without judgment. Love, then leave—probably with one less enemy. The kindness will be remembered. We're all God's children, every one of us. Some of us are born rich, some poor, a lot in-between. If we choose to mock those who have not been given as much as we have, we are insulting their Father. That's not good. If we rejoice in evil which has befallen an enemy, we are only creating more enemies. If we demonstrate kindness and mercy which mirrors that of the Father, we bring blessing to our Father, and those who have chosen to hate us begin to run out of reasons for doing that. If we're kind and merciful like God, we will enjoy a growing list of friends and a shrinking list of enemies.

The Bottom Line: We insult God when we mock the poor or rejoice in calamity.

DAY 183

Jerks in the Genealogy

About three months later Judah was told, "Tamar your daughter-in-law has been immoral. Moreover, she is pregnant by immorality." And Judah said, "Bring her out, and let her be burned." As she was being brought out, she sent word to her father-in-law, "By the man to whom these belong, I am pregnant." And she said, "Please identify whose these are, the signet and the cord and the staff." Then Judah identified them and said, "She is more righteous than I, since I did not give her to my son Shelah." And he did not know her again. Genesis 38:24-26

Oh, my. If the Israelites had gone to the trouble of sanitizing their history, Genesis chapter 38 would be missing from the Bible. It's not a pretty sight. It's a not-so-unusual tale of selfishness, sin and double standards, which were about to be applied with maximum harshness until a widowed daughter-in-law produced evidence which saved her own life and the life of her unborn twins. The evidence showed the immorality of one of the sons of Israel—the same one who casually condemned his daughter-in-law to death for her immorality—with him! When we read the whole chapter we gain some sympathy for the characters involved—but not that much. Judah, in particular, comes across as a jerk.

So, when people act like jerks and hypocrites, this is the last we hear of them in the Bible, right? Not at all. Among the twelve tribes of Israel, who rises to the top and stays there? Judah. It's the tribe of King David. It's the tribe of King Jesus, "the Lion of the tribe of Judah."Amazing. I thought the guy was a jerk! He's in the genealogy of Jesus! Why would he get such positive notoriety?

Why would any of us? It's because our God isn't interested in discarding people, but in redeeming them. Why does He redeem people? Because we need redeeming. If we were not sinners and reprobates, we wouldn't need a Savior. Since all of us fit the "jerk" category, since we all have jerks in our genealogy and come from a long line of jerks, every one of us needs a Savior. Wouldn't you know it? God so loved the world that He sent His Son. Jesus was born into a genealogy which contained nothing but sinners. One of them was Judah. Jesus then proceeded to live a sinless life, offered Himself up for all of mankind on a cross, and was raised from the dead to reign forever with the Father. He offers eternal life to all who believe, regardless of our ancestry or our track record.

We are not perfect people. We are not descended from perfect people. We are in love with a Savior who redeems absolute jerks and gives us eternal life.

The Bottom Line: Jesus redeems, regardless of our ancestry or track record.

DAY 184

Best-laid Plans

Come now, you who say, "Today or tomorrow we will go into such and such a town and spend a year there and trade and make a profit"—yet you do not know what tomorrow will bring. What is your life? For you are a mist that appears for a little time and then vanishes. Instead, you ought to say, "If the Lord wills, we will live and do this or that." As it is, you boast in your arrogance. All such boasting is evil. So whoever knows the right thing to do and fails to do it, for him it is sin. James 4:13-17

Humility is scarce in America. We assume much. Someone without grandiose plans and the braggadocio to match might be considered short-sighted, sometimes even within the church world. The power of God is sometimes assumed as being under the control of some evangelist or faith healer or TV personality with a huge amount of "faith" and an ego to match. Big plans for big churches. A big name. It means book sales and fame and money. Too often, it's nothing but arrogance, parading as Christianity.

I get tired of hearing people tell what they're going to do. There's a difference between confidence and unbridled pride. There's definitely a difference between humility and everything which is not. When we see a humble spirit, it's refreshing! Why is it so rare to find a truly humble spirit within the ranks of pastors and church leaders? "What do you mean 'boasting is evil'?! That's just confidence!" Yeah. Nauseating confidence.

Is the Bible telling us it's wrong to make plans? I don't believe so. But it's telling us that arrogance is evil, and that presuming God will rubber stamp all our plans just because we want Him to is foolish arrogance.

Arrogance will never bring revival, but humility will. Repentance will. And obedience will. If we know what we're supposed to do and we don't do it, it's sin. If we presume God has to go along with all our plans, we're just plain wrong. He doesn't. We are the ones who should be seeking His will, listening for His direction and redirection, not the other way around. Some things are guaranteed by God, but preapproval of our plans and ambitions is not one of them. "If God wills it" is the only safe attitude, when it comes to planning out the future.

God's people should be guided by God, not our egos. Obedience is expected of all disciples. We're foolish to presume on the future. The only guarantee we have is that if God wills it, it will happen. Everything beyond that is arrogance.

The Bottom Line: The only guarantee we have is that what God wills will be done.

DAY 185

Not Really Alone

Now Joseph had been brought down to Egypt, and Potiphar, an officer of Pharaoh, the captain of the guard, an Egyptian, had bought him from the Ishmaelites who had brought him down there. The LORD was with Joseph, and he became a successful man, and he was in the house of his Egyptian master. His master saw that the LORD was with him and that the LORD caused all that he did to succeed in his hands. Genesis 39:1-3

Joseph was alone. He had been sold by his own brothers into slavery. He's in a foreign country, all alone. But he's not. The LORD was with him. It was something noticeable even to a master who spoke a different language.

The saga continues. Joseph achieved as much success as was possible for a slave. Then, for being loyal to both God and his slave master, Joseph's reward is imprisonment! The lies of Potiphar's wife send Joseph to prison, alone. Except, once again, he's not. But the LORD was with Joseph and *showed him steadfast love and gave him favor in the sight of the keeper of the prison.* (Gen 39:21) A little later: *The keeper of the prison paid no attention to anything that was in Joseph's charge, because the LORD was with him. And whatever he did, the LORD made it succeed.* (Gen 39:23)

Four times in this chapter we are reminded, "The LORD was with him." But wait! Aren't these the most miserable days of Joseph's life?! Getting auctioned off by your siblings is not my idea of a good thing to happen to you. Neither is being a slave, even if you become "top slave." And to get thrown in prison for being good? How does all of this fit with "the LORD was with him"?

It fits because it was true.

It still fits. When I look back on the most miserable, difficult days of my life, there is something consistent about all of them: The LORD was with me. The worse the circumstances, the closer God's presence was felt. In the worst of times, just knowing God was there brought indescribable comfort.

Better days were coming, for Joseph. God was about to do a really impressive jailbreak, and catapult Joseph from zero status to second in command of Egypt. But I'm guessing that the times in all of Joseph's life when he felt God's presence the nearest were those difficult, lonely days when nobody was around except God, but it was enough. Our Savior promised us trouble (Jn 16:33), but He also promised something wonderful—that He would be with us, always. It's enough.

The Bottom Line: All that really matters is that the LORD is with us.

DAY 186

Just Do It

So whoever knows the right thing to do and fails to do it, for him it is sin. James 4:17

This verse has bugged me for a long time. I remember asking a pastor about it when I was seventeen. "The sin of omission," it's called. It means that not only do we need to not do the wrong thing, to avoid sin; we also need to do the right thing. It means that when we cheerfully tell God "Sure!" when He asks us to do something, but months and years have passed and we still haven't acted on our words, God doesn't just space it off and we're fine—we're actually sinning when we disobey through inaction or procrastination. That's why it bugs me. Long ago, I quit telling God "No." Procrastination? I keep intending to work on it.

God's grace is there for every sin, so it's not like I'm necessarily in eternal danger for procrastinating on stuff I know God wants me to do, but at the same time, this verse is a reminder that it matters. It's sin. Procrastination in general is not smart, but when it comes to putting off what we know God would have us do, it's sin. That's a definite problem.

What's the answer? I'm reminded of the slogan pitched by the Nike sportswear company for years: "Just do it." I always thought that would make a good church motto, particularly for folks like me. And when it comes to God's will, when we know what it is, when He's made clear to us our part, we're not needing "more prayer," "more time" or "more study"—it's time to "Just do it." And avoid the sin of omission.

I would normally write another paragraph or two to sum things up, but in keeping with the tenor of this scripture, I think we'll skip the extra verbiage, today. It's time to "Just do it." Obey God. Today.

The Bottom Line: When we know what God wants us to do, "Just do it."

DAY 187

Pray the News

And he looked down toward Sodom and Gomorrah and toward all the land of the valley, and he looked and, behold, the smoke of the land went up like the smoke of a furnace.

So it was that, when God destroyed the cities of the valley, God remembered Abraham and sent Lot out of the midst of the overthrow when he overthrew the cities in which Lot had lived. Genesis 19:28-29

Why did God tell Abraham about the impending destruction of Sodom? God knew Abraham would intercede for his nephew, Lot. Of course, God was right. Abraham bargained with God to try to spare Lot. When he had gotten God to agree to spare Sodom if ten righteous people were found in it, Abraham thought the city was safe. It wasn't, but Lot was. Why? Abraham's prayers and God's mercy. The one marginally righteous person in the city was led out by the hand. And the Word tells us God remembered–whom? Not Lot, but Abraham.

God's followers know about stuff so we can pray.

That's why the morning was such a blessing. I prayed the news.

Prompted by the Holy Spirit, I stood in front of the television for an hour, praying the news, in the same manner I was taught to prayer walk neighborhoods: when you see darkness, pray the opposite.

I was amazed at how easy and fulfilling it was. I was doing something about the problems I saw! For instance, "May Day Mayhem" was predicted for downtown Seattle. I prayed for protection for the police, wisdom for authorities.

When the weather came on, I prayed for each city on the weather map–and for people I knew in those cities. Traffic report? I held my hands out and blessed the people in the vehicles I saw on the live camera. I prayed for their safety. I prayed for their relationships, especially their relationship with God. When tragic news stories came on, I prayed for all involved. Sometimes I prayed for the reporter. I even prayed through the commercials! I prayed against gambling and alcoholism during the casino and alcohol commercials. I prayed for the children of America during the toy commercial. Laundry detergent commercial? I prayed spiritual cleansing for our nation. I prayed for cures for breast cancer and allergies, in response to TV commercials.

The hour went by quickly. The news wasn't even discouraging, because I was doing something about it! God lets us know about the hard things so we will pray.

The Bottom Line: When God lets us know about hard situations, it's so we will pray.

DAY 188

Earth's Gag Reflex

And the LORD spoke to Moses, saying, "Speak to the people of Israel and say to them, I am the LORD your God. You shall not do as they do in the land of Egypt, where you lived, and you shall not do as they do in the land of Canaan, to which I am bringing you. You shall not walk in their statutes. You shall follow my rules and keep my statutes and walk in them. I am the LORD your God. You shall therefore keep my statutes and my rules; if a person does them, he shall live by them: I am the LORD. Leviticus 18:1-5

What follows? A catalog of sexual sins. Half a chapter is devoted to what constitutes incest, and why it is sin. A prohibition is made of sexual relations during menstruation. Brief but strong mention is then made of the sins of adultery, child sacrifice, homosexuality and bestiality. Each of these latter sins is given a different label. Child sacrifice "profanes" the name of your God. Homosexual acts are "an abomination." Bestiality is "perversion."

Here's what I find interesting. After first warning the Israelites to "not do as they do in Egypt," and "not do as they do in the land of Canaan," either, the LORD informs them that the Canaanites did all these things, that this is why they are being driven out of their land, and that the land itself is "vomiting" them out, in response to their uncleanness. Here it is:

"Do not make yourselves unclean by any of these things, for by all these the nations I am driving out before you have become unclean, and the land became unclean, so that I punished its iniquity, and the land vomited out its inhabitants. But you shall keep my statutes and my rules and do none of these abominations, either the native or the stranger who sojourns among you (for the people of the land, who were before you, did all of these abominations, so that the land became unclean), lest the land vomit you out when you make it unclean, as it vomited out the nation that was before you. For everyone who does any of these abominations, the persons who do them shall be cut off from among their people. So keep my charge never to practice any of these abominable customs that were practiced before you, and never to make yourselves unclean by them: I am the LORD your God." Leviticus 18:24-30

Earth has a gag reflex when it comes to abominable practices? Guess so.

The Bottom Line: What God calls abominable practices even make the land unclean.

DAY 189

How to Guarantee a Wretched Future

"Do not make yourselves unclean by any of these things, for by all these the nations I am driving out before you have become unclean, and the land became unclean, so that I punished its iniquity, and the land vomited out its inhabitants. But you shall keep my statutes and my rules and do none of these abominations, either the native or the stranger who sojourns among you (for the people of the land, who were before you, did all of these abominations, so that the land became unclean), lest the land vomit you out when you make it unclean, as it vomited out the nation that was before you. For everyone who does any of these abominations, the persons who do them shall be cut off from among their people. So keep my charge never to practice any of these abominable customs that were practiced before you, and never to make yourselves unclean by them: I am the LORD your God." Leviticus 18:24-30

Three times Leviticus 18 mentions earth's gag reflex, whereby the land itself "vomits" out its people when they insist on practicing what God calls "abominations." Not only does sexual sin make those who practice it unclean; it even pollutes the land, with very undesirable, wretched consequences.

It goes back to the beginning, when Adam and Eve fell, brought down their perfect world with them, and found themselves expelled from Eden. Why? Sin. They started out believing God, their Friend: "Don't eat from the fruit of this tree, or you will die." With the help of the serpent, their position on sin "evolved" until it cost them everything. They couldn't say they had not been warned.

Neither can we. We can "evolve" all we want, we can enshrine abominations as the new normal, we can even try to paper over them with selected scriptures and sentiments, but the outcome is the same, because God never changes. He's just not into evolution, I guess. The outcome? You do this stuff, and the earth itself won't put up with it. You will be puked out just like those who came before you, who did these same things. Any questions?

We've been warned. "This is how it works. If you practice abominations, the land will vomit you out, because the land itself will not put up with this kind of uncleanness for long. You cause the earth to wretch when you practice these sins. Entire nations will simply be replaced with other people, for no other reason than sin. Don't do it! You are to be different. Don't do like they did in Egypt; don't do like they've been doing in Canaan. I am the LORD. You belong to me. Act like it."

The Bottom Line: Abominations make for wretched results. Guaranteed.

DAY 190

Unnatural Disasters

Do not make yourselves unclean by any of these things, for by all these the nations I am driving out before you have become unclean, and the land became unclean, so that I punished its iniquity, and the land vomited out its inhabitants. Leviticus 18:24-25

I wonder how many "natural disasters" are nothing more than "sin disasters," triggered by the revulsion of the planet against practices God terms "abominable." Are tornadoes, hurricanes and mud slides always just natural phenomena, or is there something more here? Would some of that stuff be the direct result of sin? I don't understand it, but apparently there is some sort of true connection between the practice of perversion and abominations and the expulsion of entire nations, sometimes by the earth itself, with or without attacking armies.

This earth is God's Creation. As Satan was expelled from heaven because of rebellion and sin, so man seems to be expelled from earth for the same thing. In both Egypt and Canaan, abominable practices had become acceptable customs—"laws," even. God compares His statutes to theirs, then says, "Don't be living according to their laws and customs. That's what got them kicked out of their land. That's part of what ruined them. You follow my laws, and you'll be O.K."

In our society, once-outlawed perversions have come to now be considered "constitutional rights."Although American laws have changed (abortion legal, homosexual practices legal, recognition of same-sex marriages, etc.), God's laws have not changed. They are still the same. Entire countries or world regions may adopt policies and laws which try to make sin noble and fine, but we'd better live by God's laws, or the earth itself will vomit us out! It won't be a "natural disaster," either, but an unnatural disaster, triggered by unnatural acts.

Followers of God should remember we are on a completely different system of morality. And rather than being worried about imposing our values on others, we need to not only live by God's values ourselves, but use whatever influence we have to help and guide others away from destruction. This chapter speaks of not letting the "stranger" living among you practice this stuff, either. There's a place for "live and let live," but it doesn't extend to perversion and abomination. God is definitely not "pro-choice" when it comes to child sacrifice and homosexual acts and adultery!

Sin leads to destruction every time, no matter how large the herd practicing it, or how noble they feel in the practice. Even Creation agrees... with God.

The Bottom Line: God has made clear the consequences of abominable practices.

DAY 191

What Would Jesus Do?

What would Jesus do, if He were in my county to conduct ministry for two or three years? This is what I think He would do, if He were in some sort of "in-between" trip between the Incarnation and the Second Coming. In other words, if He were here just to minister to the people in my county, how would He go about it?

He would assemble a band of disciples, and extensively train them. At the same time, He would preach to the crowds, probably starting in the churches wherever He was welcome, but also in the public square. He would heal whoever came to Him for healing. He would set people free from addictions.

He would send out disciples in groups of two to proclaim the Kingdom of God. They would go to neighborhoods locally, but they would also be sent to distant places.

He might have kind of a boot camp for disciples, where they would be alone with Him for days or weeks, even months, in order for transformation to occur.

The point is, if Jesus came to my county just to minister for a while, I think He would basically do about the same as He did, the first time He came to Earth. I think what He did through the Early Church is very, very similar to what He would do again. It was, in fact, His Spirit living in the disciples. He was ministering through them, living through them. And we have that exact same Spirit living in us.

We should learn from this mental exercise. Our method of lobbing some information and inspiration in the general direction of people a couple hours a week isn't very effective. It's kind of like 2-hour re-hab! Hey, they were sober for two hours straight! Yea. Is that the way Jesus would do it? Or even the apostles?

Jesus didn't just conduct a lot of meetings or preach to a lot of people. He *made disciples*. Then He told us to go and do the same. Why are we not doing that? Why do we persist in building big organizations and big buildings and broadcasting the message to thousands, but seldom do we make disciples? And even when we do make disciples, we make them people just like us, who will also spend most of their time in ineffective ways.

The church in America is in need of a makeover. We would do well to try to imitate Jesus more, and the world less. The Early Church lived as disciples, made disciples. That is our calling, too. We dare not ignore it.

The Bottom Line: What would Jesus do?
Probably what He did the first time.

DAY 192

Relationship Rapids

Whoever covers an offense seeks love,
but he who repeats a matter separates close friends.
A rebuke goes deeper into a man of understanding
than a hundred blows into a fool.
An evil man seeks only rebellion,
and a cruel messenger will be sent against him.
Let a man meet a she-bear robbed of her cubs
rather than a fool in his folly.
If anyone returns evil for good,
evil will not depart from his house.
The beginning of strife is like letting out water,
so quit before the quarrel breaks out.

Proverbs 17:9-14

It marks the first of the relationship rapids for many folks. About what am I talking? The first of the winter holidays: Thanksgiving. Relatives and friends are around, which is a good thing, except when it's not. Relationships between people which have drifted along for months suddenly intensify with the additional contact the holidays bring. It can get ugly. It's much like the beautiful mountain river suddenly turning into a churning cauldron of white water where you paddle for dear life and hope you picked the right guide.

Relationships are like that. And if we grab the Bible, we've picked the right guide to help us through the relationship rapids for which this season is notorious. Here are some principles to remember when we're trying to keep relationships right side up:

- Telling people about the stupid things we see folks do doesn't solve any problems, but it does separate close friends. Don't.
- Don't try to set fools straight. It doesn't work. Save your advice for those willing to listen. Except those people usually don't need advice.
- Remember that God is big enough to deal with evil people and fools, and He will. The main thing is not to be evil, or foolish, so He doesn't have to deal with us. -When you see your words are inciting an argument, quit talking while there's still time. Starting arguments is easy; stopping them, next to impossible.

Happy Holidays.

The Bottom Line: God has given us great relationship advice, if we're interested.

DAY 193

Upside-downers

He who justifies the wicked
and he who condemns the righteous
are both alike an abomination
to the LORD.

Proverbs 17:15

To see revival in America, we need people to pursue the right direction, people with right-side up priorities. Is that how it is, now? When the wicked are justified and the righteous are condemned, will a new generation choose God's moral system or the one on which they've been weaned?

Revival requires repentance—sorrow for sin and a desire to turn around. What if people don't think God's direction is good? What if they've been trained to think what God calls detestable is actually honorable? When righteousness is condemned by society, will new generations aspire to be righteous in God's sight, or will they learn a man-centered code of ethics based on political correctness?

It goes back to what is right. Is "right" what God says, or does mankind get to determine what is right by majority vote or prevailing opinion? In spiritually blessed times, we have had it both ways, in America—the majority of our society wanted to please God and abide by His rules. It was "politically correct" to have a strong faith in Christ. Scripture was present and honored throughout society.

Things have changed. Who are today's societal trend-setters? Are Americans getting their moral values from the Church or from Hollywood?

We need to go back to the Bible and its Author. There we'll find true moral values. In our present culture, being righteous in God's sight may not get us into Congress, but it'll get us into heaven! If we look to present society for moral guidance, we will be led astray! Lifestyles which God terms "an abomination" are routinely held up as "normal." Calling sin "noble" doesn't change its outcome.

The moral high ground is being claimed on an hourly basis by upside-downers who label wickedness "normal" and righteousness despicable. God will turn it all right-side up, one day. Meanwhile, we desperately need to listen to God, not the world! Sure, it means we go against the flow. But going with God is worth whatever abuse we get from those claim moral superiority while despising God. Only One has true moral superiority. Let's go with what He says.

The Bottom Line: In an upside-down culture,
we need to go with what God says.

DAY 194

Padding the Resume

Then Pharaoh sent and called Joseph, and they quickly brought him out of the pit. And when he had shaved himself and changed his clothes, he came in before Pharaoh. And Pharaoh said to Joseph, "I have had a dream, and there is no one who can interpret it." Joseph answered Pharaoh, "It is not in me; God will give Pharaoh a favorable answer." Genesis 41:14-16

"It is not in me." What do you mean? Joseph, the only reason you've been lifted out of that pit is because Pharaoh was told you could do this! And now you tell him it's not "in" you, that it's God?! Wouldn't the king be looking for confidence and performance, instead of humility? If he takes this wrong, you go back to prison, you know.

Joseph knew. If he wound up in prison again for doing it God's way instead of taking the "smart" way of self-preservation, it wouldn't be the first time he had paid that price! But Pharaoh was tired of empty boasting, anyway; he just wanted results. He wanted to know what his dreams meant.

It's interesting that Joseph was already giving glory to God before he had even heard the dreams. I wonder if that had anything to do with the fact that Joseph didn't need so much as a 15-minute recess to ponder Pharaoh's dreams before telling him exactly what was going to happen, what he needed to do, and that it was all from God. I'm reminded of a favorite promise from 1 Samuel 2:30: *Those who honor me I will honor.* I'll say! Before the day was through, the former prisoner was second in command in Egypt, all because he gave glory to God instead of himself, and he listened to God.

When Joseph gave the honest disclaimer that any ability to interpret dreams was from God and not from himself, Pharaoh didn't seem to notice, much less dock him for it. I wish it were always so. I've seen people get hammered even by other Christians for taking the humble approach rather than the boastful, resume padding one, as if humility were a weakness rather than a virtue. Just this week, a high school football player was penalized for kneeling and pointing to the sky after scoring a touchdown! It was something he had done after every touchdown all season without penalty. The world can be pretty hard on those who choose to glorify God rather than grabbing glory for themselves. It's O.K. Glorifying God can get us a penalty or prison time, or we may be totally ignored, but God *always* notices! It's always a good plan to give Him glory.

The Bottom Line: God honors those who are careful to give Him the glory.

DAY 195

Rotting Riches

Come now, you rich, weep and howl for the miseries that are coming upon you. Your riches have rotted and your garments are moth-eaten. Your gold and silver have corroded, and their corrosion will be evidence against you and will eat your flesh like fire. You have laid up treasure in the last days. Behold, the wages of the laborers who mowed your fields, which you kept back by fraud, are crying out against you, and the cries of the harvesters have reached the ears of the Lord of hosts. You have lived on the earth in luxury and in self-indulgence. You have fattened your hearts in a day of slaughter. You have condemned and murdered the righteous person. He does not resist you.

Be patient, therefore, brothers, until the coming of the Lord. See how the farmer waits for the precious fruit of the earth, being patient about it, until it receives the early and the late rains. You also, be patient. Establish your hearts, for the coming of the Lord is at hand. James 5:1-8

I don't think I've ever heard a message on the first few verses of James 5. Wonder why! Few Americans would not be "rich" by the standards of much of the world. It's hard to read this passage without guilt for our present standard of living, particularly if we're still unsatisfied, living in comparative luxury!

Though we all can point to someone else with more, this passage isn't about "Yeah, but I still don't have as much as _____." It's about establishing our hearts, so our souls get saved when everything else goes up in smoke.

We don't have long. These are "the last days" for each of us. If we clamber to obtain by corruption a pile of gold, it merely becomes evidence at the Judgment. Even before their final bell tolls, those who imitate Scrooge will often get their comeuppance. If not, at life's end it is all relinquished, anyway, left behind to infect others susceptible to an attitude which sucks the life out of life.

If we have to have it all, or we have to have it now, we're putting ourselves in danger. God isn't against riches (He made numerous people in the Bible rich), but He is most definitely against selfishness, greed, fraud and murder.

True riches are in heaven, not earth. When the Lord returns, we'll get what's coming to us. If our hearts are established with Him, our attitude toward the world right, our reward will defy imagination. If the world and its riches have a grip on our heart, it's not too soon to start mourning our coming losses. It's also not too late to reestablish our heart in a better direction. Before it's too late.

The Bottom Line: Watch out for riches!
The love or misuse of them is deadly.

DAY 196

Revival Worksheet, Page One

I resigned an 11-year pastorate to begin a new ministry, in 2005. Servant Connection was the result of this step. I was seeking the spiritual transformation of America, trying to figure out what was needed in order to see a spiritual turnaround in our nation. In this worksheet which I wrote only days before this huge transition in our lives, I outlined five things I thought needed to take place if another awakening was to come to America:

Repentance.

Outreach that connects believers with unbelievers.

A home for everybody—believers and unbelievers.

Mutual commitment. (The end of the religious consumer mentality)

A daily relationship with Jesus Christ, and a "daily" relationship with other Christians.

Repentance doesn't need much explanation. We just need to know that we are not going to "church growth" ourselves into a nationwide revival, regardless of how clever the plan or how much money is thrown into it. Without repentance there is no heart change. Without a change of the heart which only God can bring about, there is no transformation.

Outreach that connects believers with unbelievers. First, two things need to happen. In order for people to have a desire to share Christ with others, there must first be a true relationship with Him. Then, there must be a desire to connect with others who don't know Christ. If either of those things is missing, Christians stay huddled in their buildings, hoping the world will go away. On the other hand, if they are in love with Christ and they are praying for non-believers in their lives, Jesus will help them find ways to show love to their unbelieving friends. We're not lacking in plans; we're lacking in passion, both for Jesus and for a lost world. The best way to renew this passion is through prayer.

A home for everybody—believers and unbelievers. This is a tough one! How did the Early Church do it? The Early Church was a closed group, open to new members. Everybody knew who the Christians were, and "no one else dared join them," yet the Church was growing daily, as the Lord added to their number, sometimes by thousands at a time. There needs to be a place for each person, whether a mature disciple or a new believer, to connect and feel at home. More on this, tomorrow.

The Bottom Line: It all starts with repentance and a relationship with Jesus.

DAY 197

Revival Worksheet, Page Two

We're continuing a discussion of what is needed for revival. Yesterday, we left off at the need for "a home for everybody—both believers and unbelievers," which ties in with another revival need: Mutual commitment.

The religious consumer mentality has laid waste to mutual commitment in the Church. The Early Christians were committed to Christ and one another. Rather than "seeker friendly" meetings where the Cross was not mentioned for fear of offending someone, they focused on it, celebrating communion each time they met. Honest "seekers" may have been there as guests, but the meetings were certainly not designed to appeal to them, but to the Christ being worshiped. The Church was a "closed" group of only the committed, but open to new members willing to commit.

What we're lacking in the church, today, are "closed groups, open to new members." Almost all of our groups are open, and anybody can get in, sample what we've got, sniff around for awhile, and then leave, and nobody stops them or even tries. We have to lure them back to the group with something attractive to them (Prayer is never it), and even if we get them back, they often go looking for another party—somewhere they can "get fed." We have spiritual nomads everywhere, and they're mostly midgets. The majority of what we do is babysit them. We're running Christian daycare centers for adults, and calling it church.

How do you change the church from an orphanage to a family? By adoption.

In actual legal adoption, a child becomes a true member of a family. Adoption is specific—not just any child but *that* child; it's mutual—they are joining a family, they are being accepted by a family; it's committed—this is not some trial, foster-care thing, but a permanent relationship, regardless of how it turns out. There is a stability in the relationship which is reassuring to both sides.

Where is the sense of mutual commitment in the Church, today? It's sadly lacking. People can attend a church for years and still feel like a stranger, with no one who feels responsible to them for anything beyond being "friendly." People can attend a church for years and still feel absolutely no sense of obligation to anyone else in that church. That's not how it's supposed to be. God made us for mutual commitment, not to be wandering, wary consumers of spiritual products. What do we do? Commit to God, and to the people He places in our life.

One more revival necessity: A daily relationship with Jesus Christ, and a "daily" relationship with other Christians. Discipleship was daily, then. It should be now, too. And there's never been a "weekly" revival; always daily.

The Bottom Line: Revival requirements:
Mutual commitment and daily discipleship.

DAY 198

Sunday School Verse

A friend loves at all times,
and a brother is born for adversity.

Proverbs 17:17

How many times have I seen this verse on the wall of a younger kids' Sunday School classroom? Quite a few. They just use the first part because it's simple and short and self-explanatory. It's perhaps the only Bible verse which both uses the term "friend" and tells how to be one, making it very useful for Sunday School.

Since it's such standard fare in Sunday School curriculums, why is the practice of it so neglected in real-life church settings? Probably the same reason the command to "love one another" is so often overlooked, despite its many repetitions in scripture. Simply put, it's hard to love people, particularly if we're talking about "all times" or "adversity," not just when they're all warm and cuddly.

In the times when we have the good fortune to have good fortune, and we're in a benevolent mood, we will have "friends" and "brothers" aplenty, popping up to celebrate with us. When we're cheerful, folks hang around. When we're not, they don't, except for the true friends. If we garner enough true friends in a lifetime to require more than one hand to count them, we're unusually blessed (and probably a pretty good friend, ourselves).

Let's move this over to the Church. For a long time, there's been great emphasis on churches being "friendly" as a key to attracting new worshipers. Churches often congratulate themselves on their level of friendliness because smiling greeters are stationed to make folks feel welcome, which they do, if they already have friends there and they know the greeter. My observation is that when it comes to seeking a church, needy people are not looking for "friendly" nearly so much as they are looking for a friend.

"Friendly" smiles, shakes your hand and never pursues a conversation lasting more than a few seconds. A friend is the one who shows up when you're convinced everyone else in the world thinks you're a loser. *A friend loves at all times*, not just the good times. A true brother in the Lord? *Born for adversity.* It's the tough times which prove true brotherhood. Everybody wants to be your "brother" when you're rich and famous. True brothers come alongside when you're poor and stupid, and nobody else wants you. Let's keep the greeters, but what we need in the Church are more true friends and brothers.

The Bottom Line: True friendship means we are committed to love *at all times*.

DAY 199

How to Survive a Crisis

"Now therefore let Pharaoh select a discerning and wise man, and set him over the land of Egypt. Let Pharaoh proceed to appoint overseers over the land and take one-fifth of the produce of the land of Egypt during the seven plentiful years. And let them gather all the food of these good years that are coming and store up grain under the authority of Pharaoh for food in the cities, and let them keep it. That food shall be a reserve for the land against the seven years of famine that are to occur in the land of Egypt, so that the land may not perish through the famine." Genesis 41:33-36

December 7—Pearl Harbor Day, is the anniversary of "a day which will live in infamy," as the president called it. On December 7, 1941, the Japanese attacked Pearl Harbor in Hawaii, and the United States was propelled into World War II. All those old enough to remember that day still do. It was a day when their world changed, quickly and drastically. It was a day of crisis.

Another crisis is coming, for America. I don't know what, or when—just that, inevitably, events come along which rock our world and put everyone off balance. Some crises are quite predictable, others come without warning.

The crisis which faced Joseph's world came with plenty of warning—provided that those with authority promptly acted on that warning. Fortunately, they did. By the time the famine arrived, there was so much stored grain in Egypt that they had long since stopped counting. Because of the preparation God engineered through Joseph and Pharaoh, they sailed through the crisis. Egypt emerged a superpower; Jacob got his son back. All because two people heard God and obeyed.

If a crisis came upon us, what should we do to survive?

Pray. Our Father knows everything, loves us and is willing to guide those willing to follow. If we pray and ask God, He will show us exactly what to do.

Obey. Had they not carried out the plan from God, Egypt would not have been ready for the famine. If God tells us to prepare, we need to prepare. If He says to build an ark, we'd better gopher wood. And if, after prayer, we get no further assignments than the ones we already have, we're probably supposed to just keep serving God the way we have been, without worrying about crises which have not yet arrived. Christians need not worry or panic, regardless of what comes. But it's a really good idea to keep our relationships up to date, with each other, and especially with the One who can get us through anything.

**The Bottom Line: How do we get through a crisis?
Pray and obey.**

DAY 200

The Discipleship Time Machine Part One

What would the Early Church do if we suddenly fastforwarded thirty of them from about 35 A.D. to present-day America?

How often would they meet? I think they would all meet together in a large group on Sunday, but that throughout the week, small groups of two to twelve people would connect with one another on a daily basis, probably using email, etc.

Who would have a ministry? All of them. The apostles would have a ministry of oversight, plus hearing from God, prayer and teaching. I think this oversight would primarily be spiritual, with administration left to the "stewards." Teachers would teach. Evangelists would evangelize (and not much else). Prophets would hear from God, then communicate the messages to the others. Missionaries would be sent out from the group, going wherever the Spirit led them.

I don't think there would be "lay people," in the sense of "Some people are called to 'full-time' Christian service, and you're not." I think there would be the understanding that everyone is called to "full-time" Christian ministry, although those ministries are not all the same. Some have special gifts and graces, some have positions of greater responsibility and authority, but everyone has a ministry of some kind, and everyone is expected to use their spiritual gifts.

What would they do in their Sunday meetings? I think the meetings would be focused on worship and fellowship, to include congregational music. What style of music? I don't think the style would matter so much to them as the spirit, but I think they would have little interest on anything which focused on "performers" instead of on the Lord.

I think there would be opportunity for people to share with the group what they were learning, how the Lord was working in their life, and a scripture or two, with comments welcome. Though there might be regular preachers and teachers who customarily filled those roles, I don't think it would be exclusive. I don't see their weekly meetings being geared toward spectators or "seekers," but toward ministering to one another and worshiping the Lord. There would be opportunity to exercise spiritual gifts in appropriate settings. Prayer would be a natural, regular part of each meeting. They would probably celebrate the Lord's Supper each week.

The Bottom Line: The Early Church focused on worshiping the Lord together, daily.

DAY 201

The Discipleship Time Machine
Part Two

If a group of thirty Early Church disciples were somehow transported to present-day America, what would they do?

Would they have programs? I think their focus would be on being Spirit-led, as opposed to man-centered programs. Simple, relation-ship centered ministry.

Would they have buildings? Probably, but without debt or extravagance.

What would the Early Church do about finances? I'm not sure what they would do, but I'm pretty sure what they *wouldn't* do: Make it their focus. I would see them supporting some of the leaders, yet expecting everyone to be engaged in "full-time ministry." I would envision many people having some sort of employment that was basically to support their ministry habit, with even the top leadership perhaps resorting to secular work at times, if necessary to keep it all going. What I would picture would be a ministry-driven lifestyle, though, for the Church, rather than one where "ministry" was something to be hired or farmed out. I think the greater portion of church funds would also go into directly ministering to the needs of people, with minimal amounts going toward buildings or administration.

What about technology? I could see the Early Church making the most of all available technology, especially the internet, while at the same time focusing on personal, individual ministry.

What would their strategy be? Once again, I think the Early Church would focus on listening to and obeying God, rather than man-made strategy. Some things which we might consider "strategy," they would do automatically: Meeting for prayer and fellowship on a daily basis; determining what to do through prayer rather than through committee; witnessing as a lifestyle.

How about missions? As missionaries to America, I think Early Church missionaries would minister within established church settings whenever welcome, but concentrate on ministering to those outside the walls of church buildings.

Today's American situation is vastly different than what the Early Church faced at Pentecost, when the Church and the Gospel were all new. Missionaries to America today find a culture where people think they know all about Christianity, yet have never encountered Christ, and are unimpressed with His followers. Non-believers are skeptical, sometimes hostile. I think the Early Church approach would be to simply figure out where people were on their spiritual journey, start from there, and love them, one by one, into the Kingdom of God.

The Bottom Line: Is there any reason we can't do what the Early Church would do?

DAY 202

Prescription: Joy

A joyful heart is good medicine,
but a crushed spirit dries up the bones.

Proverbs 17:22

I would imagine that many pages of scientific confirmation could be written elaborating on the principle given here in one Bible sentence, but since my medical and scientific knowledge is pretty much non-existent, I'm going to just take God's Word for it and leave it at that, for today. If personal experience counts for anything, though, I have a little something to say.

Many years ago, I had allowed the circumstances of life to weigh me down to the point where I scarcely wanted to live, anymore. I had permitted a nasty convergence of disappointments and losses to drive me to desperation. Since at that time in my life I was basing my happiness upon circumstances, a bad year for circumstances meant a bad year, all around. It had been one. Coming to the end of that miserable year, having dragged bottom throughout most of it, I came to the point where I was finally willing to let go of past wounds, present discouragement and future worries, and take the extended hand of God, instead.

The Lord taught me some extremely important lessons in that time, chief among them that my joy did not have to be based upon my circumstances, but could, instead, be grounded in my relationship with Him. I could have joy, regardless of my circumstances! It was an epic transformation, which positively affected every aspect of my life, spiritual, mental and physical. It had a huge impact on my relationships, too.

The interesting thing about the whole scenario, looking back, is that the circumstances in my life didn't improve at all, right away. In fact, they got worse! But as I got better, several circumstances did, too, over time, including my health, which had suffered during the time I endured a "crushed spirit." The depression and discouragement had "dried up my bones," it seemed. When I began to focus on Jesus and the joy of living in relationship day by day with Him, it was like "good medicine" for my body, soul and mind. A few months later, I looked back in wonder at how I had allowed myself to sink so low, and what a wonderful thing it was to be on joyful ground, this time solid.

When life is so heavy that even our body is suffering, God has a prescription which is "good medicine": a joyful heart, focused on Him.

The Bottom Line: A joyful spirit is one of the best medicines around! It's a choice.

DAY 203

Asking for Vegetables

But Daniel resolved that he would not defile himself with the king's food, or with the wine that he drank. Therefore he asked the chief of the eunuchs to allow him not to defile himself. And God gave Daniel favor and compassion in the sight of the chief of the eunuchs,... Daniel 1:8-9

Considering Daniel's pitiful circumstances, it's amazing that he would attempt to hang onto any vestige of his homeland or his faith. After all, he was just a kid, a captive from Israel hauled off to Babylon, to become another Babylonian. The three-year intensive training program was supposed to transform foreigners into Chaldeans. Their overseers knew the cost if their charges failed to adequately assimilate.

The idea was to immerse these kids in all things Chaldean, even their diet. In the end, they would be true Babylonians, with scarcely a trace of their original heritage intact.

Daniel and his three friends had already lost so much, it's a wonder they would bother with such trifles as avoiding food "unclean" to Jews. After all, they were captives, exiles far from home. They had lost their families, their homeland, even their manhood. They didn't get to keep their language or their heritage; they didn't even get to keep their names! Why should they try to follow God's dietary laws for Jews in a place where they had no rights and no one cared? The same reason we should try to follow what we believe God would have us do, even when we're far from the watchful eye of parents or peers, and it seems no one cares and everyone is going the opposite direction: It honors God. Inevitably, those who honor God find themselves being honored by Him!

God could trust Daniel and his three friends, Shadrach, Meshach and Abednego. Gently, respectfully, Daniel approached the head eunuch with his simple request. Instead of cornering the overseer into some sort of showdown, Daniel suggested a 10-day test, where the Jewish boys would be given vegetables and water instead of the king's food and wine. At the end of 10 days, he could compare them with the others and act according to what he saw. The head eunuch agreed.

Ten days later, the eunuch was convinced. And when the king evaluated the crop of budding wise men, four far surpassed even the most seasoned veterans— the four who honored God when no one cared. An amazing, long career began with a polite request for vegetables, in order to honor God. He cares. He promotes.

The Bottom Line: Honoring God always matters.

DAY 204

One Tough Job

As an example of suffering and patience, brothers, take the prophets who spoke in the name of the Lord. James 5:10

Being a prophet is one tough job. It means you get to hear from God; it also means you get to tell people what God said when they don't want to hear it. Reactions vary from snide putdowns to putting people down empty cisterns, and that's just when they let you live! When they don't, imagination takes over as to how the prophet will be sent on to their heavenly reward. Hebrews 11 gives a fly-by course on some of the stuff which happens to prophets who refuse to back down. Prophets are not strangers to suffering. It comes with the territory.

Being a prophet also has its advantages—there is nothing like the rush you feel when you know God has spoken through you. And there is no way to describe what it's like when you know you've heard from God. The faithful prophet is familiar with the voice and approval of God, along with the sting of lonely suffering. Sometimes faithful prophets get their names in the Bible; always, in the Book of Life. There is a "prophet's reward."

What does any of this have to do with us? Old Testament prophets are no longer needed; Christ has come. So has the Holy Spirit. Each of us can hear from the Lord without needing to consult some guy in a camel-hair outfit, or even a pastor, for that matter. Is there still a need for prophets? Or is that a thing of the past?

Prophecy is listed in the New Testament not just as a gift, but the gift most to be desired (1 Corinthians 14:1-5). Prophecy is still around, and still important. Occasionally, prophecy will have something to do with predicting future events, as God forewarns or promises through the Spirit. Most often, "prophecy" in this New Testament era is simply relating to others truth God has revealed to us. It's still the same basic idea as in Old Testament times: Hearing from God and passing it on, for the benefit of others.

It still involves suffering and patience, though. Speaking publicly about Jesus can get you a paycheck or it can get you killed, depending on where you are in the world. But even if "prophecy" is part of our job description, welcomed and expected, we're going to need plenty of patience. Nor should suffering surprise us. Jesus promised "tribulation" even as He told us to "take heart" (John 16:33). And if we need an example of tough guys who made it, just take the prophets. Patience.

The Bottom Line: The Old Testament prophets endured suffering. So can we.

DAY 205

Grandfathered

I've seen it happen repeatedly in recent years. Here's the scene: A church with lots of seniors, long on love and tradition, gets a new pastor. The new pastor wants to serve God by reaching new people and younger people, and sees a need for change. How is the church going to attract unchurched young people and their families if everything is geared to a bunch of seniors? With best of intentions all around, the changes begin. And the conflict starts.

The new leader, sometimes the junior person of the leadership team, assumes this church wants him to lead them into the future and will eagerly follow his leadership, even if it came out of a book he just read. They're willing to give it a try, especially the young people, but the seniors are O.K. with it, too, so far.

In a matter of weeks, peace has been replaced by grumbling, conflict and the first empty pews. Long-held traditions have been replaced by whatever non-Christians were supposed to be biting on, these days. Only nibbles so far, though, and those were from unhappy denture-wearers chewing on the pastor, who feels betrayed. "I thought they wanted change!" Yeah, right. And they assumed their new pastor would care about them enough to maybe not jerk away from them everything they held dear and expect them to like it. Everybody is already starting to feel worthless, and it's just getting started. Before it's over, there will be people scattered all over the community who used to call that church home until it no longer felt like home. The pastor? He'll be asked to take his talents and scars somewhere else before long, unless he's able to attract a new following; the offended folks aren't coming back for more.

Before a church will really grow, is it necessary to remove from the existing congregation everything they like, and replace it with something new? Why take away from people things they have valued for a lifetime? At the same time, why try to force grandfather's programs on a new generation?

In construction, people don't have to tear down their old house just because the building codes have changed. They are "grandfathered" in. But if they're building something new, or doing a big remodel, the new codes apply. In the church, why jerk hymnals out of the hands of people who love hymns? And why force hymnals on people who don't know or care what they are?

If a ministry or program or method is grandfathered in, best leave it alone. But if starting a new ministry or church, it needs to be up to "code"—the new one. And if people don't feel loved and valued, none of it matters. Love is God's "code."

The Bottom Line: Any changes should be made according to God's "code": Love.

DAY 206

One Person's Junk

When I came home, they were already inside. One was brand new, the other a "trainer." The new kid hadn't yet learned to be pushy and obnoxious, while the trainer was proficient in both. Kirby vacuum cleaner salesmen.

The memorized sales pitch went like this: (1) If your current vacuum was worthless—just a piece of junk, would you keep it? Of course not. Why hang onto it if it's just junk? (2) I'm sorry to have to tell you this, but your vacuum cleaner is junk. It's worthless. (3) You really need to buy a new vacuum cleaner from us.

The sales pitch was conducted over a pile of stuff they had dumped on our carpet to prove the superiority of their new vacuum costing more than $1,000 over our inferior vacuum not yet seven years old. The new Kirby outperformed ours. This proved ours to be "junk." We didn't quite follow the reasoning that because ours wasn't the newest and best machine available, it qualified as "junk." The pitch was very effective in one way, though: Upsetting me. I grew increasingly agitated with their presence and attitude until I finally gave them five minutes to get out.

They could tell I was serious. They left. Their car was out in the street. Guess what kind of car was being driven by the Kirby salesmen. Junk! Obviously, it got them around, but it was old and ugly. Pure junk. Why would they drive such a thing, when brand new cars were available which were superior in every way?! Umm. Because they hadn't sold enough vacuum cleaners to afford a new one?

I knew what they were driving because God made me slip a note of apology under their windshield wiper before they left our neighborhood. I was ashamed of the way I had acted toward them, and told them so. It's been 20 years since that visit. We're still using the same "junk" vacuum cleaner. I've repaired it several times; it still works fine. I doubt if they're driving the same car.

Had we been looking for a new vacuum 20 years ago, the boys from Kirby would have been welcome, and might well have made a sale. As it was, they didn't sell anything; they only offended us by calling what we thought good, "junk."

And so it is in churches. When people who are perfectly satisfied with customs and traditions which have long been their way of expressing love for God are suddenly informed that because it's not new or in keeping with current fads, everything about their worship is worthless junk, would we expect them to agree with us and not be offended? Or would we get much farther toward the mutual goal of honoring God by allowing people to hang onto what's meaningful to them until they're ready to make a change? The fast track to change is love and respect.

The Bottom Line: Respect and love bring about change faster than coercion.

DAY 207

God's Kind of Hero

Behold, we consider those blessed who remained steadfast. You have heard of the steadfastness of Job, and you have seen the purpose of the Lord, how the Lord is compassionate and merciful. James 5:11

The name "Job" is synonymous with suffering. The God-fearing man suffered the loss of everything at once: His children, all his wealth, his health. Why? Was God angry with him? On the contrary, God was proud of him, so proud that God allowed Satan to attack Job, in the full knowledge that Job could and would withstand the absolute worst Satan could throw at him, and still persevere.

Satan's contention was that Job was coddled and only served God for the blessings and riches. "Remove the blessings, and he'll curse you to your face!" Wrong. Job praised God, instead. Take that, devil! Job was God's kind of hero. A second attack on Job's health produced similar results. Job: 2, Satan: 0.

When Job had withstood the test, God comforted him by answering his questions and showing him His glory, then chewed out Job's friends-turned-amateur-theologians, who had managed to add to Job's misery with their errant counsel. Three times in one verse (Job 42:8) God refers to "my servant Job" when addressing the quivering bunch of know-it-all's. He tells them He will forgive their stupidity, but only at Job's request! In other words, you'd better hope he'll pray for you! (And I'd better never hear any more of this nonsense from you, again)!

I think the key to Job's steadfastness was his self-control. His whole life smacks of discipline—before, during and after Satan's attack. Here was a man who worshiped God every single day, interceded for his children, was grateful for his wealth. He had made it a point to use his mouth to praise God as a matter of self-discipline. When every emotion within him must have screamed out to curse God for letting this happen to him, Job ignored his emotions (and his wife) and calmly proceeded to praise God, just like before. Satan watched in helpless humiliation as God's champion pounded him in a fight Satan had picked.

Afterward, God re-blessed Job with double his previous wealth. The story has a happy ending. There is always a happy ending for those who praise God, particularly when that praise comes despite suffering. Job is a hero in perseverance, but first he was a hero in self-control. There's a reason why self-control is the final gift of the Spirit listed (Gal. 5:22-23). Self-control is so powerful, the one who has it is prepared to go rounds with the devil, and win.

The Bottom Line: If we have self-control, like Job, we will persevere.

DAY 208

Simple Truth

But above all, my brothers, do not swear, either by heaven or by earth or by any other oath, but let your "yes" be yes and your "no" be no, so that you may not fall under condemnation. James 5:12

What's with the *"But above all"?* Why is refraining from swearing oaths such a big deal? James has been talking about being patient, not grumbling, enduring suffering, then suddenly breaks in with, *"But above all, my brothers, do not swear,..."* Why would that be thought so important?

What is the purpose of swearing an oath? To attempt to convince the listeners that what is being said is the truth. Something I've noticed? Those who habitually tell the truth about everything never swear that it's the truth—they don't need to. When you get to know them, you know they don't bother with lies, so there is no need to distinguish between what's true and false about their speech. If it isn't true, they don't say it. It's a good, simple plan.

The people who feel compelled to swear to the veracity of their statements are pretty much always people who mix it up: Sometimes it's the truth, sometimes not, so when they feel they need to convince us, they'll swear to it in an attempt to put it over the top. The more they swear, the more confusing it is. It's hard to believe someone who has to invoke God's name or something in order to establish that this time, at least, what they're saying is accurate. The simple, godly solution propounded by the Bible is to just tell the truth all the time, without dragging anyone else's name in as a reference.

Lying is bad enough by itself; there's no need to add to the sin by swearing it's the truth. Meanwhile, the real truth is fine on its own. It needs no embellishment or references. *Let your "yes" be yes and your "no" be no, so that you may not fall under condemnation.*

This is the simple, convincing, godly, condemnation-free approach. It's a good one to adopt; it saves us a lot of trouble. Simple truth doesn't require a co-signer. A "yes" or a "no" all on its own looks pretty good, and carries no excess baggage.

The Bottom Line: If we simply tell the truth, there's no need to swear it's truth.

DAY 209

Faces in the Wrong Places

It is not good to lift the face of the wicked
or to deprive the righteous of justice.

Proverbs 18:5

God is against face lifts? A bunch of His followers will be chagrined to discover God's displeasure at plastic surgery, nips, tucks and the liberal use of Botox. Oh, wait. It's only the *wicked* who aren't supposed to get face lifts. That's better. We're O.K.

Oh, this verse isn't about face lifts, after all? Whew. Relief.

Actually, that's not even the main text reading of the verse in my English Standard Version Study Bible; *"to lift the face of"* is the literal Hebrew rendering in the footnotes for the part of the verse translated *"It is not good to be partial to the wicked"* in the text above. I like *"to lift the face of"* better. It smacks us right in the culture.

Advertisements? Publicity? Television? Magazine covers? What an appropriate phrase for what happens to anyone famous—their face is "lifted," not by a plastic surgeon or Botox specialist but by a media-crazed culture which feasts on whatever is considered currently cool.

Often "cool" is distinctly wicked, even to the point of "that's what makes it cool." When this junk is lifted up as the targeted lifestyle and behavior for all who crave "cool," it's not good, to say the least. Another generation of lemmings follow Stupid and his guitar off a cliff. Someone told them it was cool. Whose idea was it to give a poster boy (or girl) for wickedness so much face time? Guess. The cost is really high.

Meanwhile, righteousness—or even wholesomeness—is despised, deprived of justice, and our culture suffers accordingly. Righteousness has always only been popular with God and those who love Him. It's the choice we take when we choose Christ over culture. We'll probably be deprived of justice, at least occasionally, while the world shows partiality to the "edgy," "real," wicked. The faces lifted up as models to emulate are seldom those of the righteous. It's O.K. We need to remember something: When God lifts up faces, they stay lifted. Righteousness may not be as popular, but the results are very, very long-lasting. Eternal.

The Bottom Line: When God lifts up faces, they stay lifted.

DAY 210

The Cost of Compromise

Then Nebuchadnezzar came near to the door of the burning fiery furnace; he declared, "Shadrach, Meshach, and Abednego, servants of the Most High God, come out, and come here!" Then Shadrach, Meshach, and Abednego came out from the fire. And the satraps, the prefects, the governors, and the king's counselors gathered together and saw that the fire had not had any power over the bodies of those men. The hair of their heads was not singed, their cloaks were not harmed, and no smell of fire had come upon them. Nebuchadnezzar answered and said, "Blessed be the God of Shadrach, Meshach, and Abednego, who has sent his angel and delivered his servants, who trusted in him, and set aside the king's command, and yielded up their bodies rather than serve and worship any god except their own God. Daniel 3:26-28

They wouldn't have had to be sincere in bowing before the king's idol, to save their own lives. Just the motion would have sufficed. Still, they passed. They would worship no other god but God. Instead of recanting, they witnessed. Nebuchadnezzar hadn't been expecting takers when he promised a fiery furnace for any who declined to worship the 90-foot image he had set up. Sane folks don't throw away their lives to maintain some religious convictions. Do they?

We're living in a day when non-negotiable convictions mark us an "extremist." While the cost of convictions is sometimes high, the cost of compromise is that no one ever sees that we have any convictions. Many reason that it's better to offend God, then get forgiveness, than to offend man, then get persecuted. What is lost when we compromise to save ourselves? Our testimony. The cost of compromise? We lose the opportunity to show where God ranks in our lives.

What if Shadrach, Meshach and Abednego had buckled under? They would have saved their lives and lost their witness. What happened when they didn't compromise? They saved their witness—and God saved their lives. He even sent someone "like a son of the gods" to walk with them in the furnace!

The cost of obedience to God is high; always has been. The cost of compromise? Higher. Compromise costs us the opportunity to show how deep our commitment to God really is. Compromise costs us our witness.

What did Nebuchadnezzar notice? A God who would come through and rescue men who *"yielded up their bodies rather than serve and worship any god except their own God."* This is a God we can afford to serve without compromise.

The Bottom Line: The cost of compromise is our witness. Boldly stand for God.

DAY 211

The Answer is Prayer

Is anyone among you suffering? Let him pray. Is anyone cheerful? Let him sing praise. Is anyone among you sick? Let him call for the elders of the church, and let them pray over him, anointing him with oil in the name of the Lord. And the prayer of faith will save the one who is sick, and the Lord will raise him up. And if he has committed sins, he will be forgiven. Therefore, confess your sins to one another and pray for one another, that you may be healed. The prayer of a righteous person has great power as it is working. Elijah was a man with a nature like ours, and he prayed fervently that it might not rain, and for three years and six months it did not rain on the earth. Then he prayed again, and heaven gave rain, and the earth bore its fruit.
James 5:13-18

Suffering? Pray. Cheerful? Sing your prayer. Sick? Call the elders and have them pray. Feeling convicted? Confess your sins to one another and pray. Need a drought to prime your nation for revival and remind them God is in charge? Pray. There seems to be a pattern here.

Why is the answer always "Pray"?Because when we pray, we are in contact with a God who can do absolutely anything, who hears us, loves us, and loves to answer prayer. In every situation, the best place to start is prayer. Like "stop, drop and roll," it's good to make it automatic.

As a youngster, I learned to "stop, drop and pray" at the first sign of a need. It just makes sense—when we have Someone available who knows everything, can do anything and who loves us more than we love ourselves, why would we not go to Him, first? He always knows what to do. He's big enough to handle every problem we'll ever face. He loves us, listens, understands perfectly. It makes prayer one of the grandest privileges available to humankind. When it becomes second nature to us, we're on our way to a fantastic life, guided by God.

Two days ago, a pastor friend of mine was in a situation so grim they put him in a Lear jet and got him to a hospital nearly 1500 miles away. Many prayers. As they were preparing to take him to surgery, there was a sudden, noticeable improvement in his appearance. The pastor/patient suddenly sat up and requested everyone to hold hands and pray. He asked a friend to lead in prayer as the whole medical team held hands around his bed. The procedure was completely successful. Today, I joked with him about leading the doctors and nurses in devotions. He looks really good. Prayer is the answer.

The Bottom Line: The answer to every situation begins with prayer.

Lessons in Faith

It was an adventure in faith for my family and me. With trepidation, but with assurance that this was what God wanted me to do, I resigned an 11-year pastorate, with the security that represented in finances, identity and relationships, and began relying on whatever people sent in the mail, for my income. It was a season of renewal. And it was like being in some kind of school—I feel the Lord taught me some tremendous lessons in life during the (exactly) six years I now look back on as "The Season of Faith." Here are a few of them.

1. **God will provide, just like I knew He would.**
   It's a totally different experience to rely on faith instead of a paycheck. Month after month, we would bring the pile of bills before God, ask for His provision, then see it supplied, most often as people were led to donate to Servant Connection. For those six years, we subsisted on answers to prayer. I knew God would provide, if I would obey His leading. Faith works, when it's obedience. (And it doesn't, if our "faith" is merely laziness).
2. **I have a wonderful family.**
   I already knew that, but their willingness to endure this faith adventure is tribute to the depth of their love and commitment to God and to me. I am forever grateful. Only God knows how hard it was, for each of them.
3. **Ministry is a lot more fun when you're doing it to please God rather than to please people.**
   There is a wonderful freedom in knowing that every assignment is an assignment from God. Living by faith is hard, but it's also simple, in that we're only trying to please one person, and the only thing we have to do is obey Him.
4. **Ministry has been so much more fun since I discovered God wanted me to focus on just one thing: Loving the people He has placed in my life.**
   Probably the biggest change in ministry, for me, was to realize my first assignment is to love people, in the ways that feel like love, to them. It's fun, it's effective, fulfilling, it pleases God. "Love these people and make them feel loved" may be the biggest ministry lesson I've ever learned. Thank you, God, for these lessons and many more; for my family; for providing. I love you.

The Bottom Line: God wants to teach us lessons in faith, if we are willing to obey.

DAY 213

Walking Lips

A fool's lips walk into a fight,
and his mouth invites a beating.
A fool's mouth is his ruin,
and his lips are a snare to his soul.
The words of a whisperer are like delicious morsels;
they go down into the inner parts of the body.

Proverbs 18:6-8

A fool's lips walk into a fight, and his mouth invites a beating. What a word picture! Lips stride into a surly ring of chips on shoulders, who need little provocation to pound whatever irritates them. The fool would have gone untouched, had he left them alone. Instead, *his mouth invites a beating*—and the other party obliges. *A fool's mouth is his ruin, and his lips are a snare to his soul.*

Why do fools invite conflict? What is it about fools which causes them to not just participate in all available fights, but instigate them, if no interesting fights are available? There just seems to be some kind of magnetic attraction for fools toward conflict. Do fools hate peace? Apparently so. At least peace is usually short-lived when fools are present.

I've never met someone who aspired to be a fool, though I've known a great many people whose consistent actions had achieved for them that rank. Nobody wants to be a fool, no one desires to wreck their life through saying and doing stupid things. So why is it that it so often works out that way?

One answer is in the verse which follows: *The words of a whisperer are like delicious morsels; they go down into the inner parts of the body.* There are brash fools and quiet ones. Brash ones are easily picked out, irritating even their friends and family. *Especially* their friends and family. Loud, obnoxious fools will usually bear a fool's lot in life, familiar with unemployment, relationship problems, etc., etc. Non-fools sometimes suffer the same, but malignant-tongued fools experience this stuff with predictable regularity. But that's only one kind of fool.

Another sort is quiet, discreet. In fact, the mark of this fool is not "Make my day" speeches inviting beatings and public humiliation, but quiet whispers which leave a trail of destruction all the way to the soul.

No one longs to be a fool. But if we don't control our lips, that will be our fate. The beatings taken and hurts caused will be traceable to unrestrained lips.

The Bottom Line: Unrestrained lips are going to bring nothing but hurt and trouble.

DAY 214

Bringin' 'Em Back

My brothers, if anyone among you wanders from the truth and someone brings him back, let him know that whoever brings back a sinner from his wandering will save his soul from death and will cover a multitude of sins. James 5:19-20

Notice that it says *"wanders from the truth."* People usually don't just dive into sin all at once, especially if they've had a relationship with Jesus Christ; they wander. Things happen which shake their faith, they start to have doubts, Satan fills their path with just the right people and situations to exploit their vulnerabilities, and pretty soon they're a long ways from God and have sort of forgotten the way back. Enter: A rescuer. Somebody (often Mom or another family member) isn't about to let this person trash their lives on the rocks of sin, so they go after them. No matter how far they've strayed, the rescuer will search for the wanderer, find them, and do everything in their power to reestablish the person in the path of righteousness.

Not all efforts are successful, but I have a great admiration for those stubborn souls who won't accept no for an answer, sometimes dragging their relatives to safety in a manner reminiscent of the angels pulling Lot out of Sodom. It's best to lure them back to spiritual sanity with love, of course, but sometimes there's not time for that, and sometimes hardheaded folks need someone who loves them enough to keep kicking them in the hindquarters until they feel inspired to get off the railroad tracks.

God's Word tells us there's a reward for those who bring people back: We are helping to save their soul from death! That's worth the effort! Not only that, but a *bunch* of sins are either prevented or covered when we rescue the wandering.

Evangelism has gotten really short shrift in the Church in America during the past several decades. It seems that many Christians have become much more preoccupied with their own comfort than the eternal destiny of the people around them. The culture has, meanwhile, become increasingly intolerant of those who believe in only one way to heaven—through Jesus Christ. Will we be content to remain silent in our spiritual ghettos as Satan lures souls we love toward death? If we love people like Christ loves them, we'll do whatever it takes to see them saved. Jesus stopped at nothing to bring salvation to the world. We do well to follow His example.

The Bottom Line: Bringing back spiritual wanderers is worth whatever it takes.

DAY 215

Seismic Prayer

And when they had prayed, the place in which they were gathered together was shaken, and they were all filled with the Holy Spirit and continued to speak the word of God with boldness. Acts 4:31

All across the Northwest, people were screaming at their televisions. We watched in wonderful disbelief as Seattle running back MarShawn Lynch broke tackle after tackle (8!), and went 67 yards to get into the end zone to help the Seahawks advance in the NFL playoffs (January 8, 2011). The home crowd at the stadium, known as "The 12th Man," outdid everyone in enthusiasm, though. As Lynch drove toward the end zone, shoving would-be tacklers out of his way, the geological service actually registered seismic activity below the field! I saw the graph. The cheering of the crowd generated a small earthquake. Now, that's enthusiasm!

The kind of exuberance associated with sports events is uncommon in prayer meetings, but there are at least two recorded instances of seismic prayer in the New Testament. The first is in Acts 4, when the Early Christians, following the healing of a lame man, were jailed and threatened by the authorities to either shut up about Jesus, or else! Prudent people would have complied, making sure they didn't further upset people with the power to ruin lives.

These weren't prudent people. They were disciples of Jesus Christ, completely sold out to Him, willing to pay any price to promote Jesus. The threats bounced off like those tacklers bounced off MarShawn Lynch. The Church came together, and they prayed for boldness. And got it. *And when they had prayed, the place in which they were gathered together was shaken, and they were all filled with the Holy Spirit and continued to speak the word of God with boldness.* It was seismic prayer.

That's not the only time God shook a building housing His praying servants. In Acts 16 is another account. Paul and Silas, pioneer missionaries, had been rewarded for their healing ministry by a severe beating, and imprisonment. They even got the "stocks," meaning they were unable to so much as move about in the inner prison. There was every excuse to be downtrodden, angry and bitter, but these two saints took a different tack: They prayed and sang praise to God. The prisoners, the jailer, God, were all listening. God shook the jail until everyone's chains fell off. Instead of escaping, the apostles evangelized. The church in Philippi was born that night. Seismic prayer and praise.

The Bottom Line: There is true power in prayer and praise.

DAY 216

The Hard Life of a Slacker

Whoever is slack in his work
is a brother to him who destroys.

Proverbs 18:9

The "Protestant work ethic" is real. Sure, I know it's not mentioned in the Bible as such, Protestants not being around, yet, but when it comes to having proof texts for a philosophy which puts hard work up close to godliness, there are plenty.

I've always known the Protestant work ethic was real, because I grew up surrounded with it. Not just my family or our fellow farmer neighbors—the whole state (South Dakota)! The only folks who didn't work in South Dakota resided in the graveyard, or so it seemed. It would be about the worst state I can think of to panhandle with a sign saying, "Will work for food." Supposing you found one of the few places in South Dakota where people had to stop, rather than driving by you, the first problem would be trying to survive the weather until an actual vehicle came your way. Even then, chances are, it would contain a farmer or someone else who could always use all the help they could get. A beat-up pickup truck would pull over, and instead of handing you a dollar, the guy in the baseball cap would just say, "Get in," then cart you off to his farm to treat you to all the manual labor you ever wanted until dark. He'd pay you with a good home-cooked meal and minimum wage. Well, you said you'd work for food! For some reason, I've never seen a single person use that fund-raising tactic in South Dakota.

It's a great state, if you want to work, and it cranks out notoriously good workers—even those of us who were not innately motivated to begin with, and just caved under the pressure.

Incentive to work hard and do a good job is not merely a remnant of agrarian society with strong Scandinavian influence; it goes way back to the Bible, and to a God who not only invented work, but practices it. Not only that, but everything our God does is good. That means His children should not accept shoddy, half-hearted efforts from themselves, and "call it good," when it was nowhere close and we know it. *Whoever is slack in his work is a brother to him who destroys.* We have a high standard to maintain! It's the standard of our God, who does all things well. Quality work is expected of God's children. It's a part of our identity, even if God doesn't hail from South Dakota. He made South Dakota. And everything God made is good.

The Bottom Line: Doing our best in work is part of our identity and our worship.

DAY 217

Belshazzar's Last Night

"And you his son, Belshazzar, have not humbled your heart, though you knew all this, but you have lifted up yourself against the Lord of heaven. And the vessels of his house have been brought in before you, and you and your lords, your wives, and your concubines have drunk wine from them. And you have praised the gods of silver and gold, of bronze, iron, wood, and stone, which do not see or hear or know, but the God in whose hand is your breath, and whose are all your ways, you have not honored." Daniel 5:22-23

It was Belshazzar's last night.

He was terrified of a mystical hand which appeared and wrote on his palace wall, yet he hadn't even been nervous about desecrating the vessels taken from God's Temple in Jerusalem. Nor had the difficult lessons learned by Nebuchadnezzar made any lasting impression on the heir to the throne. Once Belshazzar was in charge, people like Daniel had been quickly discarded and forgotten. Wisdom was out, partying was in. The new king was living it up, in an in-your-face banquet designed to glorify Hedonism and ridicule God. It wasn't God who ended up scared.

Once again, Daniel was summoned to solve a mystery. The last time, when he had delivered God's message to Nebuchadnezzar, Daniel had used the gentle approach; in dealing with the foolish son, there was no need for "gentle." Fools only understand blunt. Daniel read the writing on the wall like a jury foreman reading off a guilty verdict:*This is the interpretation of the matter: MENE, God has numbered the days of your kingdom and brought it to an end; TEKEL, you have been weighed in the balances and found wanting; PERES, your kingdom is divided and given to the Medes and Persians."* (Daniel 5:26-28)

Numbered, weighed, divided. The message was delivered, the king dutifully robed and honored Daniel, and before breakfast the king who had deliberately dishonored God had been killed and replaced.

Why bother with a warning? It obviously didn't change Belshazzar's destiny. He just died scared instead of haughty. Warnings don't change foolish minds, anyway. They do a lot of good, however, for those wise enough to heed them and remember that honoring the world and dishonoring God are a deadly combination. Sending lone hands to write on walls? Swapping out kings? It's all easy for the real King. Honor Him.

The Bottom Line: Let's learn from the lesson of Belshazzar and honor the real King.

DAY 218

Skating with a Witch

Before destruction a man's heart is haughty,
but humility comes before honor.

Proverbs 18:12

A roller skating party marked the end of our school years, back when I was in grade school. The public school I attended was the usual mishmash of misfits, with a couple of them dubbed "cool" and everyone else an "also-ran" or a "never-mind." At the bottom of the pecking order for the girls was a quiet, long-haired girl named Sherry, who, for whatever reason, had been labeled a "witch." Sherry was completely lacking in both "witch" qualities and social status. Her "germs" were passed from person to person with more than usual glee.

It was midway through the year-end skating party when I paused for a break from skating with several female classmates. I looked around and discovered myself alone with Sherry. She got right to the point. "Hey Ness, wanta skate with a witch?" I took half a second to gauge what being seen skating with Sherry would do to my already low social ranking, and immediately decided to save myself, at the cost of what little was left of her self-esteem.

"I'm kind of tired, right now." She understood completely. She nodded knowingly and skated off and out of my life. I never saw her again. If I had life to live over again, I'd love to skate with a witch.

But would I? One of the hazards of listening to God is that we hear what we don't want to hear. This morning, God reminded me of the long-ago episode with Sherry, plus similar missed opportunities to bless people through the years. My ego was already deflating, when God got to the point.

Dave, I love you, but you're not better than anybody else. You're also not inferior to anybody else. I love all of my children, including the weird ones. I love the ones with stuff "wrong" with them. I love the ones who seem brilliant. I love my shy kids and my proud kids (although I often bring down their pride so it doesn't ruin them). Dave, you're proud. You've been proud of your intellect, proud of your heritage, proud of your relationship with me, as if that made you special and somehow better than your brothers and sisters who struggle, spiritually.

Listen to me: If you did it to the least of one of these my children, you did it to me. If you hurt my kid, you just hurt me. If you loved my kid, you just loved me. These are all my kids.

The Bottom Line: Whatever we do is as unto Him.

DAY 219

Devoted to Prayer

Then they returned to Jerusalem from the mount called Olivet, which is near Jerusalem, a Sabbath day's journey away. And when they had entered, they went up to the upper room, where they were staying, Peter and John and James and Andrew, Philip and Thomas, Bartholomew and Matthew, James the son of Alphaeus and Simon the Zealot and Judas the son of James. All these with one accord were devoting themselves to prayer, together with the women and Mary the mother of Jesus, and his brothers. Acts 1:12-14

The beginning of spiritual transformation is always prayer, isn't it? The Church in America needs, *desperately needs*, to devote itself to prayer, instead of devoting itself to itself. We also need the unity corporate humility brings.

They had it all, in the first chapter of Acts. It was what prepared them for the second chapter of Acts. Jesus had not suggested, but commanded them to wait in Jerusalem, until they were filled with power. When people wait on God, things happen! (Isaiah 40:31)

The disciples were obediently waiting in the upper room. They were together. They were all there for the same reason. There was a spirit of humility present which had oft been absent during the heady days of Jesus' earthly ministry, when there was a constant contest for MVD ("Most Valuable Disciple").

The contest was over. It had ended on a horrible night when they had all pledged total allegiance to Jesus, then followed it up by scattering like pigeons into the night, as He was arrested. There is no way to describe the relief they must have felt to see a resurrected Lord, following Jesus' crucifixion and death! They had seen the Risen Christ over a forty-day period. Finally, He had commanded them to wait in Jerusalem, promised the Holy Spirit and promised they would be witnesses everywhere, then ascended into heaven as they looked on.

What did they do, after angels promised Jesus would return, so they might as well get on with it? They obeyed. They went and waited. What did they do while waiting? *All these with one accord were devoting themselves to prayer,...*

Wouldn't that be a good idea for the modern-day Church? Instead of devoting ourselves to the latest church growth gimmick, what if we devoted ourselves to prayer? Would we have a better chance of being filled with the Spirit? Would we have a better shot at changing the world, if we focused on what Jesus was saying to us, instead of what the latest best-selling author is promoting?

The Bottom Line: The Early Church devoted themselves to prayer. Good idea.

DAY 220

Together

When the day of Pentecost arrived, they were all together in one place.

Acts 2:1

They were all together in one place. It was vital for the disciples to be physically together, not scattered all over, for the coming of the Holy Spirit. Certain events require us to be physically together, or they won't happen. This was such an event. Under Jesus' direct orders, they stayed together.

The meeting on Pentecost was without a human agenda. God planned the whole thing from start to finish! They were just together in a house, when the Holy Spirit came upon them with tongues of fire and the sound of a violent wind. The sound drew a multitude, the Spirit did the preaching, and people heard about the mighty works of God in their own language. It was all from God. None of it was from man. That's why I think it's a mistake to try to duplicate what God has done in the past, when the original group didn't even ask Him to do that! What is *not* a mistake is to wait on God, together, in expectation. (That is, if we have been told to wait. If we've been told to "go," it's a mistake to wait.)

I don't think we've outgrown "together." We don't need another Pentecost, but we do need something we know is from God, not man. The manmade attempts to recreate Pentecost are disappointing. Any glory is quickly grabbed and branded with someone's peculiar theology, as proof of "the right doctrine." Competition is fierce for who has a corner on the Holy Spirit. Highlighted differences succeed in keeping the Church divided and powerless. Meanwhile, there's a bunch of power in "together." So what if being together with other believers makes some think we've gone over to the Dark Side. Anytime folks are united in humble worship of Jesus, good stuff happens.

We need to be together—not just the folks who wear the same denominational colors, but believers of all colors, backgrounds and persuasions. We need meetings where it's only Jesus who is in charge, rather than a band, prophet or faith healer looking for a big break. So what if there's only 120 of us instead of thousands! Were they bummed at Pentecost because more people weren't there? It hardly reads like a disappointment!

Let's focus on Jesus. Let's work on being together—not just bodies under the same roof, but humbled believers under the same God. Whatever happens will not be a disappointment.

The Bottom Line: Together as believers, no agenda but God's... What could happen?

DAY 221

Willing to Wait

And while staying with them he ordered them not to depart from Jerusalem, but to wait for the promise of the Father, which, he said, "you heard from me; for John baptized with water, but you will be baptized with the Holy Spirit not many days from now." Acts 1:4-5

When the day of Pentecost arrived, they were all together in one place. Acts 2:1

Are we willing to put our lives on hold, in order to wait on Jesus? I'm not seeing many people who appear willing to do that. In a way, I did it, several years ago, but it also took me a year before I was ready to take that jump!

Are we willing to be together with others for the sake of the Master? That includes those people who rub us in all the wrong ways. That means we're together, identified as being "one of them" (even though we're not) with those who hold very different views from ourselves, who are on the opposite end of the spectrum politically, theologically, socially. Are we willing to lay aside our doctrinal and traditional distinctive's, in order to humble ourselves and worship with others, as a way to honor Christ?

We need to humble ourselves and come together, in the name of Jesus. We need to keep our hands off God's glory, and not worry too much when somebody else is grabbing it, but not follow them, either. Jesus is the Head of the Church.

I see many Christians hungry for "Pentecost." They long to see the power of God, they want to see results, and they're willing to jump on a plane and go almost anywhere in search of God's power. But some want to bring back the Holy Spirit as a souvenir. They want power to display to their friends and enemies. There is a hunger for power, but there isn't so much hunger for God, for an intimacy that puts us down on our faces before Him in recognition of our own weakness. There's not much humility, especially in the American Church. It doesn't have to stay that way, though. We can humble ourselves, or God can do it for us—either way, humility is eventually coming to us! I'm thinking the "sooner-rather-than-later, I'll-humble-myself-so-you-don't-have-to-do-it-for-me" philosophy is the best approach.

There needs to be an army of disciples who are sold out for Christ, who would do absolutely anything for Him, who are also willing to sit on the bench for 40 years, if that's what's required of them. We need to be that army. If we were, I don't think we would have to worry about God wasting us!

The Bottom Line: Are we willing to wait on God and do it His way?

DAY 222

Deadly Devotions

When Daniel knew that the document had been signed, he went to his house where he had windows in his upper chamber open toward Jerusalem. He got down on his knees three times a day and prayed and gave thanks before his God, as he had done previously. Then these men came by agreement and found Daniel making petition and plea before his God. Daniel 6:10-11

The unalterable document awarded the lions' den for anyone who chose not to observe King Darius Month, which meant refraining from praying to anyone but the king for thirty days. Darius had thought it was a nice touch, until he discovered, too late, that the entire purpose of this decree had been to deprive him of his most trusted administrator, Daniel.

What prompted the decree was the prospect among jealous rivals of Daniel's promotion over them. Ordinary bosses could be bribed, blackmailed or whatever if they got out of hand; Daniel was so squeaky clean, competent and nice that they all knew their only chance of taking him down was to arrange a scenario in which he would have to choose between his faith and something else. They were fairly certain he would choose his faith. They were right.

Daniel's spiritual habits were so disciplined and predictable that when the neighbors heard Daniel praying they knew it must be time to eat! Morning, noon and night, every day, Daniel had his devotions, on his knees, at the window facing Jerusalem. That's the way he did it before the decree was signed. And after.

Daniel's devotional habits gave his enemies what they wanted. When they gleefully brought the news to the king of just who had openly defied his law, Daniel wasn't the only one fasting and praying—so was the king! Darius fasted all night, and instead of praying to himself, as the law required, Darius decided to try Daniel's God. *"May your God, whom you serve continually, deliver you!" he said to Daniel* (Daniel 6:16). Sounds like a prayer to me.

We know how the story turned out. God did deliver Daniel, which very much impressed the king. The lions munched on Daniel's enemies. Having his devotions was supposed to get Daniel killed; instead, it was his persecutors who were destroyed because Daniel went ahead and had his devotions.

The way the world attempts to eliminate the competition is through deceit and treachery. The way of the godly in dealing with rivals is through prayer. And God is more than adequate for dealing with all our foes, foreign and domestic.

The Bottom Line: The best way to deal with enemies is to have your devotions.

DAY 223

What Comes First

*Before destruction a man's heart is haughty,
but humility comes before honor.*

Proverbs 18:12

"Which came first, the chicken or the egg?" goes the old question. That one and its multiplied variations have been good for many an argument, but the Bible specifically weighs in on a more weighty subject, here: Which one comes first, humility or honor? The Bible's answer: Humility comes first, then honor.

The Superbowl is never an exercise in humility; it would be closer to a national pride-fest. Yet, watching an interview of a member of the winning team yesterday, I watched him twice give glory to God, rather than himself. Hmm. *Humility comes before honor.* It also comes after honor. Kind of like an "honor sandwich."

Many folks are so hungry for honor of any kind that they figure they'd better grab it for themselves while they can. A wise farmer friend whom I loved with all my heart used to start chirping, "Toot! Toot!" whenever he heard me or anyone else boasting. If we persisted in haughtiness, he would repeat the routine until we stopped and asked what was going on. To which Gib would reply, "Toot! Toot! I thought I heard someone tooting their own horn." The joking response was, "He that tooteth not his own horn, it shall not be tooted." He would grin, we would grin, and we'd shut up about our own greatness and go on to more humble topics. Every so often God just slides some great person like that into our lives.

Gib is in heaven, now. Everyone who knew him still misses him. He was one of the most humble people I ever knew, while being about the most talented person I ever knew, when it came to all things mechanical. His many friends treated him with an honor bordering on reverence. Humility first, then honor.

Those who bypass humility in order to gain honor nearly always fall short. And the haughtier the heart, the surer the destruction. "Humility, then honor, then more humility" makes a great sandwich. When we're busily describing our own grandeur and we hear a voice from above saying, "Toot! Toot!" it's either Gib or God. "He that tootheth not his own horn, it shall not be tooted." If we refrain from tooting our own horn, God has a way of doing it for us. And when God toots someone's horn, it's very impressive.

The Bottom Line: *Humility comes before honor.*

A Heart for the Harvest

And with many other words he bore witness and continued to exhort them, saying, "Save yourselves from this crooked generation." So those who received his word were baptized, and there were added that day about three thousand souls. Acts 2:40-41

What we need in America are people with Jesus in their heart and souls on their mind, who are willing to plead with bewildered non-Christians, *"Save yourselves from this crooked generation!"* I'm not talking "church growth," which often translates into nothing more than finding nice folks to help make the building payments. I'm talking about believers who love people enough that they simply do whatever it takes to get them into the Kingdom of God and out of spiritual danger.

It's humbling, and even a bit irritating, to realize we have the same Holy Spirit poured out on the Early Church, yet so pitifully few results in comparison. Our casual approach to the Great Commission is reflected in our fruitfulness. In order to effectively evangelize, someone has to care—a lot. Not enough American Christians care all that much. So, we toss a few bucks in the plate to keep the professional Christians in beans and cable TV, and figure we've done our part. That's not how they looked at it in Acts! They had a heart for the harvest. Harvest is what they saw.

We should be witnesses and harvesters. We need to lift up our voice and address the world, like Peter. But first we need to get our souls right with God, be filled with His Spirit, and have something to say!

We either don't say anything, and leave the witnessing to preachers who usually only preach to church people, anyway, or we go blabbing about our latest ideas and idiosyncracies, without even bothering with the Holy Spirit. Either way, the world isn't getting much out of us that's helpful. It's why the Church is considered so irrelevant to the world.

Telling people God is good doesn't require a seminary degree! But we need to focus on Jesus, not ourselves , our institutions or doctrines. If we point people toward Jesus, we'll do O.K. Everything else ends up being a distraction.

Peter's approach was effective: Direct, yet compassionate. Solid answers. Glorifying Christ, not himself. Preaching, not to condemn people, but to help them.

When we have a heart for the harvest, we'll see one.

The Bottom Line: When we have a heart for the harvest, we'll see one.

DAY 225

God's Weed 'n' Feed

Or do you presume on the riches of his kindness and forbearance and patience, not knowing that God's kindness is meant to lead you to repentance? Romans 2:4

"You have heard that it was said, 'You shall love your neighbor and hate your enemy.' But I say to you, 'Love your enemies and pray for those who persecute you, so that you may be sons of your Father who is in heaven. For he makes his sun rise on the evil and on the good, and sends rain on the just and on the unjust. For if you love those who love you what reward do you have? Do not even the tax collectors do the same? And if you greet only your brothers, what more are you doing than others? Do not even the Gentiles do the same? You therefore must be perfect, as your heavenly Father is perfect." Matthew 5:43-48

Kindness is God's weed 'n' feed. It helps the grass, and kills the weeds. When you apply God's kindness to the lives of healthy people, it supercharges them, and they grow like crazy. When you apply God's kindness to angry, resentful people, it works its way into their lives, going all the way down to that root of bitterness. God's kindness can eliminate the bitterness and bring new life to the very core of a person's soul.

Apply kindness and love generously everywhere! The rest of the field will eat it up and flourish, and whenever it hits bitterness or anger, it acts like weedkiller and will follow it all the way to the root and change it. Isn't this what Jesus was saying in the Sermon on the Mount? When you encounter hostility, apply love! You'll win.

The Bottom Line: Kindness is God's weed 'n' feed.

DAY 226

Not Just for Quiet People

If one gives an answer before he hears,
it is his folly and shame.

Proverbs 18:13

Back to listening. Just about the time we think we're done with that one, God brings it back to us, doesn't He? Sometimes it's a gentle nudge in the right direction. This verse is the less subtle approach we occasionally need: If we pipe up with an answer before we've even bothered to listen, we're earning ourselves "folly and shame." It sounds as if God is rather serious about our developing this habit. "Listening—it's not just for quiet people."

In fact, it's the non-quiet people who always have plenty to say who are most in need of practicing the discipline of hearing first, speaking later. The fact that it's so hard to focus on listening for some people makes the resulting wisdom that much sweeter when the discipline is practiced.

There are a couple things which make listening before speaking harder than it sounds like it should be. One of them is knowledge. The more we know, the more we wish to let others benefit from our wisdom. I've noticed that with increased education seemingly comes decreased listening capacity. Some of the poorest listeners I've ever met are gifted public speakers or academics bearing credentials. They have a whole lot to say, but if we wish to tell them something, we'd best get to the point in three sentences or less, or we'll lose their attention long before we get the message out. I believe strongly in education, but the more knowledge we possess, the harder it seems to be to listen first and fully, prior to bestowing our wisdom upon others.

Another stumblingblock to listening? Familiarity (read "marriage"). The longer and better we've known someone, the more of a struggle it is to concentrate on what they're saying before giving our response. After all, we already know everything they're going to say. Right?! Often it seems that way, especially in a relationship measured in decades. All the more precious when we follow God's advice and show our dedication to them by listening to the same story for the umpteenth time, yet catching the slight variation this time through, and letting them know we truly love them—enough to listen. Nothing communicates genuine love quite like the patience to hear someone out—not because we're so fascinated with what they're saying or because it's all new—but simply because we love them.

The Bottom Line: Listen first, before speaking.

DAY 227

Worship and Witness

Now Peter and John were going up to the temple at the hour of prayer, the ninth hour. And a man lame from birth was being carried, whom they laid daily at the gate of the temple that is called the Beautiful Gate to ask alms of those entering the temple. Seeing Peter and John about to go into the temple, he asked to receive alms. And Peter directed his gaze at him, as did John, and said, "Look at us." And he fixed his attention on them, expecting to receive something from them. But Peter said, "I have no silver and gold, but what I do have I give to you. In the name of Jesus Christ of Nazareth, rise up and walk!" And he took him by the right hand and raised him up, and immediately his feet and ankles were made strong. And leaping up he stood and began to walk, and entered the temple with them, walking and leaping and praising God. And all the people saw him walking and praising God, and recognized him as the one who sat at the Beautiful Gate of the temple, asking for alms. And they were filled with wonder and amazement at what had happened to him. Acts 3:1-10

It seems to have been a habit. At "the hour of prayer, the ninth hour" (3 P.M.), Peter and John would make their way to the temple to worship together with the other believers. Corporate worship was a vital, daily part of their lives. Witnessing, too, seems to have been a daily part of their lives.

At the Beautiful Gate, they see a familiar face, a man lame from birth who is daily carted off to the temple to beg enough money to subsist another day. The routine question is asked of the disciples, but something is different, today. It's not just the fact that Peter is broke; today there is faith in the air. Today, it's not good enough to toss a coin in the general direction of the world's pain and call it good. Today is the day to engage. Lack of money turns into the opportunity for a miracle. Through the name of Jesus in the mouth of a willing disciple, a man unable to walk for his entire life is now doing laps around the temple, screaming out praises to God. The believer engages with the world in love, and the world is suddenly listening intently to the witness. And absolutely all the credit goes to Jesus.

It's not really that hard. Worship and witness should be a daily part of our lives. How else is this world going to learn that God is good? When we daily focus on obedience to Jesus, when we engage with our world in His name and with His love, we can expect displays of His power to be a regular occurrence.

The Bottom Line: Worship and witness should be a daily part of our lives.

DAY 228

The Blessing of Being Broke

Now Peter and John were going up to the temple at the hour of prayer, the ninth hour. And a man lame from birth was being carried, whom they laid daily at the gate of the temple that is called the Beautiful Gate to ask alms of those entering the temple. Seeing Peter and John about to go into the temple, he asked to receive alms. And Peter directed his gaze at him, as did John, and said, "Look at us." And he fixed his attention on them, expecting to receive something from them. But Peter said, "I have no silver and gold, but what I do have I give to you. In the name of Jesus Christ of Nazareth, rise up and walk!" Acts 3:1-6

So, what's so good about being broke?

What if Peter would have had money, that day? Wouldn't he have just tossed the lame man a coin, instead of healing him? Perhaps that very thing had happened on numerous occasions, before. But when we're "broke," it causes us to have to depend on God, instead of ourselves. When we're out of resources, we have no choice but to turn to God's resources. Then miracles happen.

Although we may be short on money from time to time, if we make daily worship part of our lifestyle, we're never short on the awareness of God's power. We can't get close to God without a sense of awe. Daily worship keeps us spiritually charged, like plugging in a cell phone keeps the thing operable. And neglecting worship has a similar effect to losing the cell phone charger.

Many people would complain they are too busy to worship, especially daily. So what do they do instead? They daily watch the news, or read the paper, or grab the news off the radio or internet. What is the result when we get the news on a *daily* basis? We have a continuing awareness of the world's problems.

I'm not saying we should boycott the news. I'm just asking, which one of those two things better equips us to deal with life—a continuing awareness of just how many problems are in the world and how big they are, or a continuing awareness of just how big and powerful and loving our God is? Just asking!

When we engage with the world with God's love, opportunities to witness sprout around us, continually. People come to *us*. When we genuinely care about people, Christian or not, *they* ask *us* about our God. And if it takes us being broke to switch over to God's resources instead of ours, in the end being broke can be a blessing.

The Bottom Line: Being broke can be good, if it causes us to switch to God's power.

DAY 229

The Friend at the Bottom

The poor use entreaties,
but the rich answer roughly.
A man of many companions may come to ruin,
but there is a friend who sticks closer than a brother.

Proverbs 18:23-24

After watching the Academy Awards, I went to bed thinking of how few "cool" people ever seem to need God—as long as they're cool. The fashionable few whose careers are currently peaking constitute the epitome of "cool," a worldwide audience hanging onto every syllable of the acceptance speech. Wardrobe choices for one night make or break careers and companies. Extravagance of every kind is assumed; kindness is not. That's often the way it works out, too. The rich and famous are not likely to also be kind and humble (which is why it's so delightful to find one who is!).

Our star-crazed culture is good at elevating people of low character to astonishing heights, then dropping them. Those touched with fame find they don't have to be courteous to get what they want—as long as they have enough money to afford it. The rules bend behind them as they saunter down the red carpet. Except when they don't. Repeat offenders sit in disbelief as they hear judges handing out the same penalties for crimes given to lesser mortals. Big contracts get canceled when the stench of the scandal finally outweighs the former appeal which made them enough money to think they could get away with it in the first place. It's a vicious circle.

A man of many companions may come to ruin. In fact, most do. The career, the "companions," the fans and money... all gone. The wise don't surrender their integrity in order to try to gain the top, so when the spotlight has moved on, they still have a life. The really wise humble themselves before the world does it for them. And the ones headed for eternal life are those who learn, sooner or later, that the best Friend they will ever have is the One awaiting them at the bottom. When "cool" and everything that went with it is gone, Jesus is willing to be a Friend and Savior, even to fallen stars. The sooner we figure out we can have an eternal-life-long Friend, the sooner we can know we never have to be alone.

The Bottom Line: Jesus is willing to be our Friend when no one else is interested.

DAY 230

One Heart and Soul

Now the full number of those who believed were of one heart and soul, and no one said that any of the things that belonged to him was his own, but they had everything in common. And with great power the apostles were giving their testimony to the resurrection of the Lord Jesus, and great grace was upon them all. There was not a needy person among them, for as many as were owners of lands or houses sold them and brought the proceeds of what was sold and laid it at the apostles' feet, and it was distributed to each as any had need. Thus Joseph, who was also called by the apostles Barnabas (which means son of encouragement), a Levite, a native of Cyprus, sold a field that belonged to him and brought the money and laid it at the apostles' feet.
Acts 4:32-37

The "every man for himself" philosophy of Christianity currently in vogue stinks. Jesus never intended for His Church to be a roving band of consumers seeking spiritual thrills without commitment to anything or anyone, but this has become the normal attitude, for many. I don't think God is going to require us to replicate the "commune" type of lifestyle in which the Early Church engaged, but if we would just wholly commit to Jesus and to some fellow believers, it would be a huge step in the right direction!

It's no accident that the verse which describes the unity of the Early Church and their commitment to one another is followed by one telling of the power of their testimony. Their unity *was* their testimony! *There was not a needy person among them.* That statement alone makes for a great witness!

There were heroes, but they were heroes of faith, commitment and generosity, like Barnabas, who already had the nickname "Son of Encouragement" when he sealed his reputation as an encourager by selling his land and giving all to the Church.

Maybe in these days we don't need to go as far as "commune," but could we at least do "community"?! We'll have some decent power in our witness again when we start taking care of the needy among us, and we commit to one another as an act of devotion to Christ. The Church will also appear to society as much more gracious than it currently does. The *"one heart and soul"* part, we really need to work on. I have a feeling God would help us, if we're interested. I have a feeling the world would be interested, if God helped us.

The Bottom Line: "One heart and soul" commitment makes a powerful witness.

DAY 231

Fortune Cookie Wisdom

Better is a poor person who walks in his integrity
than one who is crooked in speech and is a fool.
Desire without knowledge is not good,
and whoever makes haste with his feet misses his way.
When a man's folly brings his way to ruin,
his heart rages against the LORD.
Wealth brings many new friends,
but a poor man is deserted by his friend.
A false witness will not go unpunished,
and he who breathes out lies will not escape.
Many seek the favor of a generous man,
and everyone is a friend to a man who gives gifts.

Proverbs 19:1-6

The tidbits of wisdom which make up Proverbs sometimes remind me of fortune cookies. They are short, sweet, memorable. They require little explanation. They are general in nature, applying to everyone, so it doesn't matter who the reader is. Proverbs are "tidbits for today," little droplets of wisdom which can be carried in the soul. They are great little navigational aids, both practical and plain. God wants us to do more than just "get through" in life, so our kind Father has given us pocket sized instruction. Fortune cookies are a really pale substitute for wisdom-fortified Proverbs!

In the six little proverbs which begin Proverbs 19 we are reminded:

- Poverty is not a bad thing, if a person has integrity. Better that than riches and lies, and a foolish lifestyle!
- *Desire without knowledge is not good*—we need to figure out what we're doing—and it's easy to miss the way if we get in a hurry.
- People blame God for things which are their own fault. Don't.
- Wealth brings "friends" who are not; poverty reveals who our true friends are.
- God doesn't overlook lying and false testimony, even if others do.

There is a power in generosity and gift-giving which is real. We may as well use it to be a blessing to people.

The Bottom Line: God has made so much wisdom available to us!

DAY 232

Stirred Up

Daniel declared, "I saw in my vision by night, and behold, the four winds of heaven were stirring up the great sea. And four great beasts came up out of the sea, different from one another. Daniel 7:2-3

Does it seem like things are being stirred up? Past months have seen the overthrow of a long-time dictator, with another one on the ropes. Both of these nations (Egypt and Libya) border the Mediterranean Sea, which, if Daniel had ever seen a sea, would probably have been the only one. And while a case can be made that the vision Daniel saw in chapter 7 has long since been at least partially fulfilled with a succession of kingdoms which have come and gone on the earth, it certainly looks to me (and others) like it will be fulfilled once again, except this time, completely.

The clear references to things which are "end times" in the context of the vision (*"the court sat in judgment, and the books were opened,"* for example), make me think this is an "end time" prophecy to be fulfilled. Daniel is told at the end of the vision, *"These four great beasts are four kings who shall arise out of the earth. But the saints of the Most High shall receive the kingdom and possess the kingdom forever, forever and ever."* (Dan 7:17-18) The rest of the chapter describes an interpretation I can't see as anything other than "end times."

So, things are stirred up! But who is doing the stirring? Is it mankind, the workers uniting to overthrow tyranny? Is the stirring a result of conspiracy plans?

The stirring is from God. He's the One who is able to tell someone two millennia in advance exactly what will happen, even though the knowledge gives the poor guy a headache and he has no idea of the meaning of what he's writing down. God is the One who can stir up kingdoms as easily as a human might stir up a batch of cookies. God is the One who calls His shots with 100% accuracy from thousands of years away.

While it is of interest to us to know where we fit in prophecy's time-line, what ultimately matters is our relationship with the One who stirs it up, then brings it to eternal resolution. If we know Jesus, we're fine. If we don't have a relationship with Jesus Christ, we're not fine, no matter what else we think we know.

The Bottom Line: It's God who is doing the stirring. If we know Jesus, we're fine.

DAY 233

New Ways or Old?

Many believers these days are caught between old and new. Proponents of "new" methods often seek something more effective and relevant when it comes to church, while traditionalists grasp "the good old days," grieving changes they deem pointless and ill-informed. Both sides are trying to pursue Christ. Who is right?

We should pray, but we won't all get the same answer. Some have already been led out of traditional church settings into other types of fellowships which seem "new" to Americans, yet which may actually be closer to the Church in Acts. Others are in the process of seeking ways of living out the Christian faith in community with others that seem more faith-building and challenging than anything they've previously experienced. For still others, it is clear that the place God wants them to remain is within the realm of the established church system.

It all goes back to "Follow Jesus." Wherever He leads us will be right. His individual plan for our life will not necessarily be applied to everyone else who is sincerely trying to follow Him, so we're in need of much grace when it comes to accepting one another, both those in the traditional Church and those in the one sometimes termed "organic." (By "institutional Church" I'm talking about the organized, established Church with which most of us are familiar; by "organic Church" I'm referring to small fellowships of believers who gather for worship and community without many of the trappings of the institutional Church).

I don't think God wants everyone in the Church in America to abandon their buildings, denominations and traditions and go "organic." For the most part, traditional believers would find little comfort in the changes awaiting them in the "organic" Church. Plus, there are still a lot of building payments to make, back home in the established Church! And what of the thousands of trained church leaders who would have no clue how to adapt to a new structure, even if it was "older" or more biblical? For all those who love the established church structure and feel it's the most effective place in which to serve, please stay put! If we move into what is for us "uncharted" territory, it needs to be because God called us out. Otherwise, we're liable to be even more frustrated than before!

Contentment is key. We get contentment when we pray through about God's will for us, obey Him completely, then choose to be content wherever He puts us. If He leads us to remain in our present situation, we can choose to be content (or at least at peace) in it. If God leads us to something new, we trust and obey, then choose contentment. And we have grace for those God led to the other side.

The Bottom Line: God will show us what He wants us to do. We need lots of grace.

DAY 234

Team-mates with Different Instructions

Why would God lead people in different ways, when it comes to something as big as "institutional Church versus organic Church"? Because we are individuals, and He loves us!

There are people who fit the institutional Church like a glove. They love everything about it! Ministry is a delight to them. The church building is one of their favorite places. It all makes sense to them. They are very effective in ministering to people within this framework. Why would God want them to abandon something which has brought such joy to their lives, only to replace it with something frustrating and strange to them?

Then there's the other side. For a great many unbelievers, and even some believers who have grown up in the institutional Church, the Church has little appeal to them. Why? A lot of reasons, but the point is, *the institutional Church is not reaching them.* They may tolerate what we do in the buildings with the steeples on top, but it is of no interest to them. Something much more likely to get their attention is the thought of a fellowship of people committed to each other, who are sincerely trying to find the answers to spiritual questions, but without the authoritative setting and some of the turn-offs they associate with the institutional Church.

We need to apply maximum grace to those who sense God leading them into serving Him in smaller, less organized settings, which may not look or feel very much like "church" to those of us who have spent our entire lives in the traditional setting. I also want to strongly caution those in leadership to not take away from people the things they have long loved, which in their minds constitutes "church," replace them with substitutes completely foreign to them, and expect them to like it! The end result is pretty predictable: *Nobody* will like it, and the lost aren't attracted to this train wreck, either.

Here's my summary: We should stay in the institutional Church unless God leads us out of it. We should follow Jesus wherever He leads, even if it's unfamiliar territory. We should apply lots of grace to everyone, without judging them. We should *pray!* And we should try not to react against things we don't like—God may be using them to bring people to Him. We need to remember that all of us who love Jesus are on the same team. We should ask God where He wants us to play, then choose to be content there, without questioning the spirituality of our team-mates who received different instructions from our Lord.

The Bottom Line: We should ask God where He wants us, follow Him, be content.

DAY 235

What Really Changes Society

But the high priest rose up, and all who were with him (that is, the party of the Sadducees), and filled with jealousy they arrested the apostles and put them in the public prison. Acts 5:17-18

They never like it. Unless they're John the Baptist or the same caliber, the religious leaders go jealous every time. Those in power like to stay in power.

The Sadducees tried to quarantine the Church into remission. It didn't work. The believers chose God over men. It got them jail time and revival.

Because America is a republic, in theory we get whatever we want if we get a majority and elect the right people. In practice, this means we spend a lot of energy trying to get "our" people elected, which usually results in disappointment, even if we win. Genuinely good politicians are hamstrung because they need the cooperation of a majority in all branches of government in order to do much.

The apostles skipped the whole thing. I'm sure they would have faithfully voted, had they been handed a democracy, but since they had (corrupt) government not of their choosing, they just lived with it or ignored it, as the case might be, and served Jesus without putting any trust in government as an agent for societal change. In that respect, it was a blessing that they didn't have a vote! It made it so they didn't waste any time on trying to change the system; they just changed people's hearts, one by one (which eventually changed the entire system).

Here's what I think needs to happen in America. I think believers should be more involved than ever in politics, at every level of government. I think Christians who are elected should focus on serving the people, with a strong emphasis on integrity and serving God, with the assumption that they'll only do this for one term, and with little or no effort toward getting re-elected. I think believers should vote their conscience and have the highest level of voter participation in society. *Meanwhile,* we put our hope *fully* in Jesus Christ, without illusions of political change being the solution.

What do we do? Pray, then vote. Be willing to run for public office, if directed by the Holy Spirit. If elected, focus on serving the people more than on gaining political power or being re-elected. Serve God without waiting for any kind of governmental change or even ecclesiastical change to grant "permission" to do what you know God has called you to do. Be willing to go to jail rather than disobey God. Obey God, no matter what. That's what really changes society.

The Bottom Line: Obeying God is what really changes society.

DAY 236

To Keep Us From Being Ineffective

For this very reason, make every effort to supplement your faith with virtue, and virtue with knowledge, and knowledge with self-control, and self-control with steadfastness, and steadfastness with godliness, and godliness with brotherly affection, and brotherly affection with love. For if these qualities are yours and are increasing, they keep you from being ineffective or unfruitful in the knowledge of our Lord Jesus Christ. For whoever lacks these qualities is so nearsighted that he is blind, having forgotten that he was cleansed from his former sins. Therefore, brothers, be all the more diligent to make your calling and election sure, for if you practice these qualities you will never fall.
2 Peter 1:5-10

I've been trying to figure out why the church in America is so ineffective—maybe this passage is a key. Actually, when I look at the list, many American Christians don't seem to possess much of any of these traits! No wonder we're ineffective!

What qualities? Faith, virtue, knowledge, self-control, steadfastness, godliness, brotherly affection and love. Peter arranges them like building blocks. This passage makes me think of a "faith pyramid."

It starts with faith. Regrettably, this is also where it ends for some Christians—they have a little bit of faith, just enough to feel "saved"—and they stop there. Some cling to their theology as justification for not trying too hard to act like a Christian; it's all about "believing" you are one. Wouldn't want anyone trying to work their way into heaven, you know! Um... so that means we're more spiritual if we never attempt anything which could be confused with "work"? Not according to Peter.

Peter says we are to supplement our faith with virtue. Then we add knowledge to the virtue. We add self-control to the knowledge. Steadfastness is added to self-control. Godliness is added to steadfastness. Brotherly affection is next. Last of all, we add love—not because it's least important, but because without a good foundation, there won't be much of it, nor will it endure.

Why are we so often ineffective? Maybe because we either stop at a little faith and don't go on, or we presume that the love we're supposed to have is automatic, and we can dispense with the gritty things like self-control and steadfastness, and still make it happen. Let's face it. God knows how to build stuff. Including our faith. He knows how to keep us from being ineffective.

The Bottom Line: God's list will keep us from being ineffective, if we build His way.

DAY 237

TV Discipleship

How would it feel to pay out a fortune for a 30-second Superbowl commercial, only to find that's when a great many viewers chose to take a bathroom break? If historians ever needed to know exactly when commercials were played during a Superbowl broadcast, all they would need to do is look at water usage records during the game. Every commercial break would show a spike. So, why is television commercial time worth millions? Influence.

Television is a daily, constant influence on our lives. Even those who have chosen to live without television still find themselves influenced by a society around them who watch it. It's hard to abstain from TV. I know. I've tried it.

But what if television were only available two hours a week? Not two hours of our choosing, either, but two hours chosen by someone else, and without benefit of any recording devices to make it fit our schedule. Let's say TV was only available for a couple hours, back to back, in the morning on a weekend. And then, when we did turn it on, only one channel was available: The pitiful, local cable channel, the one with no budget. What if it cost us the same as we're currently paying for cable TV with hundreds of choices, but instead of multi-million dollar productions featuring highly paid professional actors, all we got were the re-broadcasts of Winter Holiday programs of various local schools, and things on that order? Would we blow the family budget on a large screen TV, if all we got was school programs and city council meetings, for two hours a week?!

Probably not. If this were the TV situation in America, how much influence would television have on American society?

Nothing like it is, now! If all we could get on television was two hours a week of low-budget local cable, would we even bother with it? And if we did watch it, would it dramatically affect the rest of our lives?

I've just described the influence of the Church in America.

The majority of Americans have checked out, when it comes to church. They are as interested in it, and it has about as much influence on their lives, as a budget local cable TV show, available for a couple hours on Sunday mornings. Even when they do stumble across it, they just go on. The Church has little to no influence on their lives. They don't think about church, they don't wonder about it—it just has nothing to do with their lives. Influence? It doesn't even register.

What's the answer? Daily discipleship. In order to influence society, we need to serve Jesus all the time, not just a couple hours on Sunday morning.

The Bottom Line: When Christianity permeates our lives, then we have influence.

DAY 238

Full-time Influence

These days, the "faithful" are considered to be those present when the church doors are open. Two hours on Sunday morning, maybe even another hour or two on Sunday night or Wednesday night, or in a small group. The faithful attenders are regarded as deeply committed participants by the church.

But what if that's it? Two or three hours a week, faithfully attending religious services, and then you're done? What will be the influence of church on our lives, if it's two hours a week?

It will probably be noticeable, but not all that much. Right? If that's all it is—a couple hours put in every week, but that's where it stops? Kind of like the influence of a couple hours a week of one lonely local cable program on TV, vs non-stop programming on hundreds of channels, available to everybody.

There are two messages I'm getting out of the comparison between church influence and television influence:

1. Unless Christianity is something that is a constant part of the lives of Christians, all of the time, everywhere they go, we have almost no influence on the society around us, and we are only kidding ourselves if we think we do!
2. Unless Christianity is what drives our daily life, spending several hours a week in a church building is not going to have a really big impact on our life, or who we are as a person.

I've been re-reading the book of Acts, in the Bible. Christianity for them was not something they practiced on weekends; it was every day! And the Early Church had *daily results, too!* The tendency among American Christians is to come together once a week, with a very minimal commitment to one another, yet expect to see the same results the Early Church got when they met every day, with a huge commitment to one another!

It's not happening. *Weekly* discipleship is (A) not going to change the world, and (B) not going to produce the kind of Christians who influence others toward Christ. The difficult truth is, "weekly" disciples are "weakly" disciples, and discipleship is a daily deal; otherwise, it's not discipleship. Christ never called followers to part-time service. It was "Follow me"... as in, full-time, and forever.

The Bottom Line: Full-time influence requires full-time discipleship.

DAY 239

Run for the...Temple?

But during the night an angel of the Lord opened the prison doors and brought them out, and said, "Go and stand in the temple and speak to the people all the words of this Life." And when they heard this, they entered the temple at daybreak and began to teach. Acts 5:19-21

It was God who arranged the apostolic jailbreak. Once again, the Lord does the unexpected: Instead of urging the men to head for the hills, so the leadership of the Church won't be killed, the angel tells them to go preach in the Temple! That would be right under the noses of those who had jailed them, in a building under their control! I would have thought, maybe somewhere out in the woods?

Their bold obedience was part of God's plan to save them. The supposed spiritual gatekeepers of Jerusalem can't very well murder unarmed miracle workers in the middle of a sermon they are preaching to adoring fans, so they quietly cart them off and beat them up, warn them not to talk about Jesus anymore, and let them go.

Another part of God's plan was the presence of Gamaliel, who successfully reasons with the Council, and prevents further harm from coming to the disciples.

The courage of Peter and the apostles disarmed the religious leaders: *"We must obey God rather than men."* (Acts 5:29) A principle which needs to be applied!

The spiritual firestorm swirling in Jerusalem centered around the witness of the disciples. Had they been content to just do a little teaching, and not get in people's faces with the power of Jesus, a less powerful form of the Church might have existed, unharmed, for quite a while. Instead, the rage of the Sanhedrin was incited by the direct preaching of Peter and the others. Sometimes, that's just the way it needs to be! The apostles were called to be witnesses of Jesus' resurrection. Are we called to be something different? Sure, we didn't see Him in bodily form, either before or after the Resurrection, but where is the bold witness in the Church, today? And where are those who are willing to stand for Christ, even if it means getting beaten up or killed?

There are a couple pieces missing in our witness, these days. One is the kind of boldness that could possibly land us in jail, in the first place. The other is the kind of obedience which, when miraculously released, would cause us to head for the Temple instead of the trees. Boldness and obedience. It would be a good way to jumpstart our witness. And it looks like a bold witness is safer than a weak one.

The Bottom Line: Boldness and obedience to God actually make for a safer witness.

DAY 240

Neutralized by Freedom

But Peter and the apostles answered, "We must obey God rather than men." Acts 5:29

Part of our problem in America is that we are neutralized by our freedom. This nation was founded on religious freedom, yet the Constitution is used today as an excuse to shut Jesus out of public life. Our situation isn't so far off from that of the apostles—"It's fine to do miracles and stuff, but don't use the name of Jesus, at least not in public. What you do in your church buildings is different; we don't care so much about that, so long as you keep it to yourself."

So, we have religious freedom—regulated. It's quarantined, it's banned from the public square, it's personalized so that if you try to tell anyone else about it, you are looked upon as infringing upon their rights.

What if there were no religious freedom in America? What if, like some other countries, we could be tried and executed for speaking the name of Jesus in public (or even private)? Americans are naturally rebellious enough that it would be like Prohibition! People would be defiantly skirting those laws all the time! Maybe what we need in America is a law that punishes anyone who speaks the name of Jesus in love, anywhere. Maybe then we'd start talking about Him!

For much of the U.S., it's as if the courts had said, "Don't speak of Jesus anywhere unconverted people might hear you—just do it in your church buildings," and our response was, "O.K., we'll be good."

We need not pick a fight. But neither should we ignore God's commands to us, and surrender to the dictates of a society which would very much like for Jesus to just go away and leave them to their sin. If we need God's protection in the face of danger, we'll get it. If we get to be martyrs for the faith, He would give us courage and grace for that, too. Are we neutralized by our "freedom"? We have just enough of it to think it best not to make waves, to enjoy our quarantined "freedom" to speak the Good News to one another in our buildings, which gives us the perfect excuse not to bother being witnesses anywhere–not even in church. I'm glad the apostles didn't take this route. I'm sorry that I so often have.

The Bottom Line: We shouldn't let our "freedom" limit our witness.

DAY 241

God's Kind of People

If the Church in America approached the world with a bold kindness that unflinchingly pointed to Jesus, observed the secular society rules that prevent other religions from forcing their faith on people or having our tax dollars pay for their buildings, even as it prevents Christians from doing the same, we have plenty of freedom to get the name of Jesus out without even breaking any laws. Fighting for prayer in public schools or at high school graduations? I guess it's O.K. for some people to try to regain some of these privileges, but it looks like we'd be much further ahead if we just focused on praying more when we weren't at school—as in, praying in our homes, unfortunately a too rare occurrence among Christians.

I guess my point is, we have plenty of opportunities to witness for Christ in ways that don't break any laws and are winsome to society, rather than obnoxious. If we would just do that, it would have more of an effect on getting the laws reversed than any kind of protest or whining is going to have. It would also be a more powerful witness. There is a time to get in people's face with the Gospel—the apostles were talking to the very individuals who had condemned Jesus to death only months earlier; we're not talking to those people. We're talking to Gentile pagans and cultural Christians who don't know anything much about Jesus; they just know they can't stand Christians who impose their values on others for reasons they can't understand. The approach of a "bold witness" is not needed nearly so much in our case as is genuine compassion—and that's not even against the law!

What we've found with things like Servant Week (hundreds of Christians from dozens of churches coming together to do acts of service for their community) are that compassion and kindness open lots of doors, and Jesus becomes welcome because Christians are showing they care. The city council used to hate to see us coming, because we only showed up when we had a problem; now they invite us to the meeting so they can present us with an award for all we've done to help the community! Go figure.

Yes, we're supposed to be witnesses. But witnessing and demanding our rights are not the same thing. Kindness carries a lot further than shoving public officials into uncomfortable positions because we no longer have most-favored status. God's kind of people are God's kind people.

The Bottom Line: A kind witness is a bold witness!

DAY 242

Getting It Right

And the twelve summoned the full number of the disciples and said, "It is not right that we should give up preaching the word of God to serve tables. Therefore, brothers, pick out from among you seven men of good repute, full of the Spirit and of wisdom, whom we will appoint to this duty. But we will devote ourselves to prayer and to the ministry of the word." And what they said pleased the whole gathering, and they chose... (Seven men with Greek names). These they set before the apostles, and they prayed and laid their hands on them. Acts 6:2-6

The apostles not only dealt well with the food distribution issue; they also did an excellent job in communicating their reasoning to the whole Church. It wasn't that they were too good to wait tables or didn't want to do it; it was because it wouldn't be right. The reason it wouldn't be right is because it would mean giving up preaching the word of God. This not only made sense to the whole group; it pleased them.

The apostles, rather than using their own authority to pick out seven stewards, left it up to the other disciples. The criteria given was not "experience in food service administration" or business acumen or popularity, but "full of the Spirit and of wisdom." "Food service" was optional. The people chose them and presented them to the apostles, who in turn prayed and laid hands on them. The end result was that the apostles kept doing what Jesus had commissioned them to do, unhindered by administrative hassles. The needs of the Body were met, people who had wisdom and the Spirit were given responsibility that challenged them, and the Church continued to multiply. Not only that, but two of the Seven ended up being incredible evangelists, as well as being skilled in administration. One became the first martyr of the Church.

It could have all been different, had the Early Church taken a different approach! Had the apostles left off the emphasis on preaching, teaching and prayer, in order to become administrators, I think the results would have been tragic. What they did, instead, was to keep the emphasis on Christ rather than on the institution of the Church, by allowing the spiritual leaders to be spiritual leaders without burdening them with organizational administration, as well. It's a beautiful thing when the Church gets it right!

The Bottom Line: When they chose to focus on God, not "church," they got it right.

DAY 243

Three-talent Frustrations

How have we strayed so far from the Early Church example of concentrating on God, not "church," and come to consider it normal? Most pastors I know are under a groaning weight of administration, whether they want it or not. Some want it; it gives them control over the congregation they serve. Many have been trained to actually see themselves as "CEO" of "their" church. Few seem to have much time for prayer, so many are the demands of the congregation paying them to be their leader, yet also expecting fresh and powerful spiritual food.

Occasionally, we see someone who can do it all: Energetic spiritual life, the ability to preach and teach, the capacity to juggle administrative duties while maintaining a profound spiritual ministry—it all just seems to work, for them. And since we've now witnessed it, or at least heard of it being done, that expectation is then placed on less gifted mortals, and another perfectly good pastor faces a life of frustration, a three-talent steward in a five-talent position. Meanwhile, two-talent administrative people never called to preach sit glumly on the sidelines, bemoaning the failure of their minister, and wishing they could somehow have gotten "a good one" who knew how to do the job right.

How was it in the Early Church? Those called to focus on prayer and teaching were able to do just that, without also needing an MBA. People gifted in administration who were Spirit-filled and mature were selected to serve in administrative positions, to make sure things were done well, and fairly. If they also happened to be gifted in preaching, they did that, too.

In Acts 6, it was vital that the apostles continued to preach and teach about Jesus, rather than be dragged into administrative duties, because *there was no New Testament!* At this point in time, none of the New Testament had been written. All the people had was the testimony of those who had been with Jesus, who could relate His teaching and His example to others. What a tragedy it would have been to allow an administrative glitch to gobble up that testimony!

We, at least, have the New Testament. Still, I think it tragic that people called to preach end up spending so much time in administration and so little of it in talking about Jesus. When they do preach, it is generally to an audience familiar with the Gospel, looking for a new spin on it. The Church is bored; the pastor overwhelmed and frustrated; the world still doesn't know. Something wrong with this picture? It's not going to get much better until we each start to fulfill the unique ministry to which *He* called us, and decline the rest.

The Bottom Line: We need to focus on what God has called us to do. Period.

DAY 244

From Top to Bottom

And the word of God continued to increase, and the number of the disciples multiplied greatly in Jerusalem, and a great many of the priests became obedient to the faith. Acts 6:7

It was a long way down, I'm sure. This little statement has amazed me, as I've contemplated what it meant to these men and their families: *"and a great many of the priests became obedient to the faith."* Talk about a career-killing move! This decision had to have been very costly, in every way. When your whole life is based on your identity as a priest, to suddenly set that aside in order to quietly go to the bottom of society's ladder indicated the deepest sort of commitment.

Following Jesus wasn't quite so hard for those who had nothing to begin with. Their status couldn't help but rise! After all, this was a new fellowship full of life and miracles, where even a slave could be somebody. For others, it was very different. It meant laying aside wealth, prestige, even employment and ultimately life itself, in order to join with people from every segment of society in service to a Savior crucified as a criminal. People who had spent their lives climbing and striving to stay at the top of the ladder were now relinquishing everything they'd worked for, just to follow Jesus. It was inspiring. Not just a few priests were making the trip down the ladder.

It's interesting to note that the Early Church neither shunned these new converts, nor provided them with authority based on their superior scriptural knowledge and experience in leading religious organizations. They seem to have gotten in line along with everybody else. In this new Church, there was no ladder to climb, anyway! One of the tremendous strengths of the Early Church was that there was no true leader but Christ; there was only the Lord and those serving Him, without man-made positions needing to be filled. And, since basically no one was paid for "ministry," each was allowed to utilize the gifts God had granted him without also needing to worry about responsibilities or authority for which he *was* ill-suited. The way it was looks, to me, better all the time.

That was one of many reasons I felt led to resign from a 23-year career in pastoral ministry. Anyone who cared about us wanted to know what I was going to do, and how this could possibly be God's will. After all, who ever heard of being called *out* of pastoral ministry? The leading was just as clear and unmistakable, though, as the original call to preach had been. How did it turn out? Tomorrow.

The Bottom Line: Are we willing to go down the ladder for Jesus, like the priests?

DAY 245

Safe at the Bottom

It would have been nice to at least have had an income plan to share with loved ones, but it became clear that this was to be a faith venture, which meant "sight" was limited to the next step of obedience, and not much more. We jumped, but not blindly. It was at the leading of Jesus. I assured people He would provide for us—I just didn't know how, yet.

It has been a different kind of experience, one that makes me very sympathetic to the situation of first-century priests who dared to choose Christ over their career. God has provided, as I believed He would. I found that it's more demanding to freely minister to whomever God brings into your life and pray in provision for each monthly bill, than it is to be obligated to a specific group of folks who supply you with a paycheck every two weeks. I'm definitely not saying that pastoring for pay is wrong; what I am saying is that, if you're called to do it this way, the freedom to use your gifts in ministry and follow only the leading of the Lord without also needing to satisfy the expectations of others is a gratifying experience! (Warning: They quit giving you paychecks after you resign. And don't expect people to give you money just for serving Jesus—that's what they're supposed to be doing, too. Anything you get after you resign can well be considered a gift from God, because that's what it is. Nobody owes you anything, just for using your spiritual gifts, but often, God will direct kind-hearted servants to help supply your needs. It does wonders for the level of gratitude one feels!)

Well, now it's been four years.* We haven't starved or even come close; we haven't lost the house, even in this economy. The disciples didn't have medical insurance, either. As thousands of Americans, Christian and otherwise, fall off a financial ladder they've worked hard to climb, and have no choice but to rely on something different than that to which they're accustomed, take it from someone who jumped off the ladder several years ago, at God's urging. It's not bad at all at the bottom of the ladder! Whether you jumped like I did, or you got pushed, the best plan I can come up with is this: Trust God, and serve Him. Don't be lazy, but don't be faithless, either. Ask Him to show you exactly what He wants you to do, then do it. Leave the results up to Him. And one nice thing about getting to the bottom of the ladder: No more worry about falling!

The Bottom Line: If we follow God's leading faithfully, we are safe, regardless.

*Note: God once again renewed my call to pastoral ministry, after six years of "living by faith." Whatever way God leads us, it works.

DAY 246

In Need of New Wineskins

And a great many of the priests became obedient to the faith.

Acts 6:7

We in America need the kind of boldness demonstrated by those priests. We are also in need of some new wineskins. The Church's impact seems minimal here, as old methods and mentalities are recycled endlessly, with diminishing results. There's nothing wrong with the Gospel; it's the encumbrances we've picked up along the way that make bold, new approaches a hard sell to the present Church.

Are we willing to go *wherever* God is taking us, or have we placed a bunch of limits on our obedience to Him? What will these new days mean, to us?

These are days of change for the Church. I'm convinced I'm not the only pastor God will ask to resign from the pastorate, while continuing to engage in ministry. I can see God directing many more pastors to be bi-vocational. But I don't think God plans to ignore the established, traditional church or leave it without leadership. Many will be assured their place is to continue what they've been doing, ministering to the best of their ability within existing structures.

Here's a difficult one, particularly for those for whom the established church structure fits like a glove: Some folks are going to be called out of their churches in order to enter ministry at a house-church level. It's going to be hard to let those people go, and believe this is God's plan for them, especially if that's not God's plan for us. Many will be called to stay in the traditional church. Part of the mission for them will be to not allow resentment to creep in against those called to go. For all of us, it's going to mean change, even for those who don't change churches or ministries. For them, the change will be in trying to cope with new paradigms for church, trying to adapt while staying in the same place.

While we need to mobilize, I don't think we need some committee to try to control this or "strategize" the thing, any more than the apostles needed someone to plan Pentecost. What we most need to do is LET GO. We have had a death grip on the Church for so long that the Church in America has passed out! The Church has been a battle zone, with fights over music styles, tongues, traditions, theology, personal preferences of all kinds. We've not had much energy left to fight the devil. It's as if we had played into the devil's plan.

The Church in America needs to refocus on Jesus, be willing to be poured into new wineskins without complaint, and let go of everything but Jesus.

The Bottom Line: We need to let go of everything but Jesus.

DAY 247

The Learning Blessing

Whoever gets sense loves his own soul;
he who keeps understanding will discover good.

Proverbs 19:8

Learning is a reward in itself. This is coming from a kid who, for amusement, used to take the World Book encyclopedia off the shelf at the one-room country schoolhouse in South Dakota, and would read an article and write a report about it, even though no one had asked for one. It was fun! I wasn't sure what other second graders did for enjoyment.

The life-long love for learning has not diminished. The best part of school, for me, was the learning part. I got to find out things I hadn't known before. Things which previously had not made sense to me became clear. Learning has been a blessing to me.

Nowhere has that blessing been more evident than in what I have learned in my relationship with God, and through studying His Word, the Bible. It's my reason for writing these devotionals: I love learning from God, and I like to share what I've learned with others. It gives me enjoyment to learn and to write, even if no one else looks at what I've written. If some folks benefit from reading about what I'm learning, all the better—but I would have done it, anyway!

When we choose to apply ourselves to learn and to understand, it's one of the nicest gifts we can give—to ourselves! Not only that, but it blesses our Creator, who put within us a mind He would like us to exercise. When we choose to learn, we bless ourselves, our God and the people around us (particularly our teachers and parents). When we seek to understand, it pleases God. He helps us. The ability to learn is a gift from God. When we use that gift, it's one of the best gifts we can give to ourselves, too.

The Bottom Line: Learning is like a gift we give ourselves.

DAY 248

This May Sting a Bit

After this I saw in the night visions, and behold, a fourth beast, terrifying and dreadful and exceedingly strong. It had great iron teeth; it devoured and broke in pieces and stamped what was left with its feet. It was different from all the beasts that were before it, and it had ten horns. Daniel 7:7

After Daniel's vision, he found his spirit *"anxious,"* his mind *"alarmed."* Was God just trying to scare the guy? What was God's purpose in giving Daniel dreams and visions which frightened him?

When we know what's coming, it reduces fear. Take away the unknown, and most fear simply goes away. Monsters suddenly retreat back into the closets of young children as soon as the light switch is flipped on. The nurse announces, "This may sting a bit" just prior to the shot, and it's not as bad as we thought it was going to be. The surgeon who explains the surgical procedure helps calm the fears of the patient. Even the scariest horror movie isn't that scary when we've already seen it; we know what's coming. And B-grade monster movies prompt more laughter than screams, with their predictable plots and budget special effects.

So... all that prophecy in the Bible about the antichrist and the Tribulation and the end of the world... is that there to scare us? No, it's there for the opposite reason. It's there to calm us, to let us know what's coming. When the antichrist arrives on the scene to terrify the world and wreak havoc, it will be painful for all, but at least those who know their Bible will realize what's going on! "Yep. Just like his picture in the Bible. And we already know what he'll do and how it all turns out. Hang on!"

"This may sting a bit" (actually a lot). But the prophecies aren't there to scare us. Instead, they calm us. We know what's coming. We know who wins in the end. We are encouraged to stand firm until the end, and the One doing the encouraging is the same One who foretold everything which will happen from thousands of years out! If He can predict exactly what someone will do from a couple millennia away, we ought to be able to relax in the arms of "the God who told us so." Prophecy is not there to scare us, but to take away our fears.

The Bottom Line: Prophesied pain is less painful.

DAY 249

Professional Christians

And a great number of priests became obedient to the faith.
Acts 6:7

There are two treasured icons in the institutional church which seem, to me, to actually be limiting our impact on the world around us, rather than helping us: Church buildings and professional clergy.

I'm all for shelter, particularly on a nasty winter night in the Northwest, with record cold in the forecast. What bugs me is the proportion of the church's income which ends up in real estate of one form or another, particularly when the effect of a church building is generally to quarantine a congregation of believers for two or three hours a week from a world which needs what have. The inefficiency often practiced of building separate spaces for each activity (sanctuary, fellowship hall or gym, educational classrooms) and surrounding the whole thing with a parking lot used once a week doesn't help. What kind of business could pull this off? The Early Church couldn't have, either. Fortunately, they had not been trained that in order for a church to grow, it must meet a litmus test of so many acres of land and just the right sort of building. They went from 120 to 3,000 in a day. Instead of adding on to the Upper Room, they left it. The action took place not in a church building (none existed for the first 300 years of the Early Church), but in the streets, the homes of believers and the public places like the Temple in Jerusalem.

And who spoke the Good News about eternal life and salvation through a resurrected Jesus? Everyone who believed. Not only the apostles and those who had walked alongside Jesus, but people who had only come to faith in Christ days before. Two of the best preachers of the Word started out as table waiters. They just wouldn't stop talking about Jesus. That's why I think we are making a tragic mistake when we buy into the long-held tradition which reserves preaching for those who have been through extensive theological training, who are now "qualified" to talk about how good God is!

Don't get me wrong. I love preachers, I am one, and the majority of my friends are pastors. They already have a tough job, and I have no desire to see it get tougher, or for them to be unemployed. But I want to see my nation turn to God again, and leaving the bulk of the ministry in the hands of a few trained professionals is not working!

The Bottom Line: Is discipleship only for professionals, in church buildings?

DAY 250

Pigskins and People

Christianity in America is too much like pro football. Not just anybody can get on the field! The chosen play; everyone else pays to watch. And how is it in 21st Century Christianity in the U.S.? Get yourself a reverend who can really preach, build a nice building and try to pack it out, and please, please tithe so we can keep this ministry going! "Ministry?" With not enough exceptions, the only ministry is people listening to someone whom they paid to talk about Jesus. When it's over, no lives have been changed, but it was a nice "Jesus talk," anyway.

Football is a spectator sport. It's centered on the performers, not the ball. If the goal was to put a pigskin in the end zone, there are more efficient ways to do it, such as loading the thing in a Hummer and just dropping it off under the pole thingy's at the end. The goal of football is not about the ball at all; it's about the players competing against one another. That's why there are plenty of rules, one of them being that you can't have too many people on the field.

If the goal of football was for people to "get footballs into the end zone," and *everybody* could do it, you'd see people throwing footballs into the end zone, carrying them, kids carting loads of footballs in wheelbarrows, toddlers rolling them toward the goal posts. As sport, it wouldn't be too inspirational to watch— more like watching a fish processing plant run—but there would soon be an enormous pile of footballs in each end zone, if that were the goal.

But what if each football in the end zone meant something really important, like someone's life being saved, for eternity? Can you see a toddler doing an end zone dance, then going back for another one?

What if, instead of it being a boring conveyor line of football carrying drones, there was opposition, and rules to be followed? What if people of all ages and levels of ability could still get in on it? What if each person found the game represented a challenge requiring teamwork, and perfectly matched to their abilities? What if the only spectators were resting players, who would rejoin the game, later? What if?

Back to the Church. Right now, it's too much like a football game, with the pastor and about ten others out on the field, and the crowd in the stands cheering or jeering, depending on how things are going. If they don't go well for too long, the pastor will probably be looking for another team.

Which scenario is more biblical, a sacred few carrying the load, or all God's people on the field? Football is a spectator sport; Christianity shouldn't be.

The Bottom Line: What if the whole Church was on the field?

DAY 251

Spectators No More

It's time to apologize, again. I don't want to sow dis-satisfaction into anyone's life. I don't want to pile on the Church, when it seems we're already carrying too much. I don't want my pastor friends to find themselves unemployed and all of us standing out in the rain. I also want to see my nation find God, again, and they're not doing it under our present plan! What part of the Church's money does not go toward buildings, salaries and upkeep-type expenditures? Often, that's where all of it is going. It's quite rare to find a church which might spend as much as 10% on anything like outreach. It's also rare to find a pastor with much time for evangelism. How could he, with the load of maintenance responsibilities he already carries? Those in modern ministry sometimes look with longing at the early apostles, who delegated administration and went back to "prayer and the ministry of the Word." Must be nice! We forget the part about the lack of an apostolic benefit package. They didn't starve, but then, neither did the widows.

Now that I've stirred the waters more than I wanted to...

I don't know the answer. I really don't. A lot of good has been done and is being done in the Church. A lot of it is happening in church buildings. Much of it is being accomplished by very committed, highly trained, multi-talented pastors. For those who believe God wants them to continue to function in this milieu of ministry, please do! Much has been accomplished. For others—you know who you are—are you willing to get in the game and be a disciple, not a spectator? Are you willing to carry the ball for Jesus, even if you've never been trained? How about if there's no building, no title and no salary? How about if others get paid to do the exact same things you're doing for nothing?

I have no easy answers to energize the institutional church or change it back to the clear focus and effectiveness of what we see in Acts. We're a long way down the road, and institutions stink when it comes to reforming themselves. I'm hoping that what God does next in the U.S. will see new wineskins alongside old ones, with both doing well.

However it looks, I'm pretty sure God wants us all to get in the game. Institutional church? Fine. He's used this setup for hundreds of years. It's the tool under which most of us found Christ. New wineskin? Organic church? Fine, too. The Spirit will lead us to the place we need to be, if we'll let Him. *Refuse to be a spectator Christian, anymore. All* of us are called to be disciples. And Jesus wants *all* of His followers out on the field.

The Bottom Line: Refuse to be a spectator Christian, anymore.

DAY 252

Where's My Wineskin?

So, what should we do?

Don't do *anything*—unless you know you're being directed by the Holy Spirit. What I mean is, if you are in the system of the established, institutional church, don't go bailing out on it or using what I have said as an excuse to stop giving or going to the church. If you're a pastor, don't quit, *unless* you are absolutely sure that the same God who led you into ministry in the first place is now asking you to minister in a way new to you, which may be without salary. If God leads you this way, don't be surprised if it takes a while to be sure—I prayed about it constantly for a year before I was sure this was the direction I was supposed to go. And it's like jumping off a cliff—you'd better be sure *before* you leap, because it's too late on the way down.

However, if you know this is the Lord leading you to take faith and discipleship to a new level, and for you it means stepping way out of your comfort zone, don't be afraid to follow Jesus. As long as you know it's Him, and not just frustration or discontent, you can launch out in obedience even if it feels like you're walking off a cliff, and know He will catch you. Don't discard anything He has not instructed you to discard, but don't assume anything, either. We *really* need the Spirit's leading, when it comes to navigating these times. There's only one Book we can pull off the shelf which will give us the answers, and that's where we need to look! (Hint: We may not always be thrilled with what it tells us to do).

God has some amazing plans for us. Some of us will be called upon to find new ways through the wilderness, then come back to draw a map. Some of us will know without a doubt that God's plan for us is to stay put, but to ward off envy and bitterness when our friends are not so led. There is a place for all of us on the field. Christianity is not a spectator sport, and it's not just for professionals, though those (like the priests) with extra training and experience are valuable assets to the cause. We can trust God, *totally*— life, career, everything. He'll catch you. Make sure it's His voice, then obey. He'll show you which wineskin is yours.

The Bottom Line: We can trust God for clear direction.

Note: In my case, I began ministry in the established church "wineskin," was led out of it into what was for me new territory for six years, then was led back into pastoral ministry in the established church. In each case, it was the Lord's leading.

DAY 253

Disciples on the Loose

And Stephen, full of grace and power, was doing great wonders and signs among the people. Acts 6:8

I heard an astonishing figure quoted by a pastor, yesterday. He mentioned that only 2% of churches in America were experiencing growth as a result of people coming to faith in Christ. I already knew that something like 80% of churches in America were flat-lined or declining. That means that even of the 1/5 of churches which seem to be growing, the growth is through transfer rather than conversion. Bottom line? 98% of all American churches are either flat-lined, declining, or experiencing growth only through people coming from other churches. And some of us are whining about the inefficiency of the auto companies!

What's everybody doing, anyway? Pastors are some of the busiest people I know. Church calendars are crammed with activities. Some of the nicest buildings you'll ever see have crosses on the top. Some of the best music you'll ever hear is inside. And the quality of preaching? It makes me wish our politicians could speak half as well as the average pastor. Those guys can communicate!

What in the world is wrong, then? How could so much time, effort, money and skill go together to make for such a losing situation? We're even on God's side! Aren't we supposed to be winning? We're not even breaking even!

It's time to look into the Bible, at an infant Church experiencing tremendous growth, plus the beginning of severe persecution. Consider Stephen. The story of his short life is contained in Acts 6-7. The influence ripples from his life haven't stopped yet, and never will.

When the Church was looking for people to serve tables, the instructions were to look for reputable men, full of the Holy Spirit and wisdom. Stephen made the list. His responsibility was to wait tables. It didn't even pay anything, but he got to eat. He seems to have used all his free time talking to people about Jesus. Even when they brought in the championship Hebrew debate squad, he manhandled them with Spirit-anointed words. The guy had enormous grace and power, and even did wonders and signs!

His thrashing of the local intellectuals earned him some enemies, who dragged him before the Sanhedrin, along with some false witnesses. When it came time for Stephen to deliver his defense, he started with Abraham and recited the entire history of Israel, in detail and from memory.

The Bottom Line: Leaving the Gospel to the "professionals" is not working.

DAY 254

Talking About Jesus 'til it Kills Us

When Stephen accused the Sanhedrin to their faces of murdering Jesus, they interrupted his sermon to stone him, but none would forget the face of an angel, words of forgiveness echoing Jesus', the blood of the first Christian martyr. Saul, especially, couldn't forget it. He had held the coats of the stone throwers. He became so motivated to stamp out this new faith that he began a one-man vendetta against the Church that even led him to different cities when he started to run low on local Christians to persecute. Jesus intercepted him on the way (Acts 9) and the rest is history.

Back to Stephen.

Where did this incredible guy come from? Obviously, not all young Hebrews were like Stephen, but the system of training experienced in the synagogues had prepared him with a keen knowledge of spiritual history. Add Jesus, and you have an unbeatable, Spirit-filled witness. He already knew his scriptures.

I met a few (very few) young people on fire for God, who knew their Bible stories, when I was in college and seminary, but the bulk of the population, even then, had scanty knowledge and less ardor, when it came to the scriptures. Now, biblical illiteracy is at grotesque levels in all of society. Meanwhile, who is cranking out motivated young people who are familiar with their stuff and routinely expect to devote at least two years of their lives to propagating their message? That's right. The Mormons. I don't agree with their theology, but their methods are quite successful and have resulted in growth, despite the absence of clergy in their system. Could it be that it's more effective to just turn everybody loose and expect any member to talk about their faith (and know what it is), rather than consigning the whole operation to the hands of a few paid professionals?

Which would make a bigger dent in a community? 80 highly-skilled, trained professional ministers who would shepherd 80 churches, or 800 disciples who occupied every conceivable position in society, who talked about Jesus every chance they got, roughly organized by maybe twenty professional ministers?

With the 80 ministers, we'd have stability, professionalism, good recordkeeping and, according to present statistics, no growth. With the 800, society would have nowhere to run without bumping into another Christian who couldn't seem to get through the day without talking about Jesus, even if it killed them, which, if it did, would *really* shake things up!

We want the results they had in Acts, *but...*

The Bottom Line: To impact society, we need to turn all the disciples loose!

DAY 255

Easter Answers

When the Sabbath was past, Mary Magdalene and Mary the mother of James and Salome bought spices, so that they might go and anoint him. And very early on the first day of the week, when the sun had risen, they went to the tomb. And they were saying to one another, "Who will roll away the stone for us from the entrance of the tomb?" And looking up, they saw that the stone had been rolled back—it was very large. And entering the tomb, they saw a young man sitting on the right side, dressed in a white robe, and they were alarmed. And he said to them, "Do not be alarmed. You seek Jesus of Nazareth, who was crucified. He has risen; he is not here. See the place where they laid him. But go, tell his disciples and Peter that he is going before you to Galilee. There you will see him, just as he told you." And they went out and fled from the tomb, for trembling and astonishment had seized them, and they said nothing to anyone, for they were afraid. Mark 16:1-8

The tattered group of Jesus' followers didn't gather to celebrate Easter, that day, but to weep and mourn. Their lives were absolutely filled with problems. Even after being told of Jesus' resurrection by an angel, and seeing an empty tomb with the stone rolled away, their first reaction was not rejoicing but fear.

Before it was all over, they were convinced! Jesus was alive! Their problems melted away; nothing else mattered, once their Savior was with them, again.

It was only for a short while: Forty days. Then He was gone, again. This time, instead of seeing Him die, they watched Him float up into the clouds. (He promised to return)! He left His disciples with instructions, a mission: *"Go into all the world and proclaim the gospel to the whole creation."* (Mark 16:15)

We're still working on it.

Where do we fit in this Easter picture, in this present time? What are we to do? Where is our place? I could probably fill many pages with "stuff" in answer to those questions, but I'll keep it really short, instead:

Nothing matters more than that Jesus is alive. The death problem? Solved, through His death and resurrection. The sin problem? Solved through Jesus. Eternal life? Guaranteed. The same God who raised Jesus will raise all who believe. We need not be afraid. Our resurrected Lord is bigger than all our problems. And we still have a job to do, and Easter to celebrate. Forever.

The Bottom Line: Nothing matters more than that Jesus is alive.

DAY 256

The Wages of Lying

A false witness will not go unpunished,
and he who breathes out lies will perish.

Proverbs 19:9

What's the big deal about lies? In some circles of our present-day society, lying is looked upon more as a skill than a sin (politics, for example)! Surveys would lead us to believe that many people (particularly teenagers) lie on a routine, daily basis. Is it that big of a deal when people tell a lie, particularly when it seems to make things smoother for everyone?

Yes. *A false witness will not go unpunished, and he who breathes out lies will perish.* There are plenty more verses where that came from. Why is lying a big deal to God? Because we serve a God who not only always speaks the truth, but who is the Truth. Remember Jesus' words to His disciples in John 14:6? *"I am the way, and the truth, and the life. No one comes to the Father except through me."* Not stopping at just *telling* the truth, our God *is* the Truth.

Honesty matters to God. Lying, like other sins, can be forgiven by God, but lying is still sin. Getting forgiveness is not the same as having our sin overlooked. When those of us who claim to be followers of God claim alliance with Him, yet routinely tell untruths, we are reflecting on the character of God. We are telling the world, "Lying is O.K. with God." It is not. God is always truthful, and He expects His followers to be always truthful, too. (This doesn't mean we have to say everything we think)!

There is a punishment for those who choose to bear false witness, and it comes from all sides. Unforgiven, it brings the punishment all unforgiven sin brings: Death. Meanwhile, though politicians, businessmen and teenagers seem to often thrive as a result of skillfully bending the truth to their advantage, there is an earthly penalty as well. Sometimes the punishment is jail time, but most often, it's a lack of trust. "You don't trust me!" the teen wails. Wonder why. The chronic lying catches up to us, until after a while no one believes a word we say, even if we've veered onto the truth. Politics? Lies might have won the election, but not the respect needed to get anything done. Business? Same thing. It all catches up to us, eventually. Even if we get away with it, we still get to deal with God.

Who was it that said, "Honesty is the best policy"? The concept originated with God, who has no other policy. He never lies. We shouldn't, either.

The Bottom Line: Don't lie.

DAY 257

The Forty Year Wilderness Degree

Now when forty years had passed, an angel appeared to him in the wilderness of Mount Sinai, in a flame of fire in a bush. Acts 7:30

God can put our life on pause for forty years as casually as a TV program goes to a commercial break. Moses had fried his career as a prince in Egypt by trying to rescue a fellow Israelite, becoming Moses the fugitive. He had sprinted for Midian, found himself a new life, complete with family and a position in the sheep management industry, when God decided to get back to him via burning bush. Moses could have asked, "Where have you been the last forty years, God?!"

God could have replied, "Getting you trained in how to live in the desert."

How many Hebrew slaves would have known what lay beyond the Red Sea, after 400 years of captivity? Only one. Only one knew how things worked at Pharaoh's palace. Only one had Israelite blood and palace upbringing.

It's funny how God makes things work. How would God have gotten baby Moses into the household of Pharaoh, had it not been for the decree to kill the boy babies by throwing them into the Nile, a command Moses' mother embellished by first placing him in a basket? Resourceful big sister Miriam found a wet nurse who looked a lot like Mom, for the princess' new baby. Instead of death, Moses got to grow up as a prince in a palace. His real mom got paid to take care of him. Cool.

That's the Lord—able to pull together all the weird loose ends and make something incredible out of it, every time; the tough thing for most of us, though, is the *time* He takes to do it. We're racing our motor, trying to get on with life, frantically clawing at the cell walls of the wilderness pit in which we find ourselves, and God walks off and leaves us! Four decades of slow learning, seasoning and sometimes despair gets us one verse: *"Now when forty years had passed,..."*

"Where were you, God?! What have you been doing the past forty years?"

"Waiting for you."

"Waiting for *me*! Waiting for me to *what?"*

"Get done."

"Get done with what?"

"Never mind. You'll see. Now, as I was saying forty years ago, this is what I have for you to do, now that you're ready..."

The Bottom Line: God is preparing us for something. It takes time and patience.

DAY 258

Forty Year Graduate

Now when forty years had passed, an angel appeared to him in the wilderness of Mount Sinai, in a flame of fire in a bush. Acts 7:30

Time is a frequent frustration, for me. I'm frustrated by having to wait, especially needlessly; I'm frustrated when I can't accomplish all my goals because there's not enough time; I'm frustrated when I discover my time has been wasted. There are just a lot of ways I get frustrated, when it comes to time!

And then there's God. "A thousand years are like a day" (2 Peter 3:8). Why would the One who *made* time be frustrated by time? He isn't. And one of the many, many lessons He has for His children is that we also would learn to not be *(as)* frustrated by it. Forty years? It might as well be forty seconds, to God. For us, it represents half a lifetime! Yet, for pursuits of great value, the time invested seems well worthwhile.

A high school senior considering a career in medicine is looking at a pipeline which will require another twelve years of preparation, on top of the thirteen they've already put in to graduate from high school. Twenty-five years of school before they're ready to be a pediatrician? That's right. That's how long it takes to get ready. But who do you want caring for your sick baby, someone who has spent twenty-five years, plus, in getting ready through education and experience, or someone totally unprepared?

God has big plans for all of us. Fortunately, not all of them require an extra decade of hitting the books, but some do. I think all of them require time. Time to learn, time to get over things, time to mature, time to complete lessons... God's not the One who needs time; it's us. Some of His lessons are the forty year variety, just like medical careers demand years of preparation time. It would not be good for anyone if we simply forged a medical license in order to skip the schooling. First the training, then the license—that's the proper order. It would not be good for any of us if God simply waived the qualifications and qualities only learned in the wilderness, so we could sooner move forward with our dreams.

Moses had a heart for his people when he was a young man, but had God turned his staff into the rod of God then, Moses would have only used it for killing Egyptians. Moses needed some schooling—about forty years worth. When he was done, God got back to him. So, rather than being frustrated, it's time for us all to thank God for the gift of time, and get back to the sheep, the books or the bricks. We're preparing. When we're done, God will get back to us.

The Bottom Line: When we're done, God will get back to us.

DAY 259

Funeral Parties

"And I will grant authority to my two witnesses, and they will prophesy for 1,260 days, clothed in sackcloth."

These are the two olive trees and the two lampstands that stand before the Lord of the earth. And if anyone would harm them, fire pours from their mouth and consumes their foes. If anyone would harm them, this is how he is doomed to be killed. They have the power to shut the sky, that no rain may fall during the days of their prophesying, and they have power over the waters to turn them into blood and to strike the earth with every kind of plague, as often as they desire. And when they have finished their testimony, the beast that rises from the bottomless pit will make war on them and conquer them and kill them, and their dead bodies will lie in the street of the great city that symbolically is called Sodom and Egypt, where their Lord was crucified. For three and a half days some from the peoples and tribes and languages and nations will gaze at their dead bodies and refuse to let them be placed in a tomb, and those who dwell on the earth will rejoice over them and make merry and exchange presents, because these two prophets had been a torment to those who dwell on the earth. But after the three and a half days a breath of life from God entered them, and they stood up on their feet, and a great fear fell on those who saw them. Then they heard a loud voice from heaven saying to them, "Come up here!" And they went up to heaven in a cloud, and their enemies watched them. Revelation 11:3-12

The news went worldwide in seconds, this past Sunday: "They got him." The intense, decade-long manhunt for Osama bin Laden had finally ended with his death, in Pakistan, at the hands of Navy Seals. The man behind Al Quaeda and 9/11 had embittered many toward him. When word was received of his demise, jubilation broke out in some places, as crowds spontaneously gathered to celebrate the news that the one who had caused so much pain in America was gone.

As I watched news coverage of the celebrations, I thought of this prophetic passage in Revelation. One day, the world will be throwing parties because God's prophets are dead. Our world will be so far gone that when the witnesses who stand for God are killed, the reaction of the world will be to gloat, refuse the bodies burial, and celebrate by sending one another gifts.

Will the other believers in Christ still be here on earth, when this happens? I don't know. But we're here, now. We should be busy with what matters. Now.

The Bottom Line: We must be about our Father's business. Now.

DAY 260

Idols for Free

And the haughtiness of man shall be humbled,
and the lofty pride of men shall be brought low,
and the LORD alone will be exalted in that day.
And the idols shall utterly pass away.
And people shall enter the caves of the rocks
and the holes of the ground,
from before the terror of the LORD,
and from the splendor of his majesty,
when he rises to terrify the earth.

Isaiah 2:17-19

God has His ways of dealing with pride, national and otherwise. Much of our culture is saturated with haughtiness; one day it will be dealt with—all of it. *The lofty pride of men shall be brought low, and the LORD alone will be exalted in that day.*

Once again, we get the not-so-subtle hint that now would be a good time to humble ourselves before the LORD, and abandon our idols, since it's going to happen, anyway, one way or another! There is coming a time when the inhabitants of the earth will be not just respectful of God, but utterly terrified.

What of the cherished idols to which they have devoted their lives?

In that day mankind will cast away their idols of silver and their idols of gold, which they made for themselves to worship, to the moles and to the bats, to enter the caverns of the rocks and the clefts of the cliffs, from before the terror of the LORD, and from the splendor of his majesty, when he rises to terrify the earth. (Isa 2:20-21)

Think of it. Treasures of a lifetime literally tossed away, as panic-stricken people run for cover, hoping to avoid the judgment of a God they have spent their lives despising. They won't just be afraid. They will be terrified. Suddenly, only one thing will have value for them: Salvation. Escaping the judgment of God. All pride will be erased, not only from individuals, but from entire nations. Only One will be exalted in that day. It would be such a good idea to exalt Him, now. It would be such a good idea to discard worthless idols, now. There is coming a day when only God will be exalted on the earth. We are foolish if we wait until then to fear Him. Only fools cling to idols they will one day throw away.

The Bottom Line: One day all will exalt God.
Exalt Him and fear Him, now.

DAY 261

Four Alarm Persecution

And Saul approved of his execution.

And there arose on that day a great persecution against the church in Jerusalem, and they were all scattered throughout the regions of Judea and Samaria, except the apostles. Devout men buried Stephen and made great lamentation over him. But Saul was ravaging the church, and entering house after house, he dragged off men and women and committed them to prison.

Now those who were scattered went about preaching the word. Acts 8:1-4

Well, that's one way to get them out of town! It's hard to get folks motivated to leave a place where everything's perfect, but a little persecution is pretty good motivation. Suddenly, instead of one city being infected with the Gospel, now there are many. Saul ended up benefitting the Church even before he became a Christian! That was certainly not his intention, but God manages to use everything that happens in a way that moves the Kingdom forward.

The worst thing that can happen to the Church is not persecution; the worst thing that can happen is lethargy, when people settle down into their comfort zone and focus their energy on complaining, or in fighting each other, since there's no pressure on them to rely on God and hang onto each other. I don't want to call persecution a gift, but God makes it work like one when it's around.

I don't want to say we're in need of persecution in America, but I don't think it would hurt us if it came! I don't want it to come, but if that's the only way the Church will wake up in time for us to fulfill our purpose, God may be doing us an awesome favor by allowing enough of it to awaken millions of believers who seem to be caught in freedom's stupor! I'm still hoping that we'll be able to get spiritual transformation without catastrophe or persecution or both; I think God would prefer that instead of needing the fire alarm to wake us, we would just set an alarm clock. But I think He loves us enough to awaken us, and if a whisper and a gentle nudge isn't enough to rouse us, well... whatever it takes! When the house is on fire, it's no time to worry about talking too loudly. The options at the Judgment include everlasting consequences more devastating than that!

Regardless of what God does, or allows, our place is to trust Him. And if He is gently urging us out of our complacency, we would be wise to follow Him willingly, rather than waiting for four alarm persecution to really get us motivated.

The Bottom Line: We don't need to wait for persecution to move forward.

DAY 262

License to Witness

The martyrdom of Stephen could have knocked a few believers off track: "How could a loving God let one of His saints die while praising Him? If He can't protect His children better than this, how can we trust Him?" But the Early Christians had a different mentality than most of us, regarding discipleship.

Had the Church been scattered, but silent, they wouldn't have enjoyed the same results of societal change ultimately experienced. The key is that when God allowed them to be scattered, they remained the Church. Witnessing about Jesus had not been left exclusively to the apostles when they were in Jerusalem; now, they continued doing what they had been doing all along—talking about the goodness of Jesus Christ, except in a new location. *Now those who were scattered went about preaching the word.* (Ac 8:4) Who is doing the preaching? Everybody, *except* the apostles! They're still in Jerusalem! (v. 1) They're the only ones who *weren't* scattered; they're still preaching in Jerusalem, everyone else is preaching wherever they've landed. And now the Gospel is no longer limited to Jerusalem— the fire has been flung across Judea and Samaria. Next, the flame will spread to the Roman world, and who will get the torch but the man who scattered the evangelists through his persecution in the first place? "Life changing" doesn't begin to describe what happened to Saul of Tarsus.

Had it been left to the lonely apostles, persecution would have done in the Early Church. Thankfully, primitive followers of Christ knew it was the duty and privilege of every believer to testify about Jesus. It was part of being a disciple.

What if? What if all Christians considered it a privilege to preach Christ to whomever would listen? What if we talked about Jesus, even at great risk? What if we didn't wait until someone ordained us before boldly speaking about God's goodness to another person? What would Satan do with a Church like that?! If you persecute them, their message only spreads.

Our God loves us enough to wake us up. It may be gentle or it may be four alarm persecution—whatever it takes. And what we might think is the worst thing that could happen to us may just be His way of moving us into the position where we'll be most effective.

The Bottom Line: We all have a license to witness. Let's not wait for persecution!

DAY 263

Some People's Samaria

When I think of Samaria, inner cities come to mind. The mindset, environment, values—so different from suburbia! It's as if we were in separate countries. I'm among those who have been repulsed by the Inner City, a country boy who likes the wide open spaces and conservative values. I don't understand the city, don't enjoy it, don't fit—or at least don't think I do. I went through a guilt trip for awhile, in college and seminary; they were pleading with people to go to the Inner City, and I wanted to go to Alaska. I finally figured out not everyone dreamt of starting a home mission church in Alaska like I did, so it might make better sense to believe God was calling me to a place I absolutely loved, instead of somewhere which repulsed me. "Glad I went!" doesn't begin to describe how I feel about Alaska. It was an unforgettable, once-in-a-lifetime, God-driven adventure, for ten years. My loved ones thought I was heading to Samaria (or Siberia) for sure, that first trip to The Great Land. I came back thinking I'd been in heaven. To some people it was Samaria; I never wanted to leave!

Like Philip, God moved us. Kelso-Longview, Washington is a city I used to despise from the road as we sped up to get past it on I-5. "Thank you, God, that we don't have to live there!" Twenty years ago, it was as Samaritan as it gets, for me. It soon went from being "Samaria" to being "home." I'm so glad to live here! The best place on earth to be is where God has placed you.

Where do we fit? Somewhere. But it's not always the same place, and it's not usually forever. Philip was having the time of his life, but he was soon to be leaving, to accomplish another special job God had for him. He would always have Samaria to treasure as a special memory of how the Lord took him to what others considered a God-forsaken place, then showed him a bit of heaven. That's what God did for me, too, more than once!

Lessons from Samaria? Don't be taken in by the crass commercialism we sometimes see in religion. Keep the heart pure. Be open to new challenges and new people. Be willing to go among the unlovely and love them in Jesus' name—it might turn out to be the greatest experience of our life. Be willing to work as a team. God almost always uses triangulation to accomplish His purposes, with prophets predicting, then various people coming along to fulfill assignments they may not even comprehend, but which are all being managed from above. In God's book, assists seem to count as much as scoring. And don't avoid Samaria—the experience may prove to be one of the great highlights of a lifetime.

**The Bottom Line: Our new Samaria?
Seattle. Loving it. The best place to be...**

DAY 264

Puffins or People?

But God said to Jonah, "Do you do well to be angry for the plant?" And he said, "Yes, I do well to be angry, angry enough to die." And the LORD said, "You pity the plant, for which you did not labor, nor did you make it grow, which came into being in a night and perished in a night. And should I not pity Nineveh, that great city, in which there are more than 120,000 persons who do not know their right hand from their left, and also much cattle?" Jonah 4:9-11

I woke up before 5 A.M. this morning because of Canada geese nearby and couldn't go back to sleep, so decided it was time to go for a walk on the beach. I was keeping an eye out for bald eagles, which to me has long been a personal sign of God's approval and presence in my life. I was only a few minutes into my walk when I saw one. Then, later on, I saw one above Haystack Rock.

I had decided to turn around and head back toward the Cannon Beach Christian Conference Center, site of our 23rd annual Leadership Prayer Summit. I had been looking for puffins, telling God that I didn't really need to see one but that I would like to, if He wanted to show one to me. He prompted me to get my cell phone camera ready for a picture. I waited, watching Haystack Rock. No puffins. Instead, an immature bald eagle came right up over me. I didn't get the picture of Eagle #3, but I didn't need to.

That was when the Lord starting talking to me. He reminded me of Jonah and his affection for a plant, while he could care less about the people who were busy repenting as a result of his preaching! Jonah liked shade vines and hated Ninevites. He delighted in plants and didn't like people—at least not Ninevites.

The Lord told me that if I looked for people who needed Him with the same kind of excitement I had toward eagles and puffins, I would find some. And if I got as excited about people as I did about puffins, I would be more in tune with His heart. That's when I saw the first puffin. Then I saw two puffins fly by in formation, wing tip to wing tip. Then another. And another. I finally took a very poor quality cell phone picture to document puffin number 17, and started back.

The reason I've seen so many eagles and puffins through the years is because I've looked for them. I've noticed them. But I've been much more excited about eagles and puffins than I have been about lost people. It's time to start looking for the people God loves, who need someone to see them, in Jesus' name.

The Bottom Line: If I look for lost people like I look for eagles, I'll find some.

DAY 265

Eagles and Puffins and Bob's. Oh, My.

The flock of Canada geese again awakened me on the final day of the prayer summit at Cannon Beach. I thought I might as well go for one more beach walk. But this one would be a little different. Instead of focusing on wanting to see eagles or puffins, I would look for people who wanted to hear about God.

I had only been on the beach a few seconds when I saw him on the far side of the river emptying into the Pacific. I wasn't sure, but it looked like a golden eagle to me. The color of the magnificent bird as it lifted off made me think I was right. As I turned to watch it fly away, I saw a man behind me who had just appeared. For a second, I wondered if he was an angel. He walked down the beach toward Haystack Rock, the direction I was going. On his return, we met and exchanged pleasantries in front of a splendid ocean. I credited our Creator for the beautiful morning. The man seemed receptive. When I asked if he was a visitor or a local, he told me he was a visitor, working at the Christian conference center (where I was staying)! He told me his name was Bob.

Further up the beach, I exchanged smiles and greetings with a couple as they played with their three dogs.

I got to Haystack Rock and had spotted three puffins when a man and his dog came my direction. I made friends with his dog, and asked him if he was a visitor or a local. He told me had grown up in Oregon, but now lived in Manhattan, in New York City, and was here for a visit. When he asked me what brought me here, I told him I was at a pastors' prayer conference. We chatted a few more minutes, and I was able to show him a puffin. He said he needed to go, stuck out his hand and said, "I'm Bob." I grinned, told him my name and spotted three more puffins as I headed back to the conference center. I had gotten a ways down the beach when I heard commotion as the hundreds of smaller birds on Haystack Rock went into action together to ward off an intruder flying over the rock. Bald eagle.

The Bottom Line: A golden eagle, a bald eagle, seven puffins, two Bob's. Not bad.

DAY 266

The Glory of Long Fuses

Good sense makes one slow to anger,
and it is his glory to overlook an offense.
A king's wrath is like the growling of a lion,
but his favor is like dew on the grass.
A foolish son is ruin to his father,
and a wife's quarreling is a continual dripping of rain.

Proverbs 19:11-13

Patience is an often-scorned fruit of the Spirit, even among Christians. Many in our society carry the proverbial chip on their shoulder, eager to exact revenge on anyone who would dare to knock it off. It doesn't take much to get a reaction from them! The Bible counters that it makes more sense to not be so easily offended, that it's more noble to overlook an offense than it is to pick a fight, that living with someone who nurtures a quarrelsome spirit is as much fun as water torture. The Bible, of course, is right.

What can we do about a culture increasingly impatient, violent and whiny? We could choose patience, peace and the other fruits of the Spirit for ourselves. If we placed as much value on patience and kindness as we do on making sure our rights aren't trampled, we would have plenty of opportunities to display what we value. If it's all about aggression and getting even, and not so much about trying to live like God's people, man will note what we truly value—and respond accordingly.

What does God value? The Israelites in the Wilderness earned His displeasure not by being poor fighters but by refusing to stop whining and complaining! What are we teaching our young people?

A generation of young men have learned through video games that the response to everything is violence—with no lasting consequences. A son who can't control his temper or his impulses will prove to be a ruin to his father.

And it's not just the boys. Girls are allowed to be sassy and disrespectful, particularly toward men. Media fare fuels the attitude. Complaining and whining and quarreling have become trained responses to any unpleasant situation. When everything is a big deal, whining and quarreling become the automatic response.

We don't have to follow suit! We could choose to seek patience, peace and the other fruits of the Spirit. We could be examples to the world of what it looks like to be people who please the Father. Or we could be like everyone else.

The Bottom Line: Being slow to anger is much more glorious than being a hothead.

DAY 267

Please Don't Whistle

Woe to those who call evil good and good evil,
who put darkness for light and light for darkness,
who put bitter for sweet and sweet for bitter!
Woe to those who are wise in their own eyes,
and shrewd in their own sight!
Woe to those who are heroes at drinking wine,
and valiant men in mixing strong drink,
who acquit the guilty for a bribe,
and deprive the innocent of his right!

Isaiah 5:20-23

There's plenty more where that came from! One thing about the prophets: They're direct. Neither did they spare details when proclaiming the catastrophes which would befall entire nations due to the sin of some. All I can say is, "If God didn't exempt the nation He personally established through His promises, why would He spare a nation like America, if we persist in doing the same things for which Israel was judged?"

Woe to those who call evil good and good evil, who put darkness for light and light for darkness,... Our culture has been working through a process for decades in which each sin in the Bible is re-labeled "good." The entire concept of "sin" has been discarded. And what is regarded as evil? Those who would question the morality of another, who would dare to imply that biblical standards of right and wrong might apply even to people who don't like Bible standards. It's all upside down. In our society, people trying to be godly are coming to be considered evil, while those espousing evil are proclaimed to be good! Look out. Judgment is coming to a city near you!

Isaiah talks of the Lord whistling for nations to come to work destruction on His people as punishment for their national sin (Isa 5:26). As I said before, "If He would do that to His people Israel (and He did), what is keeping Him from doing the same for us?" I would guess the answer is, "His mercy." And I would think our best response should be *repentance! True, genuine, heartfelt repentance,* with actions to match! There's still time. I don't want the Lord to need to whistle something up against us. Let's call good what He calls good, and evil what He terms evil. More than that, let's live lives that show the fruit of repentance.

The Bottom Line: We need to call it the same way God calls it —or pay the price.

DAY 268

The Road to Gaza

Now an angel of the Lord said to Philip, "Rise and go toward the south to the road that goes down from Jerusalem to Gaza." This is a desert place. And he rose and went. And there was an Ethiopian, a eunuch, a court official of Candace, queen of the Ethiopians, who was in charge of all her treasure. He had come to Jerusalem to worship and was returning, seated in his chariot, and he was reading the prophet Isaiah. And the Spirit said to Philip, "Go over and join this chariot." So Philip ran to him and heard him reading Isaiah the prophet and asked, "Do you understand what you are reading?" And he said, "How can I, unless someone guides me?" And he invited Philip to come up and sit with him....

Then Philip opened his mouth, and beginning with this Scripture he told him the good news about Jesus. And as they were going along the road they came to some water, and the eunuch said, "See, here is water! What prevents me from being baptized?" And he commanded the chariot to stop, and they both went down into the water, Philip and the eunuch, and he baptized him. And when they came up out of the water, the Spirit of the Lord carried Philip away, and the eunuch saw him no more, and went on his way rejoicing. But Philip found himself at Azotus, and as he passed through he preached the gospel to all the towns until he came to Caesarea. Acts 8:26-31,35-40

I guess the road to Gaza has never been too popular, and certainly not when having the time of your life leading a breakthrough revival, only to be interrupted by a message from God to leave it and head for the desert! But Philip was a disciple, willing to obey God's instructions, logical or not. God uses one disciple to introduce a continent to Christ! God honored Philip's obedience by "poofing" him to Azotus, rather than making him walk. Obedience to God has many, many rewards!

Obedience and evangelism. One results in the other. So what of strategy? Should we never make plans? I wouldn't go that far, but I do think we spend too much time developing strategies which may ultimately only get in God's way. How many conferences or meetings have I witnessed really going somewhere, only to be shut down by the bulletin? Someone was scheduled to do something, and bless God, they were going to do it! So they took up the offering, delivered their stump speech, sold their book or whatever, and the spirit of the service went down like a grounded hot air balloon. No more soaring, today; the agenda! The Holy Spirit knows what He's doing. When He says to change plans, that's what disciples do.

The Bottom Line: One obedient disciple, willing to listen, makes a huge difference!

DAY 269

Irrelevant Adventures

I'm of the opinion that we should be consulting God before we even make any plans, then be sure to check with Him throughout the process, and more than willing to abandon the whole thing at the prompting of the Holy Spirit. If we follow this "strategy," I'm thinking we'll see at least occasional miracles, plus have the thrill of knowing without a doubt that God arranged them. If we don't want to trust God with our plans, He will probably let us keep our control, and we'll *read* about people being led of the Holy Spirit, instead of *being* that person.

It makes me think of a long-ago kids camp I helped staff, in Alaska. As we divided the camp into two teams for a massive game of "Capture the Flag," Scotty, a little space cadet known very personally to me, determined that his contribution to the game would be to wade the lake with his clothes on, clambering around the shallows, Rambo-style, in an effort to sneak up on the flag, fifty yards onshore. People were captured and freed, the flag changed hands several times, and a good time was had by all, including Scotty, who never even got out of the mud until all was done and we were headed for the next activity. Nobody chased him, he never got close to anyone else nor the flag, he was pretty much in his own world. Come to think of it, that was also true when we weren't playing "Capture the Flag." He's the only ten-year-old I've ever known who hit up a pastor for salt, to tan his mole-hide.

Back to my point. When it comes to helping God in this mission to save the world from hell, we church folks are too often taking the Scotty approach, plotting a course of action we're determined to take, based on our own ideas. It's supposed to help the cause. Meanwhile, we're oblivious to the fact that we're in our own world, completely irrelevant to what's going on in the real game. God uses those who pay attention and follow orders, sometimes giving them a free ride to their next assignment, while self-styled revolutionaries seldom get out of the swamp. Their main contribution to the cause is to leave their team one person short. God loves 'em, anyway, but instead of an MVP award, they'll probably get dry clothes.

Let's be the kind of people God can pull out of the best time of our life, send out on a road to nowhere, have us cheerfully grab the opportunity for world-changing evangelism on the first try, then spend the rest of our lives smiling about the whole deal when it's over.

The Bottom Line: To avoid irrelevant adventures, we listen to God, then obey.

DAY 270

Names and Addresses

Now there was a disciple at Damascus named Ananias. The Lord said to him in a vision, "Ananias." And he said, "Here I am, Lord." And the Lord said to him, "Rise and go to the street called Straight, and at the house of Judas look for a man of Tarsus named Saul, for behold, he is praying, and he has seen in a vision a man named Ananias come in and lay his hands on him so that he might regain his sight." But Ananias answered, "Lord, I have heard from many about this man, how much evil he has done to your saints at Jerusalem. And here he has authority from the chief priests to bind all who call on your name." But the Lord said to him, "Go, for he is a chosen instrument of mine to carry my name before the Gentiles and kings and the children of Israel. For I will show him how much he must suffer for the sake of my name." Acts 9:10-16

Saul, the fire-breathing persecutor, abruptly meets his match on the road to Damascus. Most of the time, Jesus uses the gentle approach, and other people; for Saul, He makes an exception! This disciple He calls personally, and audibly. Add to that knocking Saul down, blinding him for three days, rebuking him from the sky, then giving him a vision with details like the name of the man who will come to help Saul and what he will do when he gets there. There's not a lot left to chance— or free will, for that matter! It's just a reminder that God can do anything He wants, with or without our help, though He often lets us play a part as a favor to us.

It certainly didn't feel like a favor to Ananias when he got the vision, which he would have interpreted as just a nightmare, had God not been dropping names and addresses. "By the way, I told Saul you were coming. Yes, this is the same one you've heard about, but it's O.K., now—in the past three days he's changed his mind about a lot of things! I've picked him to carry my name to the Gentiles. So, go over to Straight Street, to Judas' house, and you'll find him there. He's praying, and I told him in a vision that it would be a man named Ananias who would lay hands on him and give him back his sight. Any questions? Good. Have fun!"

Wouldn't you know it? It worked out precisely as God had said—all of it.

The Christian life is only boring for those who haven't tried much of it. For those like Ananias, disciples so faithful, daring and obedient that God can tell someone they're coming before He even informs the disciple, there's always a thrill around the next corner.

The Bottom Line: Do you know where the fun is in discipleship? Obedience.

DAY 271

The Scariest, Best Night of His Life

Now there was a disciple at Damascus named Ananias. The Lord said to him in a vision, "Ananias." And he said, "Here I am, Lord." And the Lord said to him, "Rise and go to the street called Straight, and at the house of Judas look for a man of Tarsus named Saul, for behold, he is praying, and he has seen in a vision a man named Ananias come in and lay his hands on him so that he might regain his sight." But Ananias answered, "Lord, I have heard from many about this man, how much evil he has done to your saints at Jerusalem. And here he has authority from the chief priests to bind all who call on your name." But the Lord said to him, "Go, for he is a chosen instrument of mine to carry my name before the Gentiles and kings and the children of Israel. For I will show him how much he must suffer for the sake of my name."

So Ananias departed and entered the house. And laying his hands on him he said, "Brother Saul, the Lord Jesus who appeared to you on the road by which you came has sent me so that you may regain your sight and be filled with the Holy Spirit." And immediately something like scales fell from his eyes, and he regained his sight. Then he rose and was baptized; and taking food, he was strengthened. Acts 9:10-19

As nation after nation was opened to the Gospel through Saul of Tarsus, and a great portion of the New Testament was written by the same man, who again and again told of his conversion, including the name of the man God sent to him, Ananias the disciple must have felt a huge sense of satisfaction. Pinpoint obedience. It had started out as the scariest night of his life. Now it was his favorite memory.

Obedience is like that. Discipleship is like that. Christianity is supposed to be like that, if we don't settle for the domesticated version which would have us roll over and go back to sleep, even after a vision so clear we got names, addresses and a check-list. I wonder what we miss. We could be daring disciples, too. It all just starts with obedience. We don't even have to come up with our own adventures! Just listen, and obey. We won't be disappointed. Or bored.

The Bottom Line: The Lord has great adventures in store for all listening disciples.

DAY 272

Getting Grace on Them

It was a powerful encounter with Jesus Himself which brought Saul to a spiritual crisis, but prior to this and subsequent to it were encounters with God's grace, exemplified in the lives of disciples. First was Stephen. How would a person holding the coats of the executioners not be moved, then haunted, by the plaintive words of a young man being killed for being good: *"Lord, do not hold this sin against them"* (Acts 7:60)? Such grace!

Then, there was the disciple sent to Saul to help him regain his sight. A person who had systematically destroyed families for the crime of loving Jesus would, I think, have expected a different reception from one of their group, now that he was helpless and blind. Saul had dragged parents away from their children and thrown them in prison for refusing to deny Christ. What are the first words he hears from a Christian, a complete stranger? "Brother Saul, the Lord Jesus... sent me..." *Brother Saul?* Already? No test, no Inquisition? Talk about acceptance! That's what it looks like to be a good steward of God's grace. We do it best when we apply it liberally, letting it splash onto the bystanders. Ananias was a good steward of God's grace.

Another gracious person God put in Saul's life was Barnabas. Barnabas, whose nickname meant "Son of Encouragement", became so many things to Saul. He was an advocate, when no one else was willing to take the chance on him. Barnabas vouched for Saul's authenticity when others thought he was faking his conversion. Barnabas accompanied Saul (now called Paul) on his first missionary journey. They endured a myriad of trials, together. Barnabas proved such a loyal friend that he was even willing to sever his partnership with Paul in order to try to redeem his nephew, John Mark, when the two missionaries disagreed over whether to take another chance on him. Barnabas sidelined his own career to restore Mark's ministry. The first of the Gospels written is because someone was such a careful steward of God's grace!

How are we doing in this area? When the world peeks through the hole in the church door, are they seeing grace, inside? If they become converted, is God's grace the first thing they'll bump into, when they encounter the Church? Last of all, does the unconverted world around us get any grace on them when they rub up against us? They should. We're supposed to be good stewards of it.

The Bottom Line: When the world rubs against us, they should get grace on them.

DAY 273

Who's on First?

When it comes to discipleship, how can we tell who's ahead? First, second, third? That kind of stuff? Easy. The one who desires to be "great" gets to be the servant of all. I can show you the verses. This business of trying to be "best disciple" is like trying to divide a family up into "favorite child," "second-favorite child," and so forth; anyone dumb enough to try it would not find "winning" to be a rewarding experience.

God set it up this way *on purpose.* If we could *ever* just be satisfied to be *in* the family, without constantly jawing at each other over which one of us He likes (or should like) best! The reason we get so frustrated over the "game" of life is because it was never supposed to be a game in the first place, and God refuses to play, which means our game doesn't count. The game is our invention, not God's. Hallelujah! There's no game. There's just being part of His family, with no ranking system. Everyone in God's family receives all the love they can handle, and there's more where that came from.

I think what the Lord wants us to remember is that we are on the same team, in the same family, in the same army, and we face an enemy who is not playing games, and who is not firing blanks. This is not a drill.

How about if we channeled our competitive spirit into winning what is not a game at all, but a true battle over the souls of men, women and children? Many have a competitive nature. Surrendered to Him, God could use that spirit to rescue and protect people, while defeating the purposes of Satan. In other words, we are to beat the devil, not our teammates.

Obedience is key. The "Follow me" command of Jesus is unconditional. Christ offers no escape clause for missions which look too risky or difficult, or which don't fit with the agenda of the soldier. The soldier *has* no other agenda than to obey orders from above. Likewise, the disciple of Christ Jesus. "Follow me" is one big order. It's big enough to provide all the challenges we'll ever want, and then some.

The Bottom Line: The agenda of the disciple of Christ Jesus? "Follow me."

DAY 274

Leading with Love

The Church in Joppa took a real hit when Dorcas died. Highly respected as a woman "full of good works, and acts of charity," that lifestyle was more revered in those days than now, when anyone not holding a microphone or a book contract isn't likely to be overly noticed in the Church. Dorcas was the worker bee type, churning out articles of clothing for people behind the scenes as a ministry, in an era when clothes were scarce and valuable. Her love came through her labor, much as Mother Teresa reached out to the discarded and lonely in Calcutta, and captured the attention of the world without seeking it. This is what it is to lead with love. It can be done in a great variety of ways, with one unifying characteristic: None of them are self-seeking.

How do we lead with love? We just take whatever tools and gifts the good Lord has entrusted to us, find someone to serve, and serve them, without expecting anything in return. That's it. It's none too complicated, yet far too uncommon. Dorcas loved with a needle and thread; Peter loved by telling people all about Jesus and doing powerful works in His name; the disciples at Joppa loved by calling 911 (sending for Peter), instead of being too proud or faithless to ask for help. Because everyone did their part, not only did Dorcas regain her seamstress ministry; many believed in Jesus! The Early Church was leading in love, accompanied by power. The end result was large-scale evangelism.

If the Church will just lead with love, we'll do fine. The power of God is first of all, a display of mercy. This is not fire and signs, but healing and life. It's followed by people flocking to Jesus. If we're demonstrating the love of God, it often doesn't even require a miracle, in order to result in spiritual transformation.

The Church needs to lead with love. Power would be O.K., but I think our tendency has been to misuse power whenever we've had it, anyway, and the world seems to mistrust Christians with power, even when genuine. Love is more effective. Lead with love, and anticipate God's power showing up whenever needed.

We need to be what God has made us to be, and pursue what He has given us to do, unashamedly and with passion. Peter preached and healed, and didn't let it go to his head. Dorcas was a "beaver" type of servant, who ministered through making clothes. The disciples at Joppa exercised their faith by sending for Peter, rather than planning a funeral.

Leading with love is how to utilize every spiritual gift, and touch every life.

The Bottom Line: If the Church will lead with love, we'll do just fine.

DAY 275

Breakthrough Material?

Peter's arrival at Caesarea in Acts 10 was greeted by Cornelius trying to worship him, which Peter promptly (and wisely) averted. God interrupted Peter's sermon to the gathered crowd by just dumping the Holy Spirit on them in such an obvious way that there was no question: The Gentiles were now included in the Kingdom, too! And they hadn't even been baptized, yet! (That was soon remedied).

Is God still doing breakthrough's? Oh, yes! And we are every bit as reluctant as Peter (or more so) to barge through barriers long venerated, especially if it was a spiritual triumph to erect them in the first place. I'm talking about those personal convictions, cultural convictions, denominational standards or whatever, which have sometimes been quite useful in shielding us from temptation, or vital in keeping us within the good graces of our fellow believers. At times they may have become a sort of idol, where an otherwise flagging Christian life is reduced to the victory of "not smoking" or something else which might not have ever even been a temptation to us. As regarding outsiders to the faith, it's a two-edged sword. Sometimes they have been impressed, sometimes repulsed by our convictions, whether teetotaling our way through life or refusing to run on Sunday (a.k.a Eric Liddell, "Chariots of Fire").

Convictions have their place, and I am definitely not for displacing them, particularly for the sake of rationalizing an easier, more hedonistic lifestyle or just trying to blend in. On rare occasions, though, it's not the world which is asking us to cross the barriers we've erected, but God Himself. When it's Him, He always follows the same pattern: It's specific, not vague; He makes sure we know it's Him; He repeats the message, if necessary.

Are we the kind of people God could use to engineer a breakthrough? Pretty much all we have to do is be faithful and pay attention, and it could be any one of us. What do we need to do? We need to listen to God, that's what! He may be giving us visions, with clear, specific directions, but if we prize our personal convictions above specific orders from the Lord, we're going to miss out on breakthroughs which would have helped us all. There's a place for both convictions and breakthrough's—and it's all at God's direction, not ours. Keep alert! Whether the world notices or not, historic breakthrough's will be ours.

The Bottom Line: God uses our bold obedience to engineer breakthrough's.

An Orphanage or a Home?

In the established, organized church, are we offering people a spiritual home, or is it basically an orphanage?

In an orphanage, you get shelter, food, clothing, and a degree of care, plus the fellowship of other orphans. All of that keeps you alive, but if you're an orphan, isn't what you really want a *home*? A place where you belong, where you are accepted, where they care about what you do, where your opinion matters, where they don't feel sorry for you. If you're part of a family, you have a future. What's lacking in an orphanage is the personal, committed relationship unique to a family. In a family, you *belong*.

The larger the church, the more chance there is that people can troop in and out on Sundays, no strings attached, anonymous. It's possible to do it for weeks or months and have no one even know your name. It's not uncommon to visit a mega-church and find yourself shaking hands in the greeting time with other first-time visitors, neither one knowing it. The reason they didn't seem very friendly is because they'd never been here before, either!

With a consumer mentality in place in the Church, one expects to get music, programs and preaching which suit the tastes of the congregation, but not much in the way of relationships. Much as we might venture to Wal-Mart in search of laundry detergent at a good price but not expecting to make new friends there, the Christian consumer in America expects church services to be just that: "Services"—some music and a sermon, something for the kids, then you go home.

In the Church in Acts, people were "home" when they were with other believers. They belonged to something. It wasn't just "5,000 in attendance" in a mega-church with Peter's picture on the side of a bus; it was a family, where people knew your name and expected you to do your chores.

Unless there is mutual commitment in the Church in America, we're going to have people going home from our "services" just as lonely as they came. People long to be part of a family, where they belong, where they matter. An orphanage? It's not the same.

The Bottom Line: People need to belong to a church family, not just an "orphanage."

DAY 277

Rules to Live By

Whoever keeps the commandment keeps his life;
he who despises his ways will die.

Proverbs 19:16

God's rules are to live by. The "commandment" is what we know God wants of us, whether according to the Bible, the laws of the land, or Mom and Dad. (If it's all three, we'd best be paying attention). Those who keep God's commandments see blessings follow them throughout eternity. Those who blow off the commandments in pursuit of their personal happiness face bitter consequences—if not sooner, then definitely later. Usually both.

God's commands are not to cramp our lifestyles, but to enhance them to a degree impossible without the constraint of rules. Just as a game with no rules is neither fun nor really a game, life without rules is a frightful, unpredictable, chaotic mess, lacking in peace and in good. God has better plans for His children. He has created a world of order. It's predictable and reliable—even the fallen world brought about through man's sin. There are systems and principles which can be counted upon to be consistent and true. When we follow the commandments, we live, and live well. When we despise God's ideas in favor of our own, we die. It's our choice.

The person who chooses to bang through life carelessly, disregarding constraints, rules, God and advice, is a person successfully pursuing death. All of us know many such people. Meanwhile, the human being disciplined enough to keep the commandments—or at least pay attention to them and steer life in that general direction—will garner the benefits of a life well lived.

If we don't care where we're going, we're not going to make it to heaven, nor will we experience much of a life here on this earth. It's totally up to us; the choice is ours. The narrow way leads toward God and eternal life; the broad, careless way leads to destruction. The only way to the Father is through the Son, Jesus Christ. It starts with believing on Him, accepting His free gift of salvation. Then there are the daily choices: Will we live by God's rules or ours? The one who goes with God will find grace and life eternal; the one who despises God's ways and assumes everything will be O.K. will one day discover that salvation is only found through Jesus Christ, God's rules are to live by, and all other roads end in death.

The Bottom Line: God's rules are to live by.

DAY 278

Revival Tracks

What are the tracks left by John Wesley which distinguished the revival in 18th century England so effective in changing society?

- It was rooted in relationship with God, not in method or in theology.
- It dealt with sin. The Wesleyan revival recognized sin as the problem of mankind which only Christ could fix, and also saw sin as something to be conquered, rather than accepted as a normal part of the Christian life.
- It was outdoors. The Gospel was available to all, without any barriers.
- High expectations. The Methodist societies weren't "seeker-friendly," in terms of making people comfortable in their sin. Once people became converts, they were expected to grow up, spiritually, rather than remaining perpetual babes in Christ. The old life was to be left behind.
- Small groups. Accountability, discipling, nurturing, growth.
- Single-minded focus. Wesley told his preachers, "You have nothing to do but save souls." Itinerant evangelists played a big role in the revival.

Could revival happen in America? Of course. But it will probably only come if we want it, and if we pray. God can take dead, traditional churches, full of dead, traditional people, or sophisticated McChristians raised on psycho-babble, and make saints out of them, if He chooses. That said, if He began a revival without prayer, it would be the first time, wouldn't it? When we pray, and when we truly want revival, I don't think we'll be disappointed.

The Bottom Line: If we pray and truly desire revival, we'll get what we need.

DAY 279

On Loan to God

Whoever is generous to the poor lends to the Lord,
and he will repay him for his deed.

Proverbs 19:17

Some of the big news this week is the struggle in Washington, D.C. to raise the debt ceiling, allowing the United States government to add to its already unfathomable tab of 14.3 trillion dollars in financial obligations to others. Meanwhile, small businesses and individuals have a hard time securing loans for any amount, these days, while the U.S. continues to wallow in the deepest economic crisis since the Great Depression. Money is tight.

According to this proverb, even God is interested in getting a loan! Well, not exactly, but the terminology is there: *Whoever is generous to the poor lends to the Lord.* I've heard of "talent on loan from God" before, but God trying to get a loan?! Kind of humorous. A finance officer once told me my credit score was in the same league as God's, but I didn't think God ever used His for anything. Now God's trying to get a loan to help the poor?

Of course, the idea that God would actually need anything from us is ludicrous, along with the idea that He would ever really "owe" us anything. After all, we are His Creation, not the other way around. And God operates in a pretty much cash-less society, where if He wants something, He can just say, "Let there be...," and it appears, be it galaxy or something smaller—say, an inhabitable planet with moon accessory—or lunch for a starving child in Asia.

The Creator still has the corner on making solar systems, while allowing mankind to thrill themselves with an occasional small step on the moon or some shuttle missions. The Lord isn't asking for help in making new galaxies. But He leans on us for a really, really little thing, promising to pay us back: Be generous to the poor. Huh?

A God who has no "ceilings"—debt or otherwise—whispers to His servants, "If you'll just be generous to the poor, I'll pay you back," and obligates Himself to people who already owe Him absolutely everything. What kind of God is this? The kind that's unbelievably great to have on your side! The kind who asks us for help!

And whose responsibility is it to help the poor? The government's? No. The people of God. When we do, we're lending to the Lord. He'll pay us back. His credit rating is pretty good. And His love? Beyond comprehension.

The Bottom Line: God asks us to be generous to the poor, and He'll pay us back.

DAY 280

God's Gym

Have you not known? Have you not heard?
The LORD is the everlasting God,
the Creator of the ends of the earth.
He does not faint or grow weary;
his understanding is unsearchable.
He gives power to the faint,
and to him who has no might he increases strength.
Even youths shall faint and be weary,
and young men shall fall exhausted;
but they who wait for the LORD shall renew their strength;
they shall mount up with wings like eagles;
they shall run and not be weary;
they shall walk and not faint.

Isaiah 40:28-31

Many are the posters, plaques and coffee cups bearing the last verse of Isaiah 40. Those of us who are Christians and love eagles generally have at least a couple eagle mementoes emblazoned with Isaiah 40:31.

An eagle in the wild is something to behold. "Strong," "majestic," "graceful," are words which describe these birds. In a matter of a few wing beats, they go from perch to soaring. Their flight is best described as "effortless." They circle and float in the sky without seeming to move a wing-tip.

That's what God's children get to do. Those who wait for Him are availed of His power and majesty—all that we need. Young men relying on their youthful vigor to get them up the mountain are plopping over along the trail. Body builders have given up. The "brains rather than brawn" people are out of answers. Those who rely on God are just getting started! People without God, who only have youth or conditioning or human strength and intelligence on which to depend are exhausted, while those who wait on the LORD take off and soar effortlessly above the rest! It's not our strength; it's God's. He has plenty.

Which would we rather do? Rely on ourselves and how many times we've been to the gym, how many degrees we've collected? Or should we just wait for the Lord, and take the eagle route? Hmm. Clawing our way up the hill on our own strength, or flying with the Lord above it all? This is not a hard question.

The Bottom Line: Human strength route?
Eagle route? God's way is way better.

DAY 281

When God Does a Jailbreak

Now when Herod was about to bring him out, on that very night, Peter was sleeping between two soldiers, bound with two chains, and sentries before the door were guarding the prison. And behold, an angel of the Lord stood next to him, and a light shone in the cell. He struck Peter on the side and woke him, saying, "Get up quickly." And the chains fell off his hands. And the angel said to him, "Dress yourself and put on your sandals. And he did so. And he said to him, "Wrap your cloak around you and follow me." And he went out and followed him. He did not know that what was being done by the angel was real, but thought he was seeing a vision. When they had passed the first and the second guard, they came to the iron gate leading into the city. It opened for them of its own accord, and they went out and went along one street, and immediately the angel left him. When Peter came to himself, he said, "Now I am sure that the Lord has sent his angel and rescued me from the hand of Herod and from all that the Jewish people were expecting."
Acts 12:6-11

That's not even the whole story. It had started out tragically, with King Herod, who had a reputation to live up to with that name, singling out James, brother of John, and executing him. This garnered enough excitement among the Jewish authorities to encourage Herod to arrest Peter, too, which he did. The prospect of not living another day didn't prevent Peter from sleeping so peacefully that God's angel had to swat him to wake him up—God's peace is like that.

The dreamlike scenario continues as chains fall off, gates open by themselves (quite a novelty, back then), and the angel of the Lord leads Peter to the gathered Church desperately praying for his release, though not with sufficient faith to believe it's really him when he shows up. No matter. This whole thing is God's deal, anyway. Usually He lets people help, at least a little. This jailbreak He pulled off all on His own. Soon afterward, God also deals with the king on His own. Herod Agrippa I fancied himself a god. The Real One knocked Herod off with nothing more than a fistful of worms. Note: Real gods are not brought down by intestinal parasites. (So much for Herod being a real god).

The word of God increased and multiplied. It was going to happen. God was going to make sure it happened! Jesus didn't come to this earth to live, die and rise again, only to have it all snuffed out by ne'er do well's in royal robes! When necessary, He intervened directly. Still does.

**The Bottom Line: God can get 'er done.
Divine intervention. Prayer. Whatever.**

DAY 282

Slow Miracles

God seems to like the subtle approach. In Acts 12:25, the odd couple of Barnabas and Saul didn't leave Jerusalem alone, but purposely brought with them a young protege named John Mark. God will throw as many angels at a situation as required, in order to achieve His ends, but He seems to greatly prefer dedicated, constant service to flashy, inexplicable miracles. In other words, if the only thing that works is to knock Saul down on the road to Damascus, that's fine, He'll do it, but He'd much rather have a couple seasoned disciples take a young man under their wing and train him to be a disciple with patience and love, like Barnabas and Saul did with Mark. Compared to raising kids or disciples, miracles are easy!

We need to do a better job of bringing along younger disciples. Two generations float around out there, most of whom could care less about the Church, some because they feel the Church has never cared much about them. "What do you mean?! We've provided programs and materials. We've paid professional ministers to relate to them! How could they not get this?!"

I'm afraid that far too many times, we've wanted the younger generation to cherish our traditions more than we've wanted them to cherish our God. They always want to do everything differently, which means we lose things important to us: our traditions, our methods, our control. It's easier to warehouse them somewhere by themselves until they grow up. Then, when they've learned to see things our way, they can come join us. (Anyone notice how few are coming)?

Barnabas and Saul took the chance of letting this kid come with them. This wasn't a two-week mission trip to Mexico, with a stop at Disneyland on the way back; this was the real deal, where people would do stuff like throw rocks at disciples. John Mark couldn't cut it, and abruptly abandoned a couple disappointed missionaries in the middle of their journey. One, his relative, Barnabas, would later forego his own future career as a missionary in order to try to salvage Mark's. It worked. And the young guy from the new generation did a new thing: He wrote down what Jesus had done. The message had been circulating orally for years, but nobody had written it down, yet. Mark did it. Others followed.

God makes sure it comes out right. He can do jailbreaks, lights in the sky, anything. That's either with us or without us; He's always successful. So why bother trying to do anything for a God who doesn't really need us? Because He seems to like the "slow miracles" best—raising kids, raising disciples, patiently loving people into faith. And He almost always leaves those for us.

The Bottom Line: God seems to prefer slow miracles like parenting and discipling.

DAY 283

Abraham, My Friend

But you, Israel, my servant,
Jacob, whom I have chosen,
the offspring of Abraham, my friend;
you whom I took from the ends of the earth,
and called from its farthest corners,
saying to you, "You are my servant,
I have chosen you and not cast you off";
fear not, for I am with you;
be not dismayed, for I am your God;
I will strengthen you, I will help you,
I will uphold you with my righteous right hand.

Isaiah 41:8-10

In the midst of all God's comforting promises to His people, what stands out the most to me? *"Abraham, my friend."* Talk about honor! God calls Abraham His "friend." He would do the same for us! God is willing to be our Friend. The accompanying verses are promises of how God takes care of His friends. Not bad!

I still remember what it felt like to have Jimmy Stoddard stick up for me when we were fifth graders. I was small for my age, Jimmy was smaller still, but it didn't stop him from standing off a band of 8th grade boys who had been verbally harassing me, until Jimmy intervened by screaming at them, "You leave my friend alone!" They gave a weak retort and walked away.

"My friend." What a sweet phrase in my big, stick-out ears! I had only known Jimmy for mere weeks—his dad worked road construction building the interstate across South Dakota—and a few weeks later Jimmy moved away and out of my life, but for a while I had someone who was willing to take on multiple foes twice his size just to defend my honor.

Here is God doing the same thing. He has chosen us, identified with us. He's willing to call us His friend in front of our enemies, with not-subtle-at-all descriptions of what He will do to whomever harms us! "You leave my friend alone!" Something like that. And our God is *really big—and strong*! He takes very, very good care of His friends. There's nothing like being a friend of God.

The Bottom Line: What greater privilege than to be a friend of God?

DAY 284

Stay in the Goal

What roles does God bless? What do I mean by "roles"? Well, for one thing, are we a "settler" or an "explorer"? It helps to know. Looking at the following descriptions and seeing if one clicks with us may be helpful in finding the role God seems to bless in our lives:

Does God seem to bless it when you're the *explorer?* You try new things, at His direction, and even when they don't pan out, you still feel blessed and excited. Plus, the adventures you have with God, doing new things, are the landmark events of your whole life. You can't wait to try something new, with God.

Does God bless you when you're a manager, a *settler?* The new things you try seem to usually backfire; even when they work, you're nervous and can't wait to get back to safety. You just don't enjoy wandering around in new territory without a map. It's not fun; it's frightening. Meanwhile, what others think of as boring, you find beautiful. Routine doesn't bother you in the least. You enjoy taking care of things, even organizations. It gives you a strong sense of fulfillment, knowing that you've had a hand in the growth of something or someone. You notice and take encouragement from the slightest of improvements. It doesn't take the prospect of hair-raising experiences to motivate you to show up for work; you always show up. You can't imagine being irresponsible. You can't imagine not working.

See the contrast? God needs and uses both settlers and explorers, but the two roles are vastly different, as are the results. One blazes trails and writes stories about all the harrowing experiences along the way; the other one raises a family and keeps the nation from going hungry. Both are important.

Our roles may change over time, as well. The young, single explorer may, a decade later, be the married settler raising a family in less adventuresome circumstances. His pioneering mind set may be permanently put to rest, or it may re-emerge, later in life, or in safer avenues.

Has God given you the role of peacemaker? Inventor? Teacher? Leader? Manager? Helper? Worker? Homemaker? Husband? Wife? Parent? Student? When we find our role, it helps us relax and accomplish the work God has set before us, instead of floundering in confusion. We can find delight in our work and in our daily lives when we have the peace of knowing we are doing the will of God. God's assignments for us will often include more than one role at a time, or it may mean we move from one role to another, sequentially. (Contradictory roles mean we've probably gotten off track). Ask God to reveal His role for you. He will.

Settlers aren't keen on the idea of leaving in the middle of summer to go stake out new territory, somewhere. They know that if and when they return, all the hard work they did in planting crops will have gone to nothing, while they were out exploring a place to which they had no desire to move, anyway. Meanwhile, true adventurers can't abide the thought of spending perfectly good summers hoeing corn. Life's too short to blow it on weeds, in their estimation.

Explorer or settler? The pastor trying to be both at the same time will probably be frustrated, regardless of how many success books fill his library. The preacher who insists on leading the way into the next century and getting there first needs to be ready to go it alone, if necessary, because it's pretty well guaranteed that a placid congregation of settlers is not going to sign onto any hair-brained adventures! And the methodical, shepherd type of pastor probably would do well to skip most of the "inspirational," change-the-world conferences that fire leaflets into his mailbox. He'd do better to concentrate on being the best methodical shepherd he can be, and not pay somebody to steal his joy and help him come home feeling worn-out and worthless.

What is God calling me to be? Some answers are obvious: Husband. Wife. Father. Mother. With ministry, it gets trickier, but thanks for asking.

It's helpful if we can get it down to just a word or a short phrase— something memorable and meaningful to us. For me, it's "servant of God." To others, that term may sound like a no-brainer, but I've spent years refining the meaning of it and applying it to my life, practically.

Sports terms can help us focus. "I'm a soccer player" is different from saying, "I'm a goalie." "A forward." "A defender." All play soccer, but the roles are quite different. A goalie abandoning the goal to run down and try to score is only helping the opposing team.

Where does God have you playing, these days? If you're a goalie, quit beating yourself up for not scoring goals, and defend your own goal! If He's made you a forward, concentrate on offense, and don't expect the backfield to come help you on your favorite project. If they did, they would be wrong in leaving their assigned post! Figure out your position, and play it to the best of your ability, being ready to get switched to a new role, or the bench, at any time. Just don't try to play someone else's position for them, and don't try to play all the positions at once. Ask God for His assignment for you. Then play there with all your heart.

The Bottom Line: Play with all your heart wherever God has assigned you to play.

DAY 285

Man Bites Horse

A man of great wrath will pay the penalty,
for if you deliver him, you will only have to do it again.

Proverbs 19:19

Proverbs is a book about reality. The teachings are reminiscent of the oft-repeated sayings of parents, intent on imparting all the wisdom they can into their offspring in the usually vain hope that their own mistakes won't be repeated anew in the next generation. It's worth a try. Proverbs has that tone. Again and again, on a myriad of subjects, Proverbs puts wisdom down where we can get it, if we're interested. If we choose to go our own merry way, we can't say we weren't warned.

This is one of those "warning" proverbs—the subject: Anger. *A man of great wrath will pay the penalty, for if you deliver him, you will only have to do it again.*

What might the "penalty" be? Oh, let's see... All the way from juvenile hall to jail to prison. A trail of short-term relationships intended to be long-term ones. A long rap sheet and a short, depressing resume. A life marked by wasted potential, blown up time and time again by rage not quite under control. Out-of-control people pay the penalty in so many ways; not only that, but they are often in need of someone to bail them out. Again. Here's where the warning comes in: Until the person learns to control their own rage, you can go ahead and be their savior, but you'll just get to do it again. Just sayin'.

There is Someone big enough to handle our anger. The fruit of His Spirit includes peace, patience, gentleness and self-control, all of them really good anger inhibitors. When we surrender our lives to Jesus Christ, the makeover begins. When we get in the habit of straining our raw emotions through the filter of His love before speaking or acting, anger seldom makes it through, and when it does, remorse quickly follows. It's a beautiful thing to see it happen in someone's life! Sweeter yet when it's our own intemperate temper now under Christ's control.

I remember the days of rage. A kid whose prized possessions included half a dozen plastic horses was infuriated at his insensitive mother for ordering him to take a bath. He knew just how to get even with her. He bit the tails off all his own horses and spat them out on the floor! Kids who grow up playing with tail-less horses learn to give their temper over to God, if they're smart. It's better that way. I still have a tail-less black plastic horse. It's a reminder: Jesus saves! He's the only One who really can.

The Bottom Line: Give God your life,
including your temper. Jesus is the Savior.

DAY 286

Spirit-led Failure and Joy

Having risked their lives repeatedly to bring the Gospel to the Galatians, Barnabas and Paul are rewarded with public revilement by their own people, the Jews, whose leaders follow them from town to town, stirring up the populace and eventually causing Paul to be stoned. All the while, Gentiles are readily accepting the Gospel. In this mixed bag of blessings and trials, the reaction of the missionaries, rather than getting discouraged or going home, is simply to go to the next town when their welcome has wilted and they've done all they can do. But check out their mood: *"And the disciples were filled with joy and with the Holy Spirit"* (Acts 13:52). Really! Their missionary scorecard isn't looking that good, they are wanted in several cities (as in "wanted" posters, not wanted, nicely), but still they press on, filled with joy and the Holy Spirit. How does this work? How do you keep the joy when you're getting beat up, and your side is losing?

It goes back to the phrase, *"sent out by the Holy Spirit"* (Acts 13:4). When you're commissioned by denominational headquarters, you need something to prove this was a good idea; you need success. When you're sent out by God, all you need is obedience. As long as you didn't quit, even a "losing" effort is a successful one, and cause for joy; you did what God said.

It's hard for us to get a handle on how God's plan for us might somehow include "failure." We live in a culture which despises failure and glorifies success. The creep of that mentality into the Church makes it easy for Christians to assume everything we touch ought to result in "success," as defined by us. "God-directed failure" is a pretty hard sell these days, in America. It sounds like an oxymoron. How could an all-powerful God direct one of His own to take on a project which would result in rejection, persecution or death?! Isn't that failure?

Let's apply it to Jesus. The plan of salvation took Jesus Christ from heaven's throne room to a stable manger, then threaded Him through a life of rejection, persecution and death on a cross. Rejected by His own people, humiliated, tortured. Crucified. Failure? No, it was the greatest victory in the history of the earth, because He defeated sin and death, forever, and freed mankind from the penalty of eternal damnation, all in one afternoon. It appeared to be the ultimate defeat, from a worldly standpoint, even as Jesus successfully saved the world and exhibited perfect obedience to His Father. That's what it looks like when God directs His people toward "failure," but regards their obedience as "righteousness," the ultimate success.

The Bottom Line: If we're obeying God, it can't be failure, no matter how it looks.

DAY 287

What God Really Wants

We really need to get off the pragmatic mindset of this age, which tells us not to pursue anything unless it will bring us good results, and soon. When we adopt the "Unless it brings pleasant results, it can't be from God" frame of mind, we disqualify ourselves from the tougher assignments God uses to bring about the greatest triumphs. For some jobs, only tough disciples need apply.

Paul and Barnabas could have just gone home. After the first city, it didn't take a genius to know what was going to happen, if they persisted in this approach of going to the synagogues first, preaching to the Jews, alarming the locals to the point of obstinacy, then turning to the Gentiles, only to be frustrated and persecuted by the Jews they had been trying to help, until they were driven out of the city. The pragmatic thing to do would have been to sneak around among the Gentiles in a few towns, sharing the Gospel with people who wouldn't get upset. Instead, they felt a burden to go to their own countrymen, first. It didn't seem to do much good, judging from the rocks being thrown at them.

But self-preservation wasn't the plan. Barnabas and Paul headed straight for the synagogue in each city, to proclaim Jesus as the Messiah to their fellow Jews. Maybe a few would believe, here. Maybe not. When they inevitably got kicked out of the synagogue, they went to the non-Jews. When persecution forced them from that city, they went on to the next. It wasn't the most workable of plans, seeing as how it was so predictable, including the ignoble exit. What it did, though, was forge in Galatia a Church who understood from the start that the Christian way included suffering and hardship and demanded obedience to God always, not just when obedience brought pleasant results.

When are we going to learn that? And how? I can't count how many times I've heard the sentiment, "God wants me to be happy," usually served up as rationalization for disobedience to Him, and quoted like a Bible verse (Sorry, it isn't). The source of the Early Christians' joy was not in nice circumstances accompanying their faith, but in the satisfaction of obedience to God. When they obeyed God, they felt joyful. When they opened every aspect of their lives to the presence of the Holy Spirit, He came in and filled them with joy. It had very little to do with their results or their circumstances. Hence, they could even rejoice in "failure," if it was the outcome of obedience to God. And they could joyfully begin a process which seemed doomed from the beginning, if they knew it was the Holy Spirit sending them. Different, huh? I'll bet it would work with us, too, though.

The Bottom Line: What God really wants is our obedience. Joy follows.

DAY 288

Rock-proof Joy

In lining up for discipleship training, are we always going to check the box marked "easy level," or are we willing to spring for "difficult," if we sense God's leading? Will we go through doors of opportunity with no guarantee of success, and a high probability of pain? Do we love people to the extent that we would risk everything so they might know Christ, or are we reluctant to go through even the easy doors when it comes to witnessing? (I'm talking to myself, here).

Generations ago, circuit riding Methodist preachers scoured the countryside, evangelizing much and dying young. Where are the missionaries to America, these days? Shouldn't that be us? Some questions, based on Acts 13:

- Are we being led by the Holy Spirit or man? The answer to that question is quite important, especially when things are tough, results less than favorable. The only incentive which keeps us in the game, sometimes, is a divine commission.
- Are we committed to Christ and the mission on which He has sent us? If not, all it takes are some disappointing circumstances, a desertion or two, or one angry letter, and we're ready to bag it. Committed to Christ, regardless!
- Are we willing to forego pragmatism in favor of the leading of the Holy Spirit? In many situations in the world, the only kind of evangelism which will break through is courageous evangelism, where you're not sure you'll survive. Are we willing to obey Christ, even when we seemingly only have loss to show for it?
- Are we willing to "release" when told by Christ? This means releasing a town, a person, a ministry method, in order to go on to the next assignment. A willingness to release when led by the Spirit is important, as is the willingness to pursue ministry through pure obedience, regardless of the prospect of "success." Will we grab on or let go, according to the Spirit's will?
- Are we willing to be filled with joy and the Holy Spirit? This is not an automatic thing. It comes when the disciple invites the Spirit to have full control of his life, withholding nothing. The joy comes when we're filled with the Spirit. The joy accompanies complete obedience.

When we've opened our lives fully to the Holy Spirit, allowed Him to fill us, allowed Him to lead us; when we've completely obeyed, there is an indescribable, indestructible joy. It's circumstance-proof, desertion-proof, rock-proof. This kind of joy comes only from God. It's available for every disciple who invites God to fill him with joy and with the Holy Spirit.

The Bottom Line: For indestructible joy, we invite God's Holy Spirit into our lives.

DAY 289

Unswerving Servant

Behold my servant, whom I uphold,
my chosen, in whom my soul delights;
I have put my Spirit upon him;
he will bring forth justice to the nations.
He will not cry aloud or lift up his voice,
or make it heard in the street;
a bruised reed he will not break,
and a faintly burning wick he will not quench;
he will faithfully bring forth justice.
He will not grow faint or be discouraged
till he has established justice in the earth;
and the coastlands wait for his law.

Isaiah 42:1-4

I thought Jesus came to bring *salvation* to mankind, but here, three times in four verses, it speaks of His coming to bring *justice* to the nations. The two must be connected. Apparently, without justice there can be no salvation. Jesus brought both to this earth. In order to do it, the Servant had to be utterly unswerving. Perfect obedience to the Father marked His life. No departures from the task before Him, not even for a second. Not even for something as simple as extinguishing a burning wick about to go out, anyway, or breaking off an already-bruised reed. Not the slightest departure from the path.

There's a lesson for us, here. Sin rarely hits us head-on. Satan is far too subtle and clever to approach us with the offer to go ahead and throw away a perfectly good relationship with God in exchange for something we can see will ruin our life and the lives of those around us. No, sin starts with distraction, with curiosity. What could it hurt? We're just going to look. We won't do anything wrong, we're only stopping for a moment to finish off a broken reed. It'll only take a second. It's already broken. We're just putting it out of its misery!

The first indication of anything wrong is the sting of sin's grip.

The way to stay out of sin? Stay on the path our Savior took: Unswerving obedience to God. Eyes ahead. Ignore the offers, the ads, the "Can I have just a minute of your time?" tactics of the enemy. Jesus showed the path to victory: Follow God, without giving way to distraction or discouragement.

The Bottom Line: The way to stay free of sin's grip?
Unswerving obedience.

DAY 290

A Stone's Throw from Quitting

But Jews came from Antioch and Iconium, and having persuaded the crowds, they stoned Paul and dragged him out of the city, supposing that he was dead. But when the disciples gathered about him, he rose up and entered the city, and on the next day he went on with Barnabas to Derbe. When they had preached the gospel to that city and had made many disciples, they returned to Lystra and to Iconium and to Antioch, strengthening the souls of the disciples, encouraging them to continue in the faith, and saying that through many tribulations we must enter the kingdom of God. And when they had appointed elders for them in every church, with prayer and fasting they committed them to the Lord in whom they had believed. Acts 14:19-23

The first missionary journey was one crazy adventure! Barnabas and Paul have been journeying from town to town in Galatia, sharing the Gospel. When they hit pagan Lystra, Paul's impressive miracle of healing produces an unwanted response: Worship! The local populace, folklore-primed to expect Zeus and Hermes any day now, note that the gods have arrived, and prepare appropriate sacrifices. A horrified Barnabas and Paul are barely able to derail the worship. Meanwhile, who should appear but a troop of ne'er-do-well's, who have marched a hundred miles out of their way to harass the missionaries. They are effective in transforming the formerly worshiping crowd into a rock-hurling mob.

Paul's seemingly lifeless body is deposited outside the city gates. End of story. Ah, don't forget God. The battered missionary arises, limps into the city, then departs the next day. For home? No, the next city! Mercifully, this one is more fruitful, plus Paul's enemies, satisfied that he's dead, no longer follow him around, the only benefit to being unsuccessfully stoned to death I can think of.

They complete their mission in Derbe. It's a straight shot home. But they go to... Lystra! Where the stones were thrown. The apostles retrace their steps through each city where they've ministered, even adding a new one on the way.

Why do they go back? Follow-up is that important to them. At each stop, they strengthen the souls of the disciples and encourage them in the faith; tell them that tribulation is part of the deal, when it comes to serving Jesus (a pretty convincing message, coming from someone left for dead); appoint elders in every church; and pray (and fast) for them, committing them to the Lord. They know it could well cost them their lives to follow up on these converts. They go, anyway.

The Bottom Line: Following up is important enough to risk lives for it.

DAY 291

Careful with the Yoke
Part One

The apostles and the elders were gathered together to consider this matter. And after there had been much debate, Peter stood up and said to them, "Brothers, you know that in the early days God made a choice among you, that by my mouth the Gentiles should hear the word of the gospel and believe. And God, who knows the heart, bore witness to them, by giving them the Holy Spirit just as he did to us, and he made no distinction between us and them, having cleansed their hearts by faith. Now, therefore, why are you putting God to the test by placing a yoke on the neck of the disciples that neither our fathers nor we have been able to bear? But we believe that we will be saved through the grace of our Lord Jesus, just as they will." Acts 15:6-11

What was the cause of the debate? Some Jewish believers had determined that newly converted Gentiles needed to undergo circumcision in order to be Christians. Along with that came the implication that they should also be subject to the other laws of the Jewish faith, in effect needing to become Jews before they could become Christians. This was a big deal. It could have resulted in the first church split, or it could have severely damaged the Gospel, turning it from a free gift by faith into something based on works and rituals. There would have been little appeal to a Gentile audience, since if becoming a Jew was the drawing point, that option had been available for centuries.

The Early Church did a great job of approaching this question. Here are some of the things they did right:

1. They got right on it. People's lives had already been affected by this controversy. There wasn't time to toss this to a blue-ribbon panel of theologians to dissertate about for a few years. They called the council right away.
2. They didn't pick sides, or demonize one another. They came together as the Church, all on the same team, regardless of disagreements.
3. They listened to one another. It must have been hard to sit through some of those speeches, but they did it, respectfully.
4. They spoke up when they needed to, and where it could do some good.

The Bottom Line: To resolve differences, follow the pattern of the Early Church.

DAY 292

Careful with the Yoke
Part Two

5. They maintained a spirit of humility, prayer and worship, even as they wrestled with an uncomfortable question. This was a godly discussion. That doesn't happen by accident.
6. Though they stated their opinions, there was a willingness to submit to one another, and most importantly, submit to God. God granted them grace.
7. They came to agreement! That means a lot of people were willing to change their minds, compromise, or at least agree to stick with the group, even if they didn't see it that way.
8. They made a clear and simple decision, prayerfully, then wrote it down and communicated it clearly and consistently to everyone. They even went to the trouble of sending impartial, trusted witnesses along to confirm the accuracy of the message. The conclusion at which they arrived kept the Gospel focused on grace rather than laws and rituals, yet encouraged the new believers to abstain from particularly offensive practices. When they heard the news, they rejoiced. This decision had God's grace upon it.
9. They followed through on the decision. The letter they wrote wasn't just a piece of parchment, subsequently ignored; they lived by the decision of the Jerusalem Council.
10. They let it rest. Those who didn't get their way didn't bring it up every year, trying to get the ruling overturned, keeping the pot stirred. The Church came together, prayed together, listened to one another and voiced their opinions, made a prayerful, clear decision and communicated it, then moved on. The result was amazing. Maybe we could take a few lessons from the Early Church in how to resolve problems in the Church. We would also do well to remember that the Savior who promised "My yoke is easy and my burden is light" wants us to be pretty careful about what yokes we might place on someone else.

They did it right, when it came to resolving differences of opinion in the Church. Maybe we should try that way, more often, in churches, marriages...

The Bottom Line: This pattern really would help in resolving differences!

DAY 293

Back to School Verses

Listen to advice and accept instruction,
that you may gain wisdom in the future.
Many are the plans in the mind of a man,
but it is the purpose of the LORD that will stand.
Cease to hear instruction, my son,
and you will stray from the words of knowledge.

Proverbs 19:20-21,27

It's the first day back to school for our family. Advice is being offered freely and rebuffed just as quickly. The older we get, the harder it seems to be to listen, with teen years notoriously troublesome times for keeping the information highway open and cheerful, both ways. Ah, God will help us.

In fact, in this passage, it sounds like He is on the side of the parents. *Listen to advice and accept instruction,* that you may gain wisdom in the future. See? Even God is telling you to listen and pay attention, kid! *Cease to hear instruction, my son, and you will stray from the words of knowledge.* Do you know what is going to happen to you if you quit listening? You're going over a cliff, that's what!

But like I said, the older we get, the harder it seems to be to listen. Teen-age discontent and rebellion may be a spike on the "You won't listen to me!" chart, but it doesn't automatically settle down after high school graduation. Or college. Or marriage. Or the fortieth birthday.

It's pretty much a choice. Listening to instruction is not natural to us, like, for instance, eating. We must choose to listen, if it's going to happen. It's like choosing to go back to school, even if our assessment of the first day back, on a scale of 1-10, is a (quote) "negative three." Listen to instruction long enough—gain wisdom. Cease to listen to instruction—wind up in the ditch. Cease to listen to our spouse—marriage ends up in the ditch. Ignore God's plan and go with our own, regardless—disaster awaits us, every time.

Many are the plans in the mind of a man, but it is the purpose of the LORD that will stand. Choosing to listen to God guarantees us wisdom. Choosing to listen to the instructors He has placed in our lives also guarantees us wisdom, even on "negative three" days.

The Bottom Line: Listening to instruction and advice guarantees us wisdom.

DAY 294

Full-time Christian Service

And Judas and Silas, who were themselves prophets, encouraged and strengthened the brothers with many words. And after they had spent some time, they were sent off in peace by the brothers to those who had sent them. But Paul and Barnabas remained in Antioch, teaching and preaching the word of the Lord, with many others also. Acts 15:32-35

I wish I'd never heard the term: "Full-time Christian Service." My problem with the term is not that I don't believe in it—I do, with all my heart! The reason I wish I'd never heard it called that is because it gives the strong implication that only a few of us would have such a call, that we'll probably have to do time in a Bible college or seminary and drum up a license for it, and that *everybody else is off the hook.* In other words, if God doesn't nail you with "a call to full-time Christian service," you're free to engage in....what? "Part-time Christian service"? (Read: "Part-time follower of Jesus"—that's how it plays out in daily life).

Shouldn't "full-time Christian service" be for all "full-time Christians"? There's nothing wrong with the concept of full-time Christian service; the problem is that the existence of the concept has led to an awful lot of "part-time Christians," plus frustration on the part of many who have found their Christianity became a "career" and a way to make a living, rather than a lifestyle to be lived.

How was it in the Early Church? In the place they were first called "Christians" (Antioch), the assumption was that *everyone* was automatically called to "full-time Christian service." Had they used that term (and fortunately they didn't), it would have just been another name for discipleship. No one in the Early Church thought of "conversion" separate from discipleship; discipleship meant following and serving Jesus, full-time. If that included using a God-given gift of prophecy, people were given all the freedom they needed to exercise that gift. Same thing for teaching and preaching, or in the case of Dorcas, being pretty good with a needle and thread. A plurality of leadership meant everyone got to use the gifts God had given them. I'm liking this model!

The Bottom Line: Everyone is called to "full-time Christian service."

DAY 295

Who's Following Us?

Paul came also to Derbe and to Lystra.. A disciple was there, named Timothy, the son of a Jewish woman who was a believer, but his father was a Greek. He was well spoken of by the brothers at Lystra and Iconium. Paul wanted Timothy to accompany him, and he took him and circumcised him because of the Jews who were in those places, for they all knew that his father was a Greek. As they went on their way through the cities, they delivered to them for observance the decisions that had been reached by the apostles and elders who were in Jerusalem. So the churches were strengthened in the faith, and they increased in numbers daily. Acts 16:1-5

Whom are we bringing along with us? Hopefully, it's someone. History is strewn with the examples of great men who did outstanding deeds, then passed from the scene with no one to take up their mantle. That last figure of speech hails back to a time when someone did it right (at God's direction): Elijah, prophet of God, took on an assistant, Elisha, and poured everything of himself into the younger man. When Elisha became aware that his master would be departing, his request was that he might inherit a double portion of Elijah's spirit. Taken up to heaven in a chariot of fire, Elijah's mantle (cloak) fluttered to the ground as Elisha watched. Elisha took up the mantle of Elijah, strode to the Jordan River, and shouted, "Where is the God of Elijah" as he struck the water with the cloak. The waters parted for Elisha as they had for Elijah, previously. The onlookers remarked, "The spirit of Elijah is resting on Elisha." It wasn't a fluke. Total up the miracles and wonders done through the younger prophet, and you'll come up with about twice as many as his teacher. It's worth it to invest in the younger generation. But transferring what is meaningful from one generation to another must be done with strong commitment and on purpose, otherwise it usually won't happen. There have been lots of failures in that area through the centuries, which makes the successes stand out all the more.

Who is following us?

There are two main ingredients required on the part of a mentor, simple but vital: First, we have to have it. Then, we have to be willing to give it.

If we don't have anything to offer, spiritually, there's no need to pursue mentoring. We can't give what we don't possess. One way of putting it is like this: Would anyone want a double portion of our spirit?

The Bottom Line: Is anyone following us?
Do they have any reason to?

DAY 296

Two for Two

The way to possess an enviable relationship with God, and the life that goes with it, is to seek God with all our heart. He always makes sure we find Him. Then come the changes, as we submit to Him, body, mind and spirit. He does a makeover on every believer, some of it instant, much of it gradual. Everyone is accepted, but we have to show up and be willing. It's like my favorite light bulb joke:

"How many psychiatrists does it take to change a light bulb?"

"Only one. But the light bulb has to want to change."

In the game of passing the baton between generations, Paul and Timothy were a success story. Paul was about as "Type A" as you can get, personality-wise, which meant he wouldn't be a particularly patient teacher, nor a very willing "babysitter." If one was going to learn from Paul, he would quite probably have to do it on the run. John Mark hadn't been able to cut it, for one reason or another, but Paul took seriously the need to raise up young disciples, and he saw in Timothy someone who might be a better fit. To his credit, the apostle was willing to give it another try. It paid off. Timothy ended up being like a son to Paul. Not only that, but Barnabas' rescue effort involving his nephew, John Mark, also worked out, and earned Paul's renewed respect for Mark. Paul and Barnabas were two for two!

The main thing is they both tried. They were willing to invest heavily of themselves into younger men, in the process gifting the world with new leaders who had been trained by some of the best. There are some things you can't get in school. What Barnabas did for Mark and what Paul did for Timothy are examples.

It takes two, though. Mark had to catch the rung the second time around, with a patient uncle willing to give up being a missionary in order to nurture him, one on one. Timothy was faced with several challenges, not the least of which was undergoing circumcision, in order to not be an obstacle to ministry among the Jews. There were many sacrifices along the way, on both ends of the mentor/protege relationship. But it really paid off.

Chances are, mentoring will seem like a one-way relationship, at least for a while, with the novice supplying mostly mistakes and frustrations for the mentor. Over time, it usually changes, though sometimes people get burned. It's messy. It doesn't always work out. It's what Jesus did, though, and some of His smarter followers have done the same thing. There are a lot of Mark's and Timothy's out there who need us. They're worth it. If you've got it, give it. If you don't have it yourself, yet, get it, then give it! Timothy, Mark and Jesus will be pleased.

The Bottom Line: Mentoring is worth it.

DAY 297

Eden Entertainment

For the wages of sin is death, but the free gift of God is eternal life in Christ Jesus our Lord. Romans 6:23

Here's the lineup. A new string of shows is coming to television, aimed at the elusive "faith community" which likes to hear stuff on religious subjects, yet which is funny, edgy and true to real life.

First off, we have the show, "Adam and Eve," with two of the biggest names in Hollywood in the starring roles. Set, of course, in the beautiful Garden of Eden, Adam and Eve are two people who are drop-dead gorgeous, with a wardrobe composed mostly of flora and fauna blocking the camera shot. Filming must have been interesting.

There is in the Garden a tree, the one known in the Bible as "The Tree of the Knowledge of Good and Evil," but here shortened to just "The Tree of Knowledge." It's the one God doesn't want them to touch, since God, in this show, is paranoid of His people finding out what's really behind all this, which is not much (kind of like "Ignore that man behind the curtain," on "The Wizard of Oz"). God is against His people getting knowledge (read: Science), so He has quarantined the Tree of Knowledge, to keep the human race in perpetual stupidity (read: Believing and trusting in God, rather than in themselves).

There is another character with a major role. Through the wonders of computer animation, there is a talking snake who interacts with Adam and Eve on a daily basis. God does, too, but it's only on a remote, voice-from-the-sky basis, and usually what He says is dorky and inane. Example: A booming voice startles Adam and Eve, as out of the blue, God commands, "Thou shalt not eat the yellow snow!" Adam looks heavenward, and says, "What's snow?" There is a pause, and God replies, "Oh. Yeah. Never mind." Adam and Eve shake their heads and go about their business.

The snake, however, is cool. Cast with the voice over talent of one of the best comedians in the business, the snake is pretty much the highlight of "Adam and Eve." He comes up with the best one-liners, he's intelligent but not condescending, he's pretty much the best friend Adam and Eve have. The snake consoles them in their fate of being stuck with a clueless Creator, and agrees to help them out. Using the snake's intelligence, Adam and Eve are able to garner some of the fruit from the Tree of Knowledge, chow down, and instantly become brilliant scientists, who know the answers to everything, including how to get away from God, who starts pursuing them through the Garden, plodding along like the giant in "Jack and the Beanstalk." The snake helps them escape.

Now that they have the gift of knowledge, Adam, Eve and the snake have weekly adventures in outsmarting God, which usually isn't that hard. The show is now set for sit-com style humor, with God as the fall guy and everyone else taking turns being the hero. "Adam and Eve" is lauded as a breakthrough success. Christians by the millions watch the show, chortle at the antics, then attempt to remind themselves that it's not real, and that what the Bible says is what counts. It gets a little harder all the time, since they really do enjoy the show.

"Adam and Eve" looks to be such a hit that there are already spin-off's: "Adam and Steve," in which the growing colony of Edenites in rebellion against religion discover the wonders of same-sex relationships. "Adam and Steve" really gets in its digs at those who would dare to term such a noble lifestyle "sin," as if humans had some control over their own behavior, in reaction to bodily urges and impulses.

There is also a crime show, "CSI Eden," focused on the sad-but-true story of the first murder, when Cain killed his brother, Abel. The show's emphasis is in understanding the inner pain of the perpetrator, plus showing gory shots of the crime scene in a kind of artsy fashion. The aspect of mystery keeps viewers' attention.

Fortunately, the "Adam and Eve" show exists only in my imagination. There is no such show (I hope), nor are there spin-off's. Satan, however, is real, and he continues to spin God's good Word to make everything upside down, using every tool available, one of his favorites being the media. Consider most of the entertainment industry's offerings. Is the bottom line of the programming all that different from my imaginary "Adam and Eve" show, or would "Adam and Eve" (and spin-off's) only be a variation from what's already out there? Does most of the programming available to us agree with Biblical reality, or is everything backwards? Who is the hero in television, movies, magazines, etc.? God? The person who believes in or follows Him? Hardly ever. God's followers are consistently portrayed as narrow-minded, stupid, anti-intellectual, bigoted. God doesn't exist, except in the minds of His weak-minded followers. Smart people will look within and find what it takes to save the planet. Dumb people will stick to the manmade rules of religion. If there's a hero at all, it's the mythical, cute, clever serpent who brings us the wisdom of the ages, and encourages us to break free from the moral restraints imposed by holier-than-thou types who insist their way is the only way. Oh, yeah. In the Bible, the roles are reversed. Christians probably should try to remember that.

It's hard, though, when so much of our entertainment is geared to precisely the opposite of the scripture, and we tend to spend so little time occupied with the Bible. So we tell ourselves, "Enjoy the show, but forget each and every message it promoted. Enjoy the show, but don't believe any of it. The Bible is real, this isn't. The Bible is real, this isn't. The Bible is real? Yeah, I'm supposed to believe that. Gets harder all the time."

Find me a show or movie which *agrees* with the Bible on the subject of sin, and I'll show you a program with an uphill battle ahead of it, and probably a very short life span.

Sin, the Key Ingredient

In the Bible, sin is the key ingredient of death. In modern-day American culture, sin is the key ingredient of entertainment. Isn't it?

Check out what's available in movies and television, plus the various other media avenues. Take the Bible definition of what constitutes sin (for a starting point, we'll take the Ten Commandments), and how is sin portrayed? Once in a while, we get the Bible message that this stuff will kill you and bring you all kinds of misery, but more often this is what we see and hear:

Sin, made clever.
Sin, made funny.
Sin, made sophisticated.
Sin, made noble.
Sin, made artistic.
Sin, made interesting and exciting.
Sin, made romantic.

Only it's never called "sin." With the exception of a few sins like murder which are socially unacceptable even among the ungodly, there's usually another name for the behavior, which doesn't sound so, well,... sinful. Adultery is an "affair;" homosexual acts are a "gay" lifestyle practiced by, in real life, the unhappiest of folks, but portrayed by actors as enlightened, wise and carefree people; pre-marital sexual activity is true romance; lying is being smart; cursing is rugged, powerful and "realistic;" coveting is nothing more than the desired result of good advertising; at least murder is still "murder"—no, scratch that, I forgot about a woman's right to choose.

Hour after hour, day after day, the serpent's message blasts winsomely across our lives: Sin is great! Sin will get you "heaven." Sin brings pleasure, power. Sin is the way to get what you want and deserve. You shall be like God, you'll be as powerful as God, as smart as God, you are God, and the ever-present "There is no God, (so it doesn't matter)."

Satan's bottom line is, "Sin gains you Eden." God's bottom line is this: Sin costs you Eden, and it cost Jesus His life to get it back for you. Don't talk to God about the romance of sin. He watched His only Son being tortured to death, in order to save you from its consequences.

Camera-angle Ethics

My reason for bringing up this subject is not to harp on anyone or cast judgment on the entertainment choices of other Christians. This is a personal journey, but I realize I'm not alone. Everyone who is trying to live a holy life, trying to be closer to God, yet continually being frustrated in the attempt by the ravages of our pervasive "culture" knows what I'm talking about. I'm wondering how many times we can imbibe the latest crud served up as "entertainment," then shake it off and go back to loving God with all our heart, soul, mind and strength.

I've set limits for myself through the years, learned the hard way, as far as what my standards are to be regarding entertainment. For instance, with movies, I have refused to bring home "R" rated films, establishing the line at "PG-13." This has kept me from seeing a lot of bad movies and a few good ones. I've plugged away at PG-13, and rejoiced in the rare PG or even G film made available which was also worthy of my time. "Good entertainment" vs "bad entertainment" has been determined for me according to the letters slapped on it by the MPAA ratings board. I guess it hasn't worked that badly, but I'm rethinking some stuff. Why? Because I'm coming to see that more and more, regardless of the rating on the film, the message of so much of our media is the same: Sin is good; God and His laws are not.

Not all movies bear that underlying tone, of course, and some wonderful ones have been made over the years. But think about the message being communicated by the majority of films and television. If sin is portrayed at all, isn't it almost always either taken for granted as being natural, or romanticized? When the message of the film is directed toward making young people think sex outside of marriage is noble and there's nothing wrong with it, cutting out enough skin scenes to earn it PG-13 doesn't change that message. After we watch the thing and find ourselves vicariously celebrating fornication as being romantic, we're supposed to forget all about it, and go back to the view that the Bible standard is realistic, and the serpent's version brings heartache and death. I'm thinking that many of us have a harder time getting all the way back to the Bible, each time we enjoy another movie where sin is glamorized.

When it's all told, the damage is done by the repeated gospel that marginalizes God and exalts sin. The message is the same, whether the director graphically illustrated it or left it to the imagination.

Then there's the issue of evangelism. When sin is celebrated, when it's used as the base ingredient for nearly everything termed "entertainment," convincing a culture that we are all sinners in need of a Savior becomes increasingly difficult. The more of the "romance of sin" we accept into our lives, the harder it is to be very disturbed over a world all around us headed for eternity without God. The more we entertain ourselves with sin made cute, clever, funny or noble, the harder it is to remember that it always leads to death in real life, which is the one that counts.

Real Life Reality

Real life. This is how it works in real life: *For the wages of sin is death, but the free gift of God is eternal life in Christ Jesus our Lord* (Rom 6:23). I believe that, but the more of the world's contradictory view I willingly take in, the harder it is to have any kind of an edge to my belief. Sin is *heavily* romanticized in our culture, these days. It's a struggle to maintain a lifestyle aimed at holiness when the exact opposite message is invited to occupy many hours of our time. It pretty much kills all desire for evangelism, too. When sin "isn't that bad," why risk embarrassment or rejection to try to free people from it by pointing them to Christ?

The wages of sin is death. This is a concept usually absent from screens, big and small! It's the truth, though, and God wants us to know it. This is the outcome of sin, glamorized or not: Death. You get the pay-off, regardless of whether you want it or not. Even a part-time pursuit of sin pays the minimum wage, which happens to be death. "Yes, but Jesus our Savior paid the penalty for sin, so we're not under the Law, anymore!" Righto. The only reason we're not all toast is because of the blood of the Son of God, given for us. That's the "free gift of eternal life" part. Some have wrongly concluded, however, that "the free gift of eternal life" constitutes a coupon for unlimited free sin without consequence, that sin somehow no longer matters to God or anyone else.

The entire New Testament contradicts that thought, and since it was written after the events on Calvary, we're talking about the new reality, not the Old Testament perspective of sin. The sacrifice has been made, we are free, and Jesus our Lord is able to deliver us from sin and its penalty! Yet, in Ephesians 5, we are told not to even talk about the sins committed by the disobedient, that it's shameful to mention them. We are to have no part in the various works of darkness; instead, we live as children of light. (Awkward pause) Right?

Might I add that this was written to believers whose address was Ephesus, home to the temple of Diana, goddess of sex? And they're supposed to not even talk about all that goes on in their key local industry? Maybe sin still matters to God, even in the New Testament. Maybe it's like listening to someone you rescued from alcoholism, who is dry now, but spends all his time moaning about how great life was back when he was a drunk. So it cost you everything you had to get him clean and sober, but he insists on hanging around his old crowd and having a Coke—at the bar. You're thinking perhaps your sacrifice may have been for nothing.

Celebrating Sin

I'm tired of being part of celebrating sin. I feel God is leading me to adjust my entertainment choices to reflect compliance with His message, rather than tolerating the romanticization of sin, content just because it wasn't the worst thing available. I want to pursue the things which make me closer to God and more in love with Him, rather than the entertainments which push me away from Him and make it harder to live a holy life. I also want to give a harder look at things formerly considered "neutral," having little effect on my spiritual life. Are they really that neutral? Or is the underlying message that sin is good, God is bad or non-existent, and we're on our own?

In addition to trying to avoid what is sinful in itself, I want to try to better avoid what promotes sin, or re-characterizes it as being normal or noble. I'm thinking if I feed my mind a diet rich on God's values, I'll do better than if I practice the form of entertainment bulimia to which so many of us Christians have grown accustomed (take it in, then purge and try to get rid of the effects and go back to Biblical values).

For the wages of sin is death, but the free gift of God is eternal life in Christ Jesus our Lord. Romans 6:23

That's a realistic, reasonable philosophy, right out of the Bible. If the entertainment in question agrees with that philosophy, it may be a candidate worthy of my time; if not, probably not. I'm going to try to do a lot better in selecting entertainments which reinforce that mind set, or else do without, which is also not a bad thing. It doesn't have to be preachy or even religious; if it just doesn't romanticize sin, it would be a step above much of what's out there! I'm looking for the bottom-line message, not just the camera angle or the rating. Meanwhile, I'm glad that "Adam and Eve" is not a real TV show, even though they were real people. And I'm glad we have a real Savior named Jesus, who frees us from the law of sin and death and grants us eternal life. That's the life I want to celebrate.

The Bottom Line: Avoid whatever glamorizes sin, because sin always ends in death.

DAY 298

Spirit-led is More Fun

And they went through the region of Phrygia and Galatia, having been forbidden by the Holy Spirit to speak the word in Asia. And when they had come up to Mysia, they attempted to go into Bithynia, but the Spirit of Jesus did not allow them. So, passing by Mysia, they went down to Troas. And a vision appeared to Paul in the night: a man of Macedonia was standing there, urging him and saying, "Come over to Macedonia and help us." And when Paul had seen the vision, immediately we sought to go on into Macedonia, concluding that God had called us to preach the gospel to them. Acts 16:6-10

God likes to direct His own missionary journeys! Rather than just commissioning Paul and Silas and letting them romp where they would, the Holy Spirit carefully guides them according to His own agenda. I'm trying to imagine what it would be like to be on a missionary journey, marching 400 miles across ancient "Asia," with no other plan than following the Holy Spirit's leading. Frustrating? No, exciting! I can say that because I'm instantly reminded of my first solo "faith field trip" to Alaska, thirty years ago. My only reason for being there was I believed God wanted me to go. My main guidance system, that first summer, was the Holy Spirit, and I had the time of my life! There's nothing like being guided by the Holy Spirit and knowing without a doubt it's Him!

To the early missionaries, Spirit-led was normal. When they were "forbidden" by the Holy Spirit to engage the people of the country through which they were passing, and another plan was thwarted by the Lord, they don't seem to have rebelled or even gotten confused; they simply waited at the city of Troas. They don't seem to have had to wait long before Paul received a clear vision, and they sailed for Europe to help out the Macedonians.

Why the wandering? Only God knows for sure, but something happened between verses eight and ten which may be at least part of the story: In Troas, "they" became "we." The subtle change describing Paul's missionary journey is consistent—from here on, Luke's account of the Acts of the Apostles is in first person, not third. This seems to be where Luke got on board with the apostles. Maybe that's why they were in Troas. Perhaps God had set up a divine appointment with the person who would write down their story, plus the story of Jesus, in the books called Acts and Luke. Either way, they knew it was God doing the guiding, not Headquarters and not they themselves. It's a good feeling.

The Bottom Line: "Spirit-led" is normal, it's good and it's fun!

DAY 299

Illogical Praise

The crowd joined in attacking them, and the magistrates tore the garments off them and gave orders to beat them with rods. And when they had inflicted many blows upon them, they threw them into prison, ordering the jailer to keep them safely. Having received this order, he put them into the inner prison and fastened their feet in the stocks.

About midnight Paul and Silas were praying and singing hymns to God, and the prisoners were listening to them, and suddenly there was a great earthquake, so that the foundations of the prison were shaken. And immediately all the doors were opened, and everyone's bonds were unfastened. When the jailer woke and saw that the prison doors were open, he drew his sword and was about to kill himself, supposing that the prisoners had escaped. But Paul cried with a loud voice, "Do not harm yourself, for we are all here." And the jailer called for lights and rushed in, and trembling with fear he fell down before Paul and Silas. Then he brought them out and said, "Sirs, what must I do to be saved?" And they said, "Believe in the Lord Jesus, and you will be saved, you and your household." Acts 16:22-31

Welcome to Philippi! What happened to the pleading Macedonian who wanted Paul to "Come over and help us"?! It's a good thing this game plan came directly from the Holy Spirit, because had it come from denominational headquarters, somebody would have gotten fired over it. The missionary team had skipped over territory right in front of them, in order to sail to Europe, shortly to encounter this ignoble welcome. Their crime? Delivering a slave girl from some sort of evil spirit! (Her masters had been using her fortune-telling abilities to generate income; they didn't appreciate Paul turning her back into an ordinary slave girl).

Things quickly went from low-key evangelism along the river bank to a high-profile mini-riot, complete with being stripped, beaten with rods and thrown into jail, with the added discomfort and indignity of their feet being placed in the stocks. So this is where helping people in Jesus' name gets you!

The apostles had plenty of reasons to moan, to be angry and bitter, but they're stronger men than that. What they do is the exact opposite of what logic or their bodies must have told them to do: they sang praises to God. *Paul and Silas were praying and singing hymns to God, and the prisoners were listening to them.* It won't be long, now!...

The Bottom Line: The less likely the circumstances, the more powerful the praise.

DAY 300

Reverse Jailbreak

Acts 16 features a reverse jailbreak. Instead of breaking out of jail, God breaks in! Why? He's orchestrating a strategic conversion by placing two tough apostles face to face with a hardened, needy jailer. The jailer doesn't get out much. He's not the kind of person a couple missionaries would run into, down by the river. Nor at "church." If God wants Paul and Silas to witness to the Philippian jailer, He first needs to get them to go to Philippi; hence, the vision. Now He needs a jailbreak. He needs to get His boys into that jail! If they just show up, doing "jail ministry" or something, it will have no effect on the jailer and probably little on the prisoners; they need to go in as prisoners. That's easy—have them deliver that slave girl from her personal demon, and the owners will throw a fit.

God's plan is working, perfectly. He's getting the missionaries into position. The jailer places Paul and Silas in the stocks after they have been publicly (and illegally) beaten and humiliated for a miraculous good deed. Stripped of dignity and rights, confined, bleeding, miserably immobile in the darkest part of a foreign jail, what will the missionaries do? It's the absolute last thing anyone but God would expect them to do: pray and sing praises to God. First, God breaks into the jail with His men, then He has them put on a concert! The whole jail is listening. (Where are they going to go)? So this is what they mean by a "captive audience"!

It's all set up: people who have been cruelly mistreated, in wretched circumstances, responding by singing hymns of praise, talking to God like He's their best Friend; needy people listening to the Gospel through a message of prayer and music, and most of all, heart. God's guys have done their part perfectly—you couldn't get a better witness to the overcoming power of faith than this! Alright! It's time. For what? For God to show His own strength and power, by doing something beyond the powers of man: shaking the stinking jail so hard with an earthquake that everyone's chains rattle to the floor. They're free! Do they flee?

The jailer assumed they had, calculated his life-span if even one of his captives had crawled away in the dark, and decided to end his life before his superiors got to it. Paul doesn't blow his chance, though. This is not about getting away, but about giving the Gospel away. He yells, "Don't do it! We're all here!"

An astonished jailer calls for a light, sees his freed prisoners standing around waiting to be re-shackled, and without hesitation, kneels at the feet of Paul the missionary prisoner and asks, "What must I do to be saved?"

Mission accomplished. Nice one.

The Bottom Line: Could God entrust to me a mission like this?

DAY 301

What It Takes

What Paul and Silas did is what it takes to get to the hard ones. A soft sermon from a nice pulpit can be funny, touching and right on target, but the jailer doesn't hear it because he's not there, nor planning to be, anytime soon. The jail ministry team from the church troops through when they remember to show up, and the jailer humors them, but no deep impression is made, because this whole thing didn't cost anybody too much. But something like this... there's no explanation. How can they praise their God like nothing happened to them, when they're bruised and bloody? The earthquake. That wasn't coincidence, and he knows it. The fact that God would send two messengers to sing the Gospel to him, that they wouldn't escape when they had the chance, that they would stop their tormentor and captor from taking his own life, because,... Why? It was all too much for the Philippian jailer. He surrendered to Jesus on the spot.

This is the kind of dedication it takes to win people to Christ in the hard places. The power of the witness is proportionate to the suffering endured to give it. Anyone can drop a tract on the floor, and for some, that's all it takes. But for the hard ones, the witness that brings them to their knees is the power of God, displayed through ordinary people, reacting in ways beyond the ability of ordinary people. That one takes extraordinary courage and commitment. Would that be one of the reasons we have seen evangelism in the Church in America driddle to nearly nothing? Considering how livid I have found myself even in the past few days, prompted by nothing more than perceived incompetence or injustice adversely affecting me or mine, I wonder what my chances would be of reacting with praise and grace if I were in a situation remotely similar to Paul and Silas. I wouldn't bet on me. They did have the advantage of knowing it was because of Jesus that they were suffering, rather than just having a bad day at the auto shop or the billing office... I still wouldn't bet on me.

If I knew it was because of Jesus, and I had time to think it through and pray it through, plus I got to do it with a friend... maybe. But those times when it's just the routine bumps of life, which slime up the plans and prime the anger pump... I'm afraid those things don't turn into praise to God very often in my life. The sad bottom line, for me, is this: What does? What does it take before I praise God, *publicly?*

The Bottom Line: The power of the witness is related to its cost.

DAY 302

The Disciple's Union

Why doesn't Twenty-first Century evangelism in the U.S. look like First Century evangelism in the Roman Empire? Has the Holy Spirit lost His touch? No, I think it has more to do with the unionization of the disciples. We've banded together and talked ourselves into the mentality that we have a bill of rights as Christians, including getting to live in a "Christian nation" where we not only don't get beat up for practicing our faith; we get a tax break. Some of our other "rights" include the right to free speech, which we often interpret as not having to say anything about Jesus if we don't want to, or if it might offend someone or damage our popularity.

Because we are citizens of a nation founded on biblical principles, named or not, we have come to expect that we will be shown respect for our beliefs. Until recent generations, that was the practice. Now that public sentiment has shifted, our reaction is often more of an eagerness to regain our rights than our witness. Thus, if God allowed a couple of us to be shoved in jail on trumped up charges, rather than responding in praise to Him so we could witness to the jail population, our response would more probably be to call our attorney, post bail and start on the lawsuit. We'd probably go free. And probably no one would get saved, either.

Paul and Silas did the things which landed them in jail, didn't escape when they had the perfect opportunity (I would probably have been thinking, "Answer to prayer!" when the earthquake released my chains, and gotten out of there), and even when they were emancipated the next morning, they wouldn't go! Why? Because of their own rights? After all, their rights as Roman citizens had been grossly violated. No, it was the reputation of Christ about which Paul was concerned. He wanted to make sure no one thought Christians were criminals or seditionists, so he waited to be publicly escorted from prison by the apologetic authorities. All of this was about being a witness for Jesus, and none of it was about the rights of disciples.

What would happen to our witness if we forsook our self-granted "rights," broke ranks with the disciple's union and just focused on the reputation of Jesus? What if we talked about God's goodness freely and publicly, ignoring public opinion? *I'm talking about praising God, not berating sinners.* "Praising God" is the athlete in the winner's circle thanking Jesus publicly, while "berating sinners" is the guy carrying the sign that basically says, "God hates your sin; mine's O.K." Our witness would be much more powerful if we cared more about Jesus than our "rights."

The Bottom Line: What if we valued our witness more than our rights?

DAY 303

Disciple's Rights, More or Less

What if we allowed God to do really weird things with us like, for instance, a reverse jailbreak? God didn't get Paul and Silas out of jail, He got them in! (Then, out). If we weren't so preoccupied with our rights and the downward slope of society, we wouldn't miss as many chances to be a witness for Jesus. How many of us in Paul and Silas' shoes would have seen being slumped in a Philippian jail as a big witnessing opportunity? Pretty sure I would have missed that one! Unfortunately, I miss most of the lesser ones, too.

Why? I've grown accustomed to "disciple's rights," a concoction of our society which has determined a few things not in the Gospel, but enshrined as truth. Here are some of them:

- **God wants me to be happy.** A favorite among many, this one is used as justification for avoiding every unpleasant thing facing a Christian, including remaining married to an unpleasant person. Neither the verse nor the sentiment is found in the Bible; there is, however, a lot about God wanting us to be obedient.
- **God wants me to be financially prosperous.** The Recession has put quite a dent in that one. Also plucked out of wishful thinking and thin air, this "right" has no grounding in scripture, but many misled fans. If the prosperity gospel were accurate, when the rich young ruler came to Jesus, the Lord would have told His disciples, "Be like this guy! See what keeping the Law will get you? Wealth and honor. Good job, rich young ruler. I'll bless you with even more." Instead, Jesus told him his possessions were keeping him from being a disciple. He needed to sell all, give it to the poor, then follow Jesus. That was the road to "happiness" for the young man. He kept his wealth and rights, instead, and went away sad. Lessons?
- **I have the right to be healthy,** if I'm a Christian and I have faith. A touchy one for many people, especially those who see "promises" in scripture guaranteeing health for all who (sufficiently) believe. Health is seen by some Christians as the "right" of a believer. I'll back off a little on that one and say it's always right for us to *ask* God for healing, plus more faith, but I'm thinking that with everything Jesus has already done for us, He doesn't really owe us anything, including a healthy earthly body, particularly if we haven't bothered much to take care of it. The part of this whole discussion which bugs me is when, in effect, someone says, "I'm not going to follow Jesus unless I feel well and I don't get hurt." You can't even play football with that attitude. It doesn't cut it for discipleship, either.

"Disciple's rights" are highly overrated.

The Bottom Line: The "rights" of disciples of Jesus are mostly fictional.

DAY 304

Rights Relinquishment

There are more places we could go in exploring disciple's rights, but I'm getting tired of it. We think we have the right to not be persecuted, though Jesus assured us we would be. We have the right to be "successful," so if something isn't working to our satisfaction, we can quit. Where did that come from? We have the right to make up our own plans and follow our own agenda, so long as we ask God's blessing on it and be sure to pray "in Jesus' name," even if this is the first time He's seen the plan (kind of like an employee giving orders to his boss). We have the right to opt out of any assignment which might be dangerous or conflict with T-ball games. We have the right to not show up if we're tired. We have the right to have things go our way in all things church, or leave for where we can get better treatment and better leadership. Always, always, we have the right to air our grievances (complain) to whomever will listen, including those who were just beginning to think Jesus might be the answer, but who for some reason suddenly veer off. We have the right to speak our mind, particularly when we have been treated unfairly, unkindly or someone is just trying to bore us to death.

Really? What is the source of all these discipleship rights? It wasn't Jesus. On the contrary, Jesus instructed would-be disciples to count the cost (everything), say goodbye to the old life (all of it), pick up our cross and follow Him. Where are the "rights" in that picture?

We're not without any rights at all, though: *"But to all who did receive him, who believed in his name, he gave the right to become children of God, who were born, not of blood nor of the will of the flesh nor of the will of man, but of God."* (John 1:12-13) Now there's a right worth mentioning! The right to become children of God?! What's more, this is a right we never have to relinquish. The imaginary "rights" Christian society has assigned us? Those need to go. They're not helping anyone at all. Rather, they are hurting the cause of Christ, and they're hurting us.

When's the last time a hardened sinner, beat up by life, knelt in front of us and pleaded with us, *"What must I do to be saved?*! Tell me what I need to do to get what you have!"

I'd love to have a few examples in my own life of similar responses to my witness, but I'm coming up with blanks. It seems First Century witnessing was more powerful than Twenty-first Century American witnessing tends to be. They had fewer rights, and a lot more power. We have less power in our witness, and a lot more rights. There seems to be a pattern, here. We ought to break it.

The Bottom Line: Which would we prefer, "rights" or a powerful witness?

DAY 305

More

Have this mind among yourselves, which is yours in Christ Jesus, who, though he was in the form of God, did not count equality with God a thing to be grasped, but made himself nothing, taking the form of a servant, being born in the likeness of men. And being found in human form, he humbled himself by becoming obedient to the point of death, even death on a cross. Therefore God has highly exalted him and bestowed on him the name that is above every name, so that at the name of Jesus every knee should bow, in heaven and on earth and under the earth, and every tongue confess that Jesus Christ is Lord, to the glory of God the Father. Philippians 2:5-11

American preachers are always talking about how we could win so many more people to Christ if we just had *more*. More what? More everything. More money, more programs, a bigger building, more parking. More leaders, more training, more organization, more technology, more advertising, more public exposure, more or less contemporary music, more opportunities. I've changed my mind.

We need less. "More" is killing us. We already have more than almost anyone in the world! And less conversion results than almost anyone, too.

In order to have a more powerful witness, we need less, far less. As a rule, when it comes to witnessing, even among the few who think that's their job and not the pastor's, there is total avoidance of any witnessing where our rights might be ruffled. We're so concerned about our rights that if the mission will infringe on any of them, resulting in possible pain, embarrassment, inconvenience or whatever, this is a bad idea. If we had less rights, we'd have more converts, wouldn't we?

How many rights did Jesus give up, in order to come to earth and save us! Disciples don't have rights; we have a Savior and Lord. That's enough. And the less we hang onto "rights" and the more we focus on the Lord, the more power there will be in our witness for Him. Same Holy Spirit as in the First Century. Same rights for disciples, too. If we forget about our "rights" and focus on following the Savior, He could do really imaginative, effective stuff with us, just like He did with His First Century crew. Imagine. It could be us, being used of God to establish new churches in impossible places. We could be God's missionaries, whom He could plant anywhere, knowing that when the time came, rather than whining about our circumstances, we'd be witnessing to His power. Then comes the earthquake. It could be us. Or we could cling to our rights.

The Bottom Line: If we focus more on Jesus, less on rights, we'll see more fruit.

DAY 306

Fourth Quarter Prayers

And he told them a parable to the effect that they ought always to pray and not lose heart. He said, "In a certain city there was a judge who neither feared God nor respected man. And there was a widow in that city who kept coming to him and saying, 'Give me justice against my adversary.' For a while he refused, but afterward he said to himself, "Though I neither fear God nor respect man, yet because this widow keeps bothering me, I will give her justice, so that she will not beat me down by her continual coming.'" And the Lord said, "Hear what the unrighteous judge says. And will not God give justice to his elect, who cry to him day and night?" Will he delay long over them? I tell you, he will give justice to them speedily. Nevertheless, when the Son of Man comes, will he find faith on earth?" Luke 18:1-8

Football teams which prevail over their opponents train for the fourth quarter. Although they might be at a disadvantage in terms of talent, the team with the better conditioning will often dominate over better talent as the game draws to a close and the less well-conditioned players run out of gas. It pays to prepare for the fourth quarter.

So in the walk of a disciple of Jesus. Lots of people sign up for the free offer of eternal life, then depart at the first sign of accompanying hardship. "Free" didn't mean "free from suffering." In fact, Jesus promised trouble and a personal cross for anyone who would dare to follow Him. That wasn't in the fine print; that was in the red print.

When it comes to prayer, especially, we must be prepared for the fourth quarter. Those who toss a prayer absently in the bucket and move on will not have a very effective prayer life. Those who prevail in prayer, who refuse to give up, are people who grow stronger in their spiritual life even as life winds down for them. Their lives are "conditioned" by prayer. It shows. There is nothing quite like a fourth quarter saint on their artificial knees. They blow past immature believers who think prayer is boring, every time. Push-ups are boring, too. People who do them are stronger than those who opt out. In the spiritual realm, people who pray and don't quit wind up in the winner's circle, every time! The fourth quarter is the test.

We're in the fourth quarter. Don't give up, now! *When the Son of Man comes, will he find faith on earth?* Over here! I *told* you He was coming back!

The Bottom Line: Keep praying and don't give up! It's the fourth quarter.

DAY 307

A Little Leap

So Paul, standing in the midst of the Areopagus, said: "Men of Athens, I perceive that in every way you are very religious. For as I passed along and observed the objects of your worship, I found also an altar with this inscription, 'To the unknown god.' What therefore you worship as unknown, this I proclaim to you. Acts 17:22-23

America is seeming more like Athens all the time, increasingly open to anything, except the exclusive claims of Christianity. How do we reach people like that? What makes the difference?

During the time in my life when I was struggling the most with my faith, it wasn't the pro or con arguments which got through; it was the love, and it was the example. I looked at the love around me and knew it was real. I had experienced the love of God and knew it to be true. I had seen the example of people like my parents, and saw that their lives worked. At one point, it just became a leap of faith. Torn between what well-credentialed liberal theologians had to say and the simple faith model I had observed in the lives of my godly parents, I went with the more powerful of the two, the life that worked and the God of the Bible, as opposed to the domesticated version of Him espoused by some. I honestly felt sorry for people who had a god they could understand, and scriptures requiring the validation of their intellect in order to be true. In a moment of time, I skipped over the whole thing and went with a God I already knew and a Book I already loved. It was a "leap" of sorts, but a pretty short one, and I never looked back.

I decided to believe the Bible, just like I always had, and ignore whatever conflicted with it. That was a good choice! I think that's what will have to happen in America, in order for people to move forward in their faith. They are going to have to take the leap. Some places you can't get to, gradually. There are places we get stuck, and we never move on, if we have to have explanations for everything along the way. If we try to live by just what we can figure out about the Bible and what makes sense and what we can prove to be true, there isn't enough left over to get us through real life. If we believe the whole thing, there's plenty.

The Bottom Line: Forward spiritual progress comes when we choose to believe God.

DAY 308

Synagogue Fishing

Paul did his homework, prior to engaging the Athenians; he didn't waltz in, assuming an automatic audience. He studied their culture, their poets, their way of thinking, found a place of commonality, and went from there. He didn't leave out hard concepts like the Resurrection, but he also didn't begin there. He started where they were: so afraid of leaving something out that they had made an image to "the unknown god," just in case!

We need to do like Paul, and start from the page of those we're trying to reach. In ministering to modern-day Americans, we can make points with the church crowd if we start out by attacking the moral values of the surrounding culture, but we're not going to connect with the broken people of this age that way. Their minds are on the economy, their messed-up relationships, their loneliness, lack of purpose. Music. Their kids. Sports. Entertainment. I can't believe many of them go around thinking about how to get forgiveness for their sins. They want help, but "a Savior who died for them" doesn't compute. This doesn't mean they don't need Jesus; it just means they don't yet know why they might need Him.

The Church needs to listen, then start from where people are, not where we think they should be. The help we offer should be within their reach.

There is still a place for church ministry from the pulpit, but very little evangelism is taking place in sanctuaries in America, anymore. It's like fishermen waiting back at the house for fish to come find them. Successful fishermen go out. Likewise, successful evangelists. If we reach this generation, we need to haunt the marketplace, because they just aren't coming to find us, no more than the Gentiles were tracking down the Jews and trying to be converted to Judaism, back then. Sitting in our synagogues is not working. It's time to go to the marketplace, on purpose, and spend the days there, not marketing the Church like another commodity, but listening to a hurting world, helping them find their place in God's Kingdom by starting where they are, not where we think they should be.

We don't all fit in the same spot, but we all fit, somewhere. And whatever we do, we need to approach America as the mission field it is, rather than sitting in our synagogues expecting the world to beat down our door, anytime soon.

The Bottom Line: We reach people by starting where they are.

DAY 309

No Other God, No Other Way

Turn to me and be saved,
all the ends of the earth!
For I am God, and there is no other.
By myself I have sworn;
from my mouth has gone out in righteousness
a word that shall not return:
'To me every knee shall bow,
every tongue shall swear allegiance.'

"Only in the LORD, it shall be said of me,
are righteousness and strength;
to him shall come and be ashamed
all who were incensed against him.
In the LORD all the offspring of Israel
shall be justified and shall glory."

Isaiah 45:22-25

There *is* no other God. Believing the oft-repeated message in Isaiah would save so many people so much grief, particularly since the One True God promises that one day *all will* believe, anyway. Seekers for righteousness and strength ought to look to the One and Only God, who has a monopoly on all things holy. Seekers of salvation waste time looking for alternative routes. There's only one way out of this sinful mess mankind has created: trusting in Jesus Christ, God's Son for salvation. There's no other Savior, no other God. That's the truth, though skeptics sneer at it being "narrow-minded." Only one God. Wouldn't it make sense that if there were only one God, His Way would be the only way?

Well-meaning cultists try to talk us out of the Trinity: "See? How can you believe Jesus is God, when Jehovah says *"I am God, and there is no other"?*

Umm. Because Jehovah, Jesus and the Holy Spirit all claimed Jesus is God? Because Jehovah called Jesus His Son, and Jesus called Jehovah His Father? Because Jesus died to save all who would believe? Ultimately, *all* will believe, including current skeptics and rebels against truth. Anyone with sense should follow this plan, now: *Turn to me and be saved, all the ends of the earth!* Then get baptized, in the name of the Father and of the Son and of the Holy Spirit.

The Bottom Line: There is only one God, one way to heaven. Believe and be saved!

DAY 310

Peace in Different Directions

I'm thinking of pastor after pastor who is living in conflict with his church. The church people mistreat him, attack him, vilify him, until finally he says "Enough!", shakes out his suit at them and piles his family into the moving van to try ministry in a less hostile environment, which often isn't. The church tosses its head in bewilderment and begins the search for a replacement, the pastor trudges down the road toward his next assignment, and very few people are finding Jesus.

What's wrong? Instead of going to God in prayer, people go to each other and gripe. Lines are needlessly drawn in the sand over petty things, while the big things of the Gospel are ignored. Major decisions are based on pride, instead of leading sought through prayer.

When the answers come from God, they are specific to that situation at that time, and because they come from God, they are right. When He makes it clear what we are to do, we can rest easy—now we know what to do! Caution: It's not always the same answer for what appears to be the same scenario.

There are pastors who need to tough it out and stay until God releases them, instead of when the opposition starts doing their thing. There are others who need to let go of their pastorate and allow God to guide them into a place where they can spend their time teaching the Word of God, rather than babysitting cranky Christians. There are some, like me, who were supposed to resign, keep loving their former parishioners, and hang around town, ministering wherever there is opportunity and following only the direction of the Holy Spirit, without the benefits and banes of church boards, church politics and church salary.

What I most needed at the time of decision was solid leading from God. That's exactly what I got, through prayer. There is nothing which brings more peace to a heart than surrender to God's will, followed by clear direction from the Master. When we choose to be guided by the Holy Spirit, He makes sure we get it right. He also brings peace.

Two years have passed since I wrote the portion above. Wouldn't you know, the same God who led me to resign a pastorate led me to resume pastoral ministry in a new location, following a six-year "sabbatical" from the senior pastorate, peppered with four interim assignments and lots of faith adventures. There is peace in this new assignment, but there was also peace during the "faith years." The way it works is we have peace with God, no matter which way He takes us.

The Bottom Line: Obedience to God brings peace with God—always.

DAY 311

Occupy Gold Street

And the twelve gates were twelve pearls, each of the gates made of a single pearl, and the street of the city was pure gold, transparent as glass.

And I saw no temple in the city, for its temple is the Lord God the Almighty and the Lamb. And the city has no need of sun or moon to shine on it, for the glory of God gives it light, and its lamp is the Lamb. By its light will the nations walk, and the kings of the earth will bring their glory into it, and its gates will never be shut by day–and there will be no night there. They will bring into it the glory and the honor of the nations. But nothing unclean will ever enter it, nor anyone who does what is detestable or false, but only those who are written in the Lamb's book of life. Revelation 21:21-27

In recent weeks, the news media has often featured coverage of "Occupy Wall Street" and its various spin-off's in other cities. I was amused to receive a text from my friend, John Rogers, which read, "I'm planning on joining the 'Occupy Gold Street' crowd. I just don't know when."

Me, too, John.

One day all whose names are written in the Lamb's book of life will be assembled in the new Jerusalem. The surroundings will be astounding. Yet nothing will compare to the glory of God. Think of it. There will be no need for sun or moon. We will live forever in an environment lit by the glory of God! It makes me think of another phrase I heard used yesterday, by yet another friend, Benji Rodes. In our weekly pastors' prayer time, I heard Pastor Benji thank God that we are "condemned to victory." I love it! Because of our Savior, Jesus, we're "condemned to victory"—we literally cannot lose!

Because of God's Son, Jesus Christ, whose glory is so awesome it will light the Universe, we are "stuck" with victory over sin and death! We are heading toward an eternity with a God who loves us more than we can comprehend. The place He is preparing for those who love Him back exceeds my imagination's capacity many times over—and I have a pretty good imagination! *Whatever* we must endure at the present time is not worth comparing with the glory we will witness and receive, if we simply hang on to Jesus! Do not let go of Him! We in the "Occupy Gold Street" crowd are condemned to victory with a Lord who cannot lose. If we're with Him, we are automatically on the winning side. What a Savior!

The Bottom Line: We in the "Occupy Gold Street" crowd are condemned to victory.

DAY 312

Always a Bad Idea

"Remember this and stand firm,
recall it to mind, you transgressors,
remember the former things of old;
for I am God, and there is no other;
I am God, and there is none like me,
declaring the end from the beginning
and from ancient times things not yet done,
saying, 'My counsel shall stand,
and I will accomplish all my purpose,'
calling a bird of prey from the east,
the man of my counsel from a far country.
I have spoken, and I will bring it to pass;
I have purposed, and I will do it."

Isaiah 46:8-11

God sent the prophet Isaiah to the Israelites during worrisome times. Idolatry on a national scale was on the verge of bringing down their whole country, as God had said would happen, if they chose idols over Him. The idiocy of idol worship is highlighted in the beginning of this chapter. Does it really make sense to worship something you hired someone to make for you, which can't so much as move or speak? And for this thing you abandon the one true God?!

Sin never does make sense, though, when we come down to it. We have a wonderful, *living,* loving God who provides for us and redeems us. It makes no sense to reject His love, and it is stupid to trust in ourselves, instead of putting our trust in One able to tell us the end of a matter before its beginning!

I am God, and there is none like me, declaring the end from the beginning and from ancient times things not yet done.

Like the Israelites, we live in worrisome times. The consequences of sin are imminent. It has always been a bad idea to trust in idols. As we turn fearful corners in man's history, putting our hope in what man has made is dumber than ever! There is a living God who beckons to us, who can state to us precisely how things will end before anything has even begun! He sees it all. Whatever He says will happen, will happen. Why not just trust Him with everything? The idols won't even know we're gone.

The Bottom Line: Trusting in idols instead of God is always a bad idea.

DAY 313

How to Lose Our Country

You shall therefore keep all my statutes and all my rules and do them, that the land where I am bringing you to live may not vomit you out. And you shall not walk in the customs of the nation that I am driving out before you, for they did all these things, and therefore I detested them. But I have said to you, 'You shall inherit their land, and I will give it to you to possess, a land flowing with milk and honey.' I am the LORD your God, who has separated you from the peoples. Leviticus 20:22-24

What things, specifically, is God saying bring about judgment on the land, causing it to "vomit" out its inhabitants?

- Child sacrifice
- Adultery
- Incest
- Homosexual acts
- Bestiality

All of these abominable sins were already cited in a previous chapter, Leviticus 18, as being the cause for the expulsion of the Canaanites, with the warning to the Israelites that if they choose to practice the same things, they can well expect the same results. In Leviticus 20, an additional sin is mentioned: cursing one's father or mother.

God makes it all very clear: The Canaanites are losing their country because they have been practicing all these sins. They are being "vomited" out. Don't do as they have been doing, or the same thing will happen to you! Don't live by their laws or customs; live by mine. You are to be holy to me. Sin makes you unclean, and sin has severe consequences. If you choose to commit these sins and the penalty arrives, your blood is on your own hands. It's no one's fault but yours.

Not only do these sins make you unclean; they make the land unclean. If you choose to follow these practices and commit these sinful acts, don't be surprised when the land vomits you out, because it will. When it does, it won't be "natural disasters" and it won't be my fault; the cause of your eviction will be your sin. Am I being unfair to you? No. I'm warning you. These are the consequences of sin. Don't. And please note: The consequences of these sins apply to all nations, for all time.

The Bottom Line: If we wish to lose our country, this is the way to do it.

DAY 314

Drop the Bar, Go Where They Are

Here are some principles which seemed to work for Paul in Ephesus, which may be applicable to us as well:

Go where the people already are, or where they're going to be.

Had Paul promoted the Gospel in a remote part of Asia, where people would have had to travel far out of their way in order to find him, I don't think he would have been able to sit still for three years and reach the whole region the way he did in Ephesus. Paul's ministry wasn't to people who were on some sort of religious pilgrimage, looking for answers; it was to people who had wound up in Ephesus for one of the several reasons Ephesus was a destination city. Since they were already there (or lived there), since the hall of Tyrannus was a neutral, public kind of place, and since Paul's ministry was every day, he was able to reach people opportunistically whom he would not otherwise have reached.

Reduce barriers to the Gospel as much as possible.

There were few barriers to the Gospel, the way Paul was presenting it. He had successfully countered the obstacles which would have deterred some, such as thinking they needed to be Jewish (had he kept meeting in the synagogue); having to go find him (they were already in Ephesus); not being there at the right time (it was every day, and it included the time of day when people would not be working due to the heat). Another barrier Paul reduced was the "one-way" communication barrier, which turns many people off. Rather than lecturing for hours each day, he was "reasoning" with the people who came. This means they had a chance to talk back and ask questions. When we're asking people to adopt an entirely new lifestyle, doesn't it make sense to give them the chance to at least ask questions? It is true that some will respond well to an impassioned sermon (particularly when powered by the Holy Spirit), but there will always be those who need to be able to ask questions before they will ever be convinced. Paul was reaching both.

Two of the principles which may be applied to our present situation: (1) Go where the people are, or where they are going to be. (2) Reduce barriers to the Gospel as much as possible. Most importantly, try! Try to reach people for Jesus.

The Bottom Line: Drop the bar, go where they are!

DAY 315

More Groovy Evangelism Principles

We're learning from Paul's effective approach in Asia how to reach an area for Christ. Here are more principles to apply:

Go in the flow of God's power.

No one could deny the power of God in the ministry of Paul in Ephesus. There were genuine miracles of healing and deliverance taking place on a continuing basis, and all the credit was going to Jesus. The streaking sons of Sceva learned it took more than getting the name right to get the power. It took a relationship.

That hasn't changed. We can "Jesus' name" all we want, but if we're just repeating an incantation and expecting results without being right with God, we'd better not be poking demons! If we operate in the will of God and for His glory (not ours), we will have all the power we need. The Church will not grow without the Holy Spirit. Without Him, it's an empty lecture hall, even if it's filled with people.

The most powerful testimony is a changed life.

True spiritual transformation took place in Ephesus. Two huge examples of the effect the Gospel was having on society were the six million dollar repentance bonfire and the fact that the silversmith's union was panicking because of reduced demand for their idols. The people of Asia weren't just learning about Jesus; they were living a new life. That's the way it still should be. People shouldn't have to wonder if we're different, once we've made a commitment to serve Jesus Christ.

The most effective evangelism is daily.

Paul's ministry wasn't once a week. It was daily. Christianity is a daily walk. Limiting our relationship with Christ to one day a week makes about as much sense as being married one day a week. If we're married, we're married all the time! If we're committed to Jesus Christ, we're committed all the time, not just when we're in a church building or on Sunday. If that's not how it is, it's not "commitment."

If it's revival or an awakening we want to see in our land, we'd better be thinking "daily." I've tried to come up with a period of great evangelism, anywhere in history, which was not daily. I came up empty.

The Bottom Line: Go with God's power.
A changed life is the best witness. Daily.

DAY 316

Fools Rush In

Wine is a mocker, strong drink a brawler,
and whoever is led astray by it is not wise.
The terror of a king is like the growling of a lion;
whoever provokes him to anger forfeits his life.
It is an honor for a man to keep aloof from strife,
but every fool will be quarreling.

Proverbs 20:1-3

"Fools rush in where angels fear to tread," goes the old line. Fools don't ever seem to "get it," which is, I guess, why they're fools. Fool traps are many—it doesn't take much to catch one, because they're so... well, you know.

Strong drink has made a fool out of many who were otherwise wise, until the second or third adult beverage kicked in. Each empty glass seemed to produce a correlating drop in I.Q., judging by the aftermath. *Wine is a mocker, strong drink a brawler, and whoever is led astray by it is not wise.* That stuff can make a monkey out of someone in a hurry! Meanwhile, I've never heard of anyone whose life was ruined because he chose to be a tee-totaler. Millions have shipwrecked their lives on a bottle. They thought they were in control. They were wrong.

Does anyone who drinks alcohol classify as a fool? No, only those who allow themselves to be led astray by it. But here's the rub: people don't realize they're being led astray by it until the hangover hits. They were just having a good time! Watch out for this fool trap. It can make a mockery of your whole life in a hurry.

The second fool trap mentioned in these verses has to do with provoking kings. In king-less America, could we skip this verse and go on to something applicable? It would be wiser to consider how this verse might keep us out of jeopardy. Is there anyone in our lives who is best not provoked, due to their authority over us? Teachers? Bosses? Parents? Can you say, "policeman"? Judges? There are multiple folks in our society whom only imbeciles deliberately tick off. Fools can't seem to sense the danger, though, so they smart off to show their intelligence and "courage." Not smart at all! Rather foolish.

This brings us to Fool Trap #3: strife and quarreling. Fools find arguments irresistible! Some fools seem to feel useless if they're not quarreling. Meanwhile, wise people avoid unnecessary strife, intentionally offending authorities, binge drinking and any and all other fool traps. It's because they're wise. Let's be wise.

The Bottom Line: There are many fool traps out there: wise people avoid them.

DAY 317

Nation Changers

Now after these events Paul resolved in the Spirit to pass through Macedonia and Achaia and go to Jerusalem, saying, "After I have been there, I must also see Rome." Acts 19:21

If we will let Him, God will use us to change our nation.

How? The same way He used Paul to revolutionize the province of Asia, during Paul's three-year stay in the major city, Ephesus. Acts 19 records a major riot in Ephesus. Who caused the riot? A silversmith named Demetrius got the people stirred up, but the reason the craftsmen were upset is because one man, Paul, had been so effective in proclaiming Christ that the shrine makers for the goddess Artemis feared their business was going down the tubes. The Gospel had changed the economy. Not only that, but there had recently been a bonfire, where converts to Christianity piled six million dollars worth of their own sorcery books, etc., on it and watched their old belief system go up in smoke. You can believe that had an effect on the local populace!

God used one man to change that part of the world. Before Paul's arrival, the Ephesians were worshiping Artemis and money. By the time he had "reasoned" with them daily for three years, the whole province had been exposed to the truth of the Gospel, and paganism was on the run.

Paul's secret wasn't something he got out of a church growth seminar. He was God-powered and Spirit-led. God supplied not only the power for incredible miracles of healing and deliverance which freed people in Jesus' name; He also supplied the apostle with divine direction. How did the Early Church get it right so many times? Easy. It was the Holy Spirit who was leading the Church, not men.

Is that the way it is, now? Oh, sure, we pray before the committee meeting, but are the decisions made in that meeting coming from the Holy Spirit or from the most dominant human in the room? When it comes to future planning, isn't our usual method to go to a conference or to cook up an idea, make plans, then resolve to "get 'er done"? Paul's way was to "resolve in the Spirit." There's a difference. Rather than trying to get God to buy into and sign off on his ideas, Paul was trying to get on God's wave length; God was making sure the attempt was successful.

Often, our own plans trip us up; once we've made them, we won't listen to the Spirit. We'd be better off doing it Paul's way, learning to seek the Spirit, then following where He leads. Listening, obedient disciples change entire nations.

**The Bottom Line: If we will let Him,
God will use us to change our nation.**

DAY 318

Encouragement To Die For

After the uproar ceased, Paul sent for the disciples, and after encouraging them, he said farewell and departed for Macedonia. When he had gone through those regions and had given them much encouragement, he came to Greece. There he spent three months, and when a plot was made against him by the Jews as he was about to set sail for Syria, he decided to return through Macedonia. Acts 20:1-3

Paul's third missionary journey was winding down. After a huge riot in Ephesus in Paul's honor, it became apparent that it was time to go. Prior to the riot, Paul had already "resolved in the Spirit" to pass through Macedonia and Achaia before going to Jerusalem, though they were in the opposite direction.

There was something very important Paul wished to do in the places where he had begun churches. What was it? Encourage. The purpose of the entire trip seems to have been encouragement. It was that important to Paul. Not only did Paul focus on encouraging the disciples in Macedonia and Achaia; his last act before departing Ephesus was to encourage the disciples there.

What makes encouragement so powerful? Many times it's the difference between going on and throwing in the towel. A few words of affirmation from a leader can inspire for a lifetime. Discouragement is powerful, too. A single comment can be the tipping point which turns everything to failure.

Paul realized the power of his words. He wanted the new believers to succeed. He went far out of his way in order to bless them. They would themselves endure trials, but they would not forget the trials endured by an apostle who thought encouragement so important he was willing to risk his life just to get to them and tell them one more time that he believed in them.

Incidental encouragement is nice, but the best encouragers I know do it on purpose. They're not deciding if they should say something encouraging; they're only deciding what encouraging thing they should say or do, this time. Their lives are always pointed in the same direction. Their goal is always to build people up, never to tear them down. Bring up a bit of gossip about someone, and their customary reply is that they love that person and have been praying for them. Gossiping around a committed encourager is like spitting into the wind, except less rewarding. Committed encouragers are powerful people you love to see coming and hate to see going. They decided they were on your side before they ever met you.

The Bottom Line: We can never have too many people committed to encouragement.

DAY 319

The Procrastinating Plowman

The sluggard does not plow in the autumn;
he will seek at harvest and have nothing.

Proverbs 20:4

It isn't me who keeps dragging us back to the Protestant Work Ethic; it's the Bible! Proverbs, an instruction manual for daily life, doesn't nag; it nudges. Like the instruction manuals accompanying new products, our Bibles are too often neglected because we "don't have time." When I choose to ignore the instructions in my hand telling me how it all works, whose fault is it when things go awry?

Proverbs 20:4 tells us what happens when the lazy sluggard doesn't get around to plowing: no harvest. Sluggards are very good at excuses, so they often manage to finagle a share of someone else's harvest, anyway, but one can only play the "victim" card about so long, especially with the same people. Eventually, sluggards receive their due instead of their entitlement. It may not be in this life, but probably.

Some sluggards are intentional sluggards. It's as if they signed up for the sluggard track while still in kindergarten, majored in sluggardry, and graduated with honors. Career sluggards earn a reward commensurate with their effort.

But many are accidental sluggards. Believing their own excuses, nursing victim status, waiting until they feel well before proceeding...there are myriad ways to accomplish sluggardry and miss the fleeting opportunities to get 'er done while there's still time. Harvest time is always a disappointment for sluggards, accidental or otherwise, even with charitable neighbors.

Procrastination is one of the key elements of missing the harvest, with no one else to blame. For so many things, there is a season. Once the season is past, no amount of good intentions or whining will bring it back. Winter descends, ready or not. Better plow and plant while there's time.

The Bible, of course, is not a book focused on agriculture, but on eternal matters of the soul. There is a spiritual application to this proverb, too. It has to do with getting ready for all that lies ahead. The sluggard is counting on excuses and pity to get him through. The wise man will be found behind the plow at the right season. Rewards await the non-procrastinating plowman.

The Bottom Line: Excuses don't turn back the calendar.
Work while there's time.

DAY 320

Killer Sermons, but Fewer Funerals

On the first day of the week, when we were gathered together to break bread, Paul talked with them, intending to depart on the next day, and he prolonged his speech until midnight. There were many lamps in the upper room where we were gathered. And a young man named Eutychus, sitting at the window, sank into a deep sleep as Paul talked still longer. And being overcome by sleep, he fell down from the third story and was taken up dead. But Paul went down and bent over him, and taking him in his arms, said, "Do not be alarmed, for his life is in him." And when Paul had gone up and had broken bread and eaten, he conversed with them a long while, until daybreak, and so departed. And they took the youth away alive, and were not a little comforted. Acts 20:7-12

I've preached some pretty bad sermons, but none of them has killed anybody, at least as far as I know. On the other hand, if putting people to sleep counts as homicide—well, in that case, I'm one of those serial dudes.

At least Paul's preach-a-thon had a happy ending. The reason? His faith. How many of us, having caused somebody to nod off and plop to the ground from a third story window, would have reacted like Paul? Let's see, what would I do? First, I would be angry at myself for not foreseeing such an incident and preventing it. I might be upset at God for letting it happen. ("I was doing this for you, God, and you let somebody die on me!") I might be permanently crushed by the experience, and spend the rest of my days in grief over the loss. What did Paul do? He bent over him, took the young man up in his arms and felt God's resurrection power bring him back from the dead. Then he finished his sermon!

I have a hard time picturing myself coming up with that reaction. Why? Does the same Spirit live in me who lived in the Apostle Paul, or is this a different, 21st Century American Version of the Holy Spirit, not to be confused with the First Century Missionary Version? I'm pretty sure we're talking the same Holy Spirit. Then why the big difference in reaction to life's circumstances? I find myself going to pieces over even little stuff; Paul expects a resurrection—and gets one! How many days have I wasted in whining to God about this or that?

I think I have to face it. Same Holy Spirit, but Paul was living closer to God than I am. Paul was more dependent, more on task than I've even attempted to be. I've brushed against Paul's kind of faith a time or two; Paul *lived* there. So did many of the First Century believers. It looks like a good place to live.

The Bottom Line: Same Holy Spirit.
We could choose to depend on Him more.

DAY 321

We Matter to God

Inasmuch as many have undertaken to compile a narrative of the things that have been accomplished among us, just as those who from the beginning were eyewitnesses and ministers of the word have delivered them to us, it seemed good to me also, having followed all things closely for some time past, to write an orderly account for you, most excellent Theophilus, that you may have certainty concerning the things you have been taught. Luke 1:1-4

In the first book, O Theophilus, I have dealt with all that Jesus began to do and teach, until the day when he was taken up, after he had given commands through the Holy Spirit to the apostles whom he had chosen. Acts 1:1-2

Two of the major books of the New Testament were written to just one guy. His name was Theophilus. He was a fortunate man! I have two Bibles with my name embossed on the cover; he had two books of the Bible written just for him! To get the Gospel firsthand from someone who writes it all out just so you can know for certain what happened and what God expects... Now, that's a privilege!

We have that privilege. While our name may not be Theophilus, the Bible is so personal God might as well have had the writers address it directly to us, as He did when Luke penned two long letters to Theophilus. It's written so we can know the truth about God. The Bible is a personal book, written to *us*. It's so we can understand what we need to know about life and eternity. It's so we can not just know about God, but *know God*. We matter to God. He sees us as individuals.

In informing Theophilus of the story of the Gospel, the first story Luke relates is of the appearance of the Angel Gabriel to Zechariah in the Temple. There were no formal introductions, but in the customary seraphic greeting of "Do not be afraid," Gabriel refers to Zechariah by name, anyway, then mentions his wife Elizabeth, promises the one thing in life they desire more than anything (a son), gives the not-yet-conceived child a name (John) and more promises, then finishes by zipping Zechariah's lip until everything is fulfilled. It was all very impressive and quite personal.

God knows our name—and uses it. The first message to us is often, "Do not be afraid." What follows is a message of hope and salvation...the Gospel. And while we may not have books of the Bible written to us, if we trust in Jesus, our name is written in an even better place: The Lamb's Book of Life.

The Bottom Line: We matter to God.

DAY 322

Weights and Measures

Unequal weights and unequal measures
are both alike an abomination to the LORD.

Proverbs 20:10

Sometimes it surprises me what matters to God. For instance, the "hairs of your head are numbered" thing—who but God and a few bald guys would care? I just got my hair cut. When she got done, it looked like a fat gray mouse had exploded on the barber shop floor. I think I heard a voice from heaven saying, "Recalculating."

Anyway, although I've seen this verse and the ones like it before, it still surprises me that "unequal weights and unequal measures" would earn the status of being "an abomination to the LORD"—a term generally reserved in the Bible for "icky" sins like sexual depravity. Just having two sets of weights, one for friends and family, another for people we don't like or know, earns us this kind of rebuke from God? Yup. He's serious about a lot of things, apparently including fairness.

This verse hearkens back to earlier times when, instead of a bar code beeping across a scanner, a small business merchant would be in possession of a basket or a scale by which to measure goods. It probably wasn't that hard to have a "guest" measure available to shortchange people who looked like they could afford it. It wasn't as if a "weights and measurements" inspector was standing around the open marketplace, making sure everything was kosher. Merchants were pretty much on the honor system, when it came to fairness. It turns out that God doesn't like people getting ripped off, even if they're rich people.

So, fairness and honesty matter to God. The double standard in business which gouges customers on purpose; the insider trading which goes on; all kinds of rip-off's created to bilk people out of their money—He doesn't appreciate that? No. It's an abomination to Him. Really. His followers should have no part in cheating people, even if "they're on the other side." Fairness and honesty—to everyone. That's what God expects of His children. He expects it in business. He expects it in relationships. I'm thinking He even expects it in politics, a playground for double standards if there ever was one.

As followers of the Most High and Most Fair God, we're obligated to be just in our dealings with all people, not just the ones we like or who share our whatever. It's one more part of the price we pay in trying to live a righteous life.

The Bottom Line: God cares about, and expects, honesty and fairness from us.

DAY 323

God's Witness Protection Program

When it was day, the Jews made a plot and bound themselves by an oath neither to eat nor drink till they had killed Paul. There were more than forty who made this conspiracy. They went to the chief priests and elders and said, "We have strictly bound ourselves by an oath to taste no food till we have killed Paul. Now therefore you, along with the council, give notice to the tribune to bring him down to you, as though you were going to determine his case more exactly. And we are ready to kill him before he comes near."
Acts 23:12-15

So, it's settled. Paul, the apostle and the first missionary, is a goner.

That's what Paul's enemies thought, not comprehending the power or ingenuity of God, who is *really* good at protecting His servants. God can put the whole thing in the hands of a young boy and overcome the hatred of forty men. God's purposes are sure. Paul is His man, His apostle. No way is he going to die, until he has accomplished God's mission!

It's God's Witness Protection Program. Paul's spy kid nephew had picked up on the plot, the way kids do when no one thinks they're paying attention and adults assume they're too young to understand, anyway. The would-be lynch mob didn't know this was a dangerous young man, about to foil their whole plan. The boy told Paul, Paul discreetly got him a private audience with the tribune, the tribune sent Paul on an all-night march to safety, protected by 470 armed Roman soldiers. Pretty good bodyguard. When it comes down to it, though, all we need is God.

Paul's enemies gave it their best shot—and are defeated by a kid God sent! (Not the first time. Nor the last).

We're safe with God. We need to know that—we're safe with God. It's not that we don't have enemies—we definitely do—but we are absolutely, positively, ridiculously safe, with God. It doesn't matter how many people are trying to ruin us or even kill us. They can devote their lives to our destruction and still fail! God is a great Protector. We are utterly safe, with Him. He may use devious Roman tribunes or innocent kids with good hearing to do it, He may protect us with 470 Roman soldiers or with chariots of fire, but He will protect us. We are safe with God. Period. And when Jesus says we're going across the Lake, we're going, so we need not freak out about the storm! And when God says we're going to Rome, we're going to Rome! All the excitement is just God providing us with an armed escort and making sure we'll get in to witness to Caesar. It's all good. Part of the plan.

The Bottom Line: We're safe with God. Period.

DAY 324

Two Governors and a King

After some days Felix came with his wife Drusilla, who was Jewish, and he sent for Paul and heard him speak about faith in Christ Jesus. And as he reasoned about righteousness and self-control and the coming judgment, Felix was alarmed and said, "Go away for the present. When I get an opportunity I will summon you." At the same time he hoped that money would be given him by Paul. So he sent for him often and conversed with him. When two years had elapsed, Felix was succeeded by Portius Festus. And desiring to do the Jews a favor, Felix left Paul in prison. Acts 24:24-27

What's the theme of Acts? Acts 1:8 sums it up: *But you will receive power when the Holy Spirit has come upon you, and you will be my witnesses in Jerusalem and in all Judea and Samaria, and to the end of the earth.*

You will be my witnesses. Jesus wasn't kidding! He had a reliable one in Paul. Continued imprisonment actually meant protection for the apostle, keeping him out of the clutches of his nearby enemies, while offering him the opportunity to present his testimony before a couple governors, a king, and ultimately Caesar himself. This isn't a series of bad breaks; it's God's witnessing plan! What makes it work is Paul's refusal to compromise the way he lives out the Gospel, and his unwillingness to shut up about Jesus, even if it might have gained him his freedom.

When God gets a trustworthy witness, He really uses him! Tertullus might have been a hired spokesman for the Jewish leaders, but Paul was a bondslave spokesman for Jesus Christ. There was no contest. The lawyer couldn't even convince a corrupt governor to act against Paul, yet when Paul spoke, the governor lost his composure and had to go smother his conscience with a pillow. An uncompromising life, accompanied by a bold testimony, is the kind of witness God likes to show off—it's powerful!

Without a life of integrity, we don't have much, when it comes to spiritual power. Because Paul refused to cave in to compromise, he had so much spiritual power it was scary. He intimidated governors and kings!

God used a bold witness, disguised as a prisoner, to corner two governors and a king with the truth. God still uses faithful witnesses. He provides them with opportunities to testify about Him, often disguised as hardships.

Witnessing is not complicated, but it does take courage, which God provides. And to His faithful witnesses, God also provides something else: Opportunities.

The Bottom Line: Faithful witnesses get plenty of witnessing opportunities.

DAY 325

Chicken Brain

So on the next day Agrippa and Bernice came with great pomp, and they entered the audience hall with the military tribunes and the prominent men of the city. Then, at the command of Festus, Paul was brought in. And Festus said, "King Agrippa and all who are present with us, you see this man about whom the whole Jewish people petitioned me, both in Jerusalem and here, shouting that he ought not to live any longer. But I found that he had done nothing deserving death. And as he himself appealed to the emperor, I decided to go ahead and send him. But I have nothing definite to write to my lord about him. Therefore I have brought him before you all, and especially before you, King Agrippa, so that, after we have examined him, I may have something to write. For it seems to me unreasonable, in sending a prisoner, not to indicate the charges against him."

So Agrippa said to Paul, "You have permission to speak for yourself." Then Paul stretched out his hand and made his defense:

"I consider myself fortunate that it is before you, King Agrippa, I am going to make my defense today against all the accusations of the Jews, especially because you are familiar with all the customs and controversies of the Jews. Therefore I beg you to listen to me patiently..." Acts 25:23-26:3

Paul stands before King Agrippa II, grandson of Herod the Great, who had tried to snuff out the life of the baby Jesus. The room is filled with other prominent people. The stage is set. For what? For Paul to give his testimony. Again.

The audience won't be disappointed, nor will God. Paul was missing any kind of shyness gene, anyway, but common sense would still have dictated the necessity of keeping his mouth shut while in chains facing a hostile audience. Didn't stop him. Out came his entire testimony, a whole chapter's worth. He ended by basically asking a king to confess Christ as Savior in front of the military tribunes, city fathers and the governor. I would imagine it was the first evangelistic invitation given in that Roman audience hall, in the city named after the emperor. Nerve.

That's what I'm lacking, when it comes to witnessing. My brain has always majored in self-preservation. It would have told me to shut up and live to witness another day, in Paul's situation. It's why I've witnessed on so few days, and mostly only led people to Christ who were already on their way. My brain's a coward, a clever rationalizer and a poor evangelist. I love Jesus, but my brain's chicken. Sometimes I should disengage my chicken brain and be like Paul, for Jesus.

The Bottom Line: Faithful witnesses sometimes must disengage chicken brains.

DAY 326

Angel on Board

Since they had been without food for a long time, Paul stood up among them and said, "Men, you should have listened to me and not have set sail from Crete and incurred this injury and loss. Yet now I urge you to take heart, for there will be no loss of life among you, but only of the ship. For this very night there stood before me an angel of the God to whom I belong and whom I worship, and he said, 'Do not be afraid, Paul; you must stand before Caesar. And behold, God has granted you all those who sail with you.' So take heart, men, for I have faith in God that it will be exactly as I have been told. But we must run aground on some island." Acts 27:21-26

Paul's warning not to leave Crete had gone unheeded, but suddenly everyone is listening to him! He'd heard from God. None would ever forget the message of the prisoner, relating to them hope from God, when they thought all was lost. It all ended up happening just as Paul said the angel had said. They all got to Rome. Along the way, Paul continued to be a blessing, no matter what happened to him.

The final two chapters of Acts are a glimpse of the difference which can be made simply through one person who chooses to live for God, and not for himself. Paul had decided to be God-centered, not self-centered. Rather than noticing the unfairness of each unfair situation, Paul chose to see and seize the opportunity—to witness about Jesus; to show patience, grace and courage; to be a blessing.

That doesn't just happen, particularly for a person like Paul, an off-the-chart Type A personality, naturally impatient and ambitious. But the decision makes all the difference. "Self-centered" sees each unfair episode as yet another reason to be frustrated, angry and bitter. "God-centered" sees each unfair episode as another opportunity to tap into the grace, patience and forgiveness of God.

Self-centered produces self-centered fruit; God-centered produces the fruit of the Spirit: love, joy, peace, patience, kindness, goodness, faithfulness, gentleness and self-control (Galatians 5:22-23). The guy who wrote that lived it, too. It all came from the choice to put Christ in the center of his life. It's a choice we all can make. The same Holy Spirit who powered Paul is willing to fill us with Himself. All we have to do is choose to be God-centered instead of self-centered, and we join the ranks of the disciples of Jesus who continue to write the story of the Acts of the Holy Spirit. What a deal!

The Bottom Line: Be God-centered instead of self-centered.

DAY 327

Snakes Repenting

...the word of God came to John the son of Zechariah in the wilderness. And he went into all the region around the Jordan, proclaiming a baptism of repentance for the forgiveness of sins.

He said therefore to the crowds that came to be baptized by him, "You brood of vipers! Who warned you to flee from the wrath to come? Bear fruits in keeping with repentance. And do not begin to say to yourselves, 'We have Abraham as our father.' for I tell you, God is able from these stones to raise up children for Abraham. Even now the axe is laid to the root of the trees. Every tree therefore that does not bear good fruit is cut down and thrown into the fire."

And the crowds asked him, "What then shall we do?" Luke 3:2-3,7-10

When the evangelist's opening line to the audience is, *"You brood of vipers! Who warned you to flee from the wrath to come?"* anyone who hangs around for the conclusion is probably serious about repentance.

John the Baptist was not currying favor with anyone except the God who sent him to preach a baptism of repentance. Both repentance and the messenger who preached it were gifts to the people willing to receive them. It's still that way. While no one likes to be called a snake or told that what they are doing is sinful and will bring upon them God's wrath, those who choose to listen and respond are saved; those who stick with their own righteousness and scoff at repentance are lost. This is serious stuff. We're not talking popularity, here; this is about eternity.

It's also about action. The people asking what to do were the sinners, who, when called "a brood of vipers," didn't get defensive or antagonistic, but accepted the label as pretty accurate. "How do we change? What do we do? I'm tired of being a snake. I want to be good, not bad."

This is the attitude which leads to conversion. This is what it is to repent—to hear the bitter news that you're nothing but a snake, in imminent danger of God's wrath due to your sin, and to accept that news with sorrow—enough to be willing to do whatever it takes to live a new life. The ability to repent is a gift from God. Without His help, we aren't able to even acknowledge our sin, much less be sorry enough to change. In Christ, there is new, eternal life for snakes who repent.

We are the people who get to choose, like they did, whether we'll stick with our own righteousness, hoping it will get us through (It won't), or accept the righteousness which comes from Jesus alone.

The Bottom Line: We don't have to be snakes, anymore. Jesus saves.

DAY 328

Welcome to Nazareth

And he came to Nazareth, where he had been brought up. And as was his custom, he went to the synagogue on the Sabbath day, and he stood up to read. And the scroll of the prophet Isaiah was given to him. He unrolled the scroll and found the place where it was written,

"The Spirit of the Lord is upon me, because he has anointed me to proclaim good news to the poor, He has sent me to proclaim liberty to the captives and recovering of sight to the blind, to set at liberty those who are oppressed, to proclaim the year of the Lord's favor."

And he rolled up the scroll and gave it back to the attendant and sat down. And the eyes of all in the synagogue were fixed on him. And he began to say to them, "Today this Scripture has been fulfilled in your hearing." And all spoke well of him and marveled at the gracious words that were coming from his mouth. And they said, "Is not this Joseph's son?" Luke 4:16-22

So far, so good. Jesus has returned to his hometown, where He reads Isaiah's prophecy, announces the fulfillment of Scripture, and is able to bask in a little hometown glory—for about five seconds.

The positive vibes evaporate as Jesus explains that no prophet is accepted in his hometown, illustrating His point by referring to miracles which had happened to foreigners instead of Israelites. That's all it takes. The atmosphere instantly swings from praise to rage. Now they want to push Jesus off a cliff. Seriously! Nothing like a hometown welcome. The townspeople drive the Lord toward disgrace and death, just because He ticked them off. Not so fast. It isn't time, yet. *But passing through their midst, he went away* (Luke 4:30).

It's one thing to hear God's voice telling us He's going to set us free; it's another to hear the statements which stab our soul in conviction of sin, but the two are inter-locked. If we're unwilling to hear about sin, we'll never be free from it. Jesus comes to us and announces freedom for the captives; we can grab on and praise the name of our Rescuer, or we can try to drive Him away because it angers us to face the reality of unrighteousness and purposeful disbelief.

To all who receive Him, He grants eternal life. To those who reject Him, He goes away. We get what we choose—eternal life with a loving Savior, or the loneliness which comes when we told God to go away, and we got our wish. Good news, though. He's waiting for us, willing to set us free, if we change our mind.

**The Bottom Line: We can be free,
if we receive the truth and the Savior.**

DAY 329

Unselfish with the Savior

And reports about him went out into every place in the surrounding region.

And he arose and left the synagogue and entered Simon's house. Now Simon's mother-in-law was ill with a high fever, and they appealed to him on her behalf. And he stood over her and rebuked the fever, and it left her, and immediately she rose and began to serve them.

Now when the sun was setting, all those who had any who were sick with various diseases brought them to him, and he laid his hands on every one of them and healed them. And demons also came out of many, crying, "You are the Son of God!" But he rebuked them and would not allow them to speak, because they knew that he was the Christ.

And when it was day, he departed and went into a desolate place. And the people sought him and came to him, and would have kept him from leaving them, but he said to them, "I must preach the good news of the kingdom of God to the other towns as well; for I was sent for this purpose." And he was preaching in the synagogues of Judea. Luke 4:37-44

The folks in Capernaum were impressed beyond belief with Jesus. News about the Gospel went viral one Sabbath Day. A temporary mat shortage became a surplus as sick people were brought to Christ on mats, then walked home, grinning.

Those who saw Jesus in person were always amazed—even the *demons!* Yet somehow, so many in our culture, even among those claiming to be born again, act as if Jesus were not nearly as impressive as some stupid movie star whose life is a mess! If there were a genuine revival in the Church of impassioned commitment to Christ, of love for Him, the culture would be caught up in the vortex, I think. They're looking for something real, someone with authority and compassion at the same time—and there's no one even remotely close to Jesus Christ!

We're among the people still astonished at the goodness and authority and power and grace and compassion and love and creativity and... !!! of our Savior. We should do like the people of Capernaum did, and *tell people about Jesus!* We should appeal to Jesus on behalf of others, like they did for Simon Peter's mother-in-law. We should bring our friends to Him, knowing that if they can just meet Jesus, everything will be O.K. We should be Jesus' fan club, the groupies who worship Him, who won't shut up about Him—ever! We should be the people who love Jesus, but don't keep Him to ourselves. Because everybody needs Jesus.

The Bottom Line: Jesus is too wonderful to keep to ourselves.

DAY 330

Eternal Adventures

On one occasion, while the crowd was pressing in on him to hear the word of God, he was standing by the lake of Genessaret, and he saw two boats by the lake, but the fishermen had gone out of them and were washing their nets. Getting into one of the boats, which was Simon's, he asked him to put out a little from the land. And he sat down and taught the people from the boat. And when he had finished speaking, he said to Simon, "Put out into the deep and let down your nets for a catch." And Simon answered, "Master, we toiled all night and took nothing! But at your word I will let down the nets." And when they had done this, they enclosed a large number of fish, and their nets were breaking. They signaled to their partners in the other boat to come and help them. And they came and filled both the boats, so that they began to sink. But when Simon Peter saw it, he fell down at Jesus' knees, saying, "Depart from me, for I am a sinful man, O Lord." For he and all who were with him were astonished at the catch of fish that they had taken, and so also were James and John, sons of Zebedee, who were partners with Simon. And Jesus said to Simon, "Do not be afraid; from now on you will be catching men." And when they had brought their boats to land, they left everything and followed him. Luke 5:1-11

The enormity of the decision of those fishermen haunts me, centuries later. Up to this point in their lives, success in fishing was the goal, the achievement marker for life. Along came Someone who could grant that longing effortlessly, without even getting in the water. Simon Peter tried to disqualify himself: *"Depart from me, for I am a sinful man, O Lord."* Yeah, like Jesus didn't already know that. Instead of being excused from discipleship because of a lousy track record in holiness, Jesus gives Simon an unbelievable challenge and promise, on top of the unbelievable catch: *"Do not be afraid; from now on you will be catching men."*

That's all it took. The committed fishermen walked away from the greatest catch in their lives to follow One who could do anything, who had called sinful men to just follow Him. What an epic adventure! There has never been, nor will there ever be, anything that compares with serving God! To follow Jesus Christ is the absolute guarantee of adventure, and it's for eternity!

My mind spins with memories of what it has been like to follow Jesus. The word "adventure" doesn't do the journey justice. And to think our earthly existence is only the beginning of the trail! If it's adventure you want, follow Him!

The Bottom Line: There is nothing that compares with following Jesus Christ!

DAY 331

Get Even or Get Deliverance?

Do not say, "I will repay evil";
wait for the LORD, and he will deliver you.

Proverbs 20:22

It's easy to be discouraged and angry in today's political climate, particularly in a year with so much at stake. But bitterness, especially in politics, is very off-putting. I saw it today, as person after person testified on both sides of the gay marriage issue in my state. One person in particular typified to me the futility of trying to win an argument by coming across as prudish, harsh and bitter. I was on her side, but I knew the judgmental tone of her argument wasn't helping the cause. We lost. As it turned out, what made the difference was not the hours of impassioned testimony from citizens, but a legislator I don't believe was even present who switched sides.

So, should we skip participating in politics as Christians? No. Christians need to be more responsible and involved citizens than we have tended to be in the past several decades. We should continue to do all we can to protect religious freedom, stand for morality, and elect the best candidates available.

What I think we should do differently than we sometimes do is to let God take care of those who oppose us, instead of attempting to exact vengeance, ourselves. Those who let God handle vengeance seem to be considerably happier.

Yeah, it does seem that "nice guys" are often trounced as a reward for their civility, particularly in politics. Is waiting for the Lord still the best policy? Yup. He will deliver you. Or we can flail around in a desperate attempt to get even, and only get tired and defeated.

We get awfully concerned about our rights in America; much less concerned about people who don't know Jesus. Could it be that one of the best ways of evangelizing the "me" generations would be focusing not on "me" but on "you"?

Wait for the LORD. It's much more effective than feuding, or even winning elections. And if someone needs to be put in their place, it's not a problem at all, to God.

The Bottom Line: Getting deliverance from the LORD beats getting even.

DAY 332

Righteous Intolerance

Unequal weights are an abomination to the LORD,
and false scales are not good.
A man's steps are from the LORD;
how then can man understand his way?
It is a snare to say rashly, "It is holy,"
and to reflect only after making vows.
A wise king winnows the wicked and drives the wheel over them.
The spirit of man is the lamp of the LORD,
searching all his innermost parts.
Steadfast love and faithfulness preserve the king,
and by steadfast love his throne is upheld.
Blows that wound cleanse away evil;
strokes make clean the innermost parts.

Proverbs 20:23-28,30

God is very intolerant—when it comes to evil. What are some things which concern God? Unfairness. Rashness, particularly in sacred vows. Wickedness.

In the early days of our nation's history, our standards usually mimicked biblical standards, whether in laws or societal expectations. Evil was present, of course, but regarded as evil, not good. This has changed. In today's scramble for moral high ground in our society, some busily re-label as "good" what the Bible consistently pronounces "evil." Tolerance is lifted up as the supreme virtue, trumping all others. A country founded on godly principles now is left with popular opinion or a judge to provide a basis for right and wrong. Thus, "right" is nothing more than the prevailing opinion of the majority or a judge. "Wrong" is calling anything evil, or trying to live by God's standards, instead of the standards currently in vogue in popular culture.

Wickedness of all kinds is harbored by many leaders, as well as practiced by them. Instead of stamping out evil, those in authority often protect it and even enshrine it, calling it good! Not good. God sees it differently. So should we. We desperately need to re-adopt God's standards as our own! We can either be the people who tolerate wickedness—in ourselves and in those under our authority—or we can be the people who follow God's righteousness, applying it to each area of our lives. If we follow Him, His standard should be ours as well.

The Bottom Line: Followers of God follow His standards of righteousness.

DAY 333

Gray Glory

The glory of young men is their strength,
but the splendor of old men is their gray hair.

Proverbs 20:29

If gray hair is splendid, my splendor got started early—age 21 when it first began to show up. Added to that, on my 21st birthday a doctor doing my routine physical had casually informed me that I probably had arthritis. I thought it rather unfair to have arthritis, gray hair and acne, all at the same time!

Now I'm totally splendid (if gray hair equals splendor). People ask what color my hair used to be. They grant me senior discount status without even asking, though I may be a decade short of "senior" at their establishment. Arthritis? About the same as it was at 21. Zits? Still get one, occasionally! Once in a while I feel splendid. For a few hours.

The glory of young men is their strength. I never had a lot to glory in. I kind of missed the "glory" days of youthful strength, never possessing enough, young or old, to impress anyone. Athletics was more a source of humiliation than joy for me, as a young man. One of the nice things about growing up and graduating is no longer being forced to run gut drills, then head for the locker room to be tossed around by oversized bullies.

On the other hand, as we age, even simple things like mobility become a big deal, particularly in the company of those who have lost theirs. Yeah, *the glory of young men is their strength,* even when they don't have that much.

The splendor of old men is their gray hair. Is that true? It's not the hair; it's the journey, and the things learned along the way. It's called wisdom. It didn't come easily. Wisdom takes a long while to sink in; thus the association with gray hair. It's rare to find a wise person without it.

What I've found is that the best lessons and the wisdom all come from God. When we're young, we can glory in the strength God provided; when we're not so young, we can be glad for the gray hair and the hard-won wisdom God has granted along the way; either way, it all came from Him.

The glory of young men is their strength; of old men, their gray hair. But the glory of *wise* men, young or old, is their God.

Good thing. When I leave the barber shop, I leave a lot of "splendor" behind, these days. It looks like they shaved a gray squirrel in there.

The Bottom Line: The glory of wise men, young or old, is their God.

DAY 334

King's Hearts

The king's heart is a stream of water in the hand of the LORD;
he turns it wherever he will.
Every way of man is right in his own eyes,
but the LORD weighs the heart.
To do righteousness and justice is more acceptable to the LORD than sacrifice.
Haughty eyes and a proud heart,
the lamp of the wicked, are sin.

Proverbs 21:1-4

In the U.S. we've always prided ourselves on not having kings or queens, just presidents; some great, some good, some.... well...

This scripture is a comforting reminder that changing a king's heart (or a president's) is as easy for God as redirecting a hose! It makes me think we should pray more, complain less, when it comes to our leaders. And when it comes to voting for leaders, it also might make sense to look for the same things which impress God, instead of the things which bump up poll numbers and egos.

Pride is a very big problem when it comes to leadership. First of all, it's sin—easy to forget that in an election year, when boasting and mudslinging are standard fare, used ad nauseum by those desperately trying to move from the loser's column to the winner's. It's rather discouraging to see, time and again, that humility doesn't seem to win elections. Hmm. How often have we ever seen it? *Haughty eyes and a proud heart* are what we usually see. They are *the lamp of the wicked.* It's how they get around. Mankind is predisposed to suppose our every thought is correct. Of course we're right! Why would we think or do something if it wasn't?

There is One who weighs the heart, not the rhetoric. He frowns on pride. Sacrifices don't mean nearly as much to Him as righteousness and justice. And even when *haughty eyes and a proud heart* win the election, that One is able to direct a proud king's heart whichever way He wants it to go.

So, who will win the elections this year? I don't know. Maybe the ones with the biggest mud and money machines, or the most skillful, manipulative boasters. No matter. God can point leaders in whatever direction He wants them to go, even while their proud hearts insist it was their idea. God leads proud hearts or humble hearts with equal ease, but humble hearts get a blessing.

The Bottom Line: God easily directs even proud kings, but it's humility He blesses.

DAY 335

Idols in a Hurricane

When you cry out, let your collection of idols deliver you!
The wind will carry them off,
a breath will take them away.
But he who takes refuge in me shall possess the land
and shall inherit my holy mountain.

Isaiah 57:13

I haven't seen this verse on many coffee cups. Actually, I can't recall ever seeing a verse about idolatry on a coffee cup or plaque, although there are a great many in the Bible from which to choose. Again and again, God sent prophets to warn folks about where idolatry leads, and how good the alternative is. Usually, the people didn't listen.

Are we listening, now? In the month where we celebrate the birth of Christ, Christmas has taken on a life of its own for many, leaving Christ behind, focusing instead on what is basically the worship of stuff, of money. Idolatry. Anything which takes the place of God is an idol. Could anyone argue that we don't live in a land awash in idolatry?

Not everyone in America worships at the shrine of materialism, hedonism, education, science or whatever flavor of idol is currently in vogue for their age bracket, but a great many do. To the unbelieving crowd who stubbornly cling to their god-substitutes, God has a message: *When you cry out, let your collection of idols deliver you! The wind will carry them off, a breath will take them away.*

It makes me think of a house I saw in Mississippi, in 2005. Hurricane Katrina had just come through. The magnificent new house had been reduced to a lonely toilet bolted to the concrete slab. *Everything* else was gone.

Ultimately, it will be the same story for every single person who puts their trust in idols instead of in the one true God. Even if they manage to hang onto their idols through whatever storms life brings, death comes to all, insured and uninsured alike, prying fingers loose. After that, the Judgment. Which idol will deliver us from a Holy God?

There is a better way! Take refuge in God. An inheritance beyond our imagination waits. And along the way, peace, 'til we see what He has promised.

The Bottom Line: Put your trust in God.
Idols will ultimately just blow away.

DAY 336

Getting to God

But he would withdraw to desolate places and pray.

On one of those days, as he was teaching, Pharisees and teachers of the law were sitting there, who had come from every village of Galilee and Judea and from Jerusalem. And the power of the Lord was with him to heal. And behold, some men were bringing on a bed a man who was paralyzed, and they were seeking to bring him in and lay him before Jesus, but finding no way to bring him in, because of the crowd, they went up on the roof and let him down with his bed through the tiles into the midst before Jesus. And when he saw their faith, he said, "Man, your sins are forgiven you." And the scribes and the Pharisees began to question, saying, "Who is this who speaks blasphemies? Who can forgive sins but God alone?" When Jesus perceived their thoughts, he answered them, "Why do you question in your hearts? Which is easier, to say, 'Your sins are forgiven you,' or to say, 'Rise and walk'? But that you may know that the Son of Man has authority on earth to forgive sins"—he said to the man who was paralyzed—"I say to you, rise, pick up your bed and go home." And immediately he rose up before them and picked up what he had been lying on and went home, glorifying God. And amazement seized them all, and they glorified God and were filled with awe, saying, "We have seen extraordinary things today." Luke 5:16-26

They weren't tearing up the roof to get to the Pharisees, a point not lost on the prestigious religious leaders, who themselves had assembled from across the nation to hear the teaching of Jesus. The logjam of scholars and commoners had made it impossible to get close to the Lord, so the paralytic's friends improvised.

Dust filtered down on the packed audience Jesus taught. The distracted crowd looked up into bright daylight through a growing hole in the roof. A pallet containing a paralytic was lowered to within inches of the Master. Grinning faces looked down through the new sunroof, and were met with a smile from Jesus.

Faith. It's powerful. It's even fun. Jesus enjoyed the whole thing immensely. The Pharisees and teachers of the law didn't. "Who does he think he is?! He's forgiving sins! No one but God can do that!"

Bingo.

People didn't take drastic measures to see the scholars; they came to get to God. Forgiveness and healing followed. It was worth the effort. Always is.

The Bottom Line: People aren't desperate for scholarship, but for God.

DAY 337

The Messiah's Mission–and Ours

The Spirit of the LORD GOD is upon me,
because the LORD has anointed me
to bring good news to the poor;
he has sent me to bind up the brokenhearted,
to proclaim liberty to the captives,
and the opening of the prison to those who are bound;
to proclaim the year of the LORD's favor,
and the day of vengeance of our God;
to comfort all who mourn;
to grant to those who mourn in Zion—
to give them a beautiful headdress instead of ashes,
the oil of gladness instead of mourning,
the garment of praise instead of a faint spirit;
that they may be called oaks of righteousness,
the planting of the LORD, that he may be glorified.
They shall build up the ancient ruins;
they shall raise up the former devastations;
they shall repair the ruined cities,
the devastations of many generations.

Isaiah 61:1-4

This is all about Jesus. He even told the folks at Nazareth it was about Him, when He read from this passage in His hometown synagogue (Luke 4:16-21). Jesus of Nazareth is the perfect fulfillment of this prophecy.

But this passage is not *just* about Jesus; it's about us, too. When we choose to follow Him, His mission becomes our mission, too (thus, The Great Commission).

What's our mission? To bring good news to the poor. To bind up the broken-hearted. To proclaim liberty to the captives. To proclaim the year of the LORD's favor and the day of vengeance of our God. To bring comfort and gladness to all who mourn. To build up the ancient ruins, repair the ruined cities.

The promise if we apply ourselves to these things: *You shall be called priests of the LORD; they shall speak of you as the ministers of our God* (Isa 61:6).

We follow the Messiah. We are priests of His, with a great mission. Make that a Great Commission.

The Bottom Line: The Messiah's mission is our mission.

DAY 338

Redneck Bible Advice

It is better to live in a corner of the housetop
than in a house shared with a quarrelsome wife.

Proverbs 21:9

This is one verse I'm happy to not relate to. I love my wife, she is a joy to me and others, she's not quarrelsome. Should I just move on, or is there something I'm supposed to get out of this verse besides "Glad it's not me!"?

Scripture is here to help us, even when it sounds like something out of a "You Might be a Redneck" book. So what can a "happily-married-to-a-wonderful-woman" guy get out of this verse? And how is this little passage helpful to the guy ringed to a snarling spouse, who is seeking relief, not "I told you so!"?

Like most scripture, this passage is helpful on several levels, starting with preventive wisdom. To the lonely single guy comes a timely warning: What's worse than being single? Being married to someone who doesn't respect you, who treats you with contempt, who is always angry with you. Just sayin'!

What's worse than being poor? Living in a big house with a bitter person who doesn't act as if she likes you. The trappings of modern affluence don't counteract the pain which comes to those who have no peace with their partner.

What about the guy reading Proverbs 21:9 too late, who can only nod in sad agreement? Any hope for him? Sure.

"It takes two to quarrel." And it only takes one patient person willing to truly listen, then love, to deactivate most quarrels. Will you win the argument? Probably not. But what's worse than losing arguments? Losing relationships.

Finally, is there a message in here for the "I'm not quarrelsome—I'm right!" woman who shares a home with a husband who frequently makes himself scarce?

Yes. "Being right" matters to you. A lot. You believe in expressing your opinion and backing it up. You won't back down when you know you're right, which is, well, most of the time. One question: What's worse than people not agreeing that you're right? Wouldn't it be people you love leaving you all alone to be right by yourself? Isn't that worse?

God is always right, but never argumentative. He is love. He is peace. He is patience. Kindness. Faithfulness. Goodness. Gentleness. Self-control. He is joy. This is what we get in our own lives if we care more about being filled with His Spirit than we do about winning arguments. It's a really good deal.

The Bottom Line: The fruit of the Spirit is better than winning arguments.

DAY 339

Help is on the Way

Truth is lacking,
and he who departs from evil makes himself a prey.

The LORD saw it, and it displeased him
that there was no justice.
He saw that there was no man,
and wondered that there was no one to intercede;
then his own arm brought him salvation,
and his righteousness upheld him.
He put on righteousness as a breastplate,
and a helmet of salvation on his head;
he put on garments of vengeance for clothing,
and wrapped himself in zeal as a cloak.
According to their deeds, so will he repay,
wrath to his adversaries,
repayment to his enemies;
to the coastlands he will render payment.
So shall they fear the name of the LORD from the west,
and his glory from the rising of the sun;
for he will come like a rushing stream,
which the wind of the LORD drives.

"And a Redeemer will come to Zion,
to those in Jacob who turn from transgression," declares the LORD.

Isaiah 59:15-20

Truth is lacking, and he who departs from evil makes himself a prey. How did Isaiah know? Apparently, when nations defy God's Laws and start making up their own, it's always the same. If it were God who was delivering the State of the Union address tonight, I wonder how it would go for us. For those willing to depart from evil, it always goes well, even when the culture around them pounces. Help is on the way! Big-time help! Our God can do anything, including bringing spiritual awakening to nations in big trouble. While listening for the Lord's voice yesterday, I only got one message: "Don't give up on your country." Help is on the way.

The Bottom Line: Help is on the way, if we'll take it.

DAY 340

God's Side of the Road

I spread out my hands all the day to
a rebellious people,
who walk in a way that is not good,
following their own devices;
a people who provoke me to my face continually, ...

Isaiah 65:2-3

"These have chosen their own ways,
and their soul delights in their abominations;
I also will choose harsh treatment for them
and bring their fears upon them,
because when I called, no one answered,
when I spoke, they did not listen;
but they did what was evil in my eyes
and chose that in which I did not delight."

Isaiah 66:3-4

Judgment is coming. I just don't know when. Numerous Bible passages illustrate the outcome for people (or nations) who reject God and choose their own way. It isn't pretty. Isaiah ends with a grim prophecy for those choosing rebellion against God as their life path: *For their worm shall not die, their fire shall not be quenched, and they shall be an abhorrence to all flesh* (Isa 66:24). God is serious.

When we choose evil over good, we're choosing judgment. That goes for individuals; it goes for nations. Majority opinion doesn't change God's. We need only refer back to the time of Noah to realize that truth. If only one man on the planet cares about trying to please God, only one man and his family will be saved. The rest chose judgment when they chose evil. End of story.

Serving God in America used to be like driving on the Interstate. Pretty much everyone was going the same direction; our favorite lane was the middle one. Now, following Jesus in America is more like a 2-lane highway, with the culture coming at us like oncoming traffic. Middle of the road? No longer an option. Better get on God's side and stay there. Coming toward us are those who like God's blessings but despise His authority. We're not going the same direction. We're not on the same side. We'll also be arriving at very different destinations.

The Bottom Line: Drive on God's side of the road.

DAY 341

On the Road with God

That very day two of them were going to a village named Emmaus, about seven miles from Jerusalem, and they were talking with each other about all these things that had happened. While they were talking and discussing together, Jesus himself drew near and went with them. But their eyes were kept from recognizing him. Luke 24:13-16

This has always been one of my favorite Resurrection stories. It's easy for me to relate to a couple of weary, heart-sick disciples, going along the road, lost in their despair over the death of Jesus, the One *"we had hoped"* was to redeem Israel. The stranger has such wisdom! They don't mind His gentle rebuke about being foolish and "slow of heart;" their hungry minds are filled with peace and understanding as He opens to them the scriptures concerning Himself. The revelation is spell-binding, the road way too short.

When they arrive at their destination, they can't bear the thought of parting with the Stranger, so they plead with Him to stay with them. As He blesses the food for the evening meal, their eyes are opened–and He vanishes. They realize who it is they just spent the day with! They were on the road with God. The two disciples hurry back to Jerusalem to tell the others. While the group is cross-referencing Jesus sightings for the day, the subject of their conversation appears in their midst and floors them all once again. To prove He's not a figment of their grief-stricken imaginations, Jesus shows them His hands and feet, then polishes off the leftover fish. It was a really good day!

Every day is a good day, when you're on the road with God. It has been the story of my life. There's just nothing like walking down a lonely road, talking to the Lord of the Universe, asking Him questions and listening as He explains it to you. There have been plenty of times when I didn't realize who was walking with me, or I ignored Him, wrapped up in my own grief or confusion. There have been plenty of times when I felt my heart swell with peace and understanding, as the God of my Life revealed to me exactly what I needed.

He's alive! Not just "kind of," or "in my memory," but really alive, set-another-place-at-the-table present! There's nothing quite so great as walking life's road with Jesus.

The Bottom Line: We get to walk life's road with God.

DAY 342

For Nothing is Impossible With God

And the angel said to her, "Do not be afraid, Mary, for you have found favor with God. And behold, you will conceive in your womb and bear a son, and you shall call his name Jesus. He will be great and will be called the Son of the Most High. And the Lord God will give to him the throne of his father David, and he will reign over the house of Jacob forever, and of his kingdom there will be no end."

And Mary said to the angel, "How will this be, since I am a virgin?"

And the angel answered her, "The Holy Spirit will come upon you, and the power of the Most High will overshadow you; therefore the child to be born will be called 'holy'—the Son of God. And behold, your relative Elizabeth in her old age has also conceived a son, and this is the sixth month with her who was called barren. For nothing will be impossible with God." Luke 1:30-37

For nothing will be impossible with God. Those are sweet words when we've been told by the medical community that the odds are not good. Ten percent chance of survival in this situation? Good thing we have God—a God for whom nothing is impossible! We need Him!

Always, we need Him. But sometimes we are so out of resources and options that God is all we have left. So many times throughout history, that's exactly when He shows up. He takes the unlikely approach, often the impossible one. Why? So we know it's Him, not luck, not chance, not our own determination and skill.

Years ago, I read a book which explained to me that, according to their checklist, the church I pastored couldn't grow. I relayed this devastating finding to God in a whining prayer: "Lord, according to this book, my church can't grow! The odds are all against us!" An immediate response from the Lord slammed into my brain: I don't do odds. Just miracles.

How true! Why bother with odds when you can do *anything?*! The Bible is a book of impossibilities, all true. God speaks the Universe into existence, makes man from a pile of dirt (after creating the dirt), establishes all of Creation. God looks for an elderly, infertile couple so He can start the nation of Israel with them. God's path is strewn with the improbable and impossible. He seems to like it that way. When it comes time to send the promised Messiah, once again God begins with a couple of impossible pregnancies, just so people know it's Him. He can do anything, absolutely anything. He always keeps His promises.

So we can trust Him—with anything! He doesn't always do what we ask or expect, but He is always there. And what He does is always good, and right. We choose to trust and praise Him.

The Bottom Line: Do not be afraid. Nothing is impossible with God.

DAY 343

How To Catch Turtles

On one occasion, while the crowd was pressing in on him to hear the word of God, he was standing by the lake of Gennesaret, and he saw two boats by the lake, but the fishermen had gone out of them and were washing their nets. Getting into one of the boats, which was Simon's, he asked him to put out a little from the land. And he sat down and taught the people from the boat. And when he had finished speaking, he said to Simon, "Put out into the deep and let down your nets for a catch." And Simon answered, "Master, we toiled all night and took nothing! But at your word I will let down the nets." And when they had done this, they enclosed a large number of fish, and their nets were breaking. They signaled to their partners in the other boat to come and help them. And they came and filled both the boats, so that they began to sink. But when Simon Peter saw it, he fell down at Jesus' knees, saying, "Depart from me, for I am a sinful man, O Lord." For he and all who were with him were astonished at the catch of fish they had taken, and so also were James and John, sons of Zebedee, who were partners with Simon. And Jesus said to Simon, "Do not be afraid; from now on you will be catching men." And when they had brought their boats to land, they left everything and followed him. Luke 5:1-11

A carpenter teaching commercial fishermen how to fish! That's something you don't see every day. But this was no ordinary day, and no ordinary carpenter. That was the day the training began on how to catch men, too. On the day of Pentecost, God used Simon Peter to reel in 3,000. That was just the season opener!

In more recent times, Jesus taught a seven-year-old boy to catch turtles. The kid had spied some turtles sunning themselves beside the lake, decided he wanted one for a pet, and repeatedly tried charging toward them, only to see them scramble for safety and plop into the water, each time. Finally, he resorted to prayer. He asked God to help him catch a turtle.

Moments later, it occurred to him that since the turtles had gone into the water, perhaps he should join them. He removed shoes and socks, rolled up his pant legs and began wading the shallows, until suddenly his foot touched something both hard and slippery. He reached down to grab his first true answer to prayer. "Thanks, God!" he screamed to the sky, and raced for the house.

I became a lifelong Prayer Addict that day, with no desire for recovery. Every good thing in my life has come from Him, in answer to prayer. He's *good!*

The Bottom Line: God loves to answer our prayers.

DAY 344

How To Catch Turtles–and Men

I've always been bad at evangelism. The old spiritual gifts surveys inflicted on us at church would show my evangelism gifts at the bottom of the list, maybe off the page. It has been easy through the years to pretty much ignore evangelism, in the same way I've ignored team sports. When you stink at something, why go out and remind yourself and everyone else how bad you really are?

We're talking vastly different stakes, though. On one hand is the eternal destiny of people for whom Christ died. On the other hand is the embarrassment which comes when you dropped the easy fly ball to left field and let your team down, again. Scoring low in evangelistic "gifts" doesn't give me a pass, any more than low skills or desire in certain farm chores got me an exemption from them. Some things we need to do, whether or not we're good at it.

The other day I was asking God how to reach people for Him. The answer I got? The same way I taught you to catch turtles when you were seven.

My first real answered prayer had been when I asked God to help me catch a turtle for a pet, and He made me think of how to do it.

Until I prayed, I had been trying to catch turtles by charging down the beach toward them as fast as my second grader legs could carry me. I'd never heard turtles laugh before.

After I prayed and asked God to help me catch a turtle, the revelation hit me that since the turtles were in the water, my best bet was to go where they were, too, rather than trying to pursue them on the shore. It only took a few minutes to capture my first turtle, once I went where they were.

Now, for catching men.

I've known people so gifted in evangelism they could run toward a crowd of strangers and come back towing a convert. Me? I can't even catch turtles that way.

Here's what I need to do. Instead of charging after folks and scaring them, I should pray first, then go where they are. God's method of going where they are worked for me to catch over 100 turtles, yet I never once had a turtle approach me to be caught. Similarly, in over 30 years of ministry, I've had very few people approach me, asking me to help them find God. Pray, then go where they are–not just physically, but emotionally and spiritually. They're rarely in the church building, waiting to be caught. Instead, they're sunning themselves on the beach. They're in the water. They're at the mall. They've withdrawn into their shell. Pray. Ask God to help you help someone into His Kingdom. Go in His name. Give thanks.

The Bottom Line: Pray, then go where they are.
You'll soon scream, "Thanks, God!"

DAY 345

Moderate Righteousness

The soul of the wicked desires evil;
his neighbor finds no mercy in his eyes.
When a scoffer is punished, the simple becomes wise;
when a wise man is instructed, he gains knowledge.
The Righteous One observes the house of the wicked;
he throws the wicked down to ruin.
Whoever closes his ear to the cry of the poor
will himself call out and not be answered.
A gift in secret averts anger,
and a concealed bribe, strong wrath.
When justice is done, it is a joy to the righteous
but terror to evildoers.

Proverbs 21:10-15

There is a clear dividing line between the wicked and the righteous. On one side of the line is mercy, willingness to accept instruction, kindness to the poor, grace and wisdom in dealing with those who are angry, a love for justice, a desire for righteousness, a respect and love for the Righteous One.

On the other side of the line: a desire for evil, no mercy, scoffing, contempt for the righteous and the Righteous One, closed ears when it comes to the poor or needy, uncontrolled anger, corruption, a fear of justice.

With such a drastic contrast between sides, why would people be tempted to try to straddle the line between righteousness and evil? Why would so many attempt to be "moderates" when it comes to righteousness?

While "moderate righteousness" may at times sway men, it never appeases God. Why? Because "moderate righteousness" is an oxymoron. True righteousness is soul-deep and total. True righteousness only comes as a gift from God, granted to penitent, humble souls willing to come over to God's side of the line. All the way.

Good works don't make us righteous. God does. But God expects His people to walk with Him on the righteous side of the line, which results in a lot of good works, and forgiving grace for the not-so-good works. Justice is a relief and a joy to the righteous—and the last thing evildoers want to see. And those trying to do some kind of middle-of-the-road thing when it comes to righteousness? Roadkill. We'd better pursue righteousness, wholeheartedly, and soul-first.

The Bottom Line: Righteousness is to be pursued wholeheartedly, and soul-first.

DAY 346

Moderate Love

One of the Pharisees asked him to eat with him, and he went into the Pharisee's house and took his place at the table. And behold, a woman of the city, who was a sinner, when she learned that he was reclining at table in the Pharisee's house, brought an alabaster flask of ointment, and standing behind him at his feet, weeping, she began to wet his feet with her tears and wiped them with the hair of her head and kissed his feet and anointed them with the ointment...

Then turning toward the woman he said to Simon, "Do you see this woman? I entered your house; you gave me no water for my feet, but she has wet my feet with her tears and wiped them with her hair. You gave me no kiss, but from the time I came in she has not ceased to kiss my feet. You did not anoint my head with oil, but she has anointed my feet with ointment. Therefore I tell you, her sins, which are many, are forgiven–for she loved much. But he who is forgiven little, loves little." And he said to her, "Your sins are forgiven." Luke 7:36-38,44-48

Whatever was on the menu at Simon the Pharisee's house, it didn't include a warm welcome. Simon thought he was being quite generous simply by inviting Jesus to dinner. Hospitality stopped there, as even the most basic welcoming gestures were purposely ignored. What was on the menu? Humiliation, it seems. While it was customary to have a servant wash the feet of the guests, Jesus was not even offered any water to wash His own feet. No water, no kiss of greeting. No anointing oil for Jesus' head. Simon was a horrible host.

What Jesus received instead of welcoming love or good manners was scornful snobbery. Simon seethed as an uninvited guest–a woman, an obvious sinner–made a spectacle of herself by uninhibited demonstrations of love, honor, generosity and humility toward Jesus. Simon's conclusion? Must not be much of a prophet, if he can't even tell what kind of woman is touching him!

It didn't get better for Simon. He hadn't voiced his Pharisaical thoughts, but Jesus still knew them–and proceeded to openly contrast the level of love shown by a "sinner" woman and someone pretending to be righteous and a host.

It wasn't moderate, grudging love which purchased our salvation on Calvary. It was a Savior who held nothing back. He went far beyond anything "reasonable." The greatest commandment, according to Him, was the one about loving God back, with all our heart.

The Bottom Line: When it comes to loving God, the standard is: with all our heart.

DAY 347

Pride Overboard

Soon afterward he went on through cities and villages, proclaiming and bringing the good news of the kingdom of God. And the twelve were with him, and also some women who had been healed of evil spirits and infirmities: Mary, called Magdalene, from whom seven demons had gone out, and Joanna, the wife of Chuza, Herod's household manager, and Susanna, and many others, who provided for them out of their means. Luke 8:1-3

It was the dream of every Jewish male to grow up and be supported by some formerly demon-possessed women. Not! I'm trying to imagine how hard that must have been for some of the "I can do it myself" disciples Jesus called to follow Him. Pretty hard, I'm thinking. But being a disciple of Christ Jesus is not something we do by ourselves or on our own terms. Part of the deal is being willing to accept the help we need, whether it's coming directly from God or a somewhat spooky person He sent. Disciples learn to leave their pride behind, and accept God's provision, however and whenever it shows up.

One of the things best pitched overboard ASAP is the pride/fear/dignity which prevents us from really following Jesus. These things only weigh us down and hold us back. Disciples follow Jesus no matter what it takes, no matter what must be left behind. The original twelve got a taste of all kinds of fear and indignity. Being supported by women was only a small portion of their unsought humility. Professional fishermen yell out to God to save them because they are all going to drown in the storm, only to have a Carpenter calm the wind and sea with His voice.

They land on a strange shore and are met by a screaming naked man, a walking homeless shelter for so many demons he's called "Legion." The Master evicts the herd of demons into a herd of swine, who promptly drown themselves in the sea rather than put up with being demon-possessed. (Humans should be so smart). The villagers are more concerned with missing pigs and uncontrollable power than the fact that an outcast of society now is clothed and in his right mind. Following Jesus is both expensive and scary. It gets you so far from your comfort zone that you can't even see your comfort zone anymore! Worth it? You bet!

There's more–so much more. Following Jesus is an adventure, a scary ride where the pride and dignity and comfort get sucked out of you the longer you follow Him. There's no one like our Savior! Following God's Son is not for the faint of heart, but eternal adventures await! Starting now.

The Bottom Line: Followers of Jesus get to learn to live without their pride.

DAY 348

Forget Your Wallet

And he called the twelve together and gave them power and authority over all demons and to cure diseases, and he sent them out to proclaim the kingdom of God and to heal. And he said to them, "Take nothing for your journey, no staff, nor bag, nor bread, nor money; and do not have two tunics. And whatever house you enter, stay there, and from there depart. And wherever they do not receive you, when you leave that town shake off the dust from your feet as a testimony against them." And they departed and went through the villages, preaching the gospel and healing everywhere. Luke 9:1-6

In the adventure I've come to refer to as "Faith Field Trip One," the Twelve receive specific instructions which must have jolted most of them: Forget your wallet–on purpose. Ditto for extra clothes, a staff, a bag, bread. You're traveling light–really light. All you get to take with you is your faith. That way you'll get to see how it works.

The truth is, faith only works when we need it. Jesus knew what He was doing when He sent the Twelve out armed with nothing but the power and authority He gave them, and their faith. Had they been burdened with resources, they would have missed out on the opportunity to realize the validity of His promises, and the joy of seeing things happen which were beyond their control, but not God's.

It turned out to be quite an adventure! Faith always is. Sent out by God (this is important), the disciples quickly learned that not only does faith work when God gives you the mission and He promises provision; faith is fun! It's exciting to not know how God will do it this time–only that He will do it. It's fun to trust Him, and see Him come through again and again and again. Our faith starts to put on a little muscle. We freak out less, trust God more. We become more faithful disciples.

If we always opt out of the Faith Field Trips, we miss a lot. The faith we possess remains untested and unsteady. We would like to believe we believe, but having passed up all opportunities to find out, having always insisted on being tied off to our back-up plans, we miss the lessons only learned when there is no back-up plan, just God.

There are those who call laziness or presumption "faith," and expect God to bail them out (usually in vain). There are also those who call faith "laziness" or "presumption." They miss out. The answer, as always: Listen to Jesus, and obey.

The Bottom Line: Faith–use it according to Jesus' directions. It will grow.

DAY 349

God and Finals

The LORD by wisdom founded the earth;
by understanding he established the heavens;
by his knowledge the deeps broke open,
and the clouds drop down the dew.

Proverbs 3:19-20

Millions of students face final exams this month. They will pillage their brains, looking for the facts and principles of chemistry, biology, physics and so forth, supposedly stowed away for this occasion. It's not easy to understand these subjects in the first place; remembering it all is even harder. What do you suppose the difficulty level would be for *creating* the sciences—*all* of them? I'm not done yet, because the sciences are nothing more than the *explanation* for how things work. *How about creating the earth itself?* Complete with every system required to sustain life on the planet. Still not done. We need the Universe. Create it, please. Make it happen. And don't touch anything. Just use your knowledge. Just speak it into existence. Oh. And you have a week.

Look around. There are systems upon systems upon systems, entire fields of knowledge which are beyond the grasp of any one person to even understand. What we can't even comprehend, God invented, and He used nothing but His fantastic knowledge. Intelligent people can spend years trying to figure out tiny portions of what God did in one week. He even had to invent the "week."

He did it all with His wisdom. That's how God established the earth, the heavens, all the impossibly intricate systems we struggle even to understand. His knowledge is so vast that He just created it all, using nothing but wisdom! I am astounded at the knowledge of God.

This is a wisdom He is willing to share! If we want to understand, He opens our minds to things we could never otherwise even comprehend. It starts with knowing Him, acknowledging Him. ALL wisdom and knowledge begins in Him. If we honor the Source of all wisdom, some of it is going to rub off. If we apply what we learn from Him, not only will we find blessing and peace for ourselves; that blessing and peace will rub off on others, too.

And if you are sitting in a final exam this month, trying to remember the laws of nature, ask the One who invented every one of them. He is very, very, very smart! And helpful. Praying when you take a test is not cheating. Asking God is how smart people get through life. Especially during finals week.

The Bottom Line: Asking God is how smart people get through life.

DAY 350

Alone with God and Others

Now it happened that as he was praying alone, the disciples were with him.

Luke 9:18

I have to smile when I read this verse. Jesus was praying "alone," but the disciples were with Him. Sounds like the way I've heard motherhood described!

"Just get alone with God, dearie!"

"Yeah, right. I can't even go to the bathroom alone, these days!"

So Jesus was having a private conversation with the Father while His disciples were listening. Question. How else are the disciples ever to know what it sounds like to have the sort of intimacy in one's prayer life Jesus had? They needed to hear Him when He was praying "alone."

Many, many people have no understanding at all of what it is to pray, or how. The only prayers they've ever heard were public prayers which sounded very artificial, complicated. They automatically knew they couldn't do that—"If that's prayer, guess it's not for me!" How sad. Many of the most absolutely delightful times of my life have been in prayer, both private and public.

I heard my mother talk to God like He was her friend from my earliest days. Yes, she used a special "tone" in her voice when she was praying, but that only let me know she was praying, not talking to me. I still remember barging into her bedroom one day to find her on her knees, talking to God about me. She didn't even look up when I came in. She just kept on praying. I left, humbled. I knew the only thing rare about this occasion was that I had been present for part of it. She had begun to pray for me by name nearly nine months before I was born! She's never stopped. I know it.

Part of the point of prayer is that we are never alone, even when no other human being is present. Our God never leaves. He is always there. He is Light and Love. We're incredibly safe in His care. The One who numbers the hairs on our head is never bored with our trivia, even when our closest friends have excused themselves and sprinted for cover. Our Father hangs in there, delighting in every detail. He loves us that much.

To ignore the gift of private prayer is to cheat ourselves out of one of the greatest blessings available to man: the ability to talk to a living God who cares and listens. Prayer can be anywhere, any time. Getting to talk to a perfect person who loves you, who gives you His undivided attention and never leaves? Beat that!

The Bottom Line: To miss out on prayer is to miss out on a precious gift from God.

DAY 351

When God Commands Sloppiness

When you reap the harvest of your land, you shall not reap your field right up to its edge, neither shall you gather the gleanings after your harvest. And you shall not strip your vineyard bare, neither shall you gather the fallen grapes of your vineyard. You shall leave them for the poor and for the sojourner: I am the LORD your God. Leviticus 19:9-10

I was a seven-year-old gleaner.

I'm actually glad, now, for the experience I had as a second grader at Glee Lake School, a one-room country school out in the farmland of eastern South Dakota. The farmer whose cornfield bordered the schoolyard had agreed to let the students glean in his field after it had been mechanically picked.

So, the band of a dozen or so public school students spent our recesses and lunch periods for several days roaming a cornfield, scanning the ground for ears of corn missed by the corn picker, tucking them into the gunny sacks we dragged with us. Fellow second grader Greg and I trudged down the corn rows, having fun complaining. Our complaints soon turned to ways to make this job easier. We plotted grand gleaning inventions and dragged our meager harvest back toward the school, where it joined the more substantial results from the older kids. Ultimately, we filled and sold a sizeable trailer of ear corn. Our corn money went to buy balls and other sports equipment to use at recesses, which now resumed. We finally had some decent stuff to use! Guess who took good care of it? Guess who had a new appreciation for work and play, and possessions we had earned with our own money? When the school was closed due to low enrollment, a couple years later, who do you suppose got the games and equipment to take home as our own? The whole episode is a favorite memory of that era in my life. Rather than our rights being violated, we had been given a gift, with multiple blessings attached.

That's what gleaning is: a gift. The God who is usually such a stickler for not wasting anything commands His people to be sloppy when it comes to harvesting fields and vineyards. Why? So the poor and the sojourner will have a way to get food, while retaining their dignity, learning the joys of work, even making good memories. It's a pretty smart set-up, one which beats a non-working, entitlement mentality which cripples society from the ground up. Usually, God wants us to be pretty careful. But when He commands sloppiness, what He's really commanding is compassion, linked with work. The end result? Blessings all around. Good memories.

The Bottom Line: In this case, commanded sloppiness is commanded compassion.

DAY 352

Not That Bad

And behold, a lawyer stood up to put him to the test, saying, "Teacher, what shall I do to inherit eternal life?" He said to him, "What is written in the Law? How do you read it?" And he answered, "You shall love the Lord your God with all your heart and with all your soul and with all your strength and with all your mind, and your neighbor as yourself." And he said to him, "You have answered correctly; do this, and you will live." Luke 10:25-28

Whether it's Luke or Leviticus, the standard is the same: The greatest commandment? Love the Lord your God with all your heart, with all your soul, with all your mind, with all your strength. Right after that one: Love your neighbor as yourself.

So the constant questions should be something along the line of, "Does this help me love God with all my heart, soul, mind and strength?" "Is this 'loving my neighbor as myself'"?

How is it, then, that a standard oft applied to my lifestyle sounds more like, "How bad is this? Will it not hurt my relationship with God too much?"

Instead of a trail of holiness, the kind left by a heart desperately seeking to please God in every possible way, I see a lot of "not that bad" in my life.

Will "not that bad" still get me into heaven? That's not the point, since eternal life is through grace, anyway. The point is, in order to live a holy life, it means my life is directed toward how close I can be in my relationship with God, not how distant I can live from Him and His standards and still make it to heaven.

"Not that bad" is better than "just plain bad," but it's not a very fitting substitute for "God's best." Sadly, it often is. Just because it doesn't sink me, spiritually, isn't good enough reason to take it on board my life.

We are called to a different standard, the standard set by a holy God. What if I not only shut out of my life the "clearly bad," but also the "not that bad," allowing into my heart and mind only that which pretty certainly would enhance my relationship with Him? Would that tend to reduce the temptation load in my life? Would it result in a more victorious existence? Would my fellowship with the Lord be better if I spent all my time walking in the center of His light?

In marriage, the idea is not how much the other person will put up with and stay married to us, but how we can love them, wholeheartedly, with everything we have. Holiness? Same thing. It comes down to asking ourselves the right questions.

The Bottom Line: Replace "not that bad" with whatever helps me love God more.

DAY 353

The Promise

And Mary said, "Behold, I am the servant of the Lord; let it be to me according to your word." And the angel departed from her. Luke 1:38

Mary's ready acceptance of the angel's startling pronouncement that she, a virgin, would become mother of the Messiah, ranks among the greatest expressions of faith in the world's history. Not only did she believe God; she embraced the promise. Put those two things together, and you have all the makings of a miracle.

God loves to make promises, and He always keeps them. When He approaches us with one of His promises, there are two things He wants from us: Our belief, and our obedience. If our response to His promise is skepticism, disbelief or disqualifying ourselves, our rejection of the promise is not always enough to negate or lose the blessing intended for us, but there is usually a negative consequence to our disbelief—ask Zechariah, who couldn't speak until the angel's prediction of a miracle baby had been fulfilled. They both got the promised sons, but Mary wrote a stunningly beautiful praise poem to God before Jesus was born, while Zechariah had a rougher time, waiting in silence for John (the Baptist) to be born (Luke 1). Believing makes a difference! Sometimes that's all God requires of us.

Often, though, there is a second part: obedience, linked to our belief in the promise. Joseph's belief in the validity of the dream God gave him caused him to tear up the divorce papers and instead, take his pregnant fiancé home. The wise men followed the star. The shepherds went to Bethlehem and looked where the angel had told them to look. Joseph and the wise men fled properly and promptly, guided by divine dreams. Everything turned out splendidly at the first Christmas, because all the principal players believed God and obeyed His instructions. It's a really simple plan, which really works! *Believe Him. Obey Him*. Simple. Very effective.

As I said, God does love to make promises, and He keeps them. It was December 19, a year after my wife and I had lost a set of triplets to premature birth, when God clearly spoke to my mind, promising me that we would have a son. It was an "out-of-the-blue" message, coming unexpectedly when I was dwelling on a different subject, that of a church board meeting which had not gone so well, the previous evening. As I was on my face before God in the church prayer room, voicing my complaints to God about the church situation, He gently took my attention off the church ("It's not that big of a deal"), and gave me a simple, solid promise: "You're going to have a son. This year."

Although it was not an audible voice, the message to my mind was so strong, so clear, and so similar to previous leading's from the Lord that I had no doubt.

I wrote down the promise, word for word, in my prayer journal and went home to tell my wife. I believed. I had been praying that God would show us what to do, and now we had a plan, complete with the leading to pursue adoption if we weren't pregnant by the end of spring. A few weeks after the promise, I bought a toy fire truck for the boy we were going to have. It sat on our dresser for a long time, awaiting the arrival of a child of promise. When he got here, it became one of his favorite toys.

Just yesterday I re-told our son the story surrounding his birth, of not only the original promise, but the many other divine leading's along the way to its fulfillment. There were so many answered prayers! They have continued to this day, for everyone involved. It has been one more amazing adventure of following and trusting God. It was December 19, two years after the promise, that I completed "Healer of Hearts," the song I wrote for our son's dedication. God loves to make promises, and He keeps them.

The God who formed this Universe looked down upon a world which had gotten itself into trouble, took pity on us, and sent His only Son to save us. First, He promised. Then He made good on His promise. It's what Christmas is all about. What does God want of us? He wants us to trust Him enough to believe Him. He wants us to believe Him enough to obey. And He wants us to live with Him forever, with absolute faith in His goodness and faithfulness, wallowing in His love and in promises fulfilled. God is good. Don't ever forget it. Gotta go play with my son.

The Bottom Line: God loves to make promises—and He keeps them.

DAY 354

Annoyance in a Tree

He entered Jericho and was passing through. And there was a man named Zacchaeus. He was a chief tax collector and was rich. And he was seeking to see who Jesus was, but on account of the crowd he could not, because he was small of stature. So he ran on ahead and climbed up into a sycamore tree to see him, for he was about to pass that way. And when Jesus came to the place, he looked up and said to him, "Zacchaeus, hurry up and come down, for I must stay at your house today." So he hurried and came down and received him joyfully. And when they saw it, they all grumbled, "He has gone in to be the guest of a man who is a sinner." And Zacchaeus stood and said to the Lord, "Behold, Lord, the half of my goods I give to the poor. And if I have defrauded anyone of anything, I restore it fourfold." And Jesus said to him, "Today salvation has come to this house, since he also is a son of Abraham. For the Son of Man came to seek and to save the lost." Luke 19:1-10

When they looked up, what did they see? A traitor in a tree. A despised tax collector, who had lined his own pockets at their expense. Not only a tax collector, a sell-out to the Romans, but a *chief* tax collector, with other tax collectors working for him! When it came to sinners, the guy in the tree was among the worst, in their eyes.

The Jericho crowd wasn't interested in Zacchaeus getting saved; they wanted him to get what he deserved! They delighted in excluding the vertically challenged man from getting a glimpse of Jesus. He just climbed a tree. It wasn't like he had a lot of dignity left to lose.

When Jesus looked up, he didn't see what others did: an annoyance in a tree. Jesus saw a son of Abraham who needed a friend. He gave him one. All it took to transform Zacchaeus' life was for Jesus to invite Himself to his house for lunch.

When I encounter sinners and chief sinners, what do I see? Do I see people I wish would go away and leave me alone? Do I just see folks I wish would change— to be more like me? When I look, do I see an annoyance in a tree? Or do I see a child of God who needs a friend?

When I get better at seeing people like God sees them, I'll be doing a better job of following Christ. *For the Son of Man came to seek and to save the lost. Jesus, the Friend of sinners.*

Being a friend to sinners beats throwing sticks or insults. See the people. When we do, they see God. And respond.

The Bottom Line: Annoyance or friend?
See the people like Jesus sees them.

DAY 355

Who Gets Mercy?

He also told this parable to some who trusted in themselves that they were righteous, and treated others with contempt: "Two men went up into the temple to pray, one a Pharisee and the other a tax collector. The Pharisee, standing by himself, prayed thus: 'God, I thank you that I am not like other men, extortioners, unjust, adulterers, or even like this tax collector. I fast twice a week; I give tithes of all that I get.' But the tax collector, standing far off, would not even lift up his eyes to heaven, but beat his breast, saying, 'God, be merciful to me, a sinner!' I tell you, this man went down to his house justified, rather than the other. For everyone who exalts himself will be humbled, but the one who humbles himself will be exalted." Luke 18:9-14

Who gets mercy from God? The one who thinks he needs it, who asks for it. The self-righteous get... self-righteousness. That's it. The only reward for self-exaltation is the accompanying pride, which God will squelch, anyway. Such a deal.

The way to mercy is through humility and repentance. The way to disaster is through pride in our own righteousness, or exultation in our own unconfessed sin, with both leading to the same place.

These days, both sides vie for the role of self-righteous Pharisee. There is the religious person who thanks God he's not like the slimy tax collectors and sinners; there is the unrepentant sinner who prides himself on being inclusive and open-minded and tolerant and non-judgmental (except about people he considers judgmental), who is glad he's not a narrow-minded religious zealot. The Pharisee thanks God he's not a tax collector, and the tax collector thanks God he's not a Pharisee. And neither one is getting any mercy because neither one is asking for it.

Who gets mercy from God? People who know they need it, so they ask for it, humbly, without comparing themselves to other people or justifying themselves or telling God how good they are.

We all need God's mercy. If we assume our own righteousness is sufficient to see us through, we are sadly mistaken. The person who justifies himself doesn't get mercy, because he's not asking for it. He's self-justified. The person who is lifted up by God is the one who says, "God be merciful to me, a sinner," and means it! He knows he's a sinner, knows he is not righteous, won't even look up at God in his humility, is genuinely repentant.

The person who gets mercy is the person who thinks he needs some!

The Bottom Line: Here's a prayer God hears: " God, have mercy on me, a sinner!"

DAY 356

Not What We Wanted

And she gave birth to her firstborn son and wrapped him in swaddling cloths and laid him in a manger, because there was no room for them in the inn. Luke 2:7

"It was just what I wanted!" That's what gift givers long to hear. It's also what gift receivers want to be able to truthfully say. Variations of this line are truthfully spoken millions of times around Christmas trees, worldwide, each year. The Christmas gift received will have been the one at the top of the wish list, right down to size and color. Feigned surprise will be a staple in many households, feigned delight a forced response in many others. When it comes to Christmas presents, a little distance and enclosed gift receipts can really come in handy.

Did you get what you wanted? If so, you did a lot better than most Israelites at the first Christmas.

The first Christmas was invitation-only, the few participants having all been assembled by God's angels, late guests arriving via camel with the aid of GPS (God's Positioning Star). In the birth of Jesus, the wish of the ages, a Savior—a Messiah, came true. The prophecies and promises were all fulfilled, down to the place of birth, the blood line, the virgin. It was exactly right, though I've often imagined how frustrating it must have been for Mary and Joseph to wind up in a stable cave for the birth of God's Son. Joseph must have thought, "This is the best I can do for my family?!" It couldn't have been what either of them wanted! No matter. It was the way God wanted it. He was busily keeping all His promises. Nothing would stop Him.

That included the ruling tyrant of the time, King Herod. What Herod wanted for Christmas was to hang onto his kingdom a while longer. He wasn't above killing a few babies to eliminate the possibilities of a future rival. He had already dispatched three of his own grown sons, a wife and a mother-in-law. The guy was serious about defending his throne against all threats, real or imagined.

What the Israelites wanted for Christmas was to get rid of Herod. He could please take the ruling Romans with him, and give them back their country. The Israelites definitely wanted a Messiah, but they were thinking something more on the order of another Maccabee brother to raise a Roman-stomping army. A baby? Not at all what they had in mind! The kid would have to grow up, first!

They didn't get what they wanted; they got just what they needed. So did we. *The Word became flesh and dwelt among us (*John 1:14). He didn't have to come down here. He did it because He loves us. They were thinking an action-hero and wound up with God in swaddling clothes. He's just what we needed.

The Bottom Line: Jesus is exactly what we needed.

DAY 357

The Pursuit of ~~Happiness~~ Holiness

And the LORD spoke to Moses, saying, "Speak to all the congregation of the people of Israel and say to them, 'You shall be holy, for I the LORD your God am holy.'" Leviticus 19:1-2

Our Founding Fathers in America gave us a document which declared our independence from England, and listed some "inalienable rights,"including "the pursuit of happiness." Our Heavenly Father gave us a more noble and attainable pursuit: holiness.

I'm all for happiness, particularly compared to the alternatives, but I've found the pursuit of happiness to be a miserable dead-end. In fact, the surest way to not achieve happiness is to make it one's life goal.

Here's the problem. We've too often been in the pursuit of happiness when we should have been in the pursuit of holiness.

"Doesn't God want us to be happy?" If He does, it doesn't seem to rank very high on His priority list for us. Meanwhile, He repeatedly conveys to mankind His desire for us all: that we would be holy, like Him. He doesn't leave it as a vague wish, either, but always shows specifically what it would take for us to be holy, then provides a way to succeed in the pursuit.

This is where the pursuits of happiness and holiness greatly differ. The pursuit of happiness is elusive. The pursuit of holiness is guaranteed: If we want to be holy in God's sight, we can be. God makes sure of it.

On June 6, at age twenty-four, I was confronted with a stark choice: "Are you willing to follow Jesus alone?" The stakes were high and real; I knew God was not kidding. The decision to pursue holiness over happiness was never more clear to me. Go forward to the altar and commit to follow Jesus alone, or remain next to the girl in the pew? Pursue holiness or happiness? The long walk down the aisle felt like attending my own funeral, but it was an unconditional surrender.

I chose to pursue holiness over happiness. Wouldn't you know it? God's reward to me has been a true Joy I knew came from Him.

The Bottom Line: To find true joy, pursue holiness. Follow Jesus. Joy awaits.

DAY 358

Faith Marks

The steadfast love of the LORD never ceases;
his mercies never come to an end;
they are new every morning;
great is your faithfulness.

Lamentations 3:22-23

God's faithfulness elicits varied responses. The ancients built altars. We take pictures. Always, some have put their praise in writing. However we commemorate God's dealings in our lives, we can't follow Him very long before we have our own faith marks. A mere glance produces a flashback of His faithfulness. One of the greatest faith marks in our family took place in the devastating loss of triplets, born at just 21 weeks gestation. On the worst day of our lives we felt God's presence the closest. It was palpable.

My wife's birthday fell only five days after the loss. For a gift, I got her a picture I had seen in a Christian bookstore. The painting showed a heartbroken woman tenderly surrounded by a man's arms. The comforter's face was unseen, but obviously Jesus. A caption below the painting simply said, "I will not fail thee." The picture was placed in the intended nursery, supported by three angel figurines.

A heart-broken 3-yr-old who had intended to be the world's best big sister began petitioning God with the same prayer, morning, noon and night: "Jesus, we would like to have another baby." It wasn't just *some* of the time; it was *every* time she prayed, until three years, three months and three days after the loss of her siblings, we left the hospital with a newborn, in an adoption made in heaven. The 7-yr-old prayer warrior gave him his very first bottle, as she beamed. It was a faith mark of the biggest magnitude. We took lots of pictures.

There were many more pictures through the years, including the framed family photos documenting the breathtaking yearly changes in our children. A recent rain event prompted us to stack some of these vintage family portraits on a high dresser, in case of flooding.

It was Christmas Eve, time to celebrate the birth of the Christ child as a family. En route to the living room where we would read the Bible, pray and exchange gifts, I glanced toward the painting now mounted above a tall dresser in our bedroom, and saw a faith mark which prompted tears. I could hardly see the "I will not fail thee" painting. A tall stack of family pictures was in front of it.

The Bottom Line: He's there for us. He will not fail us. Ever.

DAY 359

Unrehearsed Life

And while they were there, the time came for her to give birth. And she gave birth to her firstborn son and wrapped him in swaddling cloths and laid him in a manger, because there was no place for them in the inn.

And in the same region there were shepherds out in the field, keeping watch over their flock by night. And an angel of the Lord appeared to them, and the glory of the Lord shone around them, and they were filled with fear. And the angel said to them, "Fear not, for behold, I bring you good news of a great joy that will be for all the people. For unto you is born this day in the city of David a Savior, who is Christ the Lord. And this will be a sign for you: you will find a baby wrapped in swaddling cloths and lying in a manger."
Luke 2:6-12

We did a Living Nativity in our church for Christmas Eve. It was totally unrehearsed. I had costumes and a background tape; the actors had no lines to say; it was just a simple re-enactment of the Christmas story, set to recorded scripture and music. It went alright, but a practice would have helped! Characters recruited moments before they were "on stage" were trying to act out parts they were hearing for the first time. This was not a high quality drama production, but it was effective in one way: it mimicked the very real, first Christmas.

Nobody knew what they were doing then, either! The whole thing was totally unrehearsed, at least for the earthly participants. Mary and Joseph were caught up in the whirlwind of events, getting over their shock and fear of one unexpected event just in time for the next—such as delivering your firstborn child in a stable a hundred miles from home. Gabriel hadn't mentioned the manger in his first shocker of an announcement. Mary and Joseph bounced from one surprise to the next, guided by angels and dreams. It was one scary deal. Not only did they not get to practice; they didn't even know what was coming, next!

No one else got to rehearse, either. The shepherds didn't have to practice looking scared; they *were* scared! Nobody told them they were going to be in a Living Nativity, which was probably good. Shepherds aren't convincing actors.

How about us? If we knew what was coming next in life, we could practice for it, but it's usually pretty much a surprise. We do best when we imitate the folks in the first Christmas story: listen when God speaks, obey Him, try not to be afraid. Yeah, this is our first time through, and we didn't get to practice. It keeps it genuine, keeps us depending on God. Life here *is* the rehearsal—for eternal life.

The Bottom Line: Life here is the rehearsal for eternal life to come.

DAY 360

A Cool Yule Spirit

Whoever restrains his words has knowledge,
and he who has a cool spirit is a man of understanding.
Even a fool who keeps silent is considered wise;
when he closes his lips, he is deemed intelligent.

Proverbs 17:27-28

I've seen the Christmas cards featuring Santa Claus or a reindeer wearing sunglasses, encouraging the reader to "Have a cool Yule!" "Cool" is a word in the English language which has marched along for decades, meaning "up to date," "fashionable," "acceptable," "good," "neat," "nifty," "swell" and "groovy!" Sorry. When I type in "cool," my thesaurus lights up with too many synonyms to fit on a page. I think it likes the word and jumps at the chance to express itself. Cool.

I think the Bible is cool. Talk about up to date! "Acceptable" in God's sight. God's wisdom is always in fashion. It's "neat" (a word I've been dragging around since high school). When I came across this proverb talking about "a cool spirit," I had to smile. The English Standard Version of the Bible which I use for study tries to translate it word for word from the original language. Our God is so cool! He even uses the word in His Book.

Although the connotations of the ancient Hebrew word translated "cool" probably have a lot more to do with "not becoming heated" in conversation, and restraining words which would hurt others, I like it that we have a page full of additional meanings which bring even more life to this verse.

At the beginning of the year, God gave me just two words as direction for it: 1. Listen 2. Love. It's hard to explain how helpful those two words have been through the course of the past twelve months! Listening first (to God, to loved ones, to others), then trying to love people based on what I've heard, has helped every relationship in my life. That simple concept has been lurking in scripture for thousands of years for anyone choosing to try it.

This Bible passage is just one of many encouraging us to listen first, and maybe not even speak at all. Silence will be mistaken for wisdom! But if we keep a cool spirit long enough, and seek to understand people, it won't be a mistake. And if we restrain our words, only letting the good ones come out, keep a cool spirit, and listen and love, we'll probably have a very cool Yule, and be thought wiser than we are. The longer we put it into practice, the more true wisdom we gain. Cool.

The Bottom Line: Silence is mistaken for wisdom,...
until it's no longer a mistake.

DAY 361

All Because We Listened

A fool takes no pleasure in understanding,
but only in expressing his opinion.
When wickedness comes, contempt comes also,
and with dishonor comes disgrace.
The words of a man's mouth are deep waters;
the fountain of wisdom is a bubbling brook.

Proverbs 18:2-4

When I asked the Lord a year ago about His direction for me for the coming year, I got just two words from Him: 1. Listen 2. Love. Those words have been my guiding principle through this year. It has not been a disappointment! Focusing on listening first (to God, to my family, to other people God has placed in my life) has brought more clarity to each relationship. After listening, it's usually clear how to express love in a way which feels like love to the recipient. Loving without listening often falls far short of the goal; listening first brings more success.

The first of these proverbs pinpoints the problem with relationships for many people: They have no desire to understand the other person; they wish only to express their opinion. A relationship between two people, neither of whom are listening to the other, is a relationship on the ropes. How can it ever improve, so long as everyone is talking but no one is listening?

There is a pleasure which comes into relationships where real listening takes place. It is the pleasure of understanding, and of being understood. A fool has no time for such things, but a wise person does. A wise person finds joy in getting to know another person at a level of understanding and vulnerability which is both refreshing and surprising. For communication to go anywhere, there must be not only a communicator but a receiver. To choose to be the receiver, not just nodding and smiling at appropriate times, but seeking to understand, is a blessing in every way: Wisdom grows, relationships deepen, new joys appear. All because we listened.

I've always loved the sound of running water (Ask my Dad). A bubbling brook produces a feeling of peace and enjoyment, for me. Wisdom is like that. Going deep with another person is like that. Only listeners experience it.

The Bottom Line: Listening, seeking to understand, blesses all.

DAY 362

Together Forever

For the Lord himself will descend from heaven with a cry of command, with the voice of an archangel, and with the sound of the trumpet of God. And the dead in Christ will rise first. Then we who are alive, who are left, will be caught up together with them in the clouds to meet the Lord in the air, and so we will always be with the Lord. Therefore encourage one another with these words. 1 Thessalonians 4:16-18

No lowly manger the second time. The first coming was very quiet; the second one won't be! When Jesus returns to this earth, the shout alone will be loud enough to wake the dead. Throw in angels and the trumpet of God... it will be like God saying "Clear!" and giving this globe the paddles.

Whether we're waiting for Him underground or over, there will be nothing we've ever experienced which will compare to the glory we will see and feel when Jesus comes back. It would be worth every bit of suffering we could ever experience for His name, to welcome Him, even if we would be spending eternity with God alone. We won't. Every human being who has ever graced the planet and chosen to trust God will be in the congregation of the saved. Not one will be missing. We will be *together*—and not just physically together, like a crowded mall at Christmas or a packed freeway—*but together* in every way, united in a unity too beautiful and pleasant for words. I don't think we are presently capable of understanding how wonderful the unity is which God has prepared for those who love Him. I heard a recording of one of those guys who was dead for something like twenty minutes, trying desperately to describe the sense of unity he felt before he got sent back. He couldn't do it. And I laughed as he talked about seeing God: "He's bigger than you think He is!" Yeah, probably.

One of the biggest blessings of Christmas time is the reunion of family and friends. With spread-out families, Christmas is sometimes the only time everyone is together in the same place. Distance and circumstances (like death, illness, broken relationships) prevent some families from being able to assemble at all. No time of year is this loss felt as keenly as during the holidays. But there is nothing quite like the beam on a mother's face when her entire family is home together, healthy and happy.

When Jesus returns, we will *all be together. Forever.* It's part of why He came in the first place. He made it so we could be together with Him, forever.

The Bottom Line: One reason He came?
So we could be together forever with Him.

DAY 363

God's Retirement Plan

The LORD spoke to Moses on Mount Sinai, saying, "Speak to the people of Israel and say to them, When you come into the land that I give you, the land shall keep a Sabbath to the LORD. For six years you shall sow your field, and for six years you shall prune your vineyard and gather in its fruits, but in the seventh year there shall be a Sabbath of solemn rest for the land, a Sabbath to the LORD. You shall not sow your field or prune your vineyard. You shall not reap what grows of itself in your harvest, or gather the grapes of your undressed vine. It shall be a year of solemn rest for the land. Leviticus 25:1-5

"Why isn't there anything in the Bible about retirement?" I asked the Lord one night as I was driving back from my interim pastoral assignment. "There is," came the reply. I thought for a moment. Sabbath. I spent the rest of the drive contemplating the ingenious system God devised for His people.

One day each week is to be spent in holy rest, acknowledging His ownership over us. Six days are for work; the seventh day for rest. "Retirement" is for everyone, and it's every week! "Remember the Sabbath Day, to keep it holy" is tucked into the Ten Commandments, along with "You shall not murder" and the one about adultery. If the rest of the Ten Commandments still apply to modern-day Gentiles, what gives us justification to disregard the one about Sabbath?

Not only did God provide for "retirement" one day every week; He went way beyond that. The commandment for the Israelites was to give the *land* a Sabbath, every seventh year, *for a year!* No planting, pruning or reaping. How will they survive? God will command such a blessing upon the land in the sixth year that they will still be eating off that harvest in Year Nine. Hmm.

He didn't stop there. The 50th year was to be a Year of Jubilee, in which society would reset; all land returned to the original family; servants set free.

As the miles ticked by, I considered. Wouldn't a Sabbath year be basically the same as a year of "retirement,"in an agrarian society? Throughout everyone's lifetime, every seventh year would be a year of "retirement"–for the whole country! Instead of plodding along through life toward retirement, God's system made retirement a lifelong process which mirrored the work week: six on, one off, whether days or years, highlighted by a Year of Jubilee in Year 50. I suddenly realized God had already implemented this system in my life! I was in Year Three of a Spirit-led faith season much like a Sabbath. It started the year I turned 49.

The Bottom Line: If we follow the God who has thought of everything, we'll be fine.

DAY 364

The Year of Jubilee

You shall count seven weeks of years, seven times seven years, so that the time of the seven weeks of years shall give you forty-nine years. Then you shall sound the loud trumpet on the tenth day of the seventh month. On the Day of Atonement you shall sound the trumpet throughout all your land. And you shall consecrate the fiftieth year, and proclaim liberty throughout the land to all its inhabitants. It shall be a jubilee for you, when each of you shall return to his property and each of you shall return to his clan. The fiftieth year shall be a jubilee for you; in it you shall neither sow nor reap what grows of itself nor gather the grapes from the undressed vines. For it is a jubilee. It shall be holy to you. You may eat the produce of the field. Leviticus 25:8-12

God set up a way for the society of the Hebrews to reset every 50 years: the Year of Jubilee. After counting off seven years of Sabbath years (49 years), they were to blow a trumpet and proclaim a "Jubilee" for a year. Everyone was to return home to their clan. All land would revert back to the ownership of the original clan. All Hebrew servants were to be freed.

It was God's plan for redistribution of wealth. In the intervening years between Jubilees, the value of land sold was to be calculated according to how many years until the next Jubilee.

What would be the effect of this bold policy, implemented nationwide and simultaneously? There would always be hope, no matter how foolish or unfortunate a family had become. There would always be a cap on capitalism; no matter how much property someone accumulated, after less than 50 years it would revert back to being the property of the original clan. And if the original clan wished to resell it, they would get a high price, since basically they were selling a 50 year lease.

It's a system of grace. It's a system where wisdom is rewarded, not punished, yet forgiveness is built in to the whole system. It's a system which continually reminds the whole nation that both the land and the people themselves belong to God. Not only is the land "on loan from God;" so is life itself.

If the Israelites ever implemented either the Sabbath Years or the Year of Jubilee, I can find no record of it. Sad. They missed out on the mind-boggling blessings such dramatic acts of obedience would have triggered, society-wide.

The same God still blesses all who obey Him, both individuals and nations. What can we do to bring blessing upon our country? Follow God. If need be, alone.

The Bottom Line: God always has a plan to bring blessing to those who obey Him.

DAY 365

Healing for a Sick Land

Thus Solomon finished the house of the LORD and the king's house. All that Solomon had planned to do in the house of the LORD and in his own house he successfully accomplished. Then the LORD appeared to Solomon in the night and said to him: "I have heard your prayer and have chosen this place for myself as a house of sacrifice. When I shut up the heavens so that there is no rain, or command the locust to devour the land, or send pestilence among my people, if my people who are called by my name humble themselves, and pray and seek my face and turn from their wicked ways, then I will hear from heaven and will forgive their sin and heal their land. Now my eyes will be open and my ears attentive to the prayer that is made in this place. For now I have chosen and consecrated this house that my name may be there forever. My eyes and my heart will be there for all time. And as for you, if you will walk before me as David your father walked, doing according to all that I have commanded you and keeping my statutes and my rules, then I will establish your royal throne, as I covenanted with David your father, saying, 'You shall not lack a man to rule Israel.'

But if you turn aside and forsake my statutes and my commandments that I have set before you, and go and serve other gods and worship them, then I will pluck you up from my land that I have given you, and this house that I have consecrated for my name, I will cast out of my sight, and I will make it a proverb and a byword among all peoples. And at this house which was exalted, everyone passing by will be astonished and say, 'Why has the LORD done thus to this land and to this house?' Then they will say, 'Because they abandoned the LORD, the God of their fathers who brought them out of the land of Egypt and laid hold on other gods and worshiped them and served them. Therefore he has brought all this disaster on them.'" 2 Chronicles 7:11-22

God's directions have always been so clear! In the Garden of Eden, Adam and Eve were warned of what would happen if they chose sin rather than obedience. It was literally a life or death choice. They chose sin. The fruit was death.

God repeatedly told Israel that if they followed His commands, their entire nation would enjoy blessing; if they mimicked the customs and idolatry of the other nations, they would suffer disaster, and ultimately lose the land. A theme in scripture from beginning to end: sin results in expulsion. The Garden of Eden; the Canaanites being ejected from their land and replaced by the Israelites; the Israelites losing the Promised Land and being sent into captivity because of their sin; the message in the Bible about the unrighteous being kept out of heaven. The message is always the same: choose God, not sin! Sin will kill you! It will ruin your whole country! Sin actually makes the land unclean, somehow, and the land itself will simply vomit out its inhabitants if sin is allowed to reign (Leviticus 18,20).

Our God never leaves His people without a way out, though! The very first sinners received the promise of a Savior. Noah's ark sheltered all who would listen–though it was only eight. The Law provided redemption through sacrifice, and paved the way for understanding how Jesus could be the ultimate sacrifice for all sin, for all time, when He died on the Cross. The Son of God laid down His life for us. He offers salvation to all willing to receive it.

God offers healing for individuals; He also offers healing for our land. The prescription is included in the famous verse frequently recited at prayer gatherings: *if my people who are called by my name humble themselves, and pray and seek my face and turn from their wicked ways, then I will hear from heaven and will forgive their sin and heal their land.* (2 Chronicles 7:14)

Sin brings death. As I observe all sorts of weird phenomena taking place these days across our nation and beyond, more and more I'm coming to the conclusion that the underlying cause of *all* our troubles is ultimately sin. Our lives, our cities, our land, have become unclean because of sin. Our land has become sick, and it's not an economic or an ecological or a political problem at the root: it's sin. Adam and Eve lost the Garden of Eden for only one reason: sin. All of Creation fell–and all because of sin! Into a perfect world, sin welcomed in death, disease, "natural disasters" and all the rest.

So, are we stuck with a sick land because so many have turned away from God to pursue sin? No! The remedy for a sick land is simple, and we don't have to wait for those who love sin to forsake it before we can experience healing. 2 Chronicles 7:14 is directed, not toward a population ignorant of God's commands, but toward "my people who are called by my name." That's us! What do we do? Humble ourselves. Pray. Seek His face. Turn from our wicked ways.

It's not a matter of slapping some sense into pagans; healing begins when those of us who already know God humble *ourselves* and repent.

Sin was never God's plan. But the remedy for it is. Through Jesus we have the promise of salvation, forgiveness for our sins, healing for our land. Deep down, we already know what to do. It's just a matter of doing it. It's time to humble ourselves and seek God's mercy for ourselves and our country. It's time to repent. Instead of raging at God or others because we are getting what we deserve, it's time to humbly seek God's mercy and healing, and turn from our wicked ways.

Jesus' earthly ministry began with healing. Let's ask Him to heal our land.

The Bottom Line: How to get healing for a sick land?
Humility. Prayer. Repentance.

DAY 366

Why Not Us?

For the eyes of the LORD search to and fro throughout the whole earth, to show himself strong in behalf of those whose heart is perfect toward him.
2 Chronicles 16:9

It's not often in life that your team wins the Super Bowl and you get to celebrate in a parade with 700,000 of your closest friends, but that's what happened in the city of Seattle. After 38 years as a franchise, the Seattle Seahawks finally won the Super Bowl! The 12th Man (the nickname for Seahawk fans) celebrated a victory they knew partially belonged to them. Numerous times throughout the season, crowd noise (loudest on record) resulted in opponents' mistakes or miscues. On two separate occasions, the exuberance of the fans when running back MarShawn Lynch was carrying the ball for a touchdown registered on the seismograph as a small earthquake under Century Link Field! That's enthusiasm! Coupled with great coaching and a great team, it made for a fun season.

My favorite part of the Seahawk saga, though, is that played by young quarterback Russell Wilson, a devout Christian. The shortest quarterback in the NFL, a late-round draft pick, Wilson gave a pep talk to his fellow teammates at the beginning of what was only Wilson's second season as a pro. The theme of his message: "Why not us? Why couldn't we be the team that wins the Super Bowl this year?" Wilson's work ethic, his character, skill and leadership ability, and maybe most of all, his optimism, helped his team achieve the elusive goal of winning the first Super Bowl in franchise history.

It was a team effort, to be sure, with everyone doing their part, including the fans. But I believe the greatest season in Seahawk history started with the attitude: "Why not us?" They set the goal, expected it, and just worked the plan.

My favorite scripture in the Bible, 2 Chronicles 16:9, reminds me that God is constantly on the alert for bold disciples willing to go out on a limb for Him, whose hearts are perfect toward Him. God always comes through! I believe He wants to send a Great Awakening, in which millions of lives are transformed.

Every day I ask God for a Great Awakening. Why not us? He is looking for people willing to be missionaries of His grace to America. He wants to start a fire somewhere–why not us?! Why couldn't we be some of the people He uses to help our hurting countrymen find spiritual peace? Why couldn't we be the people who live so counter-culturally and yet so lovingly that our nation awakens to the need for a Savior we can totally trust, who is our only hope of salvation? Why not us?

I'm asking for a Great Awakening, Father. I'm planning for it. Use me.

The Bottom Line: Why not us?

FOR SPIRITUAL LEADERS

What Would They Do?

Two of the greatest nation-changers in history were John Wesley and the Apostle Paul. John Wesley ministered in England in the 18th century, Paul in the Roman Empire in the 1st century. Both had incredible spiritual impact on entire nations. If they were transported to minister in our county, this year, what would they do? We'll start with John Wesley:

- He would preach, probably outdoors, to whomever would listen. (He might start first in the pulpits of whatever churches might be open to him.)
- He would minister through a web site, through email, probably through radio and maybe television.
- He would organize societies and bands, with leaders, accountability, and a "method" of spirituality which would result in permanently transformed lives.
- He would recruit traveling preachers, and give them the directive that they had nothing to do but save souls.
- He would refuse to compete with the established church. Instead, he would try to support it in every way, and encourage everyone else to do the same.
- On the other hand, he would not allow church membership or attendance to be a substitute for discipleship. (Unfortunately, we often have).
- He would focus his time and energies on very specific things, to the neglect of practically everything else.

He would change America.

What would Paul do?

- I think he would definitely start in the churches, preaching and teaching to whomever would listen. What would be funny would be to see people trying to debate him, using their interpretation of the scriptures Paul himself had written! "What you really meant was...!"
- Paul would engage the culture. He would spend some time in the churches, teaching on the deepest level possible, but I think he would spend the majority of his time evangelizing unbelievers, then training them to be disciples of Christ. He would seldom be alone, but would usually have ministers-in-training with him.
- I think Paul would also go for the "chiefs." He would look up the movers and shakers and give them his testimony. He would debate the intellectuals. He would write letters to the editor. I think Paul would nearly always do a frontal attack. He also probably wouldn't stay in one place for long, just long enough to see renewal in the Church. Then he would move on.

He would change America.

The Bottom Line: What could I do to change America?

Ministry Games

The "game" of ministry is all about serving Jesus. That sounds right, feels right and is right; however, in the practical, day-to-day struggle of things like pastoral ministry, what one quickly finds is that spirituality is fine, so long as the needs of the people are met, pretty much on their terms. I can see their point. Why pay a guy to serve God, if he isn't serving you? "Let him go pray or whatever, but let's get someone who will run this church the way it needs to be run, which means meeting the needs of my family." Who can blame someone for expecting service in exchange for a salary?

So, apart from the realities of church "ministry," where the church has its own set of expectations which need to be met, exactly what has God called me to do? "Follow me." Pretty basic. It's one of those "Yes" or "No" propositions. Either I'm following Jesus or I'm not.

And comparisons to other disciples are stupid: "I'm following Jesus better than you." Could it be part of God's genius that He would give us a game where we can't even figure out how we rank? Yes, that would be like Him, wouldn't it? How many times did Jesus have to get after His disciples for jockeying for position in His Kingdom? If it didn't work for the guys with apostle name tags, why would we think He would like it when we did it?

It's not about who can build the biggest ministry in the shortest amount of time, or even who can out-spiritual everyone else in his class. It's not an ecclesiastical version of "Survivor," where we try to maintain doctrinal purity, plus enough popularity to not get voted off the island (or out of the church). So what kind of game is it, and how do we win?

Here's the game: *Follow Jesus.*

That's it. That's the whole game, including the rules.

But how do we tell who's winning?! Easy. Everyone who follows Jesus wins. Whoever doesn't follow Jesus loses. I like this game.

The Bottom Line: The game of "ministry"? Follow Jesus

Having a Riot

(Church Fights Explained)

...the Jews from Asia, seeing him in the temple, stirred up the whole crowd and laid hands on him, crying out, "Men of Israel, help! This is the man who is teaching everyone everywhere against the people and the law and this place. Moreover, he even brought Greeks into the temple and has defiled this holy place." For they had previously seen Trophimus the Ephesian with him in the city, and they supposed that Paul had brought him into the temple. Then all the city was stirred up, and the people ran together. They seized Paul and dragged him out of the temple, and at once the gates were shut. And as they were seeking to kill him, word came to the tribune of the cohort that all Jerusalem was in confusion. He at once took soldiers and centurions and ran down to them. And when they saw the tribune and the soldiers, they stopped beating Paul. Then the tribune came up and arrested him and ordered him to be bound with two chains. He inquired who he was and what he had done. Some in the crowd were shouting one thing, some another. And as he could not learn the facts because of the uproar, he ordered him to be brought into the barracks. And when he came to the steps, he was actually carried by the soldiers because of the violence of the crowd, for the mob of the people followed, crying out, "Away with him!" Acts 21:27-36

Ah, yes. Nothing like a religious riot to make your day, particularly if you're a mild mannered Roman tribune responsible for keeping the peace in a powder keg like Jerusalem. And nothing like being a returning, successful missionary, worshiping God at the sanctuary, when fellow worshipers begin screaming lies about you to the crowd, which then joins them in attempting to dismantle your body!

This is the pattern of religious riots, though. History is peppered with violent acts perpetrated by those convinced God was on their side. In rare instances, He was; usually, not.

Momma Told Me Not to Come

Paul had received sufficient warning; if he were trying to avoid conflict, he knew to avoid his old stomping grounds of Jerusalem. Prophets who loved him had begged him to stay away. But Paul knew where God wanted him: Jerusalem. On his arrival, the Church elders in Jerusalem did their best to try to repair Paul's reputation among the Jewish Christians there, but in the end, it was an offshoot of Paul's success in Asia that triggered a riot which had just been awaiting a spark.

Had Paul's missionary trip to Asia been a yawner, where he mostly sat around and whined about harsh conditions and unresponsive people, then hurried home on furlough as soon as possible, the Asian Jews wouldn't have even known who he was. Instead, Paul's brilliant, Spirit-led Asian campaign had electrified the province, even shaking up the idol-making industry to the point of a riot in Ephesus sponsored by the shrine makers of Asia. Paul had given the Jews in Asia first shot at the Gospel, spending three months with them upon arrival in Ephesus, until they finally showed him the synagogue door. After that, Paul had moved next door and set up a cross-cultural ministry open to Jews and Gentiles alike—and very effective. Trophimus, his companion, was one of many, many converts to Christianity gathered from among the Asian Gentiles.

Paul's effectiveness had garnered him an assortment of enemies, as well as numerous converts. The Asian Jews who had not embraced Christianity now despised Paul. Their understanding of the situation was that Paul had rejected the laws of Judaism and was teaching other Jews to do the same. Such was not the case. Paul continued to live as a Jew, even while he offered the Gospel to Gentiles as a free gift, apart from Judaism. In other words, the Gentiles didn't need to become Jews in order to become Christians; the Jews didn't need to stop being Jews in order to become Christians. But the synagogue rulers only understood that synagogue attendance was down, it was Paul's fault, and he hung around with Gentiles. They were not interested in anything but getting rid of him. To find him in Jerusalem in the company of Gentiles, now pretending to be an honest Jew worshiping in the holy temple, must have awakened in them levels of hostility they didn't know they had. Their hatred boiled over. They had just enough disinformation to think they were right.

Response of the Defendant

Paul's response is so cool, it's like he's been through this, before. (He had). Carried out of the mob mosh pit-style by the soldiers, Paul uses his multi-lingual skills and intelligence to at least grab the chance to make a speech to the people. Before it's over, he plays the Roman citizenship card and avoids another beating, then splits the Sanhedrin over the resurrection question so they turn on one another instead of on him. Later on, he even gains an audience with Caesar by appealing to the same for justice. Through it all, the apostle is Spirit-led. It's obvious that the wisdom and courage are not coming from him, but from above. Is there any reason we can't lead lives equally Spirit-led? None I can think of.

Recipe for a Religious Riot

How do these things get started in the first place? Whether it's a vicious all-out religious riot or a garden variety church split, there are certain ingredients which make up the recipe.

Zeal

It takes a certain amount of zeal or a religious riot will never get off the ground. People have to care about something quite a bit before they're willing to inconvenience themselves to defend it. They're not going to fight for something they don't care about.

A Righteous Cause

They have to think they're on God's side. They need to be able to convince themselves that what they're doing is right. Sometimes, this takes a great degree of rationalization; sometimes, a disconnect from common sense or morality, but nevertheless, "being right" is an important ingredient.

A Willingness to Pile On

By this, I mean a willingness to pile on! A disinterest in substantiating any claims against the defendant, but merely a desire to get in a few punches before it's too late—these are characteristics of folks who are riot-hungry. It's like when certain cities have a professional sports team in a championship game. A riot is planned in advance; it'll be a victory riot if they win, a protest riot against unfairness if they lose. They only need to wait until the game is over, so they'll know which kind of riot they're having. You need people who don't particularly care why they're biting or fighting, or civility may take over and the riot may fizzle out; people who just want to argue are what keep the riot going nicely.

An Unrepentant Spirit

If the riot is supposed to continue underground even after authorities temporarily quench it, what is needed are those who choose to have an unrepentant spirit. By this I mean that no matter what, they refuse to accept any portion of responsibility for what happens. They also refuse to accept apologies from others, preferring to harbor grudges instead of starting over or making peace. Pride is key, here, because submission to God brings people to their knees, and soon it's all over. It's very hard to contribute to a riot atmosphere and repent at the same time. Repentance takes the fight right out of people.

Gossip

Gossip is the fuel necessary to keep a riot going. Usually the truth is not sufficient in itself to get people stirred up, so it has to be embellished in a convincing way to get their attention. If there isn't enough negative truth available, negative assumptions or distortions will certainly provide sufficiently interesting information to catch the interest of the zealous. Communication is important—after all, what good is a lie or a half-truth in stirring people to action if they don't know about it? It's like advertisements sitting in a drawer somewhere. Without gossip to keep it going, the riot may burn itself out.

There is a flavor to gossip. Information may start out as positive or neutral, but by the time it has gone through a link or two of the gossip chain, it inevitably picks up a bitter taste. Gossip does this to all information of all types. That's why it's such vital fuel for any kind of enduring riot or feud. When people stop talking about the situation, it's soon forgotten. Gossip makes sure they can't forget.

So, there they are, five key ingredients for a religious riot. The presence of even one of these ingredients will generate noticeable tension, but stir together all five ingredients and you'd better stand back! This will be a church fight to remember.

But then, suppose you're not trying to start a religious riot, but rather, to end one?

Enter, the Cleanup Crew

My first time-clock job was on the cleanup crew for a container corporation which canned and bottled soft drinks. We waded into some epic messes and came out better people for it.

As I look around, I see many people dealing with epic messes, these days, in the church. Like at Mid-America Container, most of the messes happened on someone else's watch; most of them were not intentional; a few we made ourselves, just to see it splatter and because we were going to have to clean it all up, anyway. Whatever happened and whoever caused it, no one would argue whether it's a genuine mess, now. That's what a lot of people face in their church—a sorry looking mess. Often, if there were intentional perpetrators, they're long gone. All that's left are innocent victims, and if you don't think they're all innocent, just ask them. (It's like at the jail).

It always falls to the innocent victims to clean up the mess. A true villain would never be found with a squeegee in his hands. If we find ourselves gazing on the scene of yet another all-church brawl, what would God have us to do?

Righting a Religious Riot

Zeal (again)

Zeal works both ways. It's required to start a church fight; it's also required to stop it. Without zeal—true passion for a cause, there is no change, there is only apathy. Everything stays the same. If we don't care enough to be involved, we'll not take the necessary risks to try to restore peace to the situation.

We are in need of some zeal in the Church, these days. There seems to be precious little of it, and what there is usually seems to be centered on some aspect of preserving, restoring or abandoning someone's version of the "good old days." This zeal is directed against the opposition, whomever they might be.

So, what little zeal we have is largely wasted, sort of like the giant intramural tug-of-war games at college, with the mud and the rope in between and competing dormitories on either side. Eventually, one group will "win" by dragging their rivals through the mud, but the end result is a lot of muddy people and not much else. Same thing for most church fights.

What we need in the Church are people with a genuine zeal for serving Jesus Christ, but whose passion is under the control of the Holy Spirit. If we act out our zeal without any sort of restraint, innocent people are going to suffer, and so will we. We need the Spirit's control, or we'll do more damage than good, especially if the fight has already started.

What does God want us to do?

He wants us to be zealous for Jesus. Being "lukewarm" about our faith is detestable to Him; ask the Laodiceans (Revelation 3). At the same time, we need to use caution in keeping our zeal under the control of the Holy Spirit. How do we do that?

Pray

When we take things before God, He has a way of revealing to us what we need to know, particularly if we ask Him! (James 1:5) Being in a church fight is like walking through a minefield, but God knows the way. He is able to thread His people through it, but paying attention is a requirement. Take exactly the number of steps God shows you to take, and only in the direction He leads. No leading? Freeze! Don't do or say anything without direction from God.

Religious riots are not fun. I tell people who are in them to keep their eyes on Jesus, and hang on! That, and "Don't do anything unless God tells you."

What are some other things we can do to bring a little peace to a messy church situation?

Learn the facts

Don't believe everything you hear. The Acts 21 riot was started by lies and rumors. Had anyone bothered to check out the facts, there would have been no riot, since Paul hadn't done anything. Learning the facts takes most of the drama out of gossip and herds it back toward the truth, which is usually pretty boring and unworthy of a fight.

Righteousness

Righteousness means a right relationship with God. This also means we are willing to do whatever we know God wants us to do. Under the direction of the Holy Spirit, righteousness is a powerful peacemaking tool. When we have repented of our own sins, bad attitudes, gossip, etc., we can then receive clear instructions regarding what to do which may be helpful to others. Until we make sure our own hearts are right before God, there's not much we can do to help anyone else.

Don't make negative assumptions

We need to be willing to live with holes in our knowledge, rather than filling them with assumptions, usually negative. (The Asian Jews assumed Paul had broken the law by bringing a Gentile into the temple. He didn't bring Trophimus into the temple; there were just people who assumed he had.) If we're going to assume something, it should at least be a positive assumption, giving them the benefit of a doubt unless proven facts indicate otherwise.

Refuse to pile on

As good as it may feel to finally be on top of those who have hurt us, we must resist the temptation to pile on. If we are in a position of authority and are actually responsible to help administer judgment, we need to be as fair and godly as possible. If it's really not our position to judge, we'd better not! If it's gossip, we would do well to let the gossip die on our watch, even when those dying to know are within whispering range.

Be a dead-end for gossip

Say nothing which does not need to be said. Do nothing which does not need to be done. We should be a dead-end for gossip. If we feel the person really needs a listening ear, we can listen to them, then let it stop with us. If there is nothing constructive which can be done about it, and nothing to be gained by anyone hearing it, we're better off to not even listen to it.

Gossip? Like with an errant e-mail, block it or listen and delete, but don't forward. Break the chain. Be a dead-end for gossip.

Refresh the person, not the quarrel

Internet browsers have a "refresh" button that updates the additions and changes on a web page. Just hit "refresh" and we know all the latest. Quarrels are like that, too. Injured people may be trying to put it out of their minds, but their friends keep hitting the "refresh" button by adding the latest tidbits of information and disinformation, since "they'd want to know." The argument (and the pain) are all renewed!

If we're wanting to keep the quarrel stirred up, all we need do is keep hitting the "refresh" button, because each time we do we're refreshing the argument. If we're wanting Jesus to use us to help calm things down instead of keeping them stirred up, a wise choice would be to refresh the people, not the quarrel. And, believe me, if you've ever been in a church fight, *everybody* is hurting and in need of refreshment! What kind of refreshment? All kinds. It's just awfully nice to have someone coming toward you who is trying to refresh you instead of trying to rebuke you, reform you or recruit you! A cup of cold water in the name of Jesus... Refresh the person, not the quarrel.

Bring in the Bitterness Bomb Squad

Examine the root of a riot; you're bound to find bitterness. Bitterness is a disease with few cures. Condemnation isn't one of them. Bitter people are not searching for facts, but for love and acceptance. The more bitter they become, the scarcer these entities are for them, since they drive everyone away, leaving only a handful of commiserators.

People aren't argued into repentance. Even when we think we've won a verbal shooting match, we find the vanquished have only crawled off to reload. I've yet to meet a person who decided to follow Christ because of the condemnation of a Christian. It's love that gets them in, and it's God's kindness that leads us toward repentance. (Romans 2:4) That same chapter details the foolishness of trying to do God's judging for Him.

Our assignment is love. Love takes many different forms, but the form which best disarms bitterness is continuing, unconditional kindness—God's kindness. It's the only thing I know that penetrates that hard shell of bitterness. God's kindness, channeled through His people, has a way of restoring hope and turning things around when nothing else can. Bitterness is like a bomb ready to go off. Condemnation is sure to set it off; so will almost any form of confrontation. What is needed is the Bitterness Bomb Squad, armed with kindness from God. Painstakingly applied kindness is the best solution to the volatile situation. Bitterness traps people. Kindness helps free them.

Conduit of Kindness

Church fights happen. People who are zealous for (or against) religious beliefs will witness confrontation from time to time. There are certain things we can do which help in reducing the amount of conflict we face, but inevitably, we'll find ourselves in the middle of a church fight of some sort, if we live long enough. What should we do, then? Hang onto Jesus, and do what He tells you! Nothing more, nothing less. If we don't know what else to do, the principles we talked about are good, biblical things to do, even if we're not in a church fight.

And we need to remember our number one tool, when it comes to resolving church fights: Kindness. Toward whom? Everyone! When it gets hot on the church scene, we need to be the fire hose God can send in as a conduit for His kindness. Will we put out the religious riot? Maybe. Maybe not. Whatever happens, God will use it. (A religious riot started the process of God getting Paul an audience with Caesar). The important thing is to be a tool God can use any way He wants. The outcome is up to Him, but if we're a conduit of kindness, He will always use us to be a blessing, regardless of our situation or the earthly outcome. What a great assignment! God has us on the cleanup crew, armed with His kindness.

The Bottom Line: God can use us to bring healing to church conflict. Or prevent it.

When God Downsizes the Staff

God's purpose is that the whole world will know about Jesus. It's going to happen, and we get to be a part! If we're ever unsure of what to do next, sharing about Jesus is an activity pretty sure to please God. Another one is worship and prayer; if we're serious, throw in fasting. After that, it's just a matter of doing what the Holy Spirit says. The nice thing is, unless He directs us to do it, we don't even have to come up with our own plan! That's often already provided.

Another nice thing is that each of us has a place in the Kingdom, but everyone doesn't have the same role. Think of the variety of responses expected of the Antioch Church (Acts 13:1-4):

Lucius and Manaen knew they weren't called to go to foreign countries. They were supposed to stay at Antioch, and they knew it. Saul and Barnabas knew they were called to go. I think most of us know what God would have us do, if we've bothered to ask. And if we don't know, that evangelism default can kick in!

It's important that the missionaries God has called actually go, not just talk about it.

It's important that not everyone goes—as in, all five prophet/teachers heading out, leaving the Antioch Church leaderless.

It's important that the Church, especially the remaining leadership, let them go, instead of trying to change their minds or hang on to them.

It's important that the Church doesn't slam a couple people into leadership after Barnabas and Saul leave, in an attempt to fill "vacancies," but wait on God for that, too.

It's a beautiful thing to belong to Jesus, to be part of His Body, the Church. The Holy Spirit is fully capable of guiding the affairs of the Church. He doesn't even need our plans, strategies, etc., though often He lets us help. We need to make sure, though, that we hold onto any plans, even Spirit-led ones, loosely. The Spirit may lead in a way that seems dangerous or difficult. He may seem to reverse directions, such as assembling a wonderful team of prophets and teachers, only to abruptly downsize the staff by 40%. We have to remember that when God downsizes the staff (or does anything else), it's because He has something even better in mind. This is a God we can totally trust! It's so nice to be on a winning team!

The Bottom Line: If we don't know what to do, sharing Christ is a great "default"!

Pray, Then Stay

When Silas and Timothy arrived from Macedonia, Paul was occupied with the word, testifying to the Jews that the Christ was Jesus. And when they opposed and reviled him, he shook out his garments and said to them, "Your blood be on your own heads! I am innocent. From now on I will go to the Gentiles." And he left there and went to the house of a man named Titius Justus, a worshiper of God. His house was next door to the synagogue. Crispus, the ruler of the synagogue, believed in the Lord, together with his entire household. And many of the Corinthians hearing Paul believed and were baptized. And the Lord said to Paul one night in a vision, "Do not be afraid, but go on speaking and do not be silent, for I am with you, and no one will attack you to harm you, for I have many in this city who are my people." And he stayed a year and six months, teaching the word of God among them.
Acts 18:5-11

What needs to happen in the Church? Christians, especially pastors, need to be guided by the Holy Spirit and not their circumstances!

This passage is one more example of how the Early Church was under the direction of the Holy Spirit, not Headquarters or even the missionaries. The vision given to Paul by the Lord helped him know just what to do, plus providing him with peace.

The way to find God's will is to pray. We need to check with God about everything. There are so many ways to get it wrong. Usually, I find that I make my mistakes when I assume the answer and don't think I need to check with God on that one!

Paul felt a keen responsibility to give his fellow Jews every opportunity to receive Christ. When they came out against him in opposition, he was released from this responsibility, and placed it back upon them. In terms of location, though, he merely moved next door! The Christians used the synagogue parking lot for their overflow meetings at Titius Justus' house, with Paul as teacher.

What does this say about some of our present situations? People need to stay put when God tells them to stay put! The conflict Paul faced in Corinth was something he had come to expect. It was coming from his own people, the Jews, and it was over the same old thing: Jealousy. Paul could have simply left Corinth, but God made it clear that his work was not finished, yet, so he stayed. The way to find God's will is to pray. Then we stay put until He gives us permission to go.

**The Bottom Line: We pray,
then stay wherever God leads until He says "Go."**

God's Traffic Lights

And they went through the region of Phrygia and Galatia, having been forbidden by the Holy Spirit to speak the word in Asia. Acts 16:6

And he entered the synagogue and for three months spoke boldly, reasoning and persuading them about the kingdom of God. But when some became stubborn and continued in unbelief, speaking evil of the Way before the congregation, he withdrew from them and took the disciples with him, reasoning daily in the hall of Tyrannus. This continued for two years, so that all the residents of Asia heard the word of the Lord, both Jews and Greeks. Acts 19:8-10

Paul and company walked across the province of Asia without preaching, on Paul's second missionary journey. Why? The Holy Spirit had forbidden them. On the way home, Paul had made a brief stop in Ephesus, received a good welcome, and had promised to return to them, "if God wills" (Acts 18:21). His third missionary journey was a beeline to Ephesus. Upon arrival, Paul jumped right into ministry among the Jews, with a three-month stint in the synagogue, until opposition arose from some in the synagogue. Paul took his disciples and left. He began a daily ministry in the hall of Tyrannus (apparently 11 A.M. to 4 P.M. each day), which continued for two years. Altogether, Paul spent three years in Ephesus. Through his ministry, the residents of Asia heard the Gospel, both Jews and Greeks.

How can one person reach a province more than 200 miles wide? If you're in the right spot, you don't even have to travel! I used to joke that if you stood in the terminal at Anchorage International Airport for a year, you would see everyone in the state of Alaska. It wasn't really a joke; it was pretty much the truth. For one reason or another, nearly everyone in the entire state would be there, usually several times in a year. Ephesus must have been like that. Ironically, one of the biggest draws to the city of Ephesus was a pagan temple which was one of the "seven wonders of the world": the temple of Artemis (also called Diana). Factors like the harbor and the temple made Ephesus a prime location through which to reach the whole region. Paul was able to sit still and teach, while the results of his ministry went everywhere. They might have come to see the temple of Artemis, but many left with the truth of the Gospel. "Project Asia" wasn't planned by apostles or denominational bureaucrats, but by a God who never misses.

The Bottom Line: We are wise to look for and follow God's leading and timing!

God-powered, God-timed Evangelism

Paul's ministry in Ephesus was accompanied by great power. Not only did he give thorough instruction each day for two years; there were so many miraculous signs and wonders being done through him in the way of healing and deliverance that people got in the habit of taking handkerchiefs or aprons which had touched Paul to their afflicted friends, and they got well! God's grace was on the apostle. The fertility god Artemis had a pretty hard time keeping up with Jesus, when it came to results! The sense of awe was only magnified when the seven sons of Sceva tried to horn in on the Gospel, and were publicly exposed (in every sense of the phrase) as frauds!

There were some key evidences of God's work among the Ephesians. One was a huge bonfire, fueled by books of magic flipped onto the flames by recent converts from sorcery to Christianity. The value of the books would today have come to around six million dollars!

Another indicator that things were changing in Ephesus was the reaction of the local silversmith's union. They were not pleased! They felt this preacher posed a threat to their livelihood, which principally consisted of making silver shrines of Artemis. Her popularity had taken a dive since the apostle hit town. Led by Demetrius, the silversmiths started a riot. Demetrius would have been better off to just start making silver handkerchiefs inscribed with "Jesus is Lord."

They had a tremendous revival in Ephesus. Question: Would this have happened had Paul gone there years before, when he first intended?

I don't think so. Apparently, the timing wasn't yet right. Also, the Spirit directed the apostles to first encircle Asia with the Gospel, before coming back to it, and there is purpose to everything God does. There was a reason for the delay. The end result was a powerful ministry which reached both Jews and Gentiles. Paul had the time of his life! It may have been his most enjoyable ministry.

What can we learn from Paul's Ephesian ministry? The pattern Paul used in Ephesus of letting people come to him, then teaching them, used to work in America. In most American ministries of today, the plan is to establish a nice facility, provide worship services and programs which people find attractive, and let them come to us so we can share with them about Jesus. *Sometimes,* this works. More often, not, particularly on the skeptical coasts, where it's hard to get anyone but Christians to come to a church service. Are we stuck? God is never stuck! It's again time to seek God's power, timing and methods for *our* situation.

The Bottom Line: God-powered, God-timed evangelism is always effective.

Reasoning with the Nation

The Ephesians didn't know about the Gospel until Paul preached to them. Now, after three years of Paul "reasoning" with them daily, they understood. He had taken pagan idol worshipers and gradually brought them into an understanding of what it meant to follow Jesus Christ. He had taught them, answered their questions. He had started where they were and led them all the way to a life-changing faith in Christ. The six million dollar repentance bonfire in Ephesus which signaled success had been three years in the making. It was ignited by a clear understanding of what it meant to be a disciple, fueled by a willingness to pay the cost. When it was over, Paul knew by the Spirit that it was time to go.

Wouldn't it be great to see revival fires burning all over this country? People confessing their sins publicly, scorning their old habits and lifestyle to the point it actually started affecting the economy? Before that happened in Ephesus, though, there was a thorough "reasoning" of the Gospel through Paul and his associates for a period of three years. I think that's a place we often overlook. Sure, it would be great to have massive repentance and the wonderful changes which follow—but does it happen that way, when people don't even really understand the Gospel or their need for a Savior? Not usually. The Wesleyan revival so effective in changing the British Isles didn't start out with repentance and societal change; in fact, I think they said the lag time between exposure to the message and conversion was an average of two years. First, they learned. Then, they committed.

We have a job to do, in America. The job is not only to evangelize the nation; first, we must "reason" with the nation. We need to present the case of the Gospel, being careful to answer all questions, starting where people are, not where we think they *should* be.

We're dealing with biblical illiteracy and the after-effects of a confusing witness. The biblical illiteracy is self-explanatory: People simply don't know what the Bible says. This includes many who attend church services. By "confusing witness" I'm referring to the many people claiming to be Christians, yet living like the world. What's a non-believer to think? If Christianity is life-changing, where's the change? It's time for the Church to live it. Then we'll be ready to reason with the nation. We'll see changes in them when they see a change in us.

The Bottom Line: Are we ready, with changed lives, to reason with the lost?

Wesley's Way

"If the world is cold, make it your business to build fires."

Horace Traubel

"There is not, on the face of the earth, another nation (at least, that we have heard of) so perfectly dissipated and ungodly; not only so totally 'without God in the world,' but so totally setting Him at defiance. There never was an age, that we read of in history, since Julius Caesar, since Noah, since Adam, wherein dissipation and ungodliness did so generally prevail, both among high and low, rich and poor."

This is how John Wesley described his native 18th century England. Wesley spent very little time in decrying the darkness; he devoted his life to building Gospel fires. Teamed with his hymn-writing brother, Charles, the Wesley's let God use them to spark a revival in Great Britain which changed the course of history.

The earliest days of the revival were confined to a dozen or so Oxford students meeting several evenings a week, in a group they called "The Holy Club." Following his Oxford days, John Wesley ventured to the American Colonies to try to bring hope to the Indians in Georgia; he came home defeated and miserable, but along the way met up with a group of Moravians who inspired him to search for a deeper holiness than he had known. An epic spiritual transformation took place in the lives of both Wesley's in 1738, which launched the powerful message of holiness in a kingdom sorely lacking in even the desire for it. John Wesley preached concerning this experience of heart cleansing in the Anglican Church, of which he was an ordained minister. He usually only got one chance. His journals from those days cheerfully record the experience of being asked "not to return," in church after church.

Meanwhile, more power accompanied his preaching than he had ever before experienced. At the urging of George Whitefield, Wesley tried "field preaching," an idea originally distasteful to him, and quickly went from reaching recalcitrant hundreds to receptive thousands. From the start, the buildings would not have contained the crowds who came to hear Wesley, anyway. (The largest crowd of his lifetime, estimated at 32,000, clearly heard a 70-year-old man without amplification preach the Gospel to them.) Wesley's 5 A.M. meetings drew thousands! He preached day and night, sometimes seven times in a day, once 23 times in a week. He wore out horses all across England, traveling some 250,000 miles on horseback in his lifetime. God used John and Charles Wesley to change their nation! Multiplied thousands began to live for Christ. Society was so powerfully transformed at the grassroots level that some historians agree that the Wesleyan revival is what spared England from the bloody revolution endured by France, following that same time period.

One of the most striking features of the Wesleyan Revival was its endurance. Throughout history, most revivals have been short-lived, with visible results lasting only a few years. The Wesleyan Revival was still going strong at the time of John Wesley's death, in 1791. Meanwhile, the American revival termed "The Great Awakening" was powerful, yet brief. In a matter of a few years, the flames had mostly gone out. Fellow Oxford student and Holy Club member George Whitefield had been a prominent figure in the American awakening, which took place very nearly the same time as the revival was taking hold in England. One lasted a few years; the other, decades. What made the difference?

Though there are other factors, the key difference was that Wesley methodically organized those who responded to his message into "societies." More than just "small groups," these cells functioned at multiple levels of cooperation, commitment and transparency. Far from being a spectator event, those admitted to the groups were queried weekly on their devotional habits and spiritual life, with each expected to give a testimony to the others as to the condition of their soul. Assignments were handed out for visiting the sick and for training the children. People spoke of the temptations they had overcome and of opportunities to do good. New converts were added regularly to the groups. These weekly society meetings were crucial to the long-lasting effects of the Gospel upon the people. When Wesley visited a town which had ignored this practice, he remarked, in disgust:

"I was more convinced than ever, that the preaching like an Apostle, without joining together those that are awakened, and training them up in the ways of God, is only begetting children for the murderer. How much preaching has there been for these twenty years all over Pembrokeshire! But no regular societies, no discipline, no order or connection; and the consequence is, that nine in ten of the once-awakened are now faster asleep than ever." (Wesley's Journal, 8/25/1763)

Our nation may not be as far gone as Wesley thought England was, but we need the same thing: an Awakening. And it seems the best way to *stay* awake is to stay awake, *together*, however that looks in America, in our present time.

The Bottom Line: Revival lasts much longer when the converts are connected.

Dave Ness has been a pastor for over 30 years, and a student of the Word since childhood. In 2005, he founded Servant Connection, a non-profit ministry dedicated to the spiritual transformation of America. Dave currently pastors North Seattle Church of the Nazarene, in Seattle, Washington.

Servant Connection
Website: PrayingforAmerica.org

Correspondence
or to purchase additional copies
of ***Answers for Today*** or ***Serving God:***

Dave Ness
13130 5th Ave. NE
Seattle, WA 98125

Email
SCJForever@centurylink.net

Donations
Servant Connection
P.O. Box 1747
Longview, WA 98632

North Seattle Church of the Nazarene
13130 5th Ave. NE
Seattle, WA 98125

NorthSeattleNazarene.org

Pray for America.